Risk and Rationality

Risk and Rationality

Lara Buchak

OXFORD
UNIVERSITY PRESS

OXFORD
UNIVERSITY PRESS

Great Clarendon Street, Oxford, OX2 6DP,
United Kingdom

Oxford University Press is a department of the University of Oxford.
It furthers the University's objective of excellence in research, scholarship,
and education by publishing worldwide. Oxford is a registered trade mark of
Oxford University Press in the UK and in certain other countries

Published in the United States of America by Oxford University Press
198 Madison Avenue, New York, NY 10016, United States of America

British Library Cataloguing in Publication Data
Data available

Library of Congress Cataloging in Publication Data
Data available

ISBN 978-0-19-967216-5 (Hbk.)
ISBN 978-0-19-880128-3 (Pbk.)

To my parents

Preface

This book is about the principles that govern decision-making in the face of risk. Our decisions involve risk more often than we might expect. Any time we make a decision while being uncertain about a relevant aspect of how the world is, such a decision involves risk. Some of these decisions are mundane, such as what time to leave for work when we do not know how much traffic there will be, or what to order from the menu at a new restaurant. Other decisions are significant, such as which career to pursue, whom to marry, or what causes to devote our time and resources to. Many decisions we make automatically; others we take days to deliberate about. A distinctive feature of all of these decisions is that we are forced to consider how our choices will turn out under various circumstances, and decide how to trade off the possibility that a choice will turn out well against the possibility that it will turn out poorly.

This book is in many ways a vindication of the ordinary decision-maker—particularly his or her attitude towards risk—from the point of view of even ideal rationality. This is a significant shift. The most widely accepted normative theory of decision-making, *expected utility theory*, claims that ordinary decision-makers are by and large irrational. This is because expected utility theory dictates a narrow way in which risk considerations can play a role in an individual's choices. It dictates that rational individuals cannot, for example, care proportionately more about what happens in the worst-case scenario than the best, or *vice versa*. But most people do pay special attention to these features of their decisions.

Are people irrational to take risk into account in the way they do, as expected utility theory claims? I argue that they are not. I show that making decisions in the way that many ordinary people do can be seen as one of many acceptable ways of picking the option with the best consequences given what one knows and does not know about the world. Furthermore, I argue that the considerations traditionally thought to support the orthodox, more stringent theory actually only support a theory which leaves more up to the individual. While the orthodox theory leaves up to the individual what to value and what to believe, the correct theory will also leave up to the individual her strategy for moving from considerations about how a choice will turn out under various circumstances to an overall evaluation of that choice. Individuals described by the orthodox theory choose according to an acceptable strategy—but so too do many individuals who are not described by the theory. Because expected utility theory is impoverished with respect to how risk can rationally be taken into account, a new theory is needed. In this book I propose and argue for a normative alternative to expected utility theory, which I call *risk-weighted expected utility theory*.

In proposing and defending this alternative to the orthodox theory of rational decision-making, I am bringing together two strains of research: one from economics and one from philosophy. Since at least the 1950s, it has been well-known that most ordinary people have preferences that violate expected utility theory. Economists and psychologists have done an excellent job of developing alternative, non-expected utility models of decision-making and analyzing their formal properties. However, there are two reasons that these developments have gone largely unnoticed by philosophers. First, philosophers are interested in what decision-makers *ought* to do, and these models are widely considered to be descriptive, not normative. Indeed, many of them allow decision-makers to violate relatively uncontroversial criteria of rationality. Second, philosophers have found models of decision-making useful in the study of individuals' beliefs about ordinary events whose probabilities are not given, such as whether there will be traffic or how likely they are to succeed in a particular career. These beliefs are usually represented as *subjective probabilities*. The non-expected utility models of economists and psychologists do not cohere well with subjective probabilities. They typically either take the probabilities to be given, so that we cannot discover an individual's beliefs at all, or they model beliefs using subjective mental states that do not behave like probabilities, so that we cannot represent *rational* belief as it is traditionally conceived.

My proposal specifically responds to these philosophical concerns, as it employs subjective probabilities and, I will argue, is normatively defensible. Therefore it should be useful to philosophers interested in rational decision-making and belief-formation. Additionally, although economists have typically been less concerned with how individuals ought to reason and with what instrumental rationality amounts to, resolving these debates can provide a much-needed explanation of what decision-makers are doing when they have preferences that violate the orthodox theory, and how and why these preferences might be justified. So this book should be useful to economists as well. Finally, although this book may not help anyone decide what time to leave for work or what career to pursue, it does show how ordinary decision-makers must think about certain kinds of decisions if they are to avoid inconsistency: decisions that take place over time and decisions that are interdependent. So the ordinary decision-maker interested in which principles follow from her general outlook may benefit from the discussion as well.

Because I am writing for a diverse audience, I have tried to assume as little background as possible given the limitations of the subject matter. A background in either philosophy or economics is sufficient. But my hope is that even readers largely unfamiliar with both philosophy and economics will be able to follow the argument, and it is for this reason that I devote significant space in the first chapter to explaining both the technical and philosophical developments in decision theory up to this point in time.

An extensive mathematical background is not required to understand the main argument of the book. Mathematical results do play a role in the argument—particularly the representation theorem in Chapter 3—and for this reason, some readers will benefit from the technical details. Nonetheless, the informal discussion of these details should be enough for less technical readers to understand the substance of the debate. Those readers can skip Sections 2.2, 2.3, 3.2, and 4.4. While Section 3.2 contains a detailed presentation of the main mathematical result of the book, readers can gain an understanding of the basic idea by following the discussion in Sections 3.3 and 3.4.

This book began as my dissertation, which I wrote at Princeton University under the guidance of Philip Pettit and Adam Elga. Both Philip and Adam were patient and encouraging, and offered invaluable feedback and advice. I continued to research for and write this book during my time as an assistant professor at UC Berkeley, and the support and encouragement I received from my colleagues—particularly Branden Fitelson—has been tremendous. In addition, while at Berkeley I received several grants that enabled me to devote time to this book. These included the UC President's Faculty Fellowship, the Doreen B. Townsend Fellowship, and several grants from the Committee on Research at Berkeley.

Several people were generous enough to read entire drafts of this book, offering sharp, careful, and insightful feedback: Kenny Easwaran, Peter Epstein, Julian Jonker, Jim Joyce, Brad Monton, Susan Vineberg, and Peter Wakker. I owe them a debt of gratitude. In many cases I was forced to rethink an argument in response to their well-formulated concerns, and my conversations with them dictated the course of several sections of the book.

I have also benefited greatly from conversations with other colleagues. These include Brad Armendt, Dave Baker, Eliza Block, Richard Bradley, Tom Dougherty, Antony Eagle, Wes Holliday, Niko Kolodny, Geoff Lee, Sarah Moss, Jennifer Nagel, Samir Okasha, Richard Pettigrew, Ted Poston, Alex Pruss, Sherri Roush, Teddy Seidenfeld, Mike Titelbaum, Paul Weirich, Seth Yalcin, Kevin Zollman, and many others. I received helpful feedback from audiences to whom I presented parts of this material, including at Bristol, Duke, Illinois-Chicago, Iowa, Massachusetts-Amherst, MIT, Missouri, North Carolina-Chapel Hill, Oxford, Peking, Penn, Pittsburgh, Rutgers, Southern Alabama, Southern Methodist, Stanford, and Toronto; the Department of Bioethics at the National Institutes of Health; the Carolina Metaphysics Workshop; the Northwest Workshop on Time and Rationality; and the Formal Epistemology Workshops in Munich and UT Austin, the latter of which is where these ideas were first presented.

A few additional people deserve thanks. The first is Kara Lindstrom, who helped create many of the images in this book. The second is Jada Twedt Strabbing, who has been a constant source of encouragement. I am especially indebted to the many friends who offered support, inspiration, and fun throughout the writing of this book. Most importantly, I could not have completed this book without the support of my brothers and my parents.

Contents

Introduction

I.1 Introduction

When an individual is making a decision and is uncertain about some relevant aspect of the world, he must consider how his choices will turn out under various circumstances. We can think of each of his possible choices as a gamble whose outcomes depend on the state of the world: for example, the choice to not bring an umbrella on one's walk is a gamble that results in getting wet if it rains and staying dry if it does not. To form preferences among various gambles, the individual must consider which outcomes he prefers and how likely each gamble is to bring about each outcome, in order to arrive at an overall evaluation of each gamble. The main subject of decision theory is what principles ought to govern these preferences. Thus, decision theories are theories of *instrumental* or *means-ends* rationality: if a rational individual is an individual who "takes the means to his ends," they formalize what it is to have consistent ends and prefer the means that realize them. Alternatively, decision theories formalize what it is to have *consistent preferences*.

The orthodox view is that *expected utility theory*, which dictates that agents prefer the gamble with the highest expected utility, is the correct theory of instrumental rationality. Expected utility (EU) theory is supposed to characterize the preferences of all rational decision-makers. And yet, there are some preferences that violate EU theory that seem both intuitively appealing and *prima facie* consistent.

An important group of these preferences stems from how ordinary decision-makers take risk into account. In EU theory, all of the information about an agent's preferences among gambles can be reduced to information about his attitude towards various outcomes (his utility function) and how likely he thinks the states that generate them are to obtain (his probability function). Thus, if a rational decision-maker does not like taking risks, this must be attributed to the fact that either the utility values he assigns to outcomes or the probability values he assigns to states are lower than their "face values." However, being averse to taking risks is intuitively neither a matter of disvaluing particular outcomes nor of being pessimistic about what will happen; rather, it is a matter of treating what will happen in the worst-case scenarios as more important to one's choices than what will happen in the best-case scenarios. More generally, it is a matter of being sensitive to "global" properties of gambles: of being sensitive not just to what happens in each particular outcome but to what the gamble looks like as a whole.

Global properties include what the worst- and best-case scenarios are, and also the extent to which the values of a gamble are spread out. And in practice, many decision-makers do care more about what happens in the worst-case scenarios, and are sensitive to global properties of gambles, in a way that on the face of it EU theory cannot capture. Thus, there seems to be an important disconnect between EU theory and the preferences of many actual decision-makers.

If one is sympathetic to the general aim of decision theory, there are three potential lines of response. The first is to claim that contrary to initial appearances, EU theory can capture decision-makers who care about global properties. There are two ways to make this argument, both of which claim that the critics of EU theory have not understood one or more of its entities. On the one hand, a defender of EU theory might point out that the utility function does not just describe a decision-maker's evaluation of outcomes; rather, it describes both his evaluation of outcomes *and* his attitude towards risk, in virtue of the way it is constructed from his preferences. Alternatively, a defender of EU theory might point out that complete specifications of the outcomes themselves include not only the prize won, but also how the individual got that prize: for example, that it was the result of a risky gamble. These first responses say that once we understand what the utility function is meant to represent or how fine-grained the outcomes to which the individual assigns value are, we understand that the theory already takes account of the individual's attitude towards risk.

The second line of response is to grant that many people care about global properties in a way that cannot be represented by EU theory, but to claim that these people are simply not rational in doing so. Expected utility theory, this response says, is the correct *normative* theory: it describes the preferences people should strive for, not the preferences ordinary people actually have. So there is no problem in its being unable to represent the preferences that most of us have, and one should only look for an alternative model when doing *descriptive* decision theory.

I find neither of these responses to be adequate: it *is* rationally permissible to take risk into account in the way many actual people do, and it *is not* possible for EU theory to accommodate the preferences of these people. The aim of this book is to argue for these claims, and to advocate a third response: modifying our normative theory to widen the range of rationally permissible preferences. In particular, I advocate widening the set of attitudes towards risk that count as rationally permissible.

As mentioned above, EU theory includes two parameters that are subjectively determined by the decision-maker: the probabilities he assigns to states, and the utilities he assigns to outcomes. The former express his beliefs about what the world is like, and the latter express his attitude towards outcomes, although in what sense they do so is a matter of some controversy, as we will see. However, there is an additional subjective judgment that an individual must make: how to weigh the fact that one act will bring about some outcome for sure against the fact that another act has some chance of a better outcome, but some chance of a worse outcome. Two individuals might attach the same value to various sums of money and agree about the likelihood of gambles to result in these amounts of money, yet one individual might think it better to take a gamble with a high potential payoff despite the risk of a low potential payoff, whereas the other might prefer a "sure-thing" sum of money with a middle-value payoff. Furthermore, both of these decision-makers can be rational in their judgments.

The theory I propose, *risk-weighted expected utility theory* (REU theory), includes three subjective parameters: a utility function of outcomes, a probability function of states, and a risk function of probabilities that represents how the individual trades off securing good worst-case scenarios against allowing for good best-case scenarios. Like others in the family of non-expected utility theories to which it belongs—the "rank-dependent" theories—risk-weighted expected utility theory is a generalization of expected utility theory: it can accommodate any set of preferences that expected utility theory can accommodate, in addition to sets of preferences, stemming from different ways of taking risk into account, that expected utility theory cannot accommodate. Expected utility maximization, then, will be a special case of risk-weighted expected utility maximization with a particular kind of risk function.

In proposing and defending this alternative to the orthodox theory of rational decision-making, I am bringing together two strains of research: one from economics and psychology and one from philosophy. Economists and psychologists have done an excellent job of developing alternative, non-expected utility models of decision-making and analyzing their formal properties. However, there are two reasons why these developments have gone largely unnoticed by philosophers. First, philosophers are interested in what decision-makers *ought* to do, and these models are widely considered to be descriptive, not normative. Indeed, many of them allow decision-makers to violate relatively uncontroversial criteria of rationality. Second, philosophers have found models of decision-making useful in the study of individuals' beliefs about ordinary events whose probabilities are not given. These beliefs are usually represented as *subjective probabilities*. The non-expected utility models of economists and psychologists do not cohere well with subjective probabilities. They typically either take the probabilities to be given, so that we cannot discover an individual's beliefs at all, or they employ probabilities that are subjective but not additive, so that we cannot represent *rational* belief as it is conceived traditionally.

REU theory is a normative theory. It aims to characterize the preferences of decision-makers with a structure that is richer than that of EU theory, and superior from the point of view of describing rational preferences. To this end, I provide *mathematical foundations* for REU theory. I show that when we are given an individual's preferences, REU theory provides a way to discover the utility values she attaches to outcomes; to discover her probabilities in such a way that they are *subjective* but also *additive*; and to discover her risk-attitudes. It does so by separating the derivation of the probability function from that of the function that measures the weight each outcome is given in decision-making. Specifically, I prove a "representation theorem" to show that if a decision-maker's preferences obey certain intuitive axioms—weaker than those required by EU theory—then she can be represented by a utility function, a probability function that is both subjective and additive, and a risk function such that she maximizes risk-weighted expected utility relative to those functions; furthermore, these functions meet the appropriate uniqueness conditions. In explicating this theorem I show that satisfying the axioms of REU theory rather than the stronger axioms of EU theory really does correspond to being sensitive to global properties of gambles. Furthermore, I provide *philosophical foundations* for REU theory. I defend the rationality of the preferences that the orthodox theory treats as irrational but that the proposed theory can accommodate, and more generally I argue that REU theory rather than EU theory correctly captures instrumental rationality. I show that some of the arguments traditionally thought to demonstrate that rational preferences must obey EU theory do not succeed, and I argue that the grounds traditionally taken to support EU theory in fact support only the more permissive REU theory.

I.2 Chapter Summary

Chapter 1 explains the problem that the orthodox theory faces. It presents examples of preferences that seem *prima facie* reasonable but that EU theory cannot accommodate. It explains why EU theory cannot accommodate these preferences by examining how the theory formally analyzes the concept of risk-aversion. Because of the formal constraints EU theory places on preferences, it dictates that once an individual has fixed beliefs about how likely a gamble is to result in various outcomes, only "local" considerations about the values of outcomes can give rise to risk-averse preferences. It rules out a different reason for having risk-averse preferences: sensitivity to global properties of gambles. This chapter investigates the range of alternative descriptive models found in the philosophy, economics, and psychology literature, and argues that none of these models can be normative: none of them provides a successful analysis of instrumental rationality.

Chapter 2 makes a positive proposal: rational agents maximize *risk-weighted expected utility*. Thus, the preferences of rational agents are captured by risk-weighted expected utility (REU) theory. REU theory separates the two different kinds of reasons for risk-averse preferences—those allowed by EU theory and those ruled out—and allows both to figure into a rational agent's decisions. I draw on work in economics to characterize precisely the relationship between the formal correlates of these two kinds of reasons on the one hand and risk-averse preferences on the other. It is then easy to see how REU theory accommodates the preferences discussed in Chapter 1. Chapter 2 also explains how REU theory characterizes the three subjective elements of instrumental rationality (reasons of the two types, as well as beliefs) and their role in decision-making. Finally, it provides some support for thinking that REU theory is not itself overly restrictive.

Chapter 3 provides a representation theorem for REU theory. This theorem outlines a set of constraints on agents' preferences—strictly weaker than the constraints of EU theory—and shows that if an individual's preferences meet these constraints, then we can represent her beliefs, her desires, and her *attitude towards risk* by precise numerical values. We will see that one way to characterize the dispute between EU theory and REU theory is in terms of whether to accept an axiom known as Tradeoff Consistency or instead a combination of two weaker axioms: Comonotonic Tradeoff Consistency and Strong Comparative Probability. We will also see how the constraints that REU theory accepts map onto allowing individuals to care about global properties of gambles, and how an REU maximizer behaves differently from an EU maximizer at the level of preferences.

Chapter 4 is devoted to a final attempt on behalf of EU theory to argue that EU theory really can accommodate preferences that result from sensitivity to global properties of gambles. This argument says that one can redescribe the "counter-example" preferences so that the properties that constitute the riskiness of a gamble attach to the outcomes themselves—accepting, we might say, that the global properties in question are really local properties. This strategy is a widely-used strategy to respond to purported counterexamples in decision theory, and I argue that while the strategy does succeed against many of the purported counterexamples in the literature, it does not succeed against the risk-related counterexamples. I provide a mathematical argument to the effect that if individuals really are REU maximizers, then they cannot be described as EU maximizers without counting equally as following many different decision rules, or as being EU maximizers with respect to many different utility functions and with respect to any probability function whatsoever.

In the second half of the book the focus shifts to the question of whether decision-makers whose preferences REU theory characterizes are genuinely rational. Chapter 5 begins with a discussion of what decision theorists take instrumental rationality to consist in. This discussion provides the background for the arguments in the remainder of the book. The chapter also explains two additional ways to see the dispute between EU theory and REU theory as a dispute about an axiom that rules out global properties— as a dispute about the Sure-Thing Principle (STP) or about the Independence Axiom. STP and Independence can each be thought of as a constraint on how agents treat risk, in the following sense: each requires that an outcome must contribute to different gambles in the same way, regardless of which other outcomes are possible on those gambles. Each requires that the values that outcomes contribute to the gambles they compose cannot be "interactive." EU theory accepts each of these constraints as a rational requirement, but REU theory accepts only a weakened version of each of them. Therefore, the remainder of Chapter 5 is devoted to responding to two arguments that STP and the Independence Axiom are self-evident constraints on instrumentally rational preferences.

Chapter 6 examines how REU maximizers perform in diachronic choice situations. In particular, it considers an argument that REU maximizers are irrational on the grounds that anyone who violates STP will be subject to diachronic inconsistency, or will be forced to choose an act that from her own point of view does not have the best consequences. I argue that there are diachronic choice strategies that allow REU maximizers to remain consistent and consequentialist while violating STP, and I consider the relationship between these strategies and philosophical views about agency.

Chapter 7 considers two arguments against REU theory that each involve choice in multi-decision scenarios: both attempt to show that REU theory will give the wrong answer in these scenarios. The first argument is a version of the classic "Dutch book" argument that betting quotients ought to be additive on pain of vulnerability to sure loss. The second argument claims that agents who conform to REU theory fare worse in the long-run. Neither of these arguments succeeds, or so I argue, but they both show us something important about how rational agents who care about global properties approach multi-decision scenarios. I close by considering the relationship between a rational individual's preferences in choice situations described so as to include everything she cares about, and her preferences in more tractable decision problems.

I.3 Terminology

Before I begin, a few preliminary notes about terminology are in order. It will help to have a canonical example of a decision problem. Consider an agent deciding whether to carry an umbrella to work. She is not sure whether it will rain, and if it rains, she is not sure how hard it will rain. If she does not carry the umbrella, then she will get slightly wet if it rains lightly, will get drenched if it rains hard, and will stay dry if it does not rain. If she carries the umbrella, she will stay dry no matter what, but she will have to deal with the unpleasantness of carrying an umbrella around.

I follow Savage's framework, which separates outcomes, acts, and states of the world.[1] **States** are descriptions of the world that are detailed enough to fix everything the agent cares about, and they are mutually exclusive and exhaustive. In our toy example, there are three states: *it does not rain* (s_1), *it rains lightly* (s_2), and *it rains heavily* (s_3). In most actual examples, states will be more fine-grained. Indeed, we will assume that the set of states is infinite. However, matters can be simplified by grouping states together. With this in mind, **events** are sets of states: the event *it rains* is the set {*it rains lightly, it rains hard*}, and the event *it does not rain* is the singleton set {*it does not rain*}. When events rather than states are used in decision problems, they will be partitioned to be mutually exclusive and exhaustive, so that the states in each event all yield a single outcome. There will naturally be many ways to form such a partition. **Outcomes**, or what Savage calls "consequences," are descriptions of all of the things the agent cares about in a particular situation that obtains. Savage refers to consequences as "states of the person as opposed to states of the world."[2] The outcomes in the above problem are *stay dry and do not carry* (x_1), *get slightly wet and do not carry* (x_2), *get drenched and do not carry* (x_3), and *stay dry and carry* (x_4). I will sometimes speak as if the outcomes of

---

[1] Savage (1954/1972: pp. 8–17); all page numbers refer to the 1972 edition. I will discuss some objections to this framework in Chapter 3.

[2] Savage, p. 14.

decision problems are particular goods or amounts of money, such as a pair of gloves or $50. This will be shorthand for the status quo altered by that prize: for example, the situation W_{gloves} consisting of the goods the agent currently has (and everything the agent cares about) altered by the addition of a pair of gloves.[3] Outcomes will be the inputs of the utility function u, and so "u(gloves)" will be shorthand for "u(W_{gloves})." Furthermore, if "A" names an outcome in which an agent receives a good, then "$\bar{A}$" names the outcome in which the agent does not receive the good. Finally, it is important to stress that outcomes include *everything* the agent cares about in a particular situation. So, for example, if an agent cares about the difference between $0 and $100, but also prefers not to get the $100 by stealing, then "$100 and I stole to get it" will be a different outcome from "$100 and I did not steal to get it."

Determining how fine-grained the outcomes are is the focus of Chapter 4. In most actual decisions, of course, agents will care about a lot of things, so the set of outcomes and states will be extremely complex. For the purposes of explaining key points and examining intuitions, most of my examples will involve artificially simple decision problems: whatever general points can be extracted from them about risk can be applied to the more complex situations that decision-makers actually face. When we are dealing with only one choice problem, this simplification will not make a difference. However, in Chapter 7 we deal with multi-decision scenarios. There I turn briefly to the problem of how to isolate a context in which a decision about a simpler, tractable problem is a good guide to a decision about the problem specified so as to include everything the agent cares about. This is the problem, in Savage's terminology, of isolating a "small-world" decision problem that is a good guide to the "grand-world" problem.

The decision an agent faces can be thought of as a decision about which act to perform. A **Savage act,** or simply an **act,** is a function from states to outcomes: the act fully determines which outcome results in each state. For example, the act of not bringing an umbrella is the function $f = \{s_1, x_1; s_2, x_2; s_3, x_3\}$, and the act of bringing an umbrella is the function $g = \{s_1, x_4; s_2, x_4; s_3, x_4\}$. I will in general write $\{s_1, x_1; s_2, x_2; \ldots\}$ for the act that yields outcome x_i in state s_i for each i, noting that the set of states might be infinite. Similarly, we can write $\{E_1, x_1; E_2, x_2; \ldots; E_n, x_n\}$ for the act that for each event E_i, yields outcome x_i in every state of E_i, where the E_i are mutually exclusive and exhaustive. Notice that the number of events in an act is finite. This is because although the set of outcomes, like the set of states, is allowed to be infinite, the set of acts with which we are primarily concerned is the set of **finite-valued acts.** A finite-valued act is an act whose possible outcomes form a finite subset of the outcome set. Finally, an act is defined by the outcomes that occur in each of its states, and need not have a "natural" description: the act $h = \{s_1, x_4; s_2, x_1; s_3, x_2\}$ is an example of such an act. In Chapter 7 it will be important to distinguish between acts, whose outcomes are described to include everything

---

[3] Since there will in general be many unknowns, in the typical decision situation, "the status quo" will itself refer to a gamble. So "a pair of gloves" as a prize will be the status quo gamble, each state altered by the addition of a pair of gloves. In most of the examples we will assume away uncertainty about the status quo, but this will be a further topic of discussion in Chapter 7.

the agent cares about (for example, her total fortune), and **bets**, whose outcomes are described as changes in wealth.

It is common to distinguish between decision-making under risk and decision-making under uncertainty. In this context, decision-making under uncertainty means that the objects of preferences are acts; and decision-making under risk means that the objects of preference are gambles in which the probability of each outcome is specified ahead of time. Following standard terminology, we will call these latter objects **lotteries**: a lottery specifies the probability with which each outcome occurs, where these probabilities sum to 1. For example, $L = \{x_1, 0.2; x_2, 0.3; x_3, 0.5\}$ is a lottery that gives its recipient a 20% chance of staying dry while not carrying an umbrella; a 30% chance of getting slightly wet while not carrying an umbrella; and a 50% chance of getting drenched while not carrying an umbrella. More generally, we will write $\{x_1, p_1; x_2, p_2; \ldots; x_n, p_n\}$ for the lottery that yields outcome x_i with probability p_i for each i.

There are two important differences between lotteries and acts. The first is that in defining a lottery we ignore which states are associated with which outcomes: we only include the probability that a particular lottery results in a particular outcome. Acts, on the other hand, are explicitly defined in terms of states. The second difference lies in whether the probabilities are "built-in"—that is, in whether we are dealing with objective or subjective probabilities. In defining a lottery the probabilities are specified ahead of time, and in defining an act they are up to the agent to supply. Even if the agent deciding between acts hears a weatherman forecast that there is a 30% chance of light rain and a 50% chance of heavy rain, it cannot be taken for granted that the agent is facing L, because it is open to her to reject the weatherman's predictions. The difference, therefore, between decisions under risk and decisions under uncertainty is not whether the agent can attach precise probabilities to the occurrence of outcomes, but rather whether there are probabilities "built-in" ahead of time. (It will not be an *assumption* of decision-making under uncertainty that the agent does attach precise probabilities, though it will follow from standard axiomatizations of EU theory, as well as the axiomatization of REU theory, that she does.) While the primary focus of this book is decision-making under uncertainty—and a decision-maker's preferences about acts—it will sometimes be helpful to talk about preferences about lotteries as well. I will use the generic term **gamble** to refer to acts or lotteries, even for the degenerate act that yields the same outcome in every state or the degenerate lottery that yields some outcome with probability 1. In each decision problem that an agent faces, she may pick among several gambles available to her; these will be her **options**. The set of options will be a subset of the total set of acts or lotteries.

The focus of this book will be an individual's **preferences** over gambles. The statement that an individual prefers f to g is ambiguous between the colloquial meaning that she strictly prefers it ($g < f$) and the sometimes-used technical meaning that she weakly prefers it ($g \leq f$), the difference being that her weakly preferring it does not rule out that she is indifferent ($f \sim g$) but her strictly preferring it does. For readability, I will use "prefers" to mean "strictly prefers" unless otherwise specified. I will also use the

Table I.1. Sample decision matrix.

	No rain (s_1)	Light rain (s_2)	Heavy rain (s_3)
Do not bring umbrella	Dry, do not carry (x_1)	Slightly wet, do not carry (x_2)	Drenched, do not carry (x_3)
Bring umbrella	Dry, carry (x_4)	Dry, carry (x_4)	Dry, carry (x_4)

locution "x is better than y" as shorthand for "the agent prefers x to y" when it is clear that we are talking about an individual's preferences, but I do not mean to take a stand on the relationship between preference and goodness.

We can represent a decision problem in matrix form (Table I.1). In general, each column corresponds to an event and each row to an act, and the intersection of the two corresponds to the outcome that results from that act in the states of that event.

One final note on the relationship between preference and choice. It seems to me that an agent's choice behavior is generally a good guide to her preferences, but a defeasible guide. However, I will not take an official stance about the relationship between preference and choice, since it will not make a difference to my arguments: I am interested in the structure of rational preference. I will sometimes describe the agent as choosing a particular option rather than preferring it when talk of preferring would result in an awkward locution, but everything I say can be recast in the language of preferences.

1

Instrumental Rationality and Expected Utility Theory

1.1 Examples

The concept of rationality that decision-theorists are concerned with encompasses two ideas. The first is rationality in the *instrumental* (rather than epistemic) sense: one ought to prefer the means to one's ends. The second is rationality in the *consistency* (rather than substantive) sense: one ought to have preferences that are consistent with each other. This book presents an alternative to the most widely accepted theory of rationality, expected utility (EU) theory. Therefore, it is natural to begin by making clear what expected utility theory says and what it is committed to. We will start with four examples of preferences that EU theory rules out. These preferences result from how decision-makers take risk into account when evaluating gambles. We will see why EU theory cannot accommodate these preferences, by way of seeing how EU theory treats preferences that display aversion to or penchant for risk.

The examples presented here will not yet be decisive counterexamples to EU theory. Although on an initial reading they violate EU theory, the EU theorist will have several tools available to capture the preferences in question—these include endorsing a particular view of what the utility function represents and redescribing the relevant outcomes—and it is also open to him to argue that the preferences are irrational. I will consider each of these responses in detail throughout the book, and ultimately argue that none of them can be successful. The main point of this section is to get several examples on the table, that seem to instantiate a common phenomenon—and to make a *prima facie* case that these are examples of preferences that rational people can have: that these preferences have a coherent rationale behind them.

1.1.1 Jeff

Jeff is a stamp collector who lives in a cold climate. He finds himself with the possibility of winning some prizes, on the basis of two coin-flips. A referee will flip one coin, and if it lands heads, Jeff will receive a rare Elvis stamp; if it lands tails, he will receive nothing. Then, the referee will flip a different coin, and if it lands tails, Jeff will receive a nice pair of gloves; if it lands heads, he will receive nothing. Jeff believes both coins to be fair. Before this happens, however, the referee offers Jeff a sort of insurance: for a few cents

Table 1.1. Jeff's decision problem.

	HH	HT	TH	TT
Deal 1	*Elvis stamp*	*Elvis stamp and gloves*	*Nothing*	*Gloves*
Deal 2	*Elvis stamp*	*Elvis stamp*	*Gloves*	*Gloves*

she will change the procedure so that the first coin determines both outcomes—if it lands heads, he gets the Elvis stamp, and if it lands tails, he gets the gloves—and therefore Jeff will be guaranteed to receive some prize (the second coin will still be flipped, but its outcome will not matter). Jeff values the two goods *independently* in the sense that having one does not add to or decrease from the value of having the other; they are not like, say, a left-hand glove and a right-hand glove. Receiving a prize does not have any value apart from the value of the prizes themselves: Jeff does not like winning for its own sake. And he is not the sort of person who experiences regret or disappointment when he might have received something but did not: he only cares about what he actually has. He decides that the referee's deal is worthwhile—it would be nice to guarantee that he gets something no matter what—so he decides to pay a few cents to allow the first coin to determine both prizes. We can represent his options schematically in Table 1.1.

Jeff prefers Deal 2 to deal 1.

1.1.2 Linda

Linda is very clear on how she values small amounts of money. Receiving $50 is just the same to her whether she starts with $0 or $50 in her pocket, as is losing $50, and she feels similarly about all small increments of money. We might say that she values money *linearly*: every dollar that she receives or loses is worth as much to her as the previous ones, at least for amounts of money less than, say, $200. And Linda is equally clear on how she values bets: she prefers $50 to a fair coin-flip between $0 and $100.[1] She reasons as follows: if I take the former, I will certainly get $50, and the possibility of getting $100 is not enough to make up for the (equally likely) possibility of getting $0—I would rather guarantee myself $50 than take that chance.

Furthermore, when Linda is making several bets she would rather not put all her eggs in one basket. For example, let us assume that she holds a bet that gives her $5, but if a dice-roll comes up one (D_1) she must pay $15 (for a loss of $10). She receives an offer of a second bet that also gives her $5, but if a particular dice-roll comes up she must similarly pay $15. The dice-roll on which she loses this bet is to be specified by her. Given that she holds the first bet, she prefers that the dice-roll on which she loses this bet be two (D_2) rather than one (D_1). That is to say, she prefers $\{D_1, \$\text{-}5; D_2, \$\text{-}5; \overline{D_1 \vee D_2}, \$10\}$ to $\{D_1, \$\text{-}20; D_2, \$10; \overline{D_1 \vee D_2}, \$10\}$. She prefers to spread out her risks.

---

[1] Unless specified otherwise, when I use the term "coin-flip" in this book I refer to a coin-flip that is fair or that the agent in question considers to be fair: that is, a 50/50 gamble.

1.1.3 Maurice

Maurice is presented with two hypothetical choices, each between two gambles.[2] He is asked first whether he would rather have L_1 or L_2:

L_1: $5,000,000 with probability 0.1, $0 with probability 0.9.
L_2: $1,000,000 with probability 0.11, $0 with probability 0.89.

He reasons that the minimum he stands to walk away with is the same either way, and there is not much difference in his chances of winning *some* money. So, since L_1 yields much higher winnings at only slightly lower odds, he decides he would rather have L_1. He is then asked whether he would rather have L_3 or L_4:[3]

L_3: $1,000,000 with probability 0.89, $5,000,000 with probability 0.1, $0 with probability 0.01.
L_4: $1,000,000 with probability 1.

He reasons that the minimum amount that he stands to win in L_4 is a great deal higher than the minimum amount he stands to win in L_3, and that although L_3 presents the possibility of much higher winnings, this fact is not enough to offset the possibility of ending up with nothing. So he decides he would rather have L_4.

1.1.4 John

Finally, John does not have a well-worked out view of how much he values money (except that he prefers more money rather than less), but he is interested in formulating some rules for himself that will help him determine when to take a gamble.[4] He thinks about how much he should pay for a 50% chance of winning some particular amount of money, and reasons that it should be somewhat less than half that amount, since he would be unwilling to give up a sure-thing sum of money for a 50% chance of twice that sum. So he formulates the following rule:

R1. Whenever faced with a coin-flip between some particular sum and nothing, be indifferent between taking the coin-flip and receiving one-third of that sum for certain.

Formally, $\{\$0, 0.5; \$x, 0.5\} \sim \{\$(\frac{1}{3})x, 1\}$.

For example, a 50% chance of $30 is worth $10, and a 50% chance of $90 is worth $30. John then thinks about how he values 50/50 lotteries in general: as an example, he considers 50/50 lotteries where the "high" value is $30 higher than the "low" value. He

---

[2] Example due to Maurice Allais (1953/1979, p. 132); all page numbers refer to the 1979 edition. Amounts of money used in the presentation of this example vary.

[3] Just to be clear, Maurice does not get one of the first gambles and *also* get to pick one of the second: he makes each choice in isolation.

[4] This example is taken from Hansson (1988, pp. 147–51). Language altered slightly, and details of John's reasoning filled in.

reasons that he would pay at least the "low" value for such a lottery, since it will yield at least that value and maybe more. But he would pay somewhat less than the average value of the lottery (somewhat less than the low value plus $15), since, again, he would not be willing to exchange a sure-thing sum of money for an even chance of getting $15 more than that sum of money and getting $15 less. So he formulates the following rule:

R2. Whenever faced with a coin-flip between one sum of money and another which is $30 larger, be indifferent between taking the coin-flip and receiving the lesser prize plus $10 for certain.

Formally, {$y, 0.5; $y + $30, 0.5} ~ {$y + $10, 1}.

For example, a coin-flip between $50 and $80 is worth $60, and a coin-flip between $100 and $130 is worth $110. These two rules have the advantage of yielding the same result in the only case in which they both apply: they both recommend that when faced with a coin-flip between $30 and $0, John should be indifferent between this lottery and $10. Furthermore, they seem to express a single attitude towards gambling: assume you are to get some fixed sum of money; then be indifferent between a 50% chance of getting some specified amount more, and simply getting one-third of that specified amount guaranteed.

On the face of it, each of these individuals has preferences that seem rational: they seem coherent and reasonable, and they seem to have been formed in a way consistent with each individual trying to do as well as he can for himself. However, according to expected utility theory, all these decision-makers are irrational.[5] I will postpone the discussion of whether these preferences, contrary to initial appearances, really are irrational to Chapter 5. First, though, I need to explain what it is about expected utility theory that rules out these preferences. Most of the remainder of this chapter will be devoted to this task. I will then focus the next two chapters on providing an alternative theory that can accommodate examples like these.

1.2 Risk-Aversion and Expected Utility Theory

It will be helpful to examine the origins of expected utility theory and its acceptance as the normative theory of decision-making.[6] The first formal decision theory was developed by Blaise Pascal in correspondence with Pierre Fermat about "the problem of the points"—the problem of how, when a game ends prematurely, to divide up the pot among the players, given the stakes they hold.[7] Pascal proposed that each gambler should be given as his share of the pot the expected monetary value of his stake, and then generalized this proposal: the monetary value of a gamble is equal to the expected

---

[5] Granting that my assumptions about them are correct. On one particular interpretation of the utility function, the constructivist interpretation, I make an assumption in Jeff's and Linda's cases that I am not entitled to without further work. This will be explained in the discussion to follow.

[6] Some of the historical discussion here appeared first in Buchak (2013).

[7] See Fermat and Pascal (1654).

value of that gamble. Formally, the value of a bet B that yields changes in wealth $\{\$x_1, p_1;$ $\$x_2, p_2; \ldots ; \$x_n, p_n\}$ is:[8]

$$EV(B) = \sum_{i=1}^{n} p_i x_i$$

Thus, Pascal proposed the following norm: one ought to choose the bet that maximizes expected monetary value.

This proposal for addressing the problem of the points exactly divides up the pot; and Pascal's more general proposal enjoins decision-makers to choose the gamble that would do better over the long-run if repeated: over the long-run, repeated trials of a gamble will average out to their expected value. However, there are several problems with the more general proposal. The first is that it does not account for the fact that which bets one should take seems to depend on what one's current fortune is: losing one's last dollar is a lot worse than losing one's millionth dollar. The second is that if we allow bets with a non-finite number of outcomes, it is easy to generate a lottery whose expected value is infinite. Consider the "St Petersburg" bet $\{\$1, {}^{1}/_{2}; \$2, {}^{1}/_{4}; \$4, {}^{1}/_{8}; \ldots\}$.[9] The expected value of this lottery is infinite; nonetheless, most people would only be willing to part with a small sum for it, and certainly very few would be willing to part with every finite sum for it. The third problem is that Pascal's proposal does not seem to account for the fact that most people would rather have a guaranteed sum of $x than a gamble whose expectation is $x.

In response to these problems, two significant modifications were suggested to Pascal's original proposal. First, bets (whose outcomes are changes in wealth) were replaced by lotteries (whose outcomes are total wealth levels).[10] Second, monetary values were replaced by a *utility function* of monetary values—a function which represents the amount of satisfaction a particular amount of money brings an individual.[11] Thus, individuals were enjoined to choose the lottery that maximizes expected utility. Daniel Bernouilli proposed that an individual's utility function of total wealth is $u(\$x) = \log(\$x)$, and along with the prescription to maximize expected utility, this answered the aforementioned problems with Pascal's proposal. Bernouilli's proposal entails that a gamble is worth a larger amount of one's money the wealthier one is, that the St Petersburg lottery is worth a finite amount of money, and that the expected utility of any lottery is less than the utility of its monetary expectation.

One significant further development produced expected utility theory in its modern form. The initial thought was that everyone ought to maximize expected utility relative to a particular, objective utility function like the one Bernouilli proposed; but this was

---

[8] Bet B is equivalent to the lottery $L = \{\$y + \$x_1, p_1; \$y + \$x_2, p_2; \ldots ; \$y + \$x_n, p_n\}$, where y is the amount of money the individual currently has.
[9] The St Petersburg Paradox was first introduced by Nicolas Bernouilli. See Joyce (1999, p. 32).
[10] This was proposed by Daniel Bernouilli (1738).
[11] This was proposed independently by Daniel Bernouilli (1738) and Gabriel Cramer (see Bernouilli 1738: 33).

replaced by the thought that the utility function could vary across people. The move to a subjective utility function also allowed a more general outcome space, so that an individual's utility function can take any outcome as input, not just her total wealth level. (The meaning of the utility function was called into question too, as I will discuss at the end of this section.) So, according to the theory in its present form, *rational agents maximize expected utility* relative to a subjective utility function.

One might worry about the move to a subjective utility function. After all, it is not clear that individuals have access to precise utility functions through introspection, and it is even less clear that decision-theorists interested in investigating the preferences of these individuals have such access. Luckily, we need not assume such introspection, or that there is any way to know an agent's utility values apart from examining her preferences. The existence of a utility function for each rational agent is *guaranteed* by any one of a number of "representation" theorems that connect pair-wise preferences to a utility function and to a probability function (assuming the latter is not given ahead of time).

Here is what these theorems say. Assume that a decision-maker's preferences between lotteries obey certain basic axioms. Then there is some way to assign values to outcomes—a numerical, subjective utility function of outcomes—such that between any two gambles the agent prefers the gamble with the higher weighted average of utility values: the higher expected utility. The expected utility of the lottery $L = \{x_1, p_1; x_2, p_2; \ldots; x_n, p_n\}$, where $\sum p_i = 1$, is given by:

$$EU(L) = \sum_{i=1}^{n} p_i u(x_i)$$

where $u(x_i)$ is the agent's subjective utility for x_i.

Philosophers usually concern themselves with the case in which probabilities are not known or given by the setup of the decision but instead are determined (consciously or not) by the decision-maker: with the case of preferences between acts. Again, as long as a decision-maker's preferences obey certain axioms (a slightly different set of axioms from those in the case of lotteries),[12] there is some way to assign subjective utility values to outcomes *and* subjective probability values to states such that the agent prefers the option whose expected utility is higher. The expected utility of the act $g = \{E_1, x_1; E_2, x_2; \ldots; E_n, x_n\}$ is given by:

$$EU(g) = \sum_{i=1}^{n} p(E_i) u(x_i)$$

where $u(x_i)$ is the agent's subjective utility for x_i, and $p(E_i)$ is the agent's subjective probability for E_i. Subjective probabilities are sometimes referred to as *credences* or *degrees of belief.*

---

[12] I will spell out these axioms in detail in Chapter 3, but I note that they include "ordering" axioms, such as completeness and transitivity; axioms that fix the relationship between gambles and outcomes; and "structural" axioms that ensure the sets of outcomes and gambles are rich enough.

In the objective probabilities version of EU theory, we say that a utility function *represents* an agent's preferences under expected utility theory just in case for all lotteries L_1 and L_2 the agent weakly prefers L_1 to L_2 iff $EU(L_2) \le EU(L_1)$, where EU is calculated relative to that utility function. In subjective expected utility theory, we say that a utility function and a probability function together represent an agent's preferences just in case for all acts f and g, the agent weakly prefers f to g iff $EU(g) \le EU(f)$, where EU is calculated relative to that utility and probability function. Because of the representation theorems, the norm *maximize expected utility* can be implemented even when an agent does not know what her utility function is. As long as she takes care to *satisfy the axioms of EU theory*, she will automatically maximize expected utility, because she will maximize the expectation of the utility function that represents her.

Technically, an agent's preferences need not adhere strictly to the axioms for her to count as having a particular utility function: the representation can tolerate some minor deviations. If an agent's preferences sometimes differ from what the utility function implies they should be, perhaps because of an inability to make precise calculations or because of a minor lapse in judgment, then we can say that the function represents her because it represents her ideal preferences or approximates her actual preferences. But there cannot be *widespread* deviation that an agent would *endorse*, even at her most clearheaded. If an agent, or an idealized version of that agent, satisfies the axioms required for the application of the representation theorem, then she can be represented by a utility function under EU theory. But if her preferences do not even approximate preferences that obey the axioms, then she is not representable by a utility function, and will be considered irrational or incoherent.

The utility function is determined by plugging an agent's *ordinal* preferences (her preferences over gambles) into the "expectation maximization" structure. According to the representation theorems, as long as an agent's preferences obey the axioms we can determine her utility function almost *uniquely*: all of the utility functions that represent her preferences will be equivalent up to unit and scale (up to *positive affine transformation*).[13] Thus, the utility functions that represent her preferences will have certain features in common. They will preserve the order of the outcomes, and they will preserve the relationship between intervals. Whatever the numerical difference between the utility of a and the utility of b, and between the utility of c and the utility of d, on a given utility function, these two numerical differences will be in the same ratio on every utility function that represents the same preferences: $\dfrac{u(a)-u(b)}{u(c)-u(d)}$ is fixed. When we speak of an agent's utility function, what we mean more precisely is the family of utility functions that represent her preferences. The only facts we will be licensed to count as facts about the agent's utility values will be the facts that these

---

[13]   To say that two utility functions u(x) and u'(x) are equivalent up to unit and scale, or equivalent up to positive affine transformation, means that there are some constants a and b where a is positive and $au(x)+b=u'(x)$. Von Neumann and Morgenstern (1944) contains an axiomatization of objective EU theory; Resnik (1987) contains a helpful exposition. Savage (1954/1972) contains an axiomatization of subjective EU theory.

functions have in common. For example, the zero point is not a "genuine" fact about the agent's utility values. Incidentally, this is also why we can simplify matters by talking about the utilities of individual goods when we mean the utilities of situations that result from adding those goods to the status quo: moving the "zero point" preserves all the genuine facts.

So, if a decision-maker has preferences that obey the axioms of expected utility theory, we can attribute to her a utility function (or family of such functions). But what does attributing a utility function to an agent mean about that agent? There are two axes along which decision theorists disagree. The first is about whether the utility function corresponds to a real mental state; for example, degree of desire, strength of preference, or amount of perceived goodness. **Psychological realists** hold that utility does correspond to a real mental state. Facts about an agent's utility function are facts about her desires or the strength of her preferences for outcomes. **Formalists**, by contrast, hold that the utility function is merely a convenient way to represent preferences: it is a theoretical construct, namely, the quantity whose mathematical expectation an agent maximizes.[14] Facts about an agent's utility function are just facts about her preferences over gambles. Formalists may be motivated by the thought that while ordinal facts about preferences correspond to something in the head, there are no mental states as precise as the utility function: I can desire something more than something else, but there is no fact of the matter about how much more I desire it. Or they may hold that there is some fact of the matter, but this is not the kind of fact captured by the utility function.

The other important disagreement about the utility function is whether facts about the utility function could in principle come apart from facts about preferences. **Constructivists** answer in the negative.[15] They hold that an agent's utility function is defined by her preferences: there is no independent source of the utility values. Regardless of whether utility corresponds to a real psychological state, utility supervenes on preferences as a matter of necessity. For constructivists, to say that the utility difference between a and b is the same as that between c and d is just to say something about the agent's preferences concerning gambles involving these outcomes. Formalists count as constructivists, clearly, but so do functionalists who hold that utility corresponds to a mental state that is constituted by its role in preferences. The latter might claim, for example, that utility corresponds to strength of desire but that what it is for an agent to have desires of a certain strength is to be disposed to have certain

---

[14] The term "formalism" comes from Hansson (1988, pp. 142–6). Wakker (1994) uses the term "the representational viewpoint" for what I call formalism, and Bérmudez (2009) uses "operationalism." A particularly clear exposition of the formalist view appears in Luce and Raiffa (1957). They write: "We are not attempting to account for [the individual's] preferences . . . We only wish to devise a convenient way to *represent* them" (p. 32). Quoted in Dreier (1996). Wakker (1994) also notes Arrow (1951) as an example of a formalist, citing Arrow thus: "the utilities assigned are not in any sense to be interpreted as some intrinsic amount of good in the outcome" (p. 425). A good example of a contemporary psychological realist is Weirich (2008), who claims that utility indicates strength of desire.

[15] The term "constructivism" comes from Dreier (1996). Good expositions of the view also appear in Maher (1993) and Dreier (2004).

preferences. **Non-constructive realists**, however, think that preferences are merely a way to discover an agent's utility function. They hold that facts about the utility function can in principle outrun facts about preferences: while preferences are a good guide to the utility function in general, there is no constitutive link between the two.[16]

One way to see the two distinctions is as distinguishing between responses to the following two questions. First, does an agent's utility function supervene on facts about her preferences? Constructivists claim that the utility function does supervene on preferences, non-constructive realists that it need not. Second, does discovering an agent's utility function tell us anything about the agent aside from her preferences about gambles? For example, does it tell us how much she prefers some outcome in choice under certainty or how much goodness she perceives in some outcome? Formalists claim that we cannot read any facts like these off of an agent's utility function, and psychological realists claim that we can. Non-constructive realism and psychological realism fit together naturally, but the former is stronger than the latter.[17]

Both of these distinctions are metaphysical, and the way a theorist comes down will commit him to a view of what it is we are doing when we determine an agent's utility function from her preferences. On the non-constructive realist picture there is some real quantity we are trying to measure, and preferences are merely a good way to measure it. On the constructivist picture (psychological realist or not), on the other hand, when we determine an agent's utility function we are primarily restating facts about her preferences.

The metaphysical distinction between non-constructive realism and constructivism is related to, though does not necessarily determine the answer to, an epistemological question that will be important in evaluating the force of the counterexamples I present. The question is to what extent the agent's own perception of her utility values needs to be accounted for when determining the agent's utility function, and, relatedly, to what extent the fact that an agent disagrees with a particular interpretation of her utility function counts against that interpretation. For a constructivist, an agent's 'perception' does not make a difference: it would be a mistake for the agent to even have pretheoretical views about her utility function, since utility functions

---

[16] There is perhaps a continuum of views between constructivism and non-constructive realism, depending on how tight the link between preferences and utility is thought to be. For example, consider a functionalist who thinks that the utility function is only partially constituted by its relationship to preferences, but also partially constituted by its relationship to utterances that agents are disposed to make about how much they desire things.

[17] Zynda (2000) uses "strong realism" for what I call non-constructive realism and "weak realism" for what I call psychological realism. Some authors fail to distinguish the two types of realism, generally because they are only interested in one of two questions: whether the utility function has any meaningful interpretations besides that which represents preferences, or whether an individual has introspective access to her utility function. Economists sometimes mention the distinction between "riskless utility" and "risky utility," where the former refers to a cardinal notion that can be determined independently of preferences over gambles and the latter is constructed from the agent's preferences over gambles. See Wakker (1994). The idea of riskless utility is only coherent for non-constructive realists, though all theorists can make sense of the notion of risky utility.

are mathematical constructs from preferences. On the other hand, it is possible for a non-constructive realist to think that an agent's perception of her utility values—her perception that she prefers an outcome to a particular extent or that she perceives a particular amount of good in it—should count as a data point when we are trying to discover what her utility values are. Although this view fits well with non-constructive realism, it is not necessary that the non-constructive realist adopt it: he might instead think that the agent's utility values are opaque to her.[18] Indeed, the non-constructive realist could take a range of views about the degree of introspective access the agent has to her utility function and the relative evidential hierarchy of the agent's preferences and the agent's perceptions in discovering the agent's utility function. But the important point is that the agent's 'perceptions' of her utility function will not sway the constructivist at all.[19]

Finally, EU theorists who adhere to any of the interpretations are committed to interpreting agents who do not obey the axioms of EU theory, and who consequently are not representable by a utility function under expected utility, as irrational. However, they may differ on one further point. A non-constructive realist can say that a decision-maker who does not obey the axioms (or approximate them closely enough) *has* a utility function but that we (the theorists) do not have a way to figure out what it is, or if we do, it is not via her ordinal preferences among gambles. But a constructivist must say that such a decision-maker cannot meaningfully be said to have a utility function at all.

In expected utility theory, in both its objective form and subjective form, the relationship between the values of outcomes and the values of the gambles they compose is fixed: the value of a gamble is a weighted average of the values of the outcomes, where each weight corresponds to the probability of getting that outcome. Given that EU theory fixes how the value of a gamble relates to the values of its constituent outcomes, it is no surprise that all facts about an agent's preferences are going to supervene on facts about her utility function: once we fix the probabilities of states, the utility function is the only thing that can vary. In particular, the fact that some agent does not like to take risks—and has preferences that reflect this—is going to show up in the values

---

[18] Dreier (1996) distinguishes between what he calls transparent realism and opaque realism on these grounds, although on his definition opaque realism encompasses both the view that the agent's introspective access to his preferences is fallible and the view that the utility function is in principle inaccessible to him.

[19] Interestingly enough, there appears to be some experimental evidence concerning whether people have introspective access to their utility functions. The evidence is this: individuals' determinations of their utility functions via introspective access appear to agree with their utility functions as determined by prospect theory (a theory that will be discussed in Sections 1.4 and 2.4): see Abdellaoui, Barrios, and Wakker (2007). The authors note (p. 361) that within the domain they consider, prospect theory agrees with what is known as anticipated utility theory, which the theory developed in this book generalizes. They suggest that the constructivist view found favor because individuals' introspective judgments of utility did not agree with their utility functions as derived from EU theory, and decision theorists were more committed to EU theory than to non-constructive realism. For theorists who are willing to abandon EU theory as descriptively accurate, and allow the utility function to be that determined by preferences along with a more descriptively accurate theory, the results of this study provide some evidence for the viability of non-constructive realism.

her utility function assigns to outcomes. For any two agents who are representable by EU theory, a difference in their preferences must show up as a difference in their utility functions. Therefore, if one does not like to take risks and the other does, we will have to interpret them as valuing outcomes differently from each other.

Many people's preferences display strict risk-aversion in the following sense: many individuals would rather have $50 than a coin-flip between $0 and $100. When this preference is plugged into the structure of EU theory, we must conclude that the utility function is such that as the size of one's winnings increases, additional amounts of money add less utility value. If one already has $50, then getting an extra $50 does not add to the value of the prospect as much as it does when one has nothing. And *vice versa*. When additional amounts of money add less utility value, the coin-flip between $0 and $100 will have an expected utility that is less than the utility of its expected dollar value. This is because the difference between the utility of $0 and the utility of $50 is larger than the difference between the utility of $50 and the utility of $100, so the increase in utility in one outcome of the gamble does not make up for the decrease in utility in the other, when computing the average utility value of the gamble: $100 is not better than $50 by as much as $0 is worse than $50.

More generally, many individuals would rather have a guaranteed $x than a risky gamble whose mean value is $x. Preferences that have this structure imply, on EU theory, a concave utility function—a utility function that diminishes marginally in monetary value.[20] (See Fig. 1.1.)

Something more general can be said about the relationship between risk-averse preferences and the utility function, as Rothschild and Stiglitz (1970) show. Consider two monetary gambles f and g (with objective or already-determined subjective probabilities) that have the same mean, but such that g is more spread out (is "riskier") in that the middle values of f are more likely to obtain, and the extreme values of g are more likely to obtain (this includes the case in which g's possible extreme values are more extreme; for example, the case in which g has a lower minimum and a higher maximum than f). More formally, assume that g can be obtained from f by a "mean-preserving spread."[21] Rothschild and Stiglitz show that if a utility function is concave,

---

[20]   A real-valued function f is concave in some interval C iff $\forall x, y \in C$ and all $\alpha \in [0, 1]$, $f(\alpha x + (1 - \alpha)y) \geq \alpha f(x) + (1 - \alpha)f(y)$. A continuous function is concave in some interval C iff $\forall x, y \in C$, $f((x + y)/2) \geq (f(x) + f(y))/2$. Concavity is strict if the inequality is strict for $x \neq y$ and $\alpha \in (0, 1)$. Definitions of convexity and strict convexity are given by reversing the inequalities. Throughout this work I will continue to use "concave" to refer to the definition that uses weak inequalities (and "strictly concave" to the definition that uses strict inequalities), so that linearity is a degenerate case of concavity. These are the standard uses. Jensen's Inequality (Jenson 1906) tells us that if u is concave, then the expected utility of a random variable (in this case, amounts of money) is no greater than the utility of its expected monetary value: if f is a gamble (with objective probabilities or already determined subjective probabilities), then $EU(f) \leq u(E(f))$, where $E(f)$ is the expected monetary value of f. And if u is convex, $EU(f) \geq u(E(f))$. Chateauneuf and Cohen (1994, p. 82) note that the converse holds: that a preference for a guaranteed $E(f)$ rather than f itself implies a concave utility function. But I do not know where this was originally shown.

[21]   This is to say: g can be obtained from f by a series of steps which consist in taking some of the probability mass from the center of f and adding it to each tail of f, while preserving the mean value. See Rothschild and Stiglitz (1970: 226–31) for a formal characterization of a mean-preserving spread.

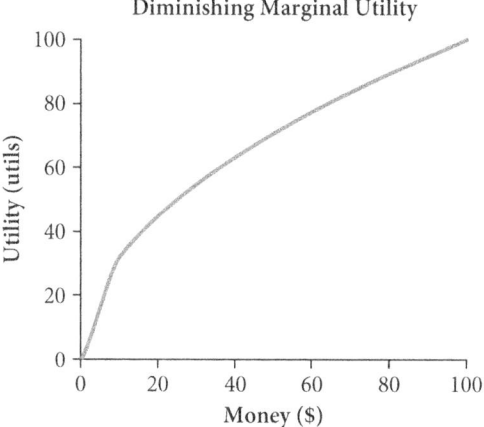

Fig. 1.1. Diminishing marginal utility.

then EU(g) ≤ EU(f). And *vice versa*. If some utility function always assigns no higher expected utility to the more "spread out" of two gambles with the same mean (if this judgment can be made, given that "more spread out" gives rise to a partial ordering), that utility function will be concave.[22]

Therefore, if a decision-maker always weakly prefers the less spread out of two gambles with the same mean monetary value, then insofar as expected utility theory can represent her preferences (that is, insofar as she satisfies the axioms of EU theory), it will represent her as having a concave utility function.

So as not to prejudge the issue of what it is to be risk-averse, I will use the term "risk-averse" to refer to a property of a preference ordering, rather than to specific features of the utility function or to the underlying psychological phenomena that might give rise to these preferences. I will say that an agent is *specifically risk-averse in money* (or any quantitative good) just in case for all *x*, the agent weakly prefers a guaranteed $x to a (non-degenerate) gamble whose mean value is $x.[23] I will say that an agent is *generally*

[22] See Rothschild and Stiglitz (1970: 240) for a summary of this result. Note that they deal with a continuous number of outcomes: that is, a definition of expected utility in terms of an integral rather than a discrete sum. In this work I deal only with the discrete case, which is a special case of this integral case. The relevant results for the discrete case appear on p. 231 of their paper. Note, interestingly enough, that the mean-preserving spread definition of risk-aversion disagrees with the definition of risk-aversion as a preference for, of two gambles with the same mean, the one with less variance. As Rothschild and Stiglitz (1970: 241) show, for any non-quadratic concave utility function, there will be gambles with the same mean such that the one with more variance has a higher expected utility. We can also, on EU theory, characterize a person's degree of risk-aversion in money, and say, of two people, when one is more risk-averse than the other. See Pratt (1954) and Ross (1981) for proposals of how to measure risk-aversion in expected utility theory. On all of these proposals, one's degree of risk-aversion will be a property of the utility function.

[23] "Weak risk-aversion" and "strong risk-aversion" are the terms used by Chateauneuf and Cohen for what I call "specific risk-aversion" and "general risk-aversion." However, since I need to disambiguate the definitions in terms of weak and strict preferences—Chateauneuf and Cohen are generally concerned with weak preference so do not need to disambiguate these—I avoid the use of their terms so as to not introduce unnecessary confusion.

risk-averse in money (or any quantitative good) just in case of any two gambles *f* and *g* such that *g* can be obtained from *f* by a mean-preserving spread, the agent weakly prefers *f*; that is, of any two gambles with the same average monetary value, the agent weakly prefers the one that is less spread out, if such a judgment can be made. When I require preference to be strict in these definitions, I will use the terms *strictly specifically risk-averse in money* and *strictly generally risk-averse in money*. The definitions will hold for any quantity which can be mapped continuously on to the real numbers—for example, lengths of life or seconds of pleasure—and my remarks about money apply to these quantities, *mutatis mutandis*. If an agent is generally risk-averse in money, she will be specifically risk-averse in money, since specific risk-aversion is a matter of behaving in a generally risk-averse way on a special kind of mean-preserving spread—one that starts from a "constant" gamble.

Since we are interested not just in continuous goods that are already ordered, we need a way to talk about risk-aversion when preferences are between gambles involving discrete goods. I will say that an agent is *generally risk-averse with respect to two goods A and B* just in case, of two gambles that yield the same probability of *A* and the same probability of *B*, the agent weakly prefers the gamble with more probability concentrated in the outcomes in which he gets at least one of the goods. (To simplify the discussion I will in general assume that for each good the agent would rather have it than not, regardless of the presence of the other.) Here is a way to think about this idea and how to capture it formally. Let us assume that an agent is facing a gamble that yields *A* with probability *a* and *B* with probability *b*. We might ask, holding fixed *a* and *b*, how much he would prefer that the states in which *A* obtains and the states in which *B* obtains overlap. In other words, if the agent could set the probability *p* of *A*&*B*, distributing probability $a - p$ to A&B̄ and $b - p$ to Ā&B, what would he prefer this probability to be? If he is generally risk-averse, he prefers to minimize *p*, to lower the chance of getting neither good even at the expense of lowering the chance of getting both. He prefers to move probability mass to the "middle" outcomes in which he receives either *A* or *B*. Formally, then, an agent is generally risk-averse with respect to *A* and *B* just in case for gambles of the form {A&B, p; A&B̄, $a - p$; Ā&B, $b - p$; Ā&B̄, $1 - a - b + p$} with any fixed *a* and *b*, he weakly prefers to minimize *p*.[24] (See Fig. 1.2.) A similar definition holds for *strict general risk-aversion* with respect to goods, with strict preference substituted for weak preference.

This definition of general risk-aversion in pairs of goods captures the same idea as the definition of general risk-aversion in money: of two gambles which yield the same goods on average, the agent weakly prefers moving probability mass from the two extreme outcomes to the middle outcomes. Notice that the two definitions agree if *A* and *B* are amounts of money: if an agent is generally risk-averse in money, she will be generally risk-averse with respect to any two sums of money considered as goods.

---

[24] Here is an equivalent way to state this definition: for any p < q, he weakly prefers {A&B, p; A&B̄, $a - p$; Ā&B, $b - p$; Ā&B̄, $1 - a - b + p$} to {A&B, q; A&B̄, $a - q$; Ā&B, $b - q$; Ā&B̄, $1 - a - b + q$}.

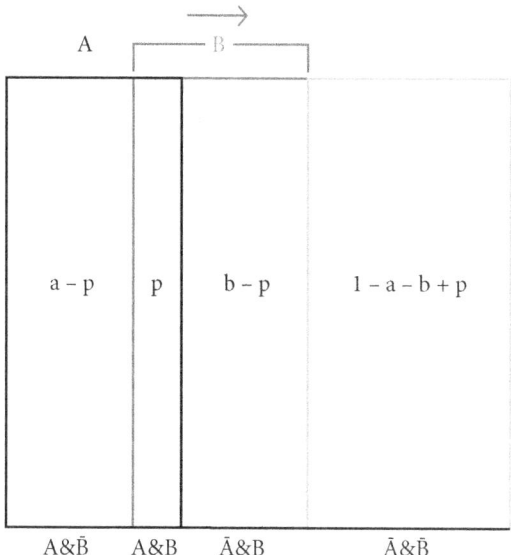

Fig. 1.2. General risk-aversion in goods.

Finally, we can give parallel definitions of risk-seeking preferences to each definition of risk-averse preferences by reversing the preference relation in the definitions of risk-averse behavior: to be generally risk-seeking in money is to prefer a mean-preserving spread, and to be generally risk-seeking in two goods is to prefer to maximize p in the above distribution. It is important to stress that all these ways of being risk-averse and risk-seeking concern properties of an agent's preferences, not (yet) of her utility function.

Again, on EU theory, an agent's being generally or strictly risk-averse in money is equivalent to her having a concave utility function, and being generally or strictly risk-seeking in money to her having a convex utility function. We can now say something about what risk-aversion in goods implies about the utility function, on EU theory. First I must define a concept that I gestured at in the "Jeff" example: *independence*. I will say that the utility function displays independence with respect to two goods A and B just in case the utility difference that having one makes is the same whether or not one has the other: $u(A\&B) - u(A\&\bar{B}) = u(\bar{A}\&B) - u(\bar{A}\&\bar{B})$. I will say that the utility function displays *dependence* with respect to two goods just in case this equivalence does not hold. (Again, let us assume that for each good the agent would rather have it than not.) One advantage of this definition is that it makes diminishing marginal utility a special case of outcome dependence: if the utility function is concave, then $u(\$x + \$y) - u(\$x) < u(\$y) - u(\$0)$. And if the utility function is in general not linear, then there exist two amounts of money x and y such that $u(\$x + \$y) - u(\$x) \neq u(\$y) - u(\$0)$. With this definition in place, it follows from EU theory that if an expected utility maximizer is strictly generally risk-averse with respect to goods A and B, then these goods are dependent.[25] More precisely, as in risk-aversion for money, receiving one of the goods adds less utility value when the agent has the other.

On EU theory, then, being generally averse to risk in money is equivalent to having a utility function that diminishes marginally, and being generally risk-averse with respect to two goods is equivalent to having a utility function with respect to which one good adds less value in the presence of the other. EU theory therefore equates a fact about an agent's preferences with a fact about her utility function. Preferring or dispreferring gambles with particular global properties (such as a particular spread) is equivalent to having a utility function with particular properties: it is equivalent to having a function that attaches values to *outcomes* in a particular way. What this equivalence means about decision-makers depends on which interpretation of utility we adopt. If we are psychological realists, then risk-aversion in money implies that the strength of an agent's desire for money diminishes marginally, and risk-aversion with respect to A and B implies that his preference for having one of the goods is less strong if he has the other.[26] Thus, on the psychological realist interpretation, diminishing marginal utility and dependence are the *psychological* correlates of risk-aversion. We might call the psychological phenomenon *saturation*: an agent's preferences display risk-aversion because money loses its value as he has more of it, or because having good A is worth less if he already has B. On the other hand, if we are formalists, then the concavity of the utility function need not correspond to a real property of the agent's values, so we cannot yet conclude anything about his psychological makeup.

1.3 Risk-Aversion and Reasons

The thesis that rational individuals maximize expected *utility* rather than expected monetary value was partially proposed to account for the phenomenon of risk-aversion. Nonetheless, in this section I will show that equating risk attitudes to properties of the utility function (for example, to diminishing marginal utility or to outcome dependence) rules out as irrational some preferences that seem to arise from risk-aversion and that initially seem reasonable. And I will show that this is true for any view of what the utility function is. These initially reasonable preferences are

---

[25] Assume that an expected utility maximizer is strictly generally risk-averse with respect to A and B.

Then, if p < q, the agent strictly prefers {A&B, p; A&B̄, a − p; Ā&B, b − p; Ā&B̄, 1 − a − b + p} to {A&B, q; A&B̄, a − q; Ā&B, b − q; Ā&B̄, 1 − a − b + q}.

Therefore, EU({A&B, p; A&B̄, a − p; Ā&B, b − p; Ā&B̄, 1 − a − b + p}) > EU({A&B, q; A&B̄, a − q; Ā&B, b − q; Ā&B̄, 1 − a − b + q}).

p(u(A&B)) + (a − p)u(A&B̄) + (b − p)u(Ā&B) + (1 − a − b + p)u(Ā&B̄) > q(u(A&B)) + (a − q)u(A&B̄) + (b − q)u(Ā&B) + (1 − a − b + q)u(Ā&B̄).

(q − p)u(A&B̄) + (q − p)u(Ā&B) > (q − p)u(A&B) + (q − p)u(Ā&B̄).

u(A&B̄) + u(Ā&B) > u(A&B) + u(Ā&B̄).

u(A&B) − u(A&B̄) < u(Ā&B) − u(Ā&B̄).

The converse also holds.

[26] Psychological realists can interpret *u* in a variety of ways, but since the difference between them does not matter for my purposes, I will use "strength of desire" to refer to the psychological realist utility function.

ruled out precisely because equating risk-aversion with a property of a function of *outcomes* rules out agents taking certain kinds of consideration into account when they choose among gambles. We will see exactly what role these considerations play in ideal practical reasoning. I will proceed by pointing out the problem for the non-constructive realist, using the examples of Jeff and Linda from Section 1.1. These two examples require assumptions that the constructivist would reject, but I begin with them even though the constructivist interpretation is more common, as they will illuminate EU theory more generally. I then show that the constructivist, even though he claims that in constructing a utility function he makes no commitments beyond those that follow from the agent's preferences, does not avoid this problem.[27] The preferences of Maurice and John, as I will explain, are ruled out as irrational on both interpretations.

It is not news that EU theory rules out some preferences that many people are initially inclined to have—Allais discovered his example (that of "Maurice") in 1953, and there has since been much psychological literature detailing other examples of EU violations. Nor am I the first to claim that this has something to do with a failure of EU theory to allow agents to "genuinely" care about risk.[28] But one problem that has been given short shrift is that of explaining what decision-makers are actually doing when they genuinely care about risk. And it is only when we can explain this that we will be able to assess whether caring about risk is rationally permissible. So, aside from laying out exactly what EU theory is committed to, one goal of this section is to explain why, from the point of view of ideal instrumental reasoning, people are violating the theory in the examples I discuss.

For the EU theorist who is a psychological realist, risk-aversion is a matter of saturation, a real psychological phenomenon. However, there is another psychological phenomenon that might give rise to risk-averse behavior. Consider two people who collect stamps. Alice is only interested in obtaining one Elvis stamp (she likes her collection to be diverse): once she has one, a second Elvis stamp is next to worthless. Bob, on the other hand, has an insatiable appetite for Elvis stamps (he does not become "saturated" with respect to Elvis stamps), but he does not like to take risks. In general, he thinks that the *possibility* of getting something good does not make up for the *possibility* of getting something bad, when the bad thing is as bad as the good thing is good, and there is an equal chance of each. He might even dislike taking risks so much that he always just wants the gamble with the best worst-case scenario. When offered a choice between one Elvis stamp on the one hand, and a coin flip between two Elvis stamps and none on the other hand, both Alice and Bob will choose the former. But they have very different reasons for this preference: Alice values outcomes in a particular way (she quickly becomes saturated with respect to Elvis stamps), while Bob cares about how outcomes of particular value are arranged across the possibility space. Expected utility theory, insofar as it can represent the preferences of these two people at all, will have to

[27] Hansson (1988) also argues that EU theory rules out what he calls "explicit risk considerations" in decision-making regardless of the interpretation of the utility function. I will discuss an example of his and the role it plays in his argument shortly.

[28] See, among others, Allais (1953/1979), Watkins (1977), Yaari (1987), and Hansson (1988).

represent them by the same utility function—a utility function that assigns less additional utility to the second Elvis stamp.

Note further that the psychological phenomenon of saturation need not always give rise to risk-averse behavior. For example, we might have a person who only slightly prefers two Elvis stamps to one, but who always prefers to take the gamble with the best best-case scenario. This person will prefer the coin flip to the certain Elvis stamp, and thus display preferences that are "risk-seeking." Expected utility theory, insofar as it can represent the preferences of this person, will have to represent him by a utility function that assigns *more* additional utility to the second Elvis stamp, even though he becomes saturated with respect to Elvis stamps. EU theory cannot distinguish between two different kinds of psychological states that give rise to the same preferences.

Is this bad? It depends partially on which kind of psychological realism we adhere to. Let us start with the stronger version: non-constructive psychological realism. On this view, there are facts apart from the agent's preferences that determine her utility function; for example, the agent's perception of how strong her preferences are. So let us assume that Linda is correct in her perception that her utility function is linear in money. She genuinely values an increase from $0 to $50 as much as she values an increase from $50 to $100. But when she evaluates the attractiveness of a gamble, she does not just care about the average of the final dollar amounts she may receive. Rather, she cares about how these amounts are arranged across the possibility space to yield that average. In particular, the possibility that she might get the higher outcome does not entirely make up for the possibility that she might get the lower outcome. Adding a good possibility to the mix does not make up for lowering the minimum value of the gamble when the mean remains unchanged. She thinks: it is really important what happens in the worst-case scenario, so the minimum value of a gamble counts a lot in my total evaluation of that gamble. Therefore, when faced with a choice between $50 and a gamble that gives her $0 if a coin lands heads and $100 if it lands tails, she would rather guarantee that she ends up with at least $50 than take the chance that she might end up with $0. And, to repeat, this is not because $0 is particularly bad (or so much worse than $50), but because the bad feature of the $0/$100 coin flip, that its minimum is lower than $50 by a particular amount, is not outweighed by the good feature of the $0/$100 coin flip, that its maximum is higher than $50 by that same amount. However, if Linda's utility function is linear, these two gambles must have the same expected utility, and therefore it would be irrational (according to EU theory) for her not to be indifferent between them.[29]

---

[29] That her utility function is linear implies that u($100) − u($50) = u($50) − u($0), which implies that (0.5)u($100) + (0.5)u($0) = u($50). Might the *subjective* expected utility theorist who is a non-constructive realist model Linda as maximizing expected utility but assigning a credence lower than 0.5 to the coin landing heads? Not if Linda is also indifferent between the coin flip that gives her $0 if the coin lands heads and $100 if it lands tails and the coin flip that gives her $0 if it lands tails and $100 if it lands heads—and we can assume she is, given her reasons as I have described them. If Linda is indifferent to which face of the coin gives her $0 and which gives her $100, the expected utility theorist is committed to modeling her as assigning probability 0.5 to the coin landing heads and probability 0.5 to the coin landing tails. Again, if Linda's psychology is as how I have described it— and it certainly seems plausible that a person would have such a psychology— then expected utility theory, in both its objective and its subjective version, must judge her to be irrational.

Provided Linda values money linearly, expected utility theory commits her to thinking that the good feature exactly outweighs the bad feature. Since she does not think this, the theory judges her to thereby be irrational. Similarly, if Linda values money linearly, then she should not be concerned about spreading out her risks. She ought to be indifferent between taking an additional risk on an already bad event and taking that risk on a different event to which she assigns the same probability: her preference about the losing dice-roll is irrational.[30]

Similarly, consider Jeff's preferences. That two goods are independent is a psychological fact about what Jeff values, and on the non-constructive realist interpretation of utility, this fact can hold independently of Jeff's preferences and should be taken into account directly by the utility function before we know what his preferences are. So let us assume that Jeff is correct that for him, an Elvis stamp and a pair of gloves are independent. It is worth noting that it is not implausible, if u corresponds to a psychological state, that agents are able to make this judgment about some goods. After all, doing so does not even involve making a direct judgment about the cardinal utilities of the goods: all Jeff has to know in order to know that he values the stamp and the gloves independently is that the presence of one does not make a difference to the value of the other. He might introspect this by realizing that when he considers how much he values a pair of gloves, he does not have to check to see if he possesses an Elvis stamp or not. It is plausible that most people are able to determine that a left-hand glove and a right-hand glove are not independent for them: the left-hand glove is more valuable if one has the right-hand glove, and *vice versa*.[31] When one considers how much a left-hand glove is worth, whether one has the right-hand glove is very relevant; but, perhaps, whether one has some other good is not. So it is plausible that Jeff is correct in his judgment that for him, an Elvis stamp and a pair of gloves are independent: that is, that $u(S\&G) - u(S\&\bar{G}) = u(\bar{S}\&G) - u(\bar{S}\&\bar{G})$. But he also prefers Deal 2 to Deal 1, and, under the assumption that the stamp and the gloves are independent, these two deals have the same expected utility.[32] So expected utility theory judges Jeff to be irrational.

---

[30] Recall that Linda (strictly) prefers {D_1, \$–5; D_2, \$–5; $\overline{D_1 \vee D_2}$, \$10} to {D_1, \$–20; D_2, \$10; $\overline{D_1 \vee D_2}$, \$10}. If her utility function is linear, then she ought to be indifferent between these two gambles: $(2/6)(u(\$–5)) + (4/6)u(\$10) = (1/6)(u(\$–20)) + (5/6)u(\$10)$. An argument analogous to the one in fn. 29 shows that we cannot explain Linda's preferences by claiming that she thinks the die is not fair.

[31] Spelling this out in utility terms: $u(R\&L)$ and $u(\bar{R}\&L)$ are each very close to $u(\bar{R}\&L)$, so $u(R\&L) - u(R\&L) > u(\bar{R}\&L) - u(\bar{R}\&\bar{L})$. As another example, for someone like Alice, an Elvis stamp and a different Elvis stamp are not independent: one is *less* valuable to her if she already has the other, since she really only needs one. In utility terms, $u(E1\&\overline{E2})$ and $u(\overline{E1}\&E2)$ are each almost as large as $u(E1\&E2)$, so $u(E1\&E2) - u(E1\&\overline{E2}) < u(\overline{E1}\&E2) - u(\overline{E1}\&\overline{E2})$.

[32] Since the results of the coin flips are probabilistically independent, each state has probability $1/4$. So:

$$EU(\text{deal 1}) = {}^1\!/_4 u(S\&G) + {}^1\!/_4 u(\bar{S}\&\bar{G}) + {}^1\!/_4 u(S\&\bar{G}) + {}^1\!/_4 u(\bar{S}\&G).$$
$$= {}^1\!/_4 [u(S\&\bar{G}) + u(\bar{S}\&G)] + {}^1\!/_4 u(S\&G) + {}^1\!/_4 u(\bar{S}\&\bar{G}) \text{ if the stamp and gloves are independent}$$
$$= {}^1\!/_2 u(S\&\bar{G}) + {}^1\!/_2 u(\bar{S}\&G)$$
$$= EU(\text{deal 2})$$

As in the previous example, the subjective expected utility theorist cannot represent Jeff's preferences by representing him as not thinking the coins are fair, assuming Jeff is indifferent about switching which states yield which outcomes.

Table 1.2. Schema for a decision problem with independent goods.

	HH	HT	TH	TT
Deal 1	*A*	*A* and *B*	*Nothing*	*B*
Deal 2	*A*	*A*	*B*	*B*

Indeed, this example gives rise to a schema for a set of preferences that expected utility theory cannot accommodate. Take any pair of goods *A* and *B* that are independent, given whatever facts are relevant to this determination aside from preferences. Then construct a deal of the form shown in Table 1.2. If the decision-maker is not indifferent between Deal 1 and Deal 2 in each of these choices, then we have a counter-example to EU theory. No utility function can simultaneously satisfy the constraint that certain goods are independent and that the agent is generally risk-averse when taking bets involving these goods. Therefore, EU theory judges these preferences to be irrational.

The non-constructivist realist will have to admit that preferences like Linda's and Jeff's violate EU theory.[33] What about the constructivist psychological realist? He can deny that introspection is a good guide to utility: independence is not the kind of property that agents have introspective access to in principle. This means he has to claim that all people with risk-averse preferences are *really* like Alice rather than Bob; that is, that no one genuinely values money linearly and at the same time has risk-averse preferences. (Or at least that all people he is interested in attributing utility functions to are like Alice rather than Bob.) However, this will not be an objection to EU theory, because the constructivist psychological realist thinks that whatever mental state utility is, the utility function is defined by its relationship to preferences. So he thinks that Alice and Bob do have the same relevant mental state, even if they profess different reasons for it.

According to the non-constructivist realist, what Jeff and Linda have in common is that they are sensitive not just to the utility values of the outcomes they might receive, and to the average utility value of a gamble, but to other global features of the gamble: for example, they are both sensitive to the *minimum* utility value a gamble might yield, preferring (when average values are equal, and perhaps when they are not) a gamble with a higher minimum value. Other features of a gamble that some decision-makers might be sensitive to include the maximum utility value a gamble might yield and the spread between the minimum and the maximum. I will call this explanation of risk-aversion *global sensitivity*. An agent is globally sensitive just in case she cares about global features of gambles—features that do not supervene on any particular outcome—besides their mean utility values.

To illustrate my point that Jeff and Linda care about global features of gambles, we can consider Jeff's choice as a choice about which of the (equally likely) states he would

---

[33] Assuming the outcomes are correctly described. I will consider a challenge to this claim in Chapter 4.

Table 1.3. Jeff's decision problem: initial setup.

	HH	HT	TH	TT
Deal	Elvis stamp	Elvis stamp	Nothing	Gloves

like to enhance with a pair of gloves, when presented with the following setup in Table 1.3.

If 'Gloves' is added to the HT state, we get Deal 1, and if it is added to the TH state, we get Deal 2, in Table 1.4.

Table 1.4. Jeff's decision problem.

	HH	HT	TH	TT
Deal 1	Elvis stamp	Elvis stamp and gloves	Nothing	Gloves
Deal 2	Elvis stamp	Elvis stamp	Gloves	Gloves

Since Jeff prefers Deal 2, he prefers that the gloves be added to the TH state. Thus, he has a preference about how values are arranged across the possibility space, given that the value of the goods does not depend on whether he has the stamp and so the value added to each state is the same, and given that the probability of each state is the same. He would like to add the gloves to a state in such a way that he increases the minimum he might receive from the gamble. Similarly, we can consider Linda as faced with an initial gamble that yields $0 if a fair coin lands heads and $50 if it lands tails. Her choice is whether to add $50 to the heads state or to the tails state—and if she would be adding the same utility value to the state in either case (that is, if her utility function does not diminish marginally), but prefers to add it to the heads state, then she cares about how the values are arranged across the possible states. In the dice-rolling example, she chooses whether to subtract $15 from D_1 or D_2, and she would rather do so from the state that is initially better: again, she cares about how the utility values are arranged across the possible states.

Of course, if an agent prefers to add a particular prize to one state rather than another, then the resultant gamble in the first case must have a higher overall value than the resultant gamble in the second case: this is what it is for our numerical assignment to gambles to accurately reflect preferences. For a globally sensitive agent, then, how much a particular prize adds to the overall value of a gamble depends not just on the utility value difference that prize makes to the outcome in which it occurs, or on the probability that outcome has of obtaining, but on the difference that prize makes to the global properties of the gamble. Again, if adding a prize to a particular state increases the minimum value of a gamble (as the addition of gloves to the TH state does in Deal 2), then it raises the value of the gamble more than adding that same prize (to a state with the same probability) does when that addition does not increase the minimum value of the gamble, even if the prize makes the same utility difference to both states.

The global sensitivity interpretation of preferences says that even holding fixed how much one likes various outcomes, and thus holding fixed the average utility value of a gamble, which outcomes constitute the gamble and how they are arranged matter. This does not rule out marginal diminishment in the value of goods. People who have diminishing marginal utility functions can still be sensitive to global properties; I suspect that most people's utility functions do diminish marginally for very large quantities of money, and yet that many people are globally sensitive. So, whereas the expected utility theorist claims that having risk-averse preferences always entails a diminishing marginal utility function, I claim that they might instead arise from global sensitivity, or from some combination of the two phenomena. (So far, this claim depends on assuming non-constructive realism, but I will show shortly that this assumption is not needed.)

EU theory claims that as long as the average utilities of the prizes in two gambles are the same, rationality requires that an agent does not care how the possibilities are arranged to yield that average: he must be indifferent as to whether all the possible value is concentrated in an outcome with small probability or whether the value is spread evenly over states. Another way of explaining the constraint that expected utility theory places on evaluating gambles is as follows: we can think of a gamble as a probability distribution over utility values. (That we can think of it this way *before* we know the agent's preferences is a non-constructive realist assumption.) This distribution will have many features: a minimum, a mean value, and a variance, to name a few. According to expected utility theory, the *only* feature of this distribution that can (rationally) matter when evaluating a gamble is its mean value (its expected utility value): we are meant to throw out any other information as useless to determining the value of the gamble. We will find preferences that violate the theory when we find agents who are sensitive to some of these other features of distributions. And since decision theory is supposed to represent all rational preferences, all of these globally sensitive agents are deemed irrational by EU theory.

I began with the examples of Jeff and Linda for two reasons: first, the preferences these examples illustrate do not depend on setting up a very unusual decision problem (for example, one involving very large sums of money): they involve ordinary decisions with run-of-the-mill outcomes and probabilities. Second, these examples illustrate two distinct psychological phenomena that could give rise to risk-averse preferences: saturation and global sensitivity. The difference between the phenomena will matter only to some decision theorists. However, these examples also illustrate something more general: that there are two different types of *reasons* behind risk-averse preferences. There are local considerations—for example, that an agent does not need very much of a particular good—and global considerations—for example, that a gamble has a particular minimum.

For the non-constructive realist, only local considerations can be captured by the utility function. The constructivist is not so restricted: it is open to him to say that *both* local and global considerations are captured by the utility function. So it is initially plausible for the constructivist to claim that the utility function accounts for attitudes towards both local and global features of gambles. If this is right, then EU theory, on the constructivist interpretation, can account for the fact that agents consider global properties when making decisions. After all, it is no strike against constructivist EU theory that it cannot distinguish cases in which an agent's risk-aversion results from local considerations from cases in which it results from global considerations: if a utility function represents both Alice's preferences and Bob's, then it does not matter to the constructivist that they have different reasons for these preferences.

However, this initially plausible position turns out to be untenable: if an agent does care about global features of gambles, then this is going to show up in her preferences in such a way as to make her preferences incompatible with having an expectational utility function of any kind, even if there are no constraints on this function other than that it be constructed from her preferences. I turn now to two examples and a theorem which demonstrate that EU theory rules out preferences that arise from global considerations—rules them out because of features of the preferences themselves, without any independent determination of utility. Examples of preferences that conflict not with some predefined utility function but with the existence of *any* expectational utility function will be problematic for both the constructivist (including the formalist) and the non-constructive realist. Since exhibiting such preferences cannot rely on any assumptions about the utility function, the examples are going to be more complex. I turn now to these examples, which expected utility theory cannot accommodate under any interpretation of the utility function.

The first example is Maurice Allais' famous paradox. Consider the agent who prefers L_1 to L_2 and L_4 to L_3:

L_1: \$5,000,000 with probability 0.1, \$0 with probability 0.9.
L_2: \$1,000,000 with probability 0.11, \$0 with probability 0.89.
L_3: \$1,000,000 with probability 0.89, \$5,000,000 with probability 0.1, \$0 with probability 0.01.
L_4: \$1,000,000 with probability 1.

Many people appear to have these preferences.[34] However, there is no way to assign utility values to \$0, \$1m, and \$5m such that L_1 has a higher expected utility than L_2 and

---

[34] Oddly enough, it is generally assumed rather than tested that people have the preferences in this exact example, though perhaps the fact that the claim that the relevant preference are the "common" preferences has gone unchallenged for sixty years is evidence for its truth. MacCrimmon and Larsson (1979) detail a catalogue of related results, which in general support Allais' contention. Furthermore, Oliver (2003) presents a study concerning an example analogous to Allais', in which the gambles are over health outcomes rather than monetary outcomes: in his study, fourteen of the thirty-eight subjects exhibited the preferences that were analogues to the Allais preference.

L_4 has a higher expected utility than L_3.[35] Allais' example does not require any background information about how the values of the outcomes relate to each other in order to produce a contradiction with EU theory: it relies only on the agent having the two preferences mentioned. As above, if decision-makers are sensitive to the minimum values of gambles (as they seem to be in preferring L_4 to L_3), then they are going to have preferences that EU theory cannot capture.[36]

The second example is adapted from an example that Hansson (1988) presents to demonstrate that expected utility maximization rules out taking certain kinds of risk-related considerations into account.[37] Recall, from Section 1.1, John's two rules for gambling:

> R1. Whenever faced with a coin-flip between some particular sum and nothing, be indifferent between taking the coin-flip and receiving one-third of that sum for certain.

> R2. Whenever faced with a coin-flip between one sum of money and another which is $30 larger, be indifferent between taking the coin-flip and receiving the lesser prize plus $10 for certain.

Hansson shows that if an agent's preferences obey both of these rules, then there will be no utility function that represents their preferences under expected utility maximization. The formal reason that the rules are incompatible is that if we assume an agent is an expected utility maximizer, then R1 and R2 each imply that the utility function diminishes marginally, but they each imply a different rate of diminishment.[38]

Surprisingly, then, each of these rules is compatible with an expectational utility function, but they are only compatible with different utility functions. This is puzzling, because not only do the rules seem reasonable in combination, they seem to express the same underlying attitude towards risk-taking: a 50% chance of getting $x more than some worst possible value makes a gamble worth $($\frac{1}{3}$)x more than its worst possible value. The problem is that this way of valuing gambles irreducibly depends on their minimum. Again, EU theory entails that an agent cannot value gambles in a way that is sensitive to global properties: the fact that a gamble yields at least some particular

---

[35] If L_1 is preferred to L_2, then we have $0.1(u(\$5m)) + 0.9(u(\$0)) > 0.11(u(\$1m)) + 0.89(u(\$0))$. Equivalently, $0.1(u(\$5m)) + 0.01(u(\$0)) > 0.11(u(\$1m))$. And if L_4 is preferred to L_3, then we have $u(\$1m) > 0.89(u(\$1m)) + 0.1(u(\$5m)) + 0.01(u(\$0))$. Equivalently, $0.11(u(\$1m)) > 0.1(u(\$5m)) + 0.01(u(\$0))$. These two contradict; so there is no utility assignment that allows for the common Allais preferences.

[36] Again, none of these examples essentially depend on objective probabilities, so we could set up analogous cases to show that subjective expected utility theory cannot accommodate preferences like these.

[37] It is important to give some context behind Hansson's consideration of this point. Watkins (1977) argued that expected utility theory rules out taking certain kinds of risk-related considerations into account, and Harsanyi (1977) replied that Watkins misunderstands that the utility function is not meant to capture strengths of preferences in isolation but also the effect of risk on an agent's preferences: in my terminology, Harsanyi's claim is that Watkins mistakenly adheres to the psychological realist conception of utility rather than the formalist conception. Hansson shows that, contra Harsanyi, Watkins's point still holds on the formalist conception.

[38] Hansson (1988).

amount of money cannot be a consideration in whether to choose that gamble over another, if preferences are to remain consistent with the theory.

Hansson's initial point in presenting R1, and later in presenting R2, is that in tweaking the utility function so that it captures either one of these rules, the EU theorist is committed to attributing some strange preferences to the agent. This phenomenon can be generalized. Rabin (2000) presents a "calibration theorem" to show that in order to describe the preferences of decision-makers that display risk-aversion in modest-stakes gambles, EU theory is committed to absurd conclusions about their preferences between gambles when the stakes are higher. As mentioned, on EU theory, modest-stakes risk-aversion must imply a concave utility function. Rabin's results assume nothing about the utility function except that it continues to be concave in higher stakes, and so does not, for example, have an inflection point above which it increases marginally.

Here are some examples of the sorts of conclusions EU theory is committed to on the assumption that the utility function is concave.[39] If an individual prefers not to take a coin-flip between losing $100 and gaining $110 (that is, if she prefers a guaranteed $0 to the coin-flip), regardless of her initial wealth level, then she must also prefer not to take a coin-flip between losing $1,000 and gaining *any amount* of money. Similarly, if an individual prefers not to take a coin-flip between losing $1,000 and gaining $1,050 for any initial wealth level, then she will also prefer not to take a coin-flip between losing $20,000 and gaining any amount of money. Furthermore, if an individual prefers not to take a coin-flip between losing $100 and gaining $105 as long as her lifetime wealth is less than $350,000, then from an initial wealth level of $340,000, she will turn down a coin-flip between losing $4,000 and gaining $635,670. In other words, she will prefer a sure-thing wealth level of $340,000 to the gamble {$336,000, 0.5; $975,670, 0.5}.[40] Most people do have these preferences in modest stakes, but do not have the high-stakes preferences Rabin cites.

Hansson's counterexample was driven by the following general idea. An agent might conform to (R1), and the EU theorist can capture the resultant behavior, but only at the expense of misinterpreting the agent's reasons for conforming to that rule. To show that getting the agent's reasons wrong is a problem even for the constructivist, add another rule (R2) which stems from the same underlying reasons as (R1), but results in preferences that require a different, and inconsistent, EU representation. Rabin's results are driven by a similar idea. The EU theorist is forced to interpret modest-stakes risk-aversion in a certain way; namely, as entailing a concave utility function. To show that this fails to represent correctly the psychology of actual agents—and that this

---

[39] Rabin (2000: 1282). While the constructivist might worry about making as assumption about the utility function, note that the assumption could be easily recast in the language of preferences under the supposition that the individual is an EU maximizer.

[40] Rabin states his results in terms of changes from initial wealth levels because he thinks that the most important explanation for people's risk-aversion in modest stakes is *loss aversion* of the kind that Kahneman and Tversky's (1979) and Tversky and Kahneman's (1992) prospect theory discusses.

failure is problematic, even for the constructivist—add another commitment that seems consistent with modest-stakes risk-aversion; namely, no *drastic* risk-aversion in high stakes. Then show that this commitment is in fact inconsistent with the required EU representation.

Expected utility theory, then, however utility is interpreted, rules out some preferences that seem at least *prima facie* reasonable: that seem to arise from a coherent set of reasons. The reason that EU theory fails to capture these preferences is that it fails to separate two different sorts of reasons for risk-averse preferences: local considerations about outcomes, like those that Alice advanced in order to determine that she prefers $50 ("this particular amount of money is more valuable . . .") and global considerations about gambles as a whole, like those that Bob advanced in order to determine that he prefers $50 ("I would rather be guaranteed $50 than risk getting less for the possibility of getting more").

Why would an agent find these considerations relevant to decision-making? Let us start with the idea that decision theory formalizes and precisifies instrumental reasoning for ideal agents. Instrumental reasoning presents us with an agent who wants some particular end and can achieve that end through a particular means. Or, more precisely, it presents us with an agent who is faced with a choice among means that lead to *different* ends, which he values to different degrees. To figure out what to do, the agent must make a judgment about which ends he cares about, and how much: he must weigh the local considerations, considerations relating to the desirability of each outcome considered on its own. This judgment is captured by the utility function.[41] In typical cases, none of the means available to the agent will lead with *certainty* to some particular end, so he must also make a judgment about the likely result of each of his possible actions. This judgment is captured by the subjective probability function. Expected utility theory makes precise these two components of means-ends reasoning: how much one values various ends, and which courses of action are likely to realize these ends.

But this cannot be the whole story: what we have said so far is not enough for an agent to reason to a unique decision, and so we cannot have captured all that is relevant to decision-making. An agent might be faced with a choice between one action that guarantees that he will get something he desires somewhat and another action that might lead to something he strongly desires, but which is by no means guaranteed to

---

[41]   This talk may faze a formalist, but we could recast this talk is terms that are acceptable to him. If risk-preferences are based only on local considerations, so that the agent obeys the axioms of EU theory, then the utility function as determined by EU theory will reflect these even if it does not correspond to anything "real." If risk-preferences are based on both kinds of considerations so that the agent does not obey the axioms of EU theory, then formalist EU theory will read the agent as not having a utility function. However, if we can define the utility function from suitable preference axioms that these preferences do obey, then the utility function will again reflect the local considerations. I present such an axiomatization in Chapter 3, and explain how each kind of consideration corresponds to preferences. Therefore, I encourage the reader who is skeptical of the talk in the remainder of this section about the desirability of ends to adopt it as shorthand for something that will be given formalist content in Chapter 3.

do so.[42] Knowing how much he values the various ends involved is not enough to determine what the agent should do in these cases: the agent must make a judgment not only about how much he cares about *particular* ends, and how likely his actions are to realize *each* of these ends, but about what *strategy* to take towards realizing his ends *as a whole*. The agent must determine how to structure the potential realization of the various aims he has. This involves deciding whether to prioritize definitely ending up with something of some value or instead to prioritize potentially ending up with something of very high value, and by how much: specifically, he must decide the extent to which he is generally willing to accept a risk of something worse in exchange for a chance of something better. This judgment corresponds to considering global or structural properties of gambles.

How should an agent trade off the fact that one act will bring about some outcome for sure against the fact that another act has some small probability of bringing about some different outcome that he cares about more? This question will not be answered by consulting the probabilities of states or the utilities of outcomes. Two agents could attach the very same values to particular outcomes (various sums of money, say), and they could have the same beliefs about how likely various acts are to result in these outcomes. And yet, one agent might hold that his preferred strategy for achieving his general goal of getting as much money as he can involves taking a gamble that has a small chance of a very high payoff, whereas the other might hold that he can more effectively achieve *this same general goal* by taking a gamble with a high chance of a moderate payoff. Knowing they can only achieve some of their aims, these agents have two different ways to structure the potential realization of them.

Importantly, when I say the agent has to determine how to structure the potential realization of his aims, I am not thinking of cases in which the means themselves have some particular interest to the agent. For example, I am not talking about cases in which the agent would rather play cards than throw dice even when the relevant probabilities are the same, or would rather work hard than schmooze his way to the top. As mentioned in the Introduction, and as I will discuss further in Chapters 4 and 5, to the extent that the agent cares about these things, they will be considered features of the outcomes, not distinguishing features of the acts that lead to these outcomes.[43] I am instead addressing the question of how an agent ought to choose between means that have different probabilities of realizing various outcomes. In particular: how should the agent take *structural* properties of acts into account?

This dimension of instrumental rationality is the dimension of evaluation that orthodox decision theory has ignored. To be precise, orthodox decision theory has not ignored it but rather assumed that there is a single correct answer for rational agents:

---

[42] For the skeptical formalist of the previous footnote: local considerations might point in the direction of one act, and considerations about the likelihood of realizing various ends might point in the direction of another.

[43] I will later consider (and rule out) the possibility that global properties can be considered features of outcomes in a similar way that considerations about "means themselves" can. See Chapter 4.

one ought to take actions that yield higher utility on average, regardless of the spread of possibilities. There may or may not be good arguments for this—I will turn to these in Chapters 5 through 7—but we will not be in a position to address them before we get clear on what exactly agents are doing when they answer the question differently, and how this relates to ideal instrumental reasoning. Presumably, clarifying this will be useful even to those who think EU maximization turns out to be the uniquely rational strategy.

In the meantime, I hope the reader is convinced that taking the means to one's ends involves making *three* evaluations rather than two. First, an individual determines which ends he wants, and how much: these are the values captured by the utility function. Second, he determines how likely various actions are to lead to various ends: how effective each means would be of realizing each particular end. This evaluation is captured by the probability function. Finally, he determines which strategy to take when choosing among actions whose outcomes are uncertain: how effective each means is towards his general aim of realizing an end he wants (an aim which is satisfied by a particular end in proportion to the degree of his desire for it). Specifically, *he evaluates the extent to which he is generally willing to accept a chance of something worse in exchange for a chance of something better.*

This way of putting things may make it sound as if an agent makes an explicit judgment about which means are most effective at realizing his goals, but I do not mean to suggest that. On the contrary, just as an agent need not make explicit probability or utility judgments to count as having a probability or utility function in expected utility theory, a globally sensitive agent need not make an explicit judgment of effectiveness to count as conceiving of some way of realizing his general aim as more effective overall.[44]

We need a decision theory that captures all three evaluations. I now turn to a catalogue of the major alternatives to expected utility theory that have been proposed. Most of these come from the fields of economics and psychology. Because these alternatives are generally proposed as descriptive rather than normative, many of them fail to satisfy some fairly obvious criteria of rationality. Of the theories that do not violate any of these criteria, I believe that some of them—in particular, the "rank-dependent" theories—partially capture what is going on when globally sensitive agents evaluate gambles, but none of them succeeds in capturing all three dimensions.

1.4 Non-Expected Utility Theories

In response to examples like the Allais paradox and to the thought that diminishing marginal utility and risk-aversion properly called are really two different concepts,

---

[44] Could an agent be globally sensitive despite having a considered judgment that this is not the most effective way to achieve his ends? This question is analogous to the question of whether an agent could have a considered judgment that some event is more likely than another but make choices that reflect a higher degree of belief in the latter; or whether an agent could have a considered judgment that some outcome is preferable to another but make choices that reflect a higher utility assigned to the latter. I will not discuss these questions here, but how we answer them will influence how we answer the analogous question about global sensitivity.

many theorists (including Allais himself) have proposed alternative models of how decision-makers evaluate gambles, maintaining the spirit of EU theory but allowing that agents are sensitive to "risk itself." One thing to keep in mind when stating these theories is that although they include a utility function, strictly speaking, the utility function can no longer be defined or measured exactly as it is in expected utility theory: it is not defined as the quantity such that the agent's preferences maximize its expectation. However, the utility function can be defined in a similar manner, provided we have a suitable representation theorem, as the quantity that represents the agent's preferences under the functional form proposed. Defined thus, the utility function is meant to explicate whichever concept of utility an EU theorist takes the utility function to explicate.

In this section I will explore whether the non-expected utility theories already present in the literature capture the additional factor in instrumental rationality beyond the value of outcomes and the likelihood with which some act will result in various outcomes.[45] I am concerned with the philosophical foundations of rational decision-making, so I will structure this section around philosophical analyses of what it is to take global properties into account in instrumental reasoning. However, since mathematical formulas do not come interpreted, some of the formal proposals might be amenable to more than one analysis.

To be clear: decision theory takes no view about how agents actually reason, just about how their preferences are structured. However, it should be apparent from the discussion in the previous section that if a decision theory does not capture everything that agents care about—everything that agents would, consciously or not, consider relevant to their decisions—then there are going to be examples of preferences that agents have but that the theory cannot accommodate. Nonetheless, my aim is not descriptive. I am interested not in how agents actually do take global properties into account, but in what are legitimate ways to take them into account from the point of view of ideal instrumental reasoning. I am interested in which "aggregation methods" might genuinely interpret agents as taking the means that they believe will be most effective in satisfying their general aims. It may turn out that any method that takes global properties into account does not survive the arguments that *rational* agents should not conform to it, and this will be the focus of the latter half of this book. But none of these arguments will claim that we cannot make sense of what agents are doing when they care about global properties, but rather that they should not actually care about them. The question for this section is how we can see what they are doing as a considered attempt to choose the means to their ends.

It is worth noting here three of the basic conditions that I think the correct normative theory must satisfy: insensitivity to framing, transitivity, and stochastic (or state-wise) dominance. In means-ends terms, these correspond to not allowing the value

---

[45] For a comprehensive survey of non-expected utility theories, see Schmidt (2004) and Sugden (2004), which were both important sources for the material in this section. Another excellent survey is Starmer (2000).

one attaches to outcomes to depend on how the outcomes are described, not allowing one's evaluation of the effectiveness of the means to depend on which alternative means are available, and not rating one means as less effective than another if for any end it is always at least as likely to yield something as good as that end (or not rating one means as less effective if it is not worse under any circumstance). I will discuss these conditions briefly in Section 2.4 and more fully in Chapter 5, but I mention them here to note that I will omit from this section theories that neither meet these three conditions nor are illuminating to the current discussion.[46]

I will consider three views about how decision-makers take global properties into account in instrumental reasoning: the view that global properties themselves add value to or take value away from a gamble, the view that the value of an outcome depends on the global properties of the gamble in which it is embedded, and the view that the value an outcome contributes to a gamble depends on the global properties of the gamble in which it is embedded.

1.4.1 First approach: global properties are valuable in themselves

Let us start with the first of these views: that global properties can themselves be valuable. This appears to be Allais' view. When he writes that decision-makers care not only about the mean utility of a gamble (I here use "utility" for what Allais calls "psychological value;" that is, psychological realist utility), but also about the dispersion of utility values, he says that caring about the latter corresponds to "the pleasure—or aversion—inherent in the fact of taking a risk, i.e. in taking part in games in which different shapes of the distribution of the psychological values are possible."[47] Moreover, he defends the claim that decision-makers care about the dispersion of utility values in a section entitled "The psychological value of dispersion considered in itself."

Formalizing this idea, many proposals take agents to maximize a function which is expected utility plus some additional term(s) that involve global properties. The functional form that Allais (1953/1979) originates and Hagen (1979) expands upon adds to expected utility a term incorporating two factors that are supposed to measure the utility of risk: a multiple of the variance of a gamble (sometimes called the "second moment" of utility) and a multiple of its skewness (sometimes called the "third moment" of utility). Let L stand for some lottery. If s stands for the standard deviation of L in terms of utility, and m for the skewness of L, then we can define some function F such that $F(s, m/s^2)$ is supposed to represent the utility of risk. The value of the lottery will then be:[48]

$$AH(L) = EU(L) + F(s, m/s^2) + \varepsilon$$

where ε is an error term.

---

[46] These include: regret theory (see Sugden (2004), Section 3.7), Fishburn's skew-symmetric bilinear utility theory (see Sugden (2004), p. 703), and Kahnemann and Tversky's (1979) prospect theory and (1992) cumulative prospect theory. I will discuss prospect theory in Section 2.4.

[47] Allais (1953/1979, pp. 52–3).

[48] Hagen (1979, p. 272).

As a different kind of example, Robert Nozick allows that if an act leads to a sure-thing, then this feature might have "symbolic utility"[49]—a more general term representing, for each act, the value of the features that an agent cares about other than its possible outcomes and their probability of obtaining. For example, symbolic utility also attaches to acting in accordance with the rules one deems ethical. Nozick's theory incorporates both evidential and causal expected utility, though the difference between these need not concern us here. Nozick claims that we assign some weight to the value of each of these three functions—symbolic utility, evidential expected utility, and causal expected utility—and so the value of an act will be:

$$DV(g) = W_C \cdot CEU(g) + W_E \cdot EEU(g) + W_S \cdot SU(g)$$

where CEU(g) is the causal expected utility of g, EEU(g) is its evidential expected utility, SU(g) is its symbolic utility, and W_C, W_E, and W_S are the weights of each and sum to 1.

My objection to these proposals is that they do not capture why global properties matter in practical reasoning. These proposals imply that the local considerations can be taken into account by averaging, and then the global considerations add some additional value. But the issue is not that EU theory has left out something the agent cares about in itself, but that it has failed to account for the fact that there are many ways of aggregating the values of the things the agent does care about (outcomes), and that these ways might depend on global properties. My contention in the previous section was that it is underdetermined how to combine the considerations of "local" outcome value in a particular gamble into a single value for that gamble, because there are different ways of trying to realize the general goal of getting the things one values more. If two gambles have different structural properties even though they have the same mean value, they present two different ways of going after this goal. But still, it need only be the outcomes themselves that are of value. An agent whose decision-making is sensitive to global properties of gambles need not value global properties for their own sake: it is possible to think that global properties matter to decision-making without thinking that value attaches to them.

1.4.2 Second approach: global properties alter the values of outcomes

The second view claims that while global properties are not in themselves valuable, they affect the values of outcomes. There are two ways to make this claim: on the one hand, one could claim that it is possible to talk about the "absolute" value of an outcome—its value apart from any gamble in which it is embedded—but that the value of this outcome when embedded in a gamble depends on the gamble. One example of a theory which could fall under this approach is Loomes and Sugden's "disappointment theory."[50] If we again let $L = \{x_1, p_1; \ldots; x_n, p_n\}$ stand for some lottery and m for its mean value, and we let D be a non-decreasing function, then the value of L will be:

---

[49] Nozick (1993).
[50] Loomes and Sugden (1986). I use the formulation in Sugden (2004).

$$DL(L) = \sum_{i=1}^{n} p_i[u(x_i) + D(u(x_i) - m)]$$

It is most natural to read this equation as a weighted sum of the values of outcomes, each adjusted to take into account the disappointment of getting that outcome in that particular gamble.[51]

One could instead deny that we can make sense of the idea of an outcome's absolute value, and claim that we can only talk about the value of an outcome within a particular gamble. We might interpret Mark Machina's generalized utility theory as fitting with this analysis.[52] Machina associates with each lottery $L = \{x_1, p_1; \ldots ; x_n, p_n\}$ a "local" utility function $u(x, L)$ and claims that in a small neighborhood around each L (a neighborhood of lotteries with nearly the same probabilities of the various outcomes), the agent approximately maximizes expected utility with respect to u.

Recall that the objection I raised to EU theory earlier in this chapter was that the theory only allows agents to subjectively value specific ends: it does not allow them to determine how to structure the potential realization of their aims. The problem with this second approach, which claims that outcomes have different values in different contexts, is that it still holds that the only thing agents can subjectively determine (aside from probabilities) is how valuable various ends are. Sure, more goes into determining these values than their values "in themselves," but we still have a picture on which agents evaluate ends, evaluate the probability with which various actions result in these ends, and then prefer the action with the highest average value. Again, though, what I claim is that an agent might reasonably aggregate outcome values in a way other than by taking the mean value, because he might think that, say, taking a gamble with a high minimum is a good way to satisfy his general goal. It is also worth noting that if this approach is correct, then there may be room to accommodate it *within* EU theory, by allowing that agents maximize expected utility, but that outcomes themselves cannot be specified without context; for example, that outcomes are not "$0" and "$100" but "$0 as part of a particular gamble g" and "$100 as part of a particular gamble g." I will discuss this possibility in Chapter 4.

The first approach claimed that agents value global properties in themselves, and the second approach claimed that global properties make a difference to the value of outcomes. But an ideal means-ends reasoner might have fixed values for outcomes and not attach any value to global properties in themselves, and still it will be underdetermined how he will aggregate value. My objection to EU theory is that it omits that there are multiple strategies for attaining one's ends when one does not know the state of

[51]   A related idea is due to David Bell, in Bell (1982) and Bell (1983), who proposes that the value of a gamble in a pairwise comparison is its expected value, but with a more complex term in the $u(x_i)$ position: $u(x_i, y_i)$, where y_i is the outcome one would have obtained in E_i if one had chosen the other gamble. Under some natural assumptions, if $v(x_i)$ is an "incremental" value function of outcomes (roughly, a function that plays the role the utility function plays in EU theory) and f is a function that measures the degree of regret, then $u(x_i, y_i)$ is equal to $v(x_i) - f(v(x_i) - v(y_i))$.

[52]   Machina (1982), Machina (1983), and Machina (1987). A helpful explanation of this theory can also be found in Sugden (2004).

the world, even once we know all the facts about an individual's ends and beliefs. So neither of these first two approaches responds to my worry.

1.4.3 Third approach: global properties determine how outcomes contribute to the value of a gamble

A third approach retains the idea that outcomes have set values to an agent. But this approach differs from EU theory in that it claims that the same outcome may make a different contribution to the overall value of a gamble, depending on the way that outcome is related to the global properties. Global properties are not to be thought of as valuable in themselves but as dictating the way in which local properties contribute to the value of a gamble. Formally, to calculate the value of a gamble, each outcome is multiplied by a factor that is not merely the probability of that outcome obtaining but instead is something else. I will refer to this factor as the outcome's importance. This is the kind of approach I favor, so I will spend some time outlining two theories that fall under this approach. My overall point will be that these theories are on the right track, but as they stand they leave us unable to account for all three subjective parameters of practical reasoning.

The two theories that I have in mind are **rank-dependent utility theory** (or **anticipated utility theory**) and **Choquet expected utility theory** (or **cumulative utility theory**). In both theories, the agent maximizes a sum of utility values of outcomes, each utility value weighted by a factor that is related to the probability of that outcome, but is not the probability itself. This factor depends on how good the outcome is relative to the other possible outcomes in the gamble: it depends on the outcome's rank among possible outcomes.

It is easiest to understand anticipated utility theory by examining some of its predecessors.[53] Handa (1977) proposed a theory that might be thought of as a "twin" to EU theory: instead of allowing that an agent subjectively values monetary outcomes, by introducing a utility function of outcomes, we allow that the agent subjectively values probabilities, by introducing a weighting function of probabilities. Handa proposed that the value of a monetary gamble should be a sum of the *monetary* values of its outcomes, each value weighted by a *function of* the probability of realizing that outcome. So, the value of a lottery $L = \{\$x_1, p_1; \$x_2, p_2; \ldots; \$x_n, p_n\}$ will be:

$$H(L) = \sum_{i=1}^{n} w(p_i)x_i$$

where w is a distortion function of probabilities (w maps the unit interval into itself), with $w(0) = 0$, $w(1) = 1$, and w increasing. Whereas u was meant to measure the true impact of each outcome on the agent's decision, w measures the true impact of each

---

[53] This explanation of the history and some of the functional forms comes from Sugden (2004). For another helpful discussion of the history of rank-dependence, see Wakker (2010, ch. 5).

probability on the agent's decision. And just as u was allowed to differ from the actual monetary value, w is allowed to differ from the actual probability value.

Naturally, one might expand this to allow that the agent subjectively evaluates both outcomes and probabilities:

$$HU(g) = \sum_{i=1}^{n} w(p_i)u(x_i)$$

This is how Kahneman and Tversky's (1979) original "prospect theory" evaluates certain "regular" gambles.[54]

However, both of these theories as stated here violate an important requirement known as "stochastic dominance." A lottery $L_1 = (x_1, p_1; \ldots; x_m, p_m)$ stochastically dominates $L_2 = (y_1, q_1; \ldots; y_m, q_m)$ with respect to the preference ordering $\geq$ if for all z,

$$\sum_{\{i | x_i \leq z\}} p_i \leq \sum_{\{j | y_j \leq z\}} q_j$$

This formalizes the idea that for any outcome, L_2 has at least as high a chance as L_1 of yielding that outcome or a worse outcome. L_1 strictly stochastically dominates L_2 if the above holds with strict inequality for some z*: if for some outcome, L_2 has a higher chance of yielding that outcome or a worse outcome than L_1 does. Another way to put this is that L_2 can be transformed into L_1 by shifting probability mass from worse outcomes to better outcomes—L_2 can be transformed into L_1 by a series of desirable alterations. The requirement of stochastic dominance is that if L_1 dominates L_2, then the agent must weakly prefer L_1 to L_2, and the requirement of strict stochastic dominance adds that if L_1 strictly stochastically dominates L_2, then the agent must strictly prefer L_1 to L_2. For both of the aforementioned formalisms it is easy to construct pairs of gambles such that one gamble stochastically dominates the other but the latter is preferred.[55]

Kahneman and Tversky's prospect theory includes an editing stage. When this stage is included, stochastic dominance may be maintained but transitivity will be violated. Therefore, as mentioned at the beginning of this section, the aforementioned theories cannot be normative theories (again, they are not intended to be).

Aside from including an editing stage, there is another way to introduce a probability weighting function without violating stochastic dominance, the way employed by anticipated utility theory. Anticipated utility theory was first formulated and axiomatized by Quiggin (1982), though Quiggin included an assumption that made the theory less general than the form I will present here.[56] The term *rank-dependent utility* (RDU)

---

[54] In prospect theory, x_i does not stand for an agent's total wealth but rather for gains and losses above some reference point. Prospect theory also includes an "editing phase" before the numerical evaluation occurs. See Kahneman and Tversky (1979). I discuss prospect theory further in Sections 2.1 and 2.4.

[55] See Kahnemann and Tversky (1979, pp. 283–4); Quiggin (1982, p. 327); Wakker (2010, pp. 153–5).

[56] In particular, Quiggin assumed that $w(1/2) = 1/2$ for a gamble with two outcomes. This assumption was crucial for Quiggin, but for purposes of introducing the functional form it can be easily dropped. It is also worth noting that Quiggin's original axiomatization required a minor modification, which Quiggin and Wakker (1994) provided. According to Quiggin and Wakker (1994), Soo Hong Chew was the first to axiomatize anticipated utility theory without the assumption that $w(1/2) = 1/2$.

is more commonly used for the theory without this assumption, so I will use that term in what follows. As in Handa's theory and Kahnemann and Tversky's theory, RDU theory allows the agent to subjectively evaluate probabilities using a distortion function $w(p)$. However, utility values are not weighted directly by w. On the contrary, the weights that outcomes get in the "expectation" equation are partially determined by the order of outcomes; that is, by how good each outcome is relative to the other possible outcomes. The worst outcome x_1 gets weighted by its distorted probability $w(p_1)$. The next worst outcome x_2 gets weighted by the distortion of the probability of getting that outcome or worse, minus the distorted probability of getting x_1: that is, x_2 is weighted by $w(p_1 + p_2) - w(p_1)$. And, in general, each outcome's weight—its importance to the evaluation of the lottery—is the distortion of the probability of getting that outcome or worse minus the distortion of the probability of getting worse. So, to calculate the rank-dependent utility of a lottery L, reorder its outcomes from worst outcome to best, and then the value of the resulting lottery $\{x_1, p_1; x_2, p_2; \ldots; x_n, p_n\}$, where $u(x_1) \leq \ldots \leq u(x_n)$ is calculated as follows:[57]

$$RDU(L) = \sum_{i=1}^{n} \left[w\left(\sum_{j=1}^{i} p_j \right) - w\left(\sum_{j=1}^{i-1} p_j \right) \right] u(x_i)$$

The "importance" values—the coefficients for the utility values—sum to 1.[58] Quiggin interprets w as a measure of how optimistic or pessimistic the agent is: given his assumption that $w(0.5) = 0.5$, the agent is pessimistic if $w(p) \geq 1 - w(1 - p)$; that is, if worse outcomes in a gamble get more weight than their probability value and better outcomes get less weight. For example, if $w(1/3) = 1/2$, and $w(2/3) = 3/4$, then $RDU(\{\$0, 1/3; \$1, 2/3\}) = 1/2 u(\$0) + 1/2 u(\$1)$, while $RDU(\{\$0, 2/3; \$1, 1/3\}) = 3/4 u(\$0) + 1/4 u(\$1)$. In the special case in which $w(p) = p$, agents are neutral and, indeed, are straightforward expected utility maximizers.

Choquet expected utility (CEU), axiomatized by Schmeidler (1989) and sometimes known as "cumulative utility theory", is similar in form to rank-dependent utility, but the entities over which agents have preferences are different.[59] To understand Schmeidler's version of this theory, it is helpful to examine Schmeidler's discussion of objective and subjective probability. Schmeidler makes a distinction between physical probability, which is "a concept like acceleration, momentum, or temperature" in that it

---

[57] Quiggin (1982). To make the notation easier, I will assume, as is fairly standard, that non-well-formed summation terms have value zero. For example, $\sum_{j=1}^{0} p_j = 0$.

[58] It is worth mentioning a special case of this functional form, Yaari's (1987) "dual theory," in which wealth levels are substituted for utility values. Yaari's theory is similar to Handa's, except that values are weighted by the rank-dependent decision weights instead of straightforward transformations of the probability function.

[59] Some authors, such as Peter Wakker, advocate using "rank-dependent utility" to include both what is called here rank-dependent utility and what is called here Choquet expected utility, calling the former RDU under risk and the latter RDU under uncertainty. Since the differences between them are important for my project, I will continue to differentiate them.

can (at least in principle) be objectively measured, and personal probability, which is "the number used in calculating the expectation . . . of a random variable."[60] He dubs the former objective probability and the latter subjective probability, and notes two things: first, that when an event has a known objective probability, this coincides with the event's subjective probability; and second, that subjective probability need not be additive. This corresponds somewhat, but not entirely, to the standard philosophical use of "subjective probability," which philosophers generally think of as an individual's degree of belief or credence in a proposition. The standard view is that this also is the number used in calculating (subjective) expected value, but the idea that subjective probability should be additive is central to probabilism.[61] This is likely because when philosophers use the term "subjective probability" they are generally interested in normative accounts of decision-making with subjective probabilities, but Schmeidler was interested in a descriptive account. Schmeidler originally proposed cumulative utility theory in response to situations like the Ellsberg paradox, in which decision-makers seemingly violate the axioms of expected utility theory because objective probabilities are unknown.[62] Although it may not be immediately obvious how this theory relates to my project, I include it here because its form will be relevant to what I discuss in the following chapters.

As mentioned earlier, in Savage's setup, agents have preferences over acts, where acts are functions from states to outcomes: each act in each state results in some outcome. In Schmeidler's setup the acts over which agents have preferences are functions from states to *lotteries*: each act in each state results in some objective-probability lottery of outcomes. For example, if the coin I am going to flip is either biased 50% towards heads or 70% towards heads, then the act of betting $10 on heads is represented as a gamble that yields the objective lottery {$10, 0.5; −$10, 0.5} if the coin is biased 50% and the objective lottery {$10, 0.7; −$10, 0.3} if the coin is biased 70%. Given this setup, the Choquet expected utility of an act is calculated in a manner similar to that of rank-dependent utility: reorder the outcomes from best to worst, and then the value of the resulting act {$E_1, x_1; E_2, x_2; . . . ; E_n, x_n$}, where E_i is the event in which the agent gets outcome x_i via some objective lottery and $u(x_1) \geq . . . \geq u(x_n)$, is calculated as follows:[63]

$$CEU(g) = \sum_{i=1}^{n} \left[v\left(\bigcup_{j=1}^{i} E_j \right) (u(x_i) - u(x_{i+1})) \right]$$

---

[60] Schmeidler (1989: 572–3).

[61] True, this might be because philosophers assume both that rational agents maximize expected utility and that degrees of belief are the coefficients, and the former assumption is precisely what is at issue here, but if additive degrees of belief come apart from the values used in calculating expectation, I suspect that most philosophers would hold that it is the additive degrees of belief that are subjective probabilities.

[62] See Ellsberg (1961) and Ellsberg (2001) and my discussion at the end of Section 2.4.

[63] Note that the outcomes here are in reverse order than anticipated utility theory: here they are ordered from best to worst, and in anticipated utility theory they are ordered from worst to best. The difference is not important from a formal point of view.

where v is a non-additive subjective probability function of events. Rearranging the terms, we can see that this is equivalent to weighting each outcome by an "importance" value, in a manner similar to RDU:

$$CEU(g) = \sum_{i=1}^{n}\left[\left(v\left(\bigcup_{j=1}^{i}E_j\right) - v\left(\bigcup_{j=1}^{i-1}E_j\right)\right)(u(x_i))\right]$$

Schmeidler's representation theorem shows that if an agent's preferences for these hybrid objective–subjective acts obey particular axioms, then she can be represented as a Choquet expected utility maximizer, with a subjective "probability" function v that is unique, and a subjective utility function u that is unique up to positive affine transformation. Schmeidler thinks that the subjective probability function v represents how averse an agent is to uncertainty, though I will omit the details of his account here.[64] In the special case in which v is additive, agents are again expected utility maximizers.

Gilboa (1987) formalizes Choquet expected utility theory in a way that only uses subjective probabilities. He starts with the same setup as Savage—acts are functions from states to outcomes—and shows that we can obtain a Choquet expected utility representation if an agent's preferences over Savage acts satisfy certain axioms. Again, if an agent satisfies the axioms we can represent her as a Choquet expected utility maximizer with a unique, not-necessarily-additive subjective "probability" function v and a utility function u that is unique up to positive affine transformation.[65]

While I think that rank-dependent utility and Choquet expected utility are on the right track in holding fixed the values of the outcomes, and in the way they allow an agent to aggregate these values other than by simply weighting them by their probability of obtaining, both theories leave us at a loss to interpret the agent as making a decision that might count as instrumentally rational. (Again, in fairness to the originators of these theories, they were not intended to do so.) To illustrate why, I first note that there are two ways in which we might interpret the weighting functions and importance coefficients of rank-dependent utility and Choquet expected utility. (Keep in mind that the weighting function and the coefficients are not the same thing, though since the latter is derived from the former, we need only interpret one or the other.) The first way is to interpret one of them as a measure of the agent's degrees of belief in the context of the decision at hand. This is suggested by Quiggin's interpretation of the weighting function as measuring optimism or pessimism (though in subsequent discussions some authors use "optimism" and "pessimism" as theoretical terms without interpretive commitments),[66] and by Schmeidler's interpretation of the weighting

---

[64]   See Schmeidler (1989), especially pp. 582–3.

[65]   Choquet expected utility gets its name because when formulated over continuous acts—acts without the restriction that there are only a finite number of outcomes—it uses the Choquet integral. I restrict myself to the finite case.

[66]   See, for example, Deicidue and Wakker (2001) and Wakker (2010).

function as a subjective probability function.[67] The second is to interpret one of them as a measure of the agent's aggregation method, but not one that necessarily corresponds to her beliefs.

Let us start with this first way, considering both the possibility that the weighting function corresponds to degrees of belief and the possibility that the importance coefficients do. The crucial formal differences between the weighting function and the importance coefficients are that the former is independent of the gamble under consideration and non-additive, and the latter are gamble-dependent (in particular, dependent on the ordering of outcomes) and additive. Given this, it will be easy to see why, if we are looking for a normative theory, we will be unhappy with taking either to correspond to beliefs. Consider first the idea of treating the importance coefficients as beliefs. Taken in this way, rank-dependent utility interprets the agent as treating events as more or less probable than their *known* probabilities, depending on how good these events will be for him. For example, a pessimistic agent (as Quiggin dubs them) believes bad things are more likely to happen to her than their objective probabilities would suggest. But the agent recognizes that how good these events are for her has no impact on how likely they are to obtain; therefore, she appears to be adopting degrees of belief that she knows are the wrong ones. It is hard to think of this as anything other than irrational. Choquet expected utility does not fare much better here: although there are no known probabilities to conflict with an agent's subjective probabilities, she is taking a factor *that she knows to be irrelevant* into account in her beliefs.

Consider next the idea of treating the weighting function as corresponding to belief. In the case of rank-dependent utility, this again has the effect of allowing that an agent has degrees of belief that differ from the known objective probabilities. Furthermore, using this strategy coupled with either RDU or CEU has an upshot that most philosophers find unpalatable: philosophers generally agree that degrees of belief should obey the probability calculus; so, they should be (at least) finitely additive.[68] Even for philosophers who are more permissive—for example, those who favor "mushy" or "fuzzy" credence—there remains a problem. On Schmeidler's version of CEU, when objective probabilities are given, the weighting function is supposed to coincide with these: a CEU maximizer is supposed to be a straightforward EU maximizer with respect to objective probability gambles. Even without this assumption, interpreting the weighting function on CEU theory as corresponding to degrees of belief has the upshot that anyone with additive or sharp credences is an EU maximizer. So there is no

---

[67] One may worry that Schmeidler's use of the term "probability" function is simply misleading here, since he is primarily referring to the weights an agent uses in decision-making. Still, he thinks that subjective probability should coincide with the objective probability function where there is one, which suggests that he really is talking about a judgment of likelihood. Schmeidler does say something about the case in which the weighting function is a distortion function of an additive function, but he does not appear to connect this to the idea of agents having separate beliefs and decision weights (Schmeidler (1989: 585–6)).

[68] All mentions of additivity in this book concern finite additivity, not countable additivity. Even for non-probabilists, who reject the claim that rational beliefs come in degrees that obey the probability calculus, the issue of not being able to represent global sensitivity will resurface, since, as we will see, beliefs and risk-attitudes are different and must be allowed to vary separately.

room to be an agent with a sharp, additive credence function who is not an expected utility maximizer. Given that the "third element" of instrumental rationality is independent of one's degrees of belief, so that an individual might be sensitive to global properties even if she *knows* the likelihoods of all of the events, this is problematic. A different *weighting method* than EU theory should not by definition correspond to having non-sharp degrees of *belief*.

Interpreting the importance coefficients or the weighting function as corresponding to degrees of belief seems hopeless if we want either RDU or CEU to count as a theory of rationality. So we might instead interpret the importance coefficients or the weighting function simply as a measure of the agent's aggregation method. What, then, could we say about the agent's beliefs? For RDU, the answer is easy: objective probabilities are given, and so the agent's beliefs coincide with these. For CEU, we might not be able to say anything, since there is no guarantee that the agent even has sharp degrees of belief (indeed, CEU was conceived to deal with precisely this problem).[69]

What this brings to the forefront is the dilemma facing interpretations of these theories as they stand. If importance coefficients are interpreted as degrees of belief, then an agent's degrees of belief about events will not be independent of the aggregation method used. This is analogous to EU theory's inability to allow an agent's judgments of the desirability of outcomes to be independent of the aggregation method. If decision weights are interpreted as degrees of belief, then an agent's degrees of belief about events will not be additive unless she is an EU maximizer. So far, neither theory yet gives us a way to derive a subjective utility function, a subjective probability function, *and* an aggregation method from the agent's preferences. And this is the crux of why these theories cannot fully capture practical reasoning: they do not allow agents to determine for themselves *all three* subjective parameters.

---

[69] I will show in Chapter 3 that if we add an additional preference axiom to an axiomatization of CEU, we will be able to derive an additive subjective probability function for an agent who satisfies the (new) axioms. In other words, the theory I will eventually present could be thought of as a restriction of CEU to the case in which the agent has sharp, additive degrees of belief.

2

Risk-Weighted Expected Utility

2.1 An Alternative Theory of Instrumental Rationality

We have just explored several approaches—alternatives to expected utility theory—for aggregating the values of the possible outcomes of a gamble to arrive at the value of the gamble as a whole. I think the rank-dependent approaches are on the right track. In these approaches, the contribution that each outcome makes to the value of the gamble as a whole depends not just on its value and its probability, but rather on where it falls in the structure of the gamble: specifically on its rank relative to the other outcomes in the gamble. But these approaches do not allow us to separate an agent's beliefs from her decision weights. They do not allow an agent to determine separately the probabilities she assigns to events and the weight that a particular outcome with a particular probability gets in the aggregation procedure. As we will see, the approach I favor bears some similarities to these approaches, though the way I arrive at it, and the interpretation of its entities, is different.

Recall my point that even if we interpret utility constructively, it is crucial to capture the reasons that an agent has for her preferences. This is why, for example, Hansson's two rules and Rabin's theorem presented problems even for constructivist expected utility theory. Therefore, it is crucial to present the theory I advocate in a way that explicates the practical reasoning it formalizes. I start with the case of gambles with only two options: gambles of the form $\{\bar{E}, x_1; E, x_2\}$. As mentioned, the subjective expected utility of these gambles is $p(\bar{E})u(x_1) + p(E)u(x_2)$. Assuming $p(\bar{E}) = 1 - p(E)$, this is equivalent to $u(x_1) + p(E)[u(x_2) - u(x_1)]$. Taking x_2 to be weakly preferred to x_1, this is equivalent to taking the minimum utility value the gamble might yield, and adding to it the potential gain above the minimum—the difference between the high value and the low value—weighted by the probability of realizing that gain.

The value of a gamble is its **instrumental value**—a measure of how the agent rates it in terms of satisfying her aims: we might say, a measure of its effectiveness as a means to her various ends. To review, on EU theory, while it is up to agents themselves how valuable each outcome is and how likely they believe each event is to obtain, these two evaluations are of set significance to the instrumental value of a gamble. If two decision-makers agree about the values of various outcomes and the probabilities involved, they must evaluate gambles in exactly the same way: they must have identical preference orderings.[1] They must agree about how the gambles rank in terms of satisfying their aims.

However, it is plausible to think that some people are more concerned with the worst-case scenario than others, again, for purely instrumental reasons: because they think that *guaranteeing* themselves something of moderate value is a better way to satisfy their general aim of getting some of the things that they value than is making something of very high value merely possible. More realistically, the minimum value will not always trump the maximum in their considerations, but it will weigh more heavily. Alternatively, an agent might be more concerned with the best-case scenario: the maximum weighs more heavily in the estimation of a gamble's value than the minimum does, even if these two outcomes are equally likely. So, it is plausible that two agents who attach the same values as each other to $100 and $0 will not both attach the same value to a coin-flip between $0 and $100. One agent will take the fact that he has a 50% chance of winning the better prize to be a weaker consideration than it is for the other. Thus, in addition to having different attitudes towards outcomes and different evaluations of likelihoods, two agents might have different attitudes towards some way of potentially attaining some of these outcomes.

A natural way to interpret these different attitudes is to postulate that different decision-makers take the fact that they might improve over the minimum to be a more or less important consideration in evaluating a gamble. Formally, they weight the potential gain above the minimum differently from each other. In EU theory, the instrumental value of a gamble is at least its minimum utility value, and the potential utility gain above the minimum is weighted by the probability of attaining the higher value. But this latter feature is too restrictive: a potential gain over the minimum *might* increase a gamble's instrumental value over the minimum value by the size of the gain multiplied by the probability of realizing that gain, but it might instead increase it by more or by less, depending on what the agent cares about. Of course, the probability and the size of the improvement will be relevant: the higher the probability of some particular gain or the larger the size of a gain with some particular probability, the better. Therefore, I propose that the possibility of a potential utility gain over the minimum improves the gamble above its minimum utility value by the size of the gain multiplied by a **function of** the probability of realizing that gain, instead of by the bare probability. This function represents the agent's attitude towards risk. Put formally, we might calculate the **risk-weighted expected utility** (REU) of a gamble $\{\bar{E}, x_1; E, x_2\}$, where $u(x_1) \leq u(x_2)$, to be $u(x_1) + r(p(E))[u(x_2) - u(x_1)]$, where r is the agent's "risk function," adhering to the constraints $0 \leq r(p) \leq 1$ for all p; $r(0) = 0$; $r(1) = 1$; and r is non-decreasing. The equation says that the instrumental value of a two-outcome gamble will be its low value plus the interval between the low value and the high value,

---

[1] For the constructivist: if two decision-makers share the same local considerations and agree on the probabilities involved, they must have identical preference orderings.

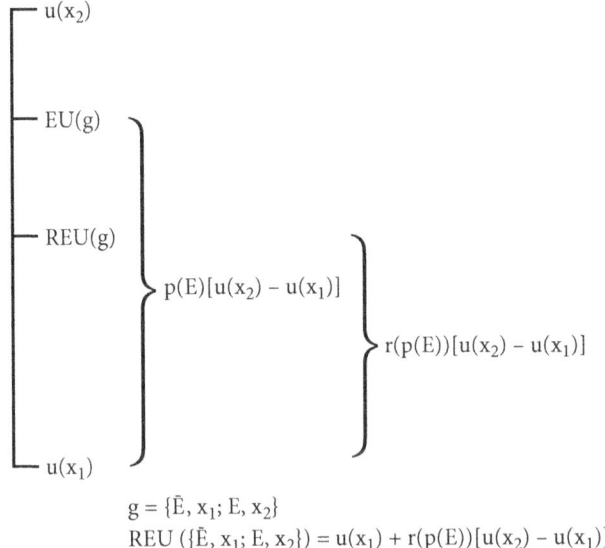

$$g = \{\hat{E}, x_1; E, x_2\}$$
$$REU\ (\{\hat{E}, x_1; E, x_2\}) = u(x_1) + r(p(E))[u(x_2) - u(x_1)]$$

Fig. 2.1. Risk-weighted expected utility for a two-outcome gamble.

this interval weighted by the output of the risk function when its input is the probability of obtaining the high value. (See Fig. 2.1.)

This equation is equivalent to $r(p(E))u(x_2) + (1 - r(p(E))u(x_1)$. So we can think of $r(p)$ either as the weight a particular improvement-possibility gets when this possibility has probability p, or as the weight that the better outcome gets when this outcome has probability p. If the risk function has a high value for some value p, then the value of the better outcome will count for a lot in the agent's evaluation of the gamble, and if it has a low value for some value p, then the value of the worse outcome will count for a lot. This formulation also makes it clear how an agent's evaluation of gambles rests on factors that are irreducibly global: the amount by which each outcome gets weighted will depend on which outcome is the minimum.[2]

Let us examine a risk function and the preferences it gives rise to. Consider the function $r(p) = p^2$ (Fig. 2.2). Now assume an agent with this risk function values amounts of money under \$1,000 linearly, so that we can represent her values by $u(\$x) = x$.[3] Then the agent will be indifferent between each gamble listed in the left-hand column of Table 2.1 and the sure-thing monetary amount listed in the right-hand column:

---

[2] If contra our supposition, $u(x_2) \le u(x_1)$, then the value of the gamble would be $r(p(\hat{E}))u(x_1) + (1 - r(p(\hat{E}))u(x_2)$: that is, $r(1 - p(E))u(x_1) + (1 - r(1 - p(E))u(x_2)$, which need not be equivalent to $r(p(E))u(x_2) + (1 - r(p(E))u(x_1)$.

[3] We will see how to derive the utility function solely from an REU maximizer's preferences in the next chapter.

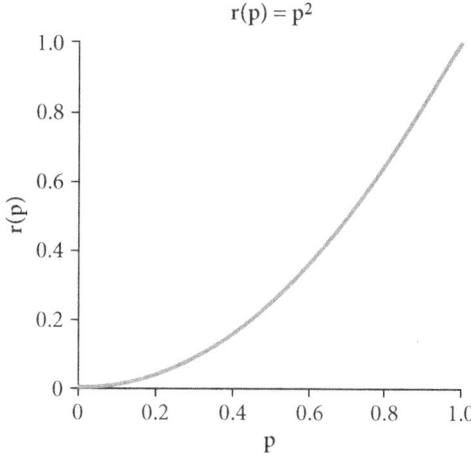

Fig. 2.2. Sample risk function: $r(p) = p^2$.

Table 2.1. Sure-thing monetary equivalents for various gambles.

Gamble {prize, probability; prize, probability}	Indifferent dollar amount
{$0, 0.5; $1,000, 0.5}	$250
{$0, 0.5; $500, 0.5}	$125
{$100, 0.5; $900, 0.5}	$300
{$0, 0.3; $1,000, 0.7}	$490
{$0, 0.5; $250, 0.5}	$63
{$250, 0.5; $1,000, 0.5}	$438
{$63, 0.5; $438, 0.5}	$157

Observe that this agent will exhibit risk-averse behavior: the sure-thing equivalents are all lower than the monetary expectations of the corresponding gambles. Also observe that the indifference facts listed in the chart are incompatible with *any* assignment of utils to dollar amounts such that the agent maximizes expected utility (assuming she prefers more money to less). For example, if she were an EU maximizer, then the preferences on lines 1, 5, and 6 entail that she must be indifferent between the gamble on line 7 ({$63, 0.5; $438, 0.5}) and a sure-thing amount of $250, but she is not.[4] We will see more examples of risk functions shortly, including risk functions that give rise to familiar decision rules and that explain the preferences in Section 1.1.

---

[4] From line 1: $0.5u(\$0) + 0.5u(\$1,000) = u(\$250)$.
From line 5: $0.5u(\$0) + 0.5u(\$250) = u(\$63)$.
From line 6: $0.5u(\$250) + 0.5u(\$1,000) = u(\$438)$.
These equations jointly imply that $0.5u(\$438) + 0.5u(\$63) = u(\$250)$. So the agent should be indifferent between {$63, 0.5; $438, 0.5} and $250, but (by line 7) he is instead indifferent between this gamble and $157 (and, presumably, prefers $250 to $157).

There is a natural way to extend this theory to gambles with more than two possible outcomes. The way I have set up the risk-weighted expected utility equation emphasizes that an agent considers his possible gain above the minimum (the interval between the low outcome and the high outcome), and weights that gain by a factor which is a function of the probability of obtaining it—a function that reflects his risk-attitude. Now consider a situation in which a gamble might result in one of *more than two* possible outcomes. It seems natural that the agent should consider the possible gain between each neighboring pair of outcomes and his chance of attaining the higher outcome or better, and, again, subjectively determine how much that chance of attaining this adds to the instrumental value of the gamble.

One way to state the value of a gamble with more than two outcomes for a standard EU maximizer is as follows. Start with the minimum value. Next, add the interval difference between this value and the next highest value, weighted by the probability of getting at least that higher value. Then add the interval difference between this value and the next highest value, weighted by the probability of getting at least *that* value. And so forth. Just as we replaced (subjective) probabilities by the agent's weights of (subjective) probabilities in the two-outcome case, we can do so in this case. So the value of a gamble for the REU maximizer will be determined by following this same procedure but instead weighting by a function of the probability at each juncture.

For example, consider the gamble that yields \$1 with probability $1/2$, \$2 with probability $1/4$, and \$4 with probability $1/4$. The agent will get at least \$1 for certain, and he has a $1/2$ probability of getting at least \$1 more. Furthermore, he has a $1/4$ probability of getting at least \$2 beyond *that*. So the EU of the gamble is $u(\$1) + 1/2[u(\$2) - u(\$1)] + 1/4[u(\$4) - u(\$2)]$, and the REU of the gamble is $u(\$1) + r(1/2)[u(\$2) - u(\$1)] + r(1/4)[u(\$4) - u(\$2)]$. This method of calculating value is a "bottom up" approach, in which the agent is treated as if he starts with the worst option, and at each stage takes a gamble to see if he "moves up" to being guaranteed the next worst option. This method emphasizes the minimum utility. We could instead emphasize the maximum utility: treat the agent as if he starts with the best option and weights the probability of doing no better than the next best option, and so forth. I find the emphasis on the minimum more intuitive. In any case, it makes no formal difference, because the "top down" and the "bottom up" approach will lead to the same risk-weighted expected utility values, if we transform the r-function accordingly[5] (see Fig. 2.3).

So the gamble $g = \{E_1, x_1; E_2, x_2; \ldots ; E_n, x_n\}$, where $u(x_1) \leq \ldots \leq u(x_n)$, is valued under expected utility theory as $\sum_{i=1}^{n} p(E_i)u(x_i)$, which is equivalent to:

$$EU(g) = u(x_1) + \left(\sum_{i=2}^{n} p(E_i)\right)(u(x_2) - u(x_1)) + \left(\sum_{i=3}^{n} p(E_i)\right)(u(x_3) - u(x_2))$$
$$+ \ldots + p(E_n)(u(x_n) - u(x_{n-1}))$$

[5] Specifically, if r(p) is an agent's risk function when we calculate risk-weighted expected utility using the "bottom up" approach, and if r'(p) = 1 − r(1 − p) is an agent's risk function when we calculate risk-weighted expected utility using the "top down" approach, the resulting values will be identical.

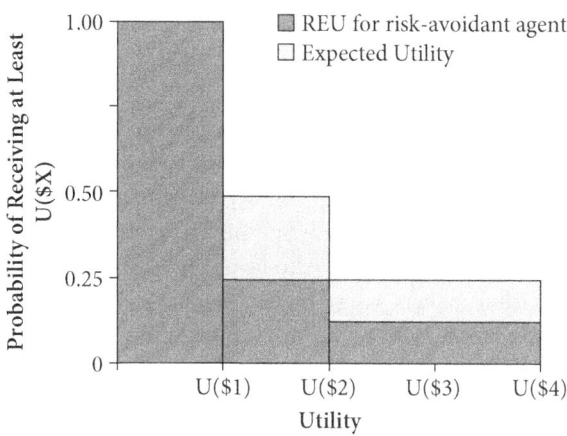

Fig. 2.3. Risk-weighted expected utility for a three-outcome gamble.

And that same gamble will be valued under risk-weighted expected utility theory as follows:

$$REU(g) = u(x_1) + r\left(\sum_{i=2}^{n} p(E_i)\right)(u(x_2) - u(x_1)) + r\left(\sum_{i=3}^{n} p(E_i)\right)(u(x_3) - u(x_2))$$

$$+ \ldots + r(p(E_n))(u(x_n) - u(x_{n-1}))$$

Again, $0 \leq r(p) \leq 1$ for all p; $r(0) = 0$; $r(1) = 1$; and r is non-decreasing. That r is non-decreasing guarantees that the agent satisfies the requirement of stochastic dominance; if we require in addition that r is increasing, then the agent will also satisfy the requirement of strict stochastic dominance.

If we set $r(p) = p$, we get the standard subjective expected utility equation. And again, for agents who are more concerned with the worse-case scenario, the possibility of getting more than the minimum will count towards the value of the gamble less than it will for the expected utility maximizer. For agents who are more concerned with the best-case scenario, this possibility will count towards the value of the gamble more. This equation also ensures that the value of a gamble is always at least its minimum and at most its maximum; that improving an outcome (given a fixed probability for that outcome) never makes a gamble worse; and, since r is non-decreasing, that increasing the probability of getting a better outcome never makes a gamble worse.

What ingredient of instrumental rationality does the risk function represent? The utility function is supposed to represent desire, according to those who think utility corresponds to something in the head, and the probability function is supposed to represent belief—both familiar propositional attitudes. We try to make beliefs "fit the world," and we try to make the world fit our desires. But the risk function is neither of these things: it does not quantify how we see the world—it does not, for example, measure the strength of an agent's belief that things will go well or poorly for him—and it does not describe how we would like the world to be. It is not a belief about how much risk one should tolerate, nor is it a desire for more or less risk. The risk function corresponds neither to beliefs nor to desires. Instead, it measures how an agent structures the potential realization of some of his aims.

Discussions of other non-expected utility theories are helpful here. Although the traditional interpretation of rank-dependent theories with objective probabilities holds that decision-makers who assign higher weights to events with unfavorable outcomes are pessimistic in that they assign higher subjective probability to events that are worse for them, a few authors who favor the rank-dependent approach have suggested that decision-makers assign higher weights to unfavorable events for reasons that do not have to do with perceptions of likelihood. For example, Lola Lopes connects a decision-maker's weightings of events to his psychological motivations rather than to his perception of probability.[6] She suggests that those who pay proportionately more attention to the worst event are motivated by a desire for security and those who pay proportionately more attention to the best event are motivated by a desire for potential. She claims that how individuals make this tradeoff is a disposition— that is, a trait that is fairly stable within a person but might vary across people. Rottenstreich and Hsee (2001) associate putting more weight on the worst-case scenario with fear, and putting more weight on the best-case scenario with hope. In non-expected utility theories that incorporate global properties directly, psychological correlates of different attitudes towards global properties have also been proposed. For example, Hagen (1979) identifies a preference for positive skewness with hope, and a preference for negative skewness with anxiety. The basic idea suggested by these authors is that there are two competing attractive features that gambles can have: one that is present in virtue of the worst-case scenario being as good as possible, and another that is present in virtue of the best-case scenario being as good as possible. And a decision-maker might be psychologically disposed to value each of these features to a different degree.

Without necessarily endorsing any of these particular views about psychological correlates of weighting functions, we need to connect the idea of psychological dispositions to my claim about its being up to an agent to choose her strategy, so that it is clear both how the risk function is psychologically explained and how it figures into ideal instrumental reasoning. And we also need to generalize the explanation, since the risk function determines the weight not just of the worst and best event, but also of every event in between. So here is my gloss. A gamble has many features of the form

---

[6] Lopes (1987). Lopes argues for a descriptive decision theory, the "security-potential/aspiration" theory, in which each individual in a decision situation is represented by a dispositional variable that reflects how he generally trades off security against potential, and a situational variable that describes his immediate needs in terms of an aspiration level that he hopes to achieve in this situation. SP/A theory shares some traits with the rank-dependent theories (in particular, with cumulative prospect theory), for example that SP/A's weighting function operates on cumulative probabilities, but it displays some differences as well, for example that SP/A theory's weighting function depends on the outcomes as well as the probabilities and that SP/A theory predicts a different pattern for how decision-maker will treat losses as compared with gains. See also Lopes and Oden (1999).

"has a p chance of yielding an outcome at least as good as x." Holding each p fixed, the better x is, the more attractive a gamble will be, precisely because having a higher x means it better satisfies the general aim of attaining the particular outcomes that one wants more. Some of these features will be particularly salient. For example, increasing the minimum ($p = 1$) means a gamble that is helpful towards satisfying one's general aim because *however* that gamble resolves, one will end up attaining an outcome that is at least that high up on one's list of desirable outcomes, and increasing the maximum is good for one's general aim because there is *some* resolution of the gamble that has one attaining an outcome that is higher on one's list. But the agent must decide how to trade off these attractive features—he must decide exactly how important what goes on in the highest p proportion of possibilities is to the realization of his aims.

There is a parallel to a familiar choice in ethics. When I am deciding how resources ought to be distributed, I face a choice between increasing the well-being of each person. And while there is something good about making the average or total well-being as high as possible, some think that we ought to pay disproportionate attention to the worst-off person. When one chooses a strategy for the realization of one's aims, one is essentially choosing how to weigh the interests of one's possible future selves. One must choose how to balance the interests of one's worst-off possible future selves against the interests of one's best-off possible future selves. And, more generally, that the best-off p proportion of possible future selves has at least some particular level of well-being is important in the evaluation of a distribution to one's possible future selves, but different agents might give different answers to the question of how much this matters for each p. Lopes (1984) presents data to suggest that decision-makers have risk-preferences that are analogous to their preferences concerning inequality in a social distribution, which seems to support the idea of thinking about a gamble as a distribution among possible future selves.

Here is a further analogy to help understand the main point. In discussing the choice of how much evidence one should require before believing a proposition, William James (1896) points out that we must choose between two competing goals: avoiding error and believing truth. These two virtues are in competition when deciding where to set the evidential threshold for belief, since once can avoid more falsehoods by setting the threshold higher, but one will thereby miss out on more truths; and one can believe more true propositions by setting it lower, but one will thereby let in more falsehoods. We face a parallel choice in the practical realm among strategies for realizing our aims. Two competing goals we have are to ensure that the worst-case scenario is as good as possible, and to ensure that the best-case scenario is as good as possible: to choose a course that is certain to go fairly well, and to choose a course that might go very well. And being drawn to each of these goals corresponds to ordinary virtue-words in the English language: a man can be prudent, or he can be venturesome. These two goals are in competition when deciding how much risk to tolerate: to the degree we care about being prudent, we must reject gambles that have some possibility of turning out very well; and to the degree that we care about being venturesome, we must accept gambles that might turn out very poorly. (In the practical realm, there are goals in between: to choose a course that will *almost* certainly go fairly well, and so forth. But it is telling that there is a "virtue" name for each of the "endpoint" goals.) And just as some epistemic agents privilege avoiding believing falsehoods over believing truth and some *vice versa*, without on James' view being criticizable, some instrumental agents privilege prudence over venturesomeness and some *vice versa*, without on my view being criticizable.

Thus, we can see that this "third ingredient" of instrumental rationality does correspond to a class of folk-psychological concepts, and that it does figure in instrumental reasoning. This does not mean that we need to be non-constructive realists about *r*: we can hold that *r* is determined purely from preferences. In Chapter 3, when we see exactly how the *r*-function can be determined from preferences, we will see more directly how the *r*-function corresponds to trading off attractive features in different structural parts of a gamble.

On REU theory, the agent subjectively determines *three* things: which outcomes he prefers, how likely he believes various acts are to result in various outcomes, and the extent to which he is generally willing to accept the risk of something worse in exchange for the possibility of something better. First, like EU theory, REU theory allows agents to attach subjective values to outcomes. It is up to agents themselves to choose their ends, and hence, REU theory includes a subjective utility function, which is not necessarily linear in money (or any other good). Second, also like EU theory, REU theory allows agents to set their credences, and hence, REU theory includes a subjective probability function. Third, *unlike* EU theory, REU theory allows agents to decide how to structure the potential realization of the outcomes they care about. It allows them to judge which gamble is better from the point of view of their general aim of getting more money (which includes their particular aims of, say, getting $50 or of getting $100, which they may value twice as much). It is up to them whether they will better fulfill their general aim by prioritizing a high minimum or by prioritizing a high maximum. And it is up to them exactly how these two features of gambles—and those concerning rank-levels in between—trade off: how much weight to put on what happens in the top p proportion of outcomes. Hence, REU theory includes a subjective risk function, which is not necessarily linear in probability.

Every agent has beliefs and desires, and determines for himself a norm for translating these two things into preferences. EU theory claims that aggregation with $r(p) = p$ is the correct norm: that we ought to be globally neutral. But just as rationality does not dictate a single utility function or credence function for all agents, I claim that it also does not dictate a unique norm.

In summation form, the risk-weighted expected utility of a gamble $g = \{E_1, x_1; E_2, x_2; \ldots ; E_n, x_n\}$, where $u(x_1) \leq \ldots \leq u(x_n)$, is:

$$REU(g) = \sum_{j=1}^{n} \left[r\left(\sum_{i=j}^{n} p(E_i) \right) (u(x_j) - u(x_{j-1})) \right]$$

Here, "$u(x_0)$" is stipulated to be 0. Note the similarity to rank-dependent utility:

$$RDU(L) = \sum_{j=1}^{n}\left[w\left(\sum_{i=1}^{j}p_i \right) - w\left(\sum_{i=1}^{j-1}p_i \right)\right]u(x_j)$$

If we rearrange the terms of the RDU equation and replace subjective probabilities by objective probabilities, then REU is formally equivalent to RDU.[7] Given the similarity in the formalism, I could present REU theory as a generalization of rank-dependent utility theory to decision-making with subjective probabilities: that is, as "subjective" rank-dependent utility theory. But to do so would be misleading about what the functions in Quiggin's theory are generally taken to refer to; furthermore, the philosophical foundations of REU theory—the way in which it analyzes means–ends reasoning—are very different from Quiggin's. I am committed not just to a formalism but to the thesis that there are three ingredients of instrumental rationality, represented by u, p, and r (though this does not commit me to realism about any of the functions); and that by understanding what instrumental rationality is like we can understand why having preferences representable by this formalism is rational. Most importantly, the difference between formulating a decision theory with objective probabilities and formulating a decision theory with subjective probabilities is not merely a matter of taking more or less for granted. It also concerns the question of what we can discover about an agent from her preferences. With respect to the formalism of RDU theory, we cannot tell from the agent's *preferences* whether her decision weights are different from the objective probabilities because she is pessimistic (in the ordinary sense of the term) or because she obeys a different norm than the EU maximizer. This is because RDU theory cannot separate two agent-determined components that together determine the weights of the outcomes: it cannot formally characterize what it is to have a belief separately from what it is to have a decision weight. (Again, this will not matter to anyone whose aims are descriptive.) However, we will see in Chapter 3 that the representation theorem for REU theory tells us exactly how to distinguish between the agent's beliefs and her decision weights on the basis of her preferences, and tells us why the former really should count as beliefs and the latter as reflecting how the agent structures the realization of her aims. As a result, if objective probabilities are given, REU theory allows us to formulate and answer the question of whether an agent believes in accordance with them despite not maximizing expected utility with respect to them.

---

[7] Some authors present anticipated utility theory with the terms rearranged in this way. See, for example, Chateauneuf and Cohen (1994), who present the formalism in terms of utility differences, and write: "With this formulation, we can interpret the decision-maker's behavior: Obtaining the minimum satisfaction $u(x_1)$ with certainty, the decision-maker then evaluates the successive additional utility differences as weighted by the associated transformed cumulative probabilities" (80). This formal equivalence also allows us to see how we would evaluate acts with continuous outcomes (rather than finite-valued acts): integrate with respect to utility values. However, such acts are not covered in this book, and they are incompatible with the setup of the representation theorem in Chapter 3. Finally, I note that the RDU weighting function is the inverse of the REU weighting function, so that we would have to set $r(p) = 1 - w(1 - p)$.

One might instead think of the REU formalism as a restriction of Choquet expected utility theory to the case in which the agent has an additive probability function over events in addition to assigning subjective weights to events. Again, since Schmeidler and Gilboa are not concerned with analyzing the components of instrumental rationality and determining how agents might be seen as competently taking the means to their ends, but rather in describing and modeling behavior mathematically, there are a few differences between REU theory and a "restricted" CEU theory. Most crucially, since non-expected utility theories under uncertainty are generally formulated to allow agents to have non-sharp beliefs, the weighting function of CEU theory is generally seen as reflecting beliefs, but non-sharp and hence non-additive beliefs. However, I am interested in allowing agents to be interpreted as having sharp degrees of belief about events and using those to determine how outcomes ought to be weighted, without being EU maximizers. As I stressed in my discussion of instrumental reasoning, it is possible to have sharp degrees of belief but to weight the outcomes by some other quantity: weighting outcomes differently than EU theory advises should not be tied to having beliefs that are different in form from a standard probability function. Again, I am interested in deriving both an agent's beliefs and her decision weights from her preferences, and since CEU (like RDU) has only one subjective parameter that goes into fixing the weight each outcome gets, this will not be possible using CEU. (Although the project of allowing both *non-sharp* degrees of belief and global sensitivity is beyond the scope of this project, I do not think the answer is to use CEU theory directly, because this project still requires two separate factors: one that measures non-sharp beliefs *and* one that corresponds to decision weights given these beliefs.) Nonetheless, if it is helpful to the reader who is familiar with these two theories to think of this work as defending "subjective RDU" or "CEU with probabilistic sophistication" as normative, that is in fact the *formalism* I am defending.

It is also worth discussing the relationship of risk-weighted expected utility theory to prospect theory, since prospect theory is empirically well-supported as a theory of actual behavior, and if the reader is familiar with only one non-expected utility theory, it is probably prospect theory. Prospect theory, put forth by Kahneman and Tversky (1979), posits that agents approach lotteries in two stages. In the first stage the lotteries are "edited" to be cognitively simpler. Doing so involves at least two important features: first, editing involves setting a reference point, so that outcomes are thought of as gains and losses relative to this reference point. This presumably makes the resultant outcomes simpler: instead of thinking about his entire fortune, the agent just thinks about small changes from a specified point. Second, editing involves making the lotteries numerically simpler: for example, by rounding probabilities or dollar amounts, or by ignoring components that are common to all of the choices under consideration. After editing, the second stage of evaluation consists in arriving at a value for each "edited" lottery. In two-outcome "edited" bets $B = \{\$x, p; \$y, q\}$,[8]

---

[8] It need not be the case that p and q sum to 1, in part because there is an implied $0 outcome (the reference point) that is not included in the PT equation.

where, again, \$x and \$y are incremental changes in value rather than total worlds, this value is given by:

If $p + q < 1$, or $x \leq 0 \leq y$, or $y \leq 0 \leq x$: $PT(B) = w(p)u(x) + w(q)u(y)$.

If $p + q = 1$ and either $0 < y < x$ or $x < y < 0$: $PT(B) = u(y) + w(p)[u(x) - u(y)]$.

where w is a weighting along the same lines as Quiggin's.

Prospect theory is generalized by cumulative prospect theory (CPT), which drops the assumption that the agent eliminates dominated prospects in the editing phase, since this assumption is redundant in the new theory.[9] In CPT, the value of an act g is given by first separating the set of outcomes that are above the reference point (g^+) from the set of outcomes that are below the reference point (g^-). Next, the value of each of these sets is calculated using CEU. For g^+ the decision weights are the standard ones, so $CEU^+(g^+)$ is $CEU(g^+)$ calculated with the decision weights $W^+(E) = v(E)$; and for g^- the decision weights are the inverse of the standard ones, so $CEU^-(g^-)$ is $CEU(g^-)$ calculated with the decision weights $W^-(E) = 1 - v(\mathcal{S} \setminus E)$, where $\mathcal{S}$ is the entire state space. Finally, these two values are summed:

$$CTP(g) = CEU^+(g^+) + CEU^-(g^-)$$

CPT can also be defined in a parallel manner on lotteries, by calculating the RDU values of L^+ and L^- using the decision weights $W^+(p) = w(p)$ and $W^-(p) = 1 - w(1 - p)$.

Again, CPT is formally similar to REU. However, aside from CPT not including both subjective probabilities and separate decision weights, the important difference between cumulative prospect theory and the theory I defend here is that REU theory does not treat gains differently from losses: in REU theory, there is no privileged reference point. REU theory takes as input gambles over total situations rather than changes in wealth relative to some reference point. Given this, we might think of REU theory as CPT under uncertainty with probabilistic sophistication, in which the reference point is defined to be at or below the worst possible outcome (we could think of this outcome as having utility value negative infinity): that is, in which all outcomes are thought of as gains. We might think of REU theory as prospect theory stripped of tendencies that (as I will later argue) are genuinely irrational.

I think it is best to view REU theory as belonging to the same formal family as the rank-dependent theories present in the literature but different from them both in that beliefs and decision weights can be separated and in that it is put forth as a normative theory. Luckily, though, the similarity in formalism means that we can make use of mathematical results pertaining to these theories, and many of the results discussed in the next section, as well as an essential piece of the representation theorem in Chapter 3, arise directly from such work. I turn now to a more precise characterization of the risk function, and how it corresponds to the agent's attitude towards risky gambles.

---

[9] Tversky and Kahneman (1992). I use the formulation found in Köbberling and Wakker (2003).

2.2 The Risk Function

In this section we will examine particular risk functions and the preferences they give rise to. Furthermore, we will see under what conditions an agent's utility function and risk function together give rise to risk-averse behavior. For ease of exposition, since nothing here depends on how the probability function is determined, I will assume that it is given. But first a few clarifications are in order to avoid some possible misunderstandings of what the theory implies. Each is associated with a potential worry about globally sensitive agents.

The first worry is that even for agents who care about risk, the fact that outcomes are offered as the result of gambles should not always affect the role those outcomes play, particularly if the outcomes are more fine-grained than the agent's preferences. Consider, for example, the gamble that yields a 2003 dollar bill if a fair coin lands heads, and a 2004 dollar bill if a fair coin lands tails. Assuming there is nothing special about either bill, it would seem irrational to value this gamble less than receiving either dollar bill for certain. And it seems that globally sensitive agents must be committed to discounting both possible outcomes simply because the outcomes are not guaranteed.

However, this objection misunderstands the theory: the globally sensitive agent does not discount the weight attached to each uncertain outcome because it is uncertain; rather, he discounts (or amplifies) the weight attached to intervals between adjacent outcomes. In this case, since the outcomes are of equivalent value to the agent, the interval between them has length zero. So, since both the 2003 dollar bill and the 2004 dollar bill have the same utility value, REU({HEADS, 2003 dollar; TAILS, 2004 dollar}) = u(2003 dollar) + r($^1/_2$)(u(2004 dollar) − u(2003 dollar)) = u(2003 dollar). Similar reasoning shows that the gamble also has an REU equivalent to u(2004 dollar). Any gamble whose outcomes all have the same utility value must be equal in value to each of those outcomes. More generally, dividing a single outcome within a gamble into two outcomes of the same utility value does not change the REU of the gamble: as long as two gambles yield outcomes of the same utility values with the same probabilities, the gambles will have the same REU, regardless of whether each gamble contains few distinct outcomes or many.

A related worry is that on REU theory a sure bet will be worth much more than a gamble between two outcomes that are both very close in value to the sure bet. Presumably, the possibility of doing slightly worse should not dramatically lower the overall value of an option. However, this worry is also unfounded. Observe that because of the constraint that $0 \leq r(p) \leq 1$, the REU of a gamble will never be less than the utility of every constituent outcome, and it will never be greater than the utility of every constituent outcome. The best and worst possible outcomes are upper and lower bounds on the REU of a gamble. Furthermore, if two of the outcomes in a gamble are arbitrarily close to each other, then the value of the gamble will be arbitrarily close to the value of a gamble that contains just one of these outcomes in place of both.[10] So, for example, if we take a gamble which contains a possible outcome of $1,000, and subdivide that outcome into a possible outcome of $1,000 and a possible outcome of $999.99, we will not change the REU of the gamble by more than a tiny amount.

The next worry is that dramatically lowering the minimum value of a gamble will dramatically lower the REU of that gamble, even if the probability of the worst-case scenario is close to zero. And since (we might think) nearly every act has some extremely tiny probability of a terrible outcome—there is always a *possibility* that given the state of the world and the act performed, a disaster will occur—REU theory implies that most acts have very low value. There are two things to say in response to this worry. First, many gambles carry with them the same risk of a disaster: taking a $0/$100 coin-flip does not raise your probability of sudden death, for example. When two gambles have the same probability of a very bad outcome, the REU equation for each will include the same first term and the same weight applied to the second term, so the bad outcome will count against them by the same amount. Second, we can point out that if the risk-function is continuous, then as the probability of a bad consequence gets arbitrarily close to zero, the value of the gamble gets arbitrarily close to that of the gamble that does not include that consequence at all.[11] (One might worry that the values of these two gambles *should not* be arbitrary close, if one thinks there is an important difference between no risk of a bad possibility and some arbitrarily small risk. We could accommodate this with an *r*-function that is discontinuous near 1, though at the end of this section I will provide reasons for thinking such a function is irrational.) The upshot is that we can approximate the value of a gamble without considering extremely unlikely bad events. Relatedly, if two gambles differ in the probability they assign to a bad outcome by only a very small amount, then, again as long as the

---

[10]   More formally, consider the two gambles $g_1 = \{x_1, p_1; x_2, p_2; x_3, p_3; x_4, p_4\}$ and $g_2 = \{x_1, p_1; x_3, p_2 + p_3; x_4, p_4\}$, where $u(x_1) \leq u(x_2) < u(x_3) \leq u(x_4)$ and $u(x_3) = u(x_2) + \varepsilon$. Then

$$REU(g_2) = u(x_1) + r((p_2 + p_3) + p_4)[u(x_3) - u(x_1)] + r(p_4)[u(x_4) - u(x_3)]$$
$$REU(g_1) = u(x_1) + r(p_2 + p_3 + p_4)[u(x_2) - u(x_1)] + r(p_3 + p_4)[u(x_3) - u(x_2)] + r(p_4)[u(x_4) - u(x_3)]$$
$$= u(x_1) + r(p_2 + p_3 + p_4)[u(x_3) - \varepsilon - u(x_1)] + r(p_3 + p_4)[\varepsilon] + r(p_4)[u(x_4) - u(x_3)]$$
$$= u(x_1) + r(p_2 + p_3 + p_4)[u(x_3) - u(x_1)] + r(p_4)[u(x_4) - u(x_3)] + \varepsilon[r(p_3 + p_4) - r(p_2 + p_3 + p_4)]$$

Therefore, the REU of g_1 is arbitrarily close to that of g_2. This point generalizes to show that if a gamble is altered by moving all the probability from one outcome to an arbitrarily close outcome, the REU of the resulting gamble will be arbitrarily close to the REU of the original gamble.

[11]   That is, hold fixed the probability of all the options except the worst and next-worst option. As the probability of the worst option goes to zero (and the probability of the next-worst option goes to the remainder), the REU of the resulting gamble will approach the REU of the gamble that has the next-worst option as a minimum, instead of the bad consequence. Formally:

Consider two gambles, $f = \{x_1, \varepsilon; x_2, p_2 - \varepsilon; x_3, p_3; \ldots; x_n, p_n\}$ and $g = \{x_2, p_2; x_3, p_3; \ldots; x_n, p_n\}$, where $u(x_1) \leq u(x_2) \leq u(x_3) \ldots \leq u(x_n)$. Provided $r(1 - \varepsilon) \to r(1)$, which holds if (but not only if) r is continuous, we will have: As $\varepsilon \to 0$, $u(x_1) + r(1 - \varepsilon)(u(x_2) - u(x_1)) + r(1 - p_2)(u(x_3) - u(x_2)) + \ldots + r(p_n)(u(x_n) - u(x_{n-1}))$
$\to u(x_2) + r(1 - p_2)(u(x_3) - u(x_2)) + \ldots + r(p_n)(u(x_n) - u(x_{n-1}))$.
So as $\varepsilon \to 0$, $REU(f) \to REU(g)$.

risk-function is continuous, this difference makes an arbitrarily small difference in the REU of the two gambles.[12]

A final worry concerns the fact that the risk function just takes probabilities as input. One might have thought that since riskiness is partially a matter of large utility differences between outcomes in a gamble, r should depend not just on p but on some properties of u as well. In response, an important point to note is that while r takes probability values as input, utility *intervals* are multiplied by r. This means that the value that a particular outcome adds to the instrumental value of gamble—its value contribution—depends both on the risk function and on the interval between that outcome and the next best outcome. One way to express this is that the risk function "shrinks" or "distorts" the contribution of utility intervals (relative to their contribution in EU theory) by a factor that reflects the risk attitude. For a given $r(p)$ that is smaller than p, larger intervals will be shrunk by more: the larger the interval, the less value it will add to a gamble's total instrumental value, relative to the value it adds for an EU maximizer. For example, for an EU maximizer, {HEADS, -10 utils; TAILS, 10 utils} and {HEADS, $-1,000,000$ utils; TAILS, $1,000,000$ utils} both have an expected utility of 0. But for an REU maximizer with $r(0.5) = r(0.25)$, the first gamble has REU -5, and the second has REU $-500,000$. Of two gambles with the same mean utility value, the gamble with the much larger interval between best and worst prize is much worse.

With these clarifications out of the way, we can turn to some examples of risk functions, and a formal characterization of what sorts of preferences they give rise to in an REU maximizer. In this section I assume that r, p, and u are given, and focus on the properties of the resulting preferences. In the next chapter I will assume preferences are given, and explore when agents can be represented by a unique r, p, and u.

Recall that the REU formalism is a generalization of the RDU formalism to subjective probabilities. Because we are taking p as given in this section, and events play no special role in REU theory once we know their probabilities, the preferences that result from a given r and u on REU theory will be the same as the preferences that result from the equivalent w and u on RDU theory. Therefore, we can make use of results from RDU theory about the relationship of its weighting function and utility function to preferences to say something about the relationship of r and u to REU preferences for a fixed p. Much of the remainder of this section draws on such results, the main exception being the discussion of risk-aversion in discrete goods.

To remind the reader of the definitions from 1.2: preferences display specific risk-aversion if the agent weakly prefers a guaranteed sum of money $\$x$ to

---

[12] Consider two gambles, $f = \{x_1, p_1 + \varepsilon; x_3, p_3; \ldots; x_n, p_n\}$ and $g = \{x_1, p_1; x_2, \varepsilon; x_3, p_3; \ldots; x_n, p_n\}$, where $u(x_1) \leq u(x_2) \leq u(x_3) \ldots \leq u(x_n)$. Provided $r(1 - p_1 - \varepsilon) \to r(1 - p_1)$, which holds if (but not only if) r is continuous, we will have: As $\varepsilon \to 0$, $u(x_1) + r(1 - p_1 - \varepsilon)(u(x_3) - u(x_1)) + \ldots + r(p_n)(u(x_n) - u(x_{n-1}))$
$\to u(x_1) + r(1 - p_1)(u(x_2) - u(x_1)) + r(1 - p_1 - \varepsilon)(u(x_3) - u(x_2)) + \ldots + r(p_n)(u(x_n) - u(x_{n-1}))$.
So as $\varepsilon \to 0$, REU(f) $\to$ REU(g).

any (non-degenerate) gamble with expected monetary value $x. Preferences display general risk-aversion in money if when one gamble is a mean-preserving spread of another, the agent weakly prefers the latter. Preferences display general risk-aversion in two goods if the agent weakly prefers that probability be concentrated in the events in which she gets one of the goods rather than in the events in which she gets neither and the events in which she gets both. Analogous definitions hold for strict risk-aversion in all three forms, and for risk-seeking preferences.

We have already seen an example of a risk function. Now let us examine a few more examples, including some that characterize particularly important attitudes.

The example above is $r(p) = p^2$ (Fig. 2.2). If utility is linear in money, then this agent's preferences will display strict specific risk-aversion: if the expected monetary value of (non-degenerate) gamble g is $x, then REU($g$) < REU($x$).[13] Equivalently, the agent will strictly prefer a sure-thing amount of money $x to a gamble with expected monetary value $x. And no matter what her utility function is, she will be strictly specifically risk-averse in *utility*: she will strictly prefer to receive an outcome with utility value x than to take a (non-degenerate) gamble whose expected utility is x.[14] In general, an agent will be specifically risk-averse in utility if $r(p) \leq p$ for all p: for any gamble g, REU(g) $\leq$ REU(EU(g)), which is to say, REU(g) $\leq$ EU(g). Similarly for $r(p) < p$ and strict specific risk-aversion in utility: if $r(p) < p$ for all $p \neq 0$ or 1, then for any (non-degenerate) gamble g, REU(g) < EU(g).[15] Using some results from work on RDU theory, we can also show that an agent will be strictly generally risk-averse in utility if r is strictly convex.[16]

We can also make use of results about RDU theory to say something more general about how the utility function and the risk function interact to yield risk-averse behavior in money (or any continuous good). An REU maximizer with a differentiable utility function is specifically risk-averse only if $r(p) \leq p$ for all p.[17] An REU maximizer with a

---

[13] We are assuming that g is not the degenerate gamble {$x, 1}.

$$REU(g) = u(x_1) + r(\sum_{i=2}^{n} p_i)(u(x_2) - u(x_1)) + r(\sum_{i=3}^{n} p_i)(u(x_3) - u(x_2)) + \ldots + r(p_n)(u(x_n) - u(x_{n-1}))$$
$$= x_1 + (\sum_{i=2}^{n} p_i)^2[x_2 - x_1] + (\sum_{i=3}^{n} p_i)^2[x_3 - x_2] + \ldots + (p_n)^2[x_n - x_{n-1}]$$
$$< x_1 + (\sum_{i=2}^{n} p_i)[x_2 - x_1] + (\sum_{i=3}^{n} p_i)[x_3 - x_2] + \ldots + (p_n)[x_n - x_{n-1}] = EV(g)$$

[14] The very idea of being risk-averse in *utility* will be anathema to formalist EU theorists like Luce and Raiffa who thought that the utility function was supposed to capture attitudes both towards outcomes and towards risk. Even for formalists, though, we can make sense of the idea of being risk-averse in utility on non-expected utility theories.

[15] $r(p) \leq p$ implies that REU(g) $\leq u(x_1) + (\sum_{i=2}^{n} p_i)[u(x_2) - u(x_1)] + (\sum_{i=3}^{n} p_i)[u(x_3) - u(x_2)] + \ldots + (p_n)[u(x_n) - u(x_{n-1})] = EU(g)$. If $r(p) < p$ for $p \neq 0, 1$: REU(g) $< u(x_1) + (\sum_{i=2}^{n} p_i)[u(x_2) - u(x_1)] + (\sum_{i=3}^{n} p_i)[u(x_3) - u(x_2)] + \ldots + (p_n)[u(x_n) - u(x_{n-1})] = EU(g)$.

[16] Chew, Karni, Saffra (1987: 375, Corollary 2) show that in RDU theory, the preference relation displays strict general risk-aversion iff (1) the utility function is concave and the weighting function is concave and (2) the utility function is strictly concave or the weighting function is strictly concave. This assumes that u is differentiable. Note that the risk function is the "reverse" of their weighting function f as defined. It follows from the Corollary that an agent with a linear utility function and a strictly convex risk function will display strict risk-aversion in money. Similarly, an agent with a strictly convex risk function will be strictly risk-averse in utility, since utility is a linear function of itself.

[17] Chateauneuf and Cohen (1994: 82, Proposition 2(ii)).

concave differentiable utility function is specifically risk-averse *if and* only if r(p) ≤ p for all p.[18] Furthermore, a decision-maker may be specifically risk-averse even if she has a strictly convex utility function, though there are some utility functions that are too convex to allow for risk-averse behavior regardless of r.[19] All of this suggests that the risk function plays a more important role in specific risk-averse behavior than does the utility function: one does not need a concave utility function to be risk-averse, but one does need r(p) ≤ p for all p. There are also results about RDU theory and general risk-averse behavior in money, which we can adapt. An REU maximizer with a differentiable utility function is generally risk-averse if and only if her utility function is concave and her risk function is convex, and she is strictly generally risk-averse if she is generally risk-averse and her utility function is strictly concave or her risk function is strictly convex.[20]

Results about risk-seeking behavior mirror those about risk-averse behavior. An REU maximizer will be specifically risk-seeking in *utility* if r(p) ≥ p for all p: for all *g*, REU(*g*) ≥ EU(*g*). And she will be strictly specifically risk-seeking in utility if r(p) > p for all p ≠ 0, 1.[21] Using results about RDU theory, a decision-maker with a differentiable utility function is specifically risk-seeking only if r(p) ≥ p for all p.[22] And if she has a convex differentiable utility function, she is specifically risk-seeking if and only if r(p) ≥ p for all p.[23] Again, a decision-maker may be specifically risk-seeking even if she has a strictly concave utility function.[24] And the results for general risk-seeking behavior are also similar: an agent with a differentiable utility function is generally risk-seeking if and only if the utility function is convex and the risk function is concave, and is strictly generally risk-seeking if one of these holds strictly.[25] Finally, if r(p) = p for all p, then, as pointed out above, the agent will be a standard expected utility maximizer (Fig. 2.4).

We can also say something about risk-aversion in goods. An REU-maximizer is generally risk-averse with respect to two goods that are independent if and only if her risk function is convex; furthermore, if her risk function is convex she will be risk-averse with respect to all independent pairs of goods. The same holds for

---

[18] Chateauneuf and Cohen (1994: 86, Corollary 1). Chateauneuf and Cohen mention that Quiggin (1989) already proved this result.

[19] Chateauneuf and Cohen (1994: 86, Corollary 2).

[20] Under the assumption that the RDU function (that is, the REU function with fixed probabilities) is Gateaux differentiable. This is shown by Chew, Karni, and Safra (1987: 375, Corollary 2). Note that the risk function is the "reverse" of their weighting function *f* as defined, so the stated results are that a decision-maker is strictly risk-averse if and only if *u* and *f* are both concave. A result from Yaari (1987) independently shows that (linear u + and convex weighing function) iff = generally risk-averse preferences (106–8), since his "dual theory" is RDU restricted to a linear u (see Chapter 1, fn. 58 of this book). See also Wakker (1994) for results on comparative risk-aversion.

[21] Simply reverse the inequalities in Chapter 2, fn. 13.

[22] Chateauneauf and Cohen (1994: 87, Proposition 4(ii)).

[23] Chateauneuf and Cohen (1994: 88, Corollary 3). Chateauneuf and Cohen mention that Quiggin (1989) already proved this result.

[24] Chateauneuf and Cohen (1994: 88, Corollary 4).

[25] Chateauneuf and Cohen (1994: 82) claim that this is shown by Chew, Karni, and Saffra (1987).

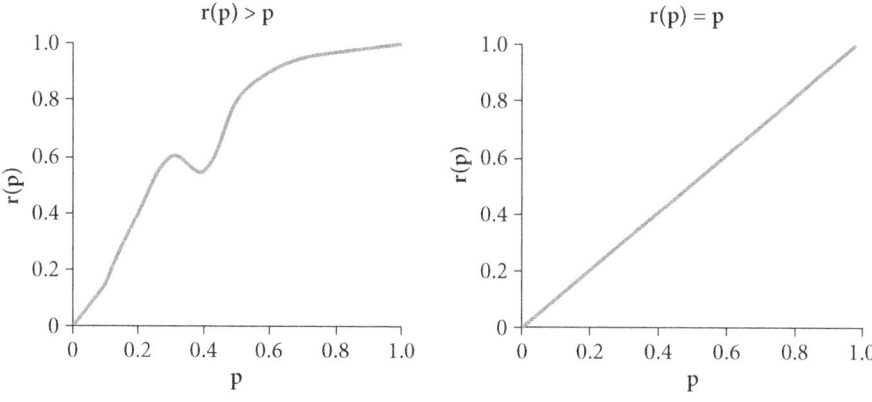

Fig. 2.4. $r(p) > p$ and $r(p) = p$.

strict general risk-aversion and strict convexity.[26] And similarly with risk-seeking behavior in goods: an REU maximizer is generally risk-seeking with respect to independent goods if and only if her risk function is concave, and similarly for strict general risk-seeking and strict concavity.[27]

We now have two interpretive possibilities for general risk-averse behavior: a concave or dependent utility function on the one hand or a convex risk function on the other hand—or some combination of the two. And here we come to the crux of the difference between the phenomenon that EU theory thinks is properly called risk-aversion and the phenomenon that I think merits the term. *On EU theory, to be generally risk-averse is to have a concave utility function, or, in the case of discrete goods, a utility function that displays non-independence. On rank-dependent theories like REU theory, to be generally risk-averse is to have a convex risk function.* The psychological intuition behind the diminishing marginal utility analysis of risk-aversion was that adding money to an outcome is of less value the more money that outcome already contains; or that getting an additional good is of less value if one already has some other good.

---

[26] If an agent is generally risk-averse with respect to A and B, she weakly prefers, for any a and b and for any $p' < p$, {A&B, p'; A&B̄, $a - p'$; Ā&B, $b - p'$; Ā&B̄, $1 - a - b + p'$} to {A&B, p; A&B̄, $a - p$; Ā&B, $b - p$; Ā&B̄, $1 - a - b + p$}.

Assume we have two independent goods, A and B. So u(A&B) − u(Ā&B) = u(A&B̄) − u(Ā&B̄) and u(A&B) − u(A&B̄) = u(Ā&B) − u(Ā&B̄). Let c = u(A&B) − u(Ā&B) and let d = u(A&B) − u(A&B̄). Without loss of generality, let us assume u(Ā&B) ≤ u(A&B̄). Then u(A&B) − u(Ā&B) = c − d, and d ≤ c.

Let $p' < p$. We want to show:

REU({A&B, p; A&B̄, $a − p$; Ā&B, $b − p$; Ā&B̄, $1 − a − b + p$}) ≤ {A&B, p'; A&B̄, $a − p'$; Ā&B, $b − p'$; Ā&B̄, $1 − a − b + p'$} ⇔ r(p) is convex (strictly convex).

We know that the left-hand side of the equivalence holds if and only if:

u(Ā&B̄) + r(a + b − p)(d) + r(a)(c − d) + r(p)(d) ≤ u(Ā&B̄) + r(a + b − p')(d) + r(a)(c − d) + r(p')(d)

This holds if and only if r(p) − r(p') ≤ r(a + b − p') − r(a + b − p).

r is convex iff given any 2 subintervals of equal length, [s, s+h] and [t, t+h] with t > s, it is the case that: r(t + h) − r(t) ≥ r(s + h) − r(s). Definition from Bruckner (1964). Here the relevant intervals are [p', p] and [a+b−p, a+b−p'], that is, set $p' = s$, $p = h + s$, $a + b − p = t$.

A similar proof holds for strict preference and strict convexity, replacing "≤" with "<".

[27] Simply reverse the relevant inequalities in the previous footnote.

The intuition behind the rank-dependent analysis of risk-aversion is that adding *probability* to a preferred outcome is of more value the more likely that outcome already is to obtain. Risk-averters care proportionately more about improving the lot of a *p*-portion of their futures possible selves the lower they are in the rank-ordering. Of course, rank-dependent theories like REU theory also allow the utility function to be concave: one can have any combination of utility function shape and risk function shape. But I claim that the concavity of the utility function, which describes how an agent evaluates *outcomes*, pulls apart from her attitude towards *risk* properly called. What we appropriately describe as an agent's attitude towards risk is captured by the shape of her risk function.[28]

That REU theory allows both the shape of the utility function and the shape of the risk function to be up to the agent means that we can formally separate what were intuitively two different phenomena: saturation in money or goods, and being sensitive to structural properties of gambles. Separating these two elements allows us to ask whether a particular agent's "risk-averse" preferences are due to saturation or to global sensitivity: to go back to an example in Section 1.3, whether they are like Alice's or like Bob's. This is not a question that the EU theorist can even pose on his theory.

So as not to confuse the reader, I will continue to use the term **risk-aversion** to refer to a property of behavior or of preferences. I will use the term **globally sensitive agents** to refer to REU maximizers with non-linear risk functions, $r(p) \neq p$. I will use the term **globally neutral agents** to refer to REU maximizers with linear risk functions, $r(p) = p$. Globally neutral agents are EU maximizers. I will bestow a special name on agents with convex risk functions.[29] I will call these agents **risk-avoidant**. (Formally equivalent agents are called *pessimistic* in treatments of RDU theory, but it will be one of my goals to show that these agents are not appropriately termed pessimistic!)[30] Risk-avoidant agents can have any utility function, but regardless of what their utility functions are, these agents will be risk-averse in utility. I will also bestow a special name on agents with concave risk functions. I will call them **risk-inclined**. These agents are risk-seeking in utility. (See Fig. 2.5.)

Naturally, agents need not fall into one of these two classifications. Experimental evidence suggests that typical individuals maximize the cumulative prospect theory equation defined on lotteries and have S-shaped weighting functions,[31] and so it is worth considering what this means for REU theory. Recall that REU theory is formally equivalent to cumulative prospect theory defined on lotteries with two modifications. First, REU theory makes no distinction between gains and losses, and so could be thought of as CPT with the reference point at or below the worst possible outcome.

---

[28] See Prelec (1998) for a further analysis of the properties of the weighting function in rank-dependent utility theory.

[29] Note that risk functions that are convex and continuous are also super-additive: that is, $r(x + y) \geq r(x) + r(y)$: Bruckner and Ostrow (1962) show that if f is non-negative, continuous, and convex, and $f(0) = 0$ then f is super-additive. Risk functions are by definition non-negative and have $r(0) = 0$.

[30] See, for example, Yaari (1987). Chateauneuf and Cohen (1994) call this "strong pessimism," where pessimism is AU theory's equivalent of $r(p) \leq p$.

[31] See Kahneman and Tversky (1979) and Tversky and Kahneman (1992).

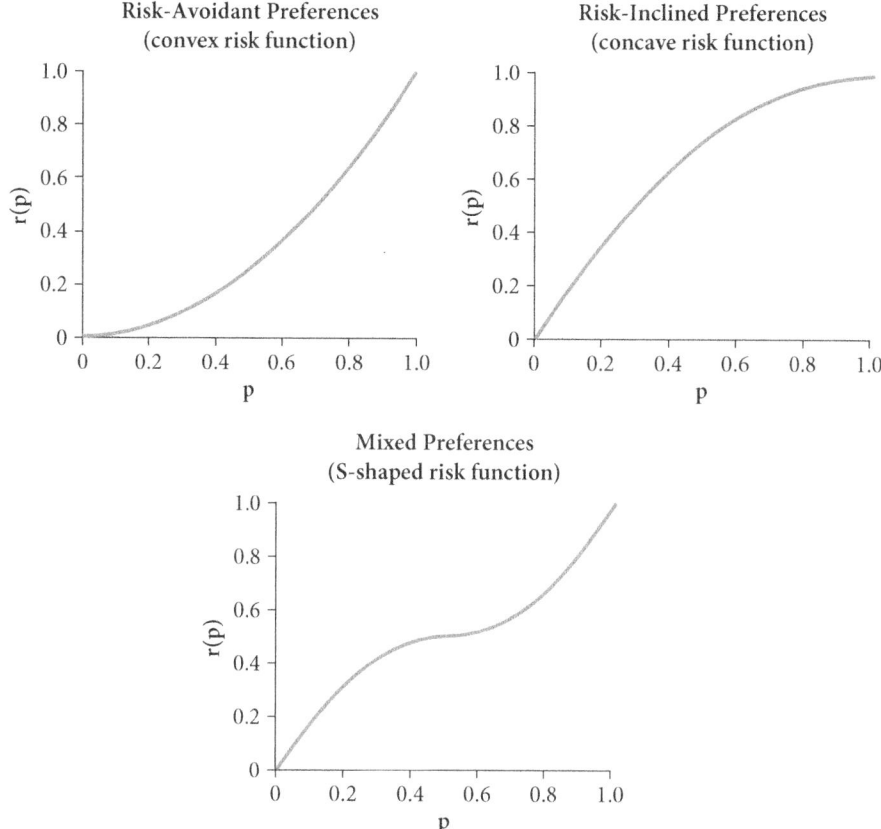

Fig. 2.5. Risk-avoidant agent (convex risk function), risk-inclined agent (concave risk function), mixed agent (s-shaped risk function).

Second, REU preferences are defined on acts, and REU theory separately derives subjective beliefs and decision weights. What these second facts mean in combination is that an S-shaped weighting function in CPT over lotteries could correspond to one of two features of REU maximizers, or some combination thereof: (1) having degrees of belief that are not in line with objective probabilities; or (2) having an S-shaped risk function. To the extent that the first feature is present, preferences are not rational and do not tell us anything about the ideal instrumental reasoner. To the extent that the second feature is present, we can ask what attitude it corresponds to. An individual with an S-shaped risk function will be risk-inclined in small probabilities and risk-avoidant in large probabilities. This reflects that an individual pays proportionately more attention to the best and worse outcomes than to the middle outcomes. The thought is that one cares a lot about ensuring that the poorly off future selves are not too badly off, and cares a lot about ensuring that there are at least some future selves that do extremely well.

I have noted that r(p) = p yields expected utility maximization. In addition, we can see other familiar decision rules as special cases of REU maximization. Consider maximin and maximax: someone who follows maximin always prefers the gamble with the highest minimum, and someone who follows maximax always prefers the gamble with the highest maximum. If the individual in question has a probability distribution, we can represent each of these rules as conforming to risk-weighted expected utility maximization, the former as a risk-avoidant rule and the latter as a risk-inclined rule. An agent who follows maximin can be represented as an REU maximizer with r(p) = {0 if p ≠ 1, 1 if p = 1}. An agent who follows maximax can be represented as an REU maximizer with r(p) = {0 if p = 0, 1 if p ≠ 0}. A related rule found in the literature is the "Hurwicz criteria."[32] An agent sets a coefficient of "optimism" α, weights the best possible outcome by α, weights the worst possible outcome by 1 − α, and sums them. We can represent an agent using the Hurwicz criteria by setting r(p) = α for all p ≠ 0, 1[33] (Fig. 2.6).

There is, however, a potential issue with the rationality of decision-makers who conform to one of the three aforementioned rules. None of the corresponding *r*-functions are continuous. Therefore, agents who use or can be represented by any of these rules will fall prey to versions of a worry mentioned at the beginning of this section. For the maximinimizer and the agent who uses the Hurwicz criteria, a very small chance of a bad consequence will make the gamble much worse. Indeed, since the value of a gamble for someone using maximin is simply the value of the worst possible outcome of that gamble, then if we think (quite understandably) that there is always at least some chance of death involved in any act, a maximinimizer will be indifferent among all acts.[34] Someone who supports maximin-like behavior but wants to dispense with this unfortunate upshot might support a modified version of the decision rule, in which r(p) = {0 if p < 1 − ε, 1 if p ≥ 1 − ε} for some ε close to 0. On this decision rule, only bad outcomes that have some threshold chance of occurring will drag down the value of a gamble. And this might accord with how some people behave: until the risk of death is, say, 0.01%, they do not take notice; but they rule out any act that has a chance of death above this threshold. However, it is implausible that there should be a sharp cut-off

---

[32] Discussed in Ellsberg (2001).

[33] There is a technical issue here. The Hurwicz criteria is generally used for decisions for which the agent has no assignment of probabilities to states (except 0 and 1), but the REU equation requires a probability function of states. We can get around this problem by pointing out that we can represent an agent who uses the Hurwicz criteria as maximizing risk-weighted expected utility relative to the *r*-function stated above and *any* probability function of states, provided that probability function assigns 1 and 0 to the states the agent treats as certain or impossible. Relatedly, maximin and maximax are also often thought to be justified only in the context in which the agent has no probability function. In these contexts we can again represent the agent as maximizing REU relative to the *r*-functions given above and any probability function of states. Unfortunately, in all these cases the agent will not meet the conditions for the theorem in Chapter 3, and so there will be no unique probability function that we can represent the agent as having (perhaps unsurprisingly, since their behavior only registers the difference between states they think are certain and uncertain, or the difference between states they think are possible and impossible).

[34] A similar worry arises for maximax. We might think that every act has at least some chance of leading to some really great outcome. And if that is true, then anyone following the maximax strategy will again be indifferent among all acts.

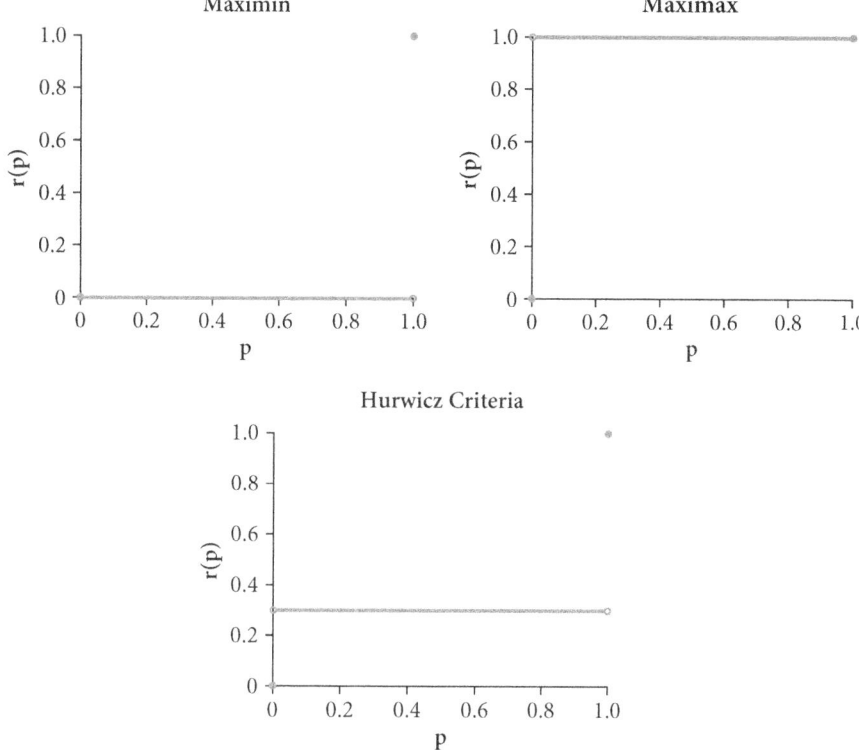

Fig. 2.6. Maximin, maximax, Hurwicz criteria.

between when a bad consequence has no effect on the value of the gamble and when it has such an effect that it drags the value of the gamble down to that of the bad consequence.[35] Indeed, it seems that small differences in probability ought not make a large difference to the value of a gamble.

It is a worry like this that might lead one to think that a rational agent should have a continuous risk function. I will not take a stand on this here, though the theorem in the next chapter relies on assuming that the r-function is continuous. It is also, in my mind, an open question whether the r-function of a rational agent ought to be strictly increasing rather than simply non-decreasing; that is, whether a shift in probability from a worse outcome to a better outcome ought to increase the value of the gamble, or whether it is enough that it does not decrease its value. (The requirement that r be increasing would also rule out maximin and maximax.) My initial thought is that the r-function ought to be increasing, since it seems that if two gambles yield the same outcome in every event except one—an event which has some probability of obtaining

---

[35] Perhaps it is more plausible that there would be behavior that approximates that of a maximiner, where the r-function is continuous, but stays mostly at 0 and 1 except for a steep but continuous increase at some point close to 1.

and yields a better outcome in one of the gambles—then being indifferent between the two gambles would amount to disavowing one's preferences between the outcomes in that event. Unless r is increasing, the resultant preferences will violate the strict stochastic dominance requirement, though a non-decreasing r will be enough to satisfy the weak stochastic dominance requirement. I will not take up the question in further detail in this work.[36]

Now that the reader is more familiar with how the r-function helps represent agent's preferences, we can turn to examining how REU theory can accommodate and explain the examples from the first chapter.

2.3 Examples Explained

REU theory can accommodate the preferences of Jeff, Linda, John, and Maurice from the previous chapter. Since REU theory is more permissive than EU theory, it will naturally be able to accommodate more preferences, and thus counterexamples will be harder to construct. So it is important that REU theory accommodate them in a way that is not *ad hoc* and that makes understandable why the agents could have the preferences they have from the point of view of ideal instrumental reasoning. Again I note that everything in this section applies equally to RDU as to REU, since we can take the agent's probabilities for granted.

It is easy to see that Linda can be represented as a risk-weighted expected utility maximizer: if $u(\$x) = x$ and $r(1/2) < {}^1/_2$, then she values money linearly but \$50 has a higher REU than a fair coin-flip between \$0 and \$100. In the general spirit of the example, if we set $u(\$x) = x$ and let $r(p) < p$ for $p \neq 0$ or 1, then Linda will value money linearly and still strictly prefer \$x for certain to a gamble whose average monetary value is \$x. And this fits the intuition behind the case: the reason that she displays risk-averse preferences is that the possibility of the bad result is not made up for by the possibility of the good result, even though, in combination, these two possibilities have an average value of \$50. That is, she is risk-avoidant. Her preference for $\{D_1, \$\text{-}5; D_2, \$\text{-}5; \overline{D_1 \vee D_2}, \$10\}$ rather than $\{D_1, \$\text{-}20; D_2, \$10; \overline{D_1 \vee D_2}, \$10\}$ can be explained in a similar fashion. If $u(\$x) = x$ and $[1 - r(5/6) > r(5/6) - r(2/3)]$—an inequality which holds if the risk function is convex—then the preference fits with the theory.[37] And this, too, coheres with the idea that even though both gambles have the same average monetary value, she prefers the gamble in which the worst-case scenario is less bad.

---

[36] The representation theorem I produce in the next chapter rules out any r-function that is not strictly increasing, so the axioms I produce for REU theory will rule out maximin, maximax, and the Hurwicz criteria as being irrational. However, it is still useful to mention these strategies and their relationship to REU theory because (1) that the REU equation can capture them makes it plausible that we have captured the intuition behind these strategies, even if they turn out to be irrational; (2) the axioms of REU theory do allow strategies that are very close to these, and that approximate these in the limit; and (3) it might turn out that these strategies are rational, in which case we would have to conclude that the task of coming up with axioms that represent rational attitudes towards risk has not been completed here.

[37] $(-5) + r(2/3)(15) > (-20) + r(5/6)(30) \Rightarrow r(2/3) > -1 + 2r(5/6) \Rightarrow 1 - r(5/6) > r(5/6) - r(2/3)$.

Table 2.2. Jeff's decision problem.

	HH	HT	TH	TT
Deal 1	*Elvis stamp*	*Elvis stamp and gloves*	*Nothing*	*Gloves*
Deal 2	*Elvis stamp*	*Elvis stamp*	*Gloves*	*Gloves*

Similarly, Jeff's preferences can be captured by a utility function and a risk function under risk-weighted expected utility theory. To remind the reader, Jeff values an Elvis stamp and a pair of gloves independently, but prefers Deal 2 to Deal 1 (Table 2.2).

Jeff can strictly prefer Deal 2 to Deal 1 without contradiction. More specifically, he can prefer Deal 2 to Deal 1 as long as $r(0.75) + r(0.25) < 1$, which will hold if Jeff is risk-avoidant with a strictly convex risk function.[38]

Next, consider the Allais paradox. Again, to remind the reader, the Allais agent prefers L_1 to L_2 and L_4 to L_3:

L_1: \$5,000,000 with probability 0.1, \$0 with probability 0.9.
L_2: \$1,000,000 with probability 0.11, \$0 with probability 0.89.
L_3: \$1,000,000 with probability 0.89, \$5,000,000 with probability 0.1, \$0 with probability 0.01.
L_4: \$1,000,000 with probability 1.

On risk-weighted expected utility theory, these preferences give us the following two inequalities:[39]

$$r(0.1)[u(\$5m) - u(\$0)] > r(0.11)[u(\$1m) - u(\$0)].$$
$$(1 + r(0.1) - r(.99))[u(\$1m) - u(\$0)] > r(0.1)[u(\$5m) - u(\$0)].$$

These inequalities hold jointly only if $r(0.11) - r(0.1) < 1 - r(0.99)$. (They are unsatisfiable when the risk function is linear.) They hold jointly only if the incremental change in the r-function between 0.99 and 1 is greater than the incremental change from 0.10 to 0.11. This will be true when the risk function is convex (indeed, it falls out of the definition of convexity). Furthermore, the inequalities hold jointly if and only if the risk function is convex and $\dfrac{r(0.1)}{1 + r(0.1) - r(0.99)} < \dfrac{u(\$1M) - u(\$0)}{u(\$5M) - u(\$0)} < \dfrac{r(0.1)}{r(0.11)}$.[40] For example, $r(p) = p^2$, $u(\$0) = 0$, $u(\$1m) = 1$, $u(\$5m) = 2$.

---

[38] Follow the steps in the proof in fn. 26, setting $a = b = 0.5$, $p' = 0$ and $p = 0.25$. The conclusion will be that $r(0.25) - r(0) < r(1) - r(0.75)$.

[39] $L_1 > L_2 \Leftrightarrow u(\$0) + r(.1)[u(\$5m) - u(\$0)] > u(\$0) + r(.11)[u(\$1m) - u(\$0)]$
$\Leftrightarrow r(.1)[u(\$5m) - u(\$0)] > r(.11)[u(\$1m) - u(\$0)]$.
$L_4 > L_3 \Leftrightarrow u(\$1m) > u(\$0) + r(.99)[u(\$1m) - u(\$0)] + r(.1)[u(\$5m) - u(\$1m)] \Leftrightarrow (1 - r(.99))[u(\$1m) - u(\$0)] > r(.1)[u(\$5m) - u(\$1m)]$.

[40] Segal (1987) and Prelec (1998) also make this point.

Finally, recall the example that Hansson provides. An individual's preferences adhere to the following two rules:

R1. Whenever faced with a coin-flip between some particular sum and nothing, be indifferent between taking the coin-flip and receiving one-third of that sum for certain.

R2. Whenever faced with a coin-flip between one sum of money and another which is $30 larger, be indifferent between taking the coin-flip and receiving the lesser prize plus $10 for certain.

These rules are jointly satisfied by a utility function $u(\$x) = x$ and a risk function that has $r(1/2) = 1/3$ (for example, $r(p) \approx p^{1.58}$).[41] Indeed, this way of formalizing the constituent elements of John's preferences fits naturally with the intuition that Hansson attributes to the agent in question. As discussed above, a person with these preferences might think that a 50% chance of getting $x more than some worst possible value makes a gamble worth $x/3 more than its worst possible value, and this fact is easily read off the risk function: $r(1/2) = 1/3$.

Similarly, REU theory can accommodate the modest-stakes risk-aversion that Rabin mentions without committing agents to extreme risk-aversion in higher stakes.[42] Recall that on EU theory, an agent who declines a lose $100/gain $110 coin-flip regardless of her initial wealth level, and who has a concave utility function, must also decline a coin-flip between losing $1,000 and gaining any amount of money. And recall that an agent who declines a lose $100/gain $105 coin-flip for total wealth less than $350,000 must also decline a lose $4,000/gain $635,670 coin-flip if her initial wealth level is $340,000. REU theory does not share these implausible upshots. If we assume that the utility function is linear in modest stakes, then the fact that an agent would decline the lose $100/gain $110 coin-flip entails only that her risk function sets $r(1/2) < 100/210$.[43] She need only be mildly risk-avoidant. Let us assume $r(1/2) = 0.4$, so that this coin-flip is worth −$16, i.e. she would rather pay $16 than accept this coin-flip; and she would only accept a 50% chance of losing $100 when paired with a 50% chance of gaining at least $150. If the utility function remains linear, then in order for her to accept a coin-flip that carries with it a 50% chance of losing $1,000, this possibility needs to be paired with a 50% chance of gaining at least $1,500. If the utility function diminishes marginally, then the offsetting amount will need to be higher, but there will be some offsetting amount that will make the coin-flip acceptable as long as there is some amount of money that is better than the status quo by 1.5 times the utility difference between −$1,000 and the status quo. In general, for an individual with $r(1/2) = 0.4$, the utility difference between the "good" prize and the status quo will need to be at least

---

[41] For the first rule, REU({$0, 0.5; $x, 0.5}) = 0 + r(0.5)(x − 0) = x/3 = REU({$x/3}). For the second rule, REU({$x, 0.5; $x + 30, 0.5}) = x + r(0.5)(x + 30 − x) = x + 10 = REU({$x + 10}).

[42] I note again that Rabin thinks the most important explanation for modest-stakes risk-aversion is loss aversion, which REU theory does not include. See Rabin (2000) and Rabin and Thaler (2001).

[43] REU({$0, 1}) > REU({$−100, 0.5; $110, 0.5}) ⇒ 0 > −100 + r(1/2)(210) ⇒ r(1/2) < 100/210.

1.5 times the utility difference between the status quo and the "bad" prize in order for the individual to accept the gamble.[44]

REU theory thus accommodates the counterexamples discussed in Chapter 1. It explains them as a result of the interaction between utility functions and risk functions that are both fairly simple and intuitive. It thus explains why an ideal means-ends reasoner might have these preferences.

I briefly mention one final example that often arises in discussions about risk: the St Petersburg Paradox. The St Petersburg gamble is as follows. I am going to flip a fair coin until it lands heads. If it lands heads for the first time on the first turn, you get $2. If it lands heads for the first time on the second turn, you get $4. On the third turn, $8. On the nth turn, $2^n. How much are you willing to pay for this gamble? The expected monetary value is infinite: it is equal to $1/2(\$2) + 1/4(\$4) + 1/8(\$8) + \ldots = \sum_{i=1}^{\infty} (1/2^i)\$2^i$. So if you are an expected monetary value maximizer, you should be willing to pay any finite amount of money for this gamble: you should prefer it to any finite amount of money. If utility diminishes marginally, then the gamble need not have infinite expected utility. However, as long as utility is unbounded—as long as for any utility value there is a prize with that value—the paradox can be reformulated in terms of utility. Let f be the gamble that yields a prize with utility value 2^i if the coin lands heads on the ith turn. This reformulated gamble has infinite expected utility: $EU(f) = \sum_{i=1}^{\infty} (1/2^i)(2^i)$. So if you are an expected utility maximizer, you should be willing to give up an infinite amount of utility for this gamble: you should prefer it to any finite-valued prize. Since bounding the utility function seems _ad hoc_, the reformulated paradox still needs a solution.

One might wonder whether REU theory can help resolve the reformulated paradox. How does REU theory evaluate this gamble? Technically, we have not said how to evaluate gambles that have infinite possible outcomes, but there is a natural extension, particularly when there is a worst possible outcome. We will have

$$REU(f) = 2 + r(0.5)(4-2) + r(0.25)(8-4) + \ldots = 2 + \sum_{j=1}^{\infty} r\left(\frac{1}{2^j}\right)(2^j).$$ Now, the immediate thought is that if r is convex enough, then this sum will be finite. Could we reformulate the gamble in a similar manner as we did in response to the EU solution to the original paradox, to reintroduce the paradox? Yes: all we need to do is let the initial prize (the "heads on the first toss" prize) have some positive utility value, and let the ith prize have a utility value that is better than that of the $(i-1)$th prize by $\dfrac{1}{r\left(\frac{1}{2^{i-1}}\right)}$. The REU of this new gamble will be $u(\text{initial prize}) + \sum_{j=1}^{\infty}\left[r\left(\frac{1}{2^j}\right)\left(\frac{1}{r\left(\frac{1}{2^j}\right)}\right)\right]$, which will be infinite. However, there is a way to block this move: we could allow that there is some $\varepsilon > 0$ such

---

[44] Note, incidentally, that as the coin-flips get riskier—that is, as they carry with them the possibility of a higher loss—the difference between the risk-weighted expected utility of a gamble and its expected utility increases.

that for all $p < \varepsilon$, $r(p) = 0$. In non-technical terms, this means that there will be some probability so small that the best p-portion of events does not make a difference to the overall value of the gamble. This will make it the case that for events in the St Petersburg series with small enough probability, there will be no utility value we can assign to their prizes high enough to make the sum of the series infinite: after a finite number of terms in the series, the remaining terms will all have zero value. So there is a way for the REU theorist to block a St Petersburg-type Paradox. And the assumption it requires is not crazy: we might think that we ought not consider the chance of a good outcome in our calculations if that good outcome is extremely unlikely to happen. Still, this does come at a cost: one must allow that rational r-functions can be merely non-decreasing rather than strictly increasing, and as I mentioned at the end of Section 2.2, I am not sure how plausible this is ultimately.

2.4 Deviations from REU Theory

We have seen how REU theory accommodates more of the preferences that people actually have than EU theory does, and provides a way for people who have these preferences to count as genuinely preferring the means to their ends. A natural worry, though, is that REU theory has not gone far enough. After all, there are choices that people make, and make quite predictably, that do not cohere with EU theory *or* REU theory, and an even more permissive theory could accommodate these. So why stop at allowing REU maximization? The short answer is that I think deviations from REU theory are irrational: normative EU theory has it wrong in how it handles risk-aversion, but right otherwise. REU theory is the appropriately permissive theory of ideal rationality. It will still be an interesting question how humans ought to behave given their limitations; for example, what time-saving heuristics to use in decision-making. But one of the purposes of this work is to argue that deviations from EU theory in how agents take risk into account ought not to be thought of as non-ideal heuristics or misfires; unlike other deviations that psychologists have uncovered, deviations that stem from different attitudes towards risk are part of the theory of ideal rationality.

Let me elaborate by discussing five of the additional factors of actual human decision-making that REU theory does not accommodate, and explaining why I think these factors give rise to irrational preferences. But first let me outline two basic criteria of rational preferences, which I will discuss in detail in Chapter 5.

Instrumental rationality involves preferring the means to one's ends. One clear way in which a person could fail to prefer the means to her ends is by preferring a gamble that she disprefers in every respect to some other gamble. And one way a gamble could be worse than another gamble in every respect is that the outcome of the former is dispreferred in every state of the world to the outcome of the latter: no matter how the world might turn out, the latter is preferred. (I remind the reader that an outcome includes everything that the agent potentially cares about, including, perhaps, the way in which the agent came to obtain a particular monetary amount). So, rational preferences obey **betterness-for-reasons**: one gamble is strictly preferred to another only if it is strictly preferred in some state. A second way in which a person could fail to prefer the means to her ends is by having preferences that could not possibly give rise to a plan to choose. In particular, an agent could let her preferences depend on how the options are described. For example, if you prefer two yards of licorice to six feet of licorice, while recognizing that two yards and six feet are the same, then you do not have a coherent evaluation of what is in fact a single option. Let us call the condition that describing an option differently cannot change its place in one's preference ordering the **minimal condition of consistency**. In its most general form, it says that if "f" and "h" describe the same gamble, and if "g" and "j" describe the same gamble, and if a rational agent knows this, then she prefers f to g if and only if she prefers h to j, for both strict and weak preference. I have described these as conditions of instrumental rationality, but they may alternatively be thought of as conditions of consistency. To evaluate the same gamble differently depending on its description is to be of two minds about it, and to prefer one gamble even though its outcomes are all worse is to disavow one's evaluation of outcomes in one's preferences between the gambles.

To see the first two of the features of actual human psychology that REU theory cannot capture, it is helpful here to contrast REU theory with prospect theory, in both its original and cumulative version. For purposes of discussing these two features, we can assume that probabilities are given, and so restrict both REU theory and prospect theory to their objective counterparts; and we can also simplify things by framing the discussion in terms of monetary outcomes only. Prospect theory is more permissive than REU theory in two respects. First, prospect theory allows individuals to treat losses differently than gains. In particular, individuals fix a reference point, and think of outcomes not in terms of their total monetary value, but in terms of their relationship to this reference point.[45] For most individuals, monetary gains are less good than monetary losses are bad, so the utility function for most people tends to increase slowly to the right of the reference point, and drop sharply to the left of the reference point: the utility graph is concave to the right of the reference point and convex to its left. The second respect in which prospect theory is more permissive than REU theory is that it allows that an individual facing a decision problem starts by engaging in an "editing" phase, in which she simplifies the decision problem by (among other things) rounding off some of the probabilities and dollar amounts to more cognitively manageable numbers.[46]

Let us consider the first idea, that individuals treat losses differently than they treat gains. The reason that REU theory cannot accommodate this is that in REU theory, as in EU theory, individuals have preferences concerning total wealth levels rather than changes in wealth. But outcomes in prospect theory are things like "I get $5 more than the reference point." One natural reference point is the individual's wealth level at the

---

[45] For a further discussion of framing effects, see Tversky and Kahneman (1981).

[46] This phase plays a much larger role in the original prospect theory than in its cumulative version, since editing is needed in the original theory to avoid violating the requirement of stochastic dominance.

start of the experiment eliciting her preference. But choice situations can be set up to elicit different reference points. For example, Kahneman and Tversky offered choices to two different groups of subjects.[47] Subjects in the first group were asked to imagine that in addition to whatever they currently owned, they were given $1,000; and they were asked to then choose between $500 and the bet {($1,000, 0.5; $0, 0.5)}. Most subjects chose the former. Subjects in the second group were asked to imagine that in addition to whatever they currently owned, they were given $2,000; and they were asked to choose between −$500 and the bet {(−$1,000, 0.5; $0, 0.5)}. Most subjects chose the latter. If we assume these preferences hold across the two groups, these experimental subjects fail the minimal condition of consistency. Described in one way, they prefer $1,500 more than their current wealth level to a coin-flip between $1,000 and $2,000 more than their current wealth level, but described in a different way, they prefer the latter to the former. If one's preferences over total wealth levels are sensitive to which wealth level gets counted as the reference point, and different descriptions can elicit different reference points, then they are sensitive to how gambles are described. A related phenomenon is the endowment effect, in which individuals who are given an item set the monetary equivalent (price at which they are willing to sell it) higher for this item than individuals who are not given the item set the monetary equivalent (price at which they are willing to buy it). Individuals demand more to give up an item than they would be willing to pay to buy it.[48] The item is preferred to some amount of money when it is thought of as already part of one's possessions, and dis-preferred to that amount when it is not thought of in that way.

The second way in which prospect theory differs from REU theory is that it allows that the agent begins her deliberations with an editing phase. Some of what goes on during the editing phase serves to fix the reference point, and thus runs afoul of the minimal condition of consistency. But other features of editing, such as rounding complicated numbers, serve to make the decision cognitively easier. If editing results in a preference that the ideal agent would not have, then the resulting preference is irrational (with respect to ideal rationality) by definition; if it does not, then rounding is inessential to the predictions of the theory, even though it tells us something interesting about human psychology: namely, how people can arrive at instrumentally rational choices despite facing complex decision problems.

Again, Kahneman and Tversky's reason for including the editing phase in their theory is not because they believe it to be a feature of ideal rationality. Prospect theory is intended to be descriptive, but I am here interested in what rational agents ought to do if they are not bound by cognitive limitations. Nonetheless, it is useful to consider the question of how agents can approximate ideal rationality given their limitations. It is clear how editing helps decision-makers with limited computational capacities: in most cases, editing will lead to the same decision that ideal computation will lead to,

---

[47] Kahneman and Tversky (1979: 273).
[48] See, for example, Kahneman, Knetsch, and Thaler (1991).

but in a much shorter time. So if REU maximization is the correct prescription, then editing may allow agents with limited cognitive capacities to approximate this prescription. (There is nothing special about REU theory here: this is, of course, also true if EU maximization is the correct prescription.)

Might we also explain the endowment and framing effects as results of tools that ordinarily help agents with cognitive limitations approximate ideal rationality? While this is speculative, here is one thought about how to explain the endowment effect. Acquiring a particular item is a gamble on its condition. For example, purchasing a car can be thought of as a gamble on how the car performs in a variety of situations, how often the car needs repairs, and so forth. In general, owning a particular item means that you know more about it, and doing so resolves, to a certain degree, the gamble that having that item consists of. Typically, one discovers that many of the unlikely but very bad possibilities do not obtain—that the seller was not trying to unload an item with a serious defect—but also that many of the unlikely but very good possibilities do not obtain. (I say "typically" because this is what it is for these possibilities to be unlikely). Therefore, in typical cases, one's credence distribution concerning the value of the item "settles" around the mean. So when a risk-avoidant agent faces a choice between the item in his possession and an unfamiliar item of the same type, it will typically be true that the gamble "keep the current item" and the gamble "acquire the new item" have the same average value, but that the latter gamble is more spread out. Therefore, the heuristic "of two items with the same EU, stick with what you have" will typically maximize risk-weighted expected utility for the risk-avoidant agent. Conversely, the heuristic "of two items with the same EU, pick the one you do not have" will typically maximize risk-weighted expected utility for the risk-inclined agent. So while I am not defending the preferences of the experimental subjects who learned no new information but assigned a higher value to the item once it came into their possession, I think we may be able to explain why the heuristic that led to that choice is *generally* useful to agents who aim at REU maximization but have cognitive and time-based limitations.

A similar point might be made about framing effects. Recall first that outcomes in REU (and EU) theory include not just total wealth levels but whatever features of the world an agent cares about. Then notice that many of one's plans are made by considering the amount of money one expects to have, for example, when one plans one's mortgage payments. Having less than one expects therefore often has the additional ill effect of thwarting or complicating one's plans: there are generally utility costs to having less than one expects to have, beyond the utility of the wealth level itself.[49] The outcome "wealth level x having planned on higher wealth level y" is generally worse than "wealth level x having planned on wealth level x." So we might conjecture that the heuristic "treat going under your reference point as particularly bad" generally allows one to maximize REU (or EU) but "misfires" in certain cases. As I said, this is all speculative,

---

[49] This is an adaptation of a point made in Armendt (forthcoming), though Armendt suggests it as an argument that REU theory does not take into account all of the features of our risk-attitudes that matter.

but in order to know how the experimental data bear on the extent to which decision-makers are generally rational, it is worth exploring the relationship between norms of ideal rationality and heuristics for cognitively limited agents further.

The fact that decision-makers tend to be subject to framing effects brings up another worry: that contrary to the assumptions of REU theory (and most normative decision theories), decision-makers do not in general have an underlying stable preference ordering. Though I will not discuss this point in detail, I offer two considerations in favor of the claim that people in general do have stable underlying preferences. First, when we notice we have preferences that appear unstable under different descriptions, we are generally motivated to change them, and we do so in part by thinking about what matters. Part of what we do when we make decisions is try to figure out the right way of framing them.[50] Second, although this is tentative, at least some recent research in psychology suggests that framing effects go away when choices are presented in a foreign language, the idea being that thinking in a foreign language reduces the influence of the emotions on decision-making.[51] This tentatively suggests that there may be an underlying stable preference ordering that is sometimes distorted by non-rational influences.

Let us set prospect theory aside and turn to the other ways in which REU theory is less permissive than it might be. The third way in which REU theory might be made more permissive is in allowing agents to care about *other* global properties besides those having to do with a gamble's riskiness. For example, someone might consider it an attractive feature of a gamble that it contains exactly four possible outcomes. Or it might be an attractive feature that it contains fewer rather than more outcomes. Why not allow the agent to take these things into account?

My reply depends on the agent's reasons for caring about these global properties. If the agent prefers, say, fewer outcomes to more because the cognitive costs of making a decision are lower, then we can say the same thing as above. While taking this into account might be interesting in thinking about how individuals make decisions in light of their natural cognitive limitations, I am interested in how they would make decisions if these limitations were not present: I am interested in ideal rationality. On the other hand, if the agent prefers fewer outcomes to more because he finds thinking about gambles with fewer outcomes to be less anxiety-producing, then this will already be taken into account in the outcome descriptions. Although the number of outcomes is a global property of the gamble, its value will show up as a "local" property of each outcome, because the fact that there were a particular number of outcomes will make a difference to the value associated with *each* monetary outcome: "$100 and having

---

[50] For a discussion of how we might privilege a particular description of an act, see Schick (1991).

[51] See the study by Keysar, Hayakawa, and An (2012). The authors claim that their experiments show that when choices are presented in a foreign language, individuals are not influenced by framing manipulations and display less "myopic loss aversion," the tendency to reject bets with a positive expected value when they are presented with a series of many such bets. (See Chapter 7 of this book for a discussion of how rational agents evaluate series of bets.) They propose "that these effects arise because a foreign language provides greater cognitive and emotional distance than a native tongue does" (661).

undergone anxiety" is worse than "$100 without having undergone anxiety."[52] Finally, the agent may prefer fewer outcomes to more but not in such a way that the disvalue of a gamble with many outcomes shows up in any of the outcomes. In this case, the individual in question will violate betterness-for-reasons. To see this, consider the following two gambles: one has two distinct outcomes, x if event $\bar{E}$ occurs and y if event E occurs; the other has three distinct outcomes, x if $\bar{E}$, y if $E\&F$, and z if $E\&\bar{F}$; and the agent is indifferent between y and z. Then our agent will prefer the first gamble to the second, but will not prefer it in any particular state. In general, if a critic claims that we ought to take account of other irreducibly global features besides those that contribute to riskiness, she will have to say why they matter to instrumental value.

The fourth way in which one might wonder whether REU theory is permissive enough is particular to the issue of risk. One might agree that ruling out risk avoidance/inclination is the only thing EU theory gets wrong, but think that I have overlooked an important fact: namely that rational individuals can have different risk functions in different domains. For example, an individual might be more risk-avoidant when it comes to his health than when it comes to money. Or he might have different risk functions when the stakes are different: he might be more risk-avoidant the higher the stakes are. So, says the criticism, an individual's r-function should be indexed to particular domains or stakes, and there need not be any specific relationship between r_{health} and r_{money}, or between $r^{low\ stakes}$ and $r^{high\ stakes}$. That we accept different levels of risk in different situations is born out by empirical evidence: a study by Rottenstreich and Hsee (2001) found that the shape of the weighting function in prospect theory depends on the kind of decision being made. For example, even though individuals preferred $50 to a kiss with their favorite movie star, they tended to be willing to pay more for a chance of the kiss than for an equivalent chance of $50: they were more risk-seeking with respect to the kiss. More generally, the weighting function deviated more from linearity when the possible outcomes were more emotionally laden.

I do not have space to explore this possibility in detail, but there are a few ways to respond to these suggestions. First, some of the preferences that may be driving this objection are already accounted for by REU theory. As we will see in Chapter 7, if a gamble is to be repeated many times the risk-avoidant agent will appear less risk-avoidant on any particular instance of that gamble; and the risk-inclined agent will appear less risk-inclined. So an individual may appear to have different norms in different domains but will actually be instantiating the same norm. In addition, for most globally sensitive agents, it is usually true that the larger the spread of possibilities in a gamble, the larger the difference will be between the REU of that gamble and

---

[52] One might wonder whether the EU theorist who thinks my theory is overly permissive might have a similar rejoinder to my claim that we ought to allow the agent to care about risk-related global features of a gamble: for example, its minimum value. Might he say that either these features can be taken into account in our description of the outcomes? I will examine this argument in detail in Chapter 4, and show that the argument does not succeed and is importantly different from arguments like the one I make here.

its EU. The risk-avoidant agent will pay a larger premium to avoid a risky gamble, relative to its expected utility, when the stakes are large than when the stakes are small.

This may not account for all of the relevant intuitions, and I do grant that I am ruling out certain preferences as irrational. For example, an REU maximizer cannot value a gamble below its EU in large stakes and value a gamble above its EU in small stakes, if the probabilities of the analogous outcomes are the same. So the second thing to say is that in the end this debate should not take place at the level of which preferences seem reasonable anyway: it should proceed via a discussion of whether the axioms that underlie REU theory are rational requirements. I will present these in the next chapter, but it is worth mentioning that the axiom that the proponent of this objection is likely to challenge is Axiom (A1), the Ordering Axiom, which entails that all gambles are comparable. If one thinks that risk-attitudes may be different in different domains, one might be drawn to thinking that we cannot compare outcomes that fall within different domains; otherwise, it would seem odd to have different preference norms in different domains. Finally, I might respond to the objector who wants to allow different risk-attitudes in different domains by pointing out that some gambles will be hybrid gambles, that might result in a health outcome but might result in a monetary outcome—for example, the purchase of medical insurance—and the objector will have to say how the agent values these.

The final way in which one might wonder whether REU theory is permissive enough concerns an assumption it inherits from EU theory: namely, that rational agents act as if they assign a sharp probability to each outcome. That most actual people violate this assumption in making decisions is shown by the Ellsberg paradox. In Ellsberg's (1961) example, you are presented with an urn filled with ninety balls of various colors. You know that thirty of the balls are red, and the rest are black and yellow but in unknown proportion. A ball is to be drawn at random, and you are asked which of the following two acts you prefer:

f_1: $100 if the ball is red; $0 if the ball is black or yellow.
f_2: $100 if the ball is black; $0 if the ball is red or yellow.

You are also asked which of the following two acts you prefer:

f_3: $100 if the ball is red or yellow; $0 if the ball is black.
f_4: $100 if the ball is black or yellow; $0 if the ball is red.

Most people prefer f_1 to f_2 and prefer f_4 to f_3, but this violates EU theory.[53] People appear not to assign a stable value to p(RED), and appear to prefer a gamble in which the probability of the good outcome is known to one in which the probability of the good

---

[53] $EU(f_1) > EU(f_2)$
$\Rightarrow p(red)u(\$100) + p(black)u(\$0) + p(yellow)u(\$0) > p(red)u(\$0) + p(black)u(\$100) + p(yellow)u(\$0)$
$\Rightarrow p(red) > p(black)$
$EU(f_3) < EU(f_4)$
$\Rightarrow p(red)u(\$100) + p(black)u(\$0) + p(yellow)u(\$100) < p(red)u(\$0) + p(black)u(\$100) + p(yellow)u(\$100)$
$\Rightarrow p(red) < p(black)$

outcome is unknown. The majority choices also violate REU theory.[54] As in EU theory, a decision-maker can only be represented as a risk-weighted expected utility maximizer by acting as if she assigns sharp probabilities to states, and assigns them consistently across different decisions. Whether instrumental rationality ought to allow that agents do not assign sharp probabilities to states is beyond the scope of this work.[55] I am primarily interested in showing that if an agent does have sharp probabilities, then she is not rationally required to use *those* as decision weights, and that we can discover her probability function from her preferences if she is an REU maximizer. Perhaps REU theory can be extended to the case in which subjective probabilities are not sharp.

The discussion in this section may not have put to rest the reader's worry that REU theory is not permissive enough. If the reader still thinks we ought to adopt a more permissive normative theory, I encourage her to take the arguments in this book, to the effect that preferences conforming to REU theory are rationally permissible, as the first step in arguing for a sufficiently permissive theory. Furthermore, it is important to note the role of counterexamples in decision theory; this point applies to the present work as much as it does to anyone arguing for a more permissive theory. While we may be motivated to *consider* the question of whether we need a different normative theory by the existence of preferences that violate some current theory, ultimately the *justification* of any particular normative decision theory depends on justifying its axioms.

---

[54] $REU(f_1) > REU(f_2)$
$\Rightarrow u(\$0) + r(p(black) + p(red))[u(\$0) - u(\$0)] + (r(p(red))[u(\$100) - u(\$0)] > u(\$0) + r(p(black) + p(red))[u(\$0) - u(\$0)] + (r(p(black))[u(\$100) - u(\$0)]$
$\Rightarrow r(p(red)) > r(p(black))$
$\Rightarrow p(red) > p(black)$ (assuming that r is non-decreasing)
$REU(f_3) < REU(f_4)$
$\Rightarrow u(\$0) + r(p(yellow) + p(red))[u(\$100) - u(\$0)] + (r(p(red))[u(\$100) - u(\$100)] < u(\$0) + r(p(yellow) + p(black))[u(\$100) - u(\$0)] + (r(p(black))[u(\$100) - u(\$100)]$
$\Rightarrow r(p(yellow) + p(red)) < r(p(yellow) + p(black))$
$\Rightarrow p(red) < p(black)$ (assuming that r is non-decreasing)

[55] See Levi (1974), Gärdenfors and Sahlin (1982), White (2009), Elga (2010), and Joyce (2010) on the question of whether rational agents are required to have sharp probabilities.

3

Representation

3.1 From Preferences to Beliefs and Desires

We have so far been focusing on the question of how a decision-maker might aggregate his beliefs (credence function) and desires (utility function) to arrive at a single value for a gamble. I have argued that agents need not aggregate according to the expected utility principle, but instead might weight the values of outcomes by a function of their probabilities. Thus we might model decision-makers as using a more general decision rule, which includes a utility function, a credence function, and a risk function. However, philosophers are interested not only in what a decision-maker's preferences ought to be given his beliefs and desires, but also what his beliefs and desires are given his preferences.

Recall the discussion of representation in Chapter 1. A utility and probability function represent an agent under EU theory just in case for all acts f and g, the agent weakly prefers f to g iff $EU(f) \geq EU(g)$, where expected utility is calculated relative to the agent's subjective probability and utility functions. A *representation theorem* provides a set of axioms on the preference relation over acts such that if an agent's preferences obey these axioms, he will be represented under expected utility theory by a unique probability function and a utility function that is unique up to positive affine transformation: he will be an EU maximizer relative to these functions.[1] So the question that arises for REU theory is what general conditions on preferences allow us to extract beliefs, desires, and an attitude towards risk from particular sets of preferences. A utility, probability, and risk function represent an agent under REU theory just in case for all acts f and g, the agent weakly prefers f to g if and only if $REU(f) \geq REU(g)$, where risk-weighted expected utility is calculated relative to these functions. Are there axioms such that if an agent's preferences obey them, he will be represented under REU theory by unique probability and risk functions and a utility function unique up to positive affine transformation?

The role of representation theorems depends on the use to which decision theory is put. The reader will no doubt be familiar with the distinction between *normative* and

---

[1] See Savage (1954/1972); Ramsey (1926). A similar point holds for the objective probabilities case: a representation theorem provides a set of axioms on the preference relation over lotteries that entail that the agent is represented under expected utility theory by a utility function that is unique up to positive affine transformation (see, e.g., von Neumann and Morgenstern (1944). Also see Fishburn (1981) for a survey of representation theorems for EU theory.

descriptive decision theory: the former concerns what individuals ought to do and the latter what individuals in fact do. Philosophers tend to be primarily concerned with normative decision theory, and that is the subject of this book. However, there are at least two very different ways in which normative decision theory has been used, which I refer to as the *prescriptive* use and the *interpretive* use.

When the theory is taken prescriptively, it has both a first-person and a third-person use. An agent uses it to identify the choice he should make or the preferences he should have: he judges whether his preferences accord with the theory, and brings them in line with it if not. A third party uses the theory to ascertain whether the agent's preferences in fact accord with the theory, and it is by this criterion that she judges whether the agent's preferences are rational.[2] Representation theorems are useful for prescriptive decision theory because they provide a criterion for determining when an agent has preferences that accord with the theory. This criterion does not require knowing the agent's precise numerical values ahead of time. Furthermore, it can be employed even if we think there are no precise numerical values to know aside from those that result from the theorem. This is why representation theorems are especially useful to the constructivist. For the constructivist, rationality *just is* conformity to the axioms of decision theory, and it is merely a convenience that a rational agent can be represented as maximizing a particular utility function. Since representation theorems provide an alternative criterion to the maximization criterion, they allow us to refocus the debate about rationality: instead of arguing about whether a rational agent ought to maximize expected utility or some other quantity, we can argue about whether a rational agent ought to conform to the axioms of EU theory or some other axioms.

In contrast to prescriptive decision theory, a portion of the modern philosophical literature treats decision theory *interpretively*: as a framework to interpret an agent's desires, his beliefs, and perhaps even the options that he takes himself to be deciding among.[3] This use is only available to the psychological realist. For the non-constructivist psychological realist, the interpretive use of decision theory arises in response to a worry about how to discover what an agent believes and desires, given that we have no direct access to these mental states, and the agents themselves have at most only limited access to them via introspection. However, it seems that it is relatively easy to discover agents' *preferences*: preferences do manifest themselves directly (if not perfectly) in behavior, and are ordinarily open to introspection. For the constructivist psychological realist, the interpretive use of decision theory arises in response to the question of how

---

[2] Some authors make finer distinctions within what I call the prescriptive use of decision theory: for example, Bermúdez (2009) distinguishes between the action-guiding use of decision theory and the normative use, which appear to correspond roughly to the first-person prescriptive use and the third-person prescriptive use. I do not mean to minimize the difference between these two uses of the theory, but for my purposes, the important question for both the agent and the theorist is whether the agent is doing what he *ought*: the agent is trying to answer this question so that he can shape his behavior appropriately, and the theorist is trying to answer this question so that she can assess the agent.

[3] This seems to be the major innovation of decision theory for Ramsey (1926): the theory provides a way to measure an agent's degrees of belief. For examples of the interpretive use, see Davidson (1973) and Lewis (1974). See also the discussion in Hurley (1989), especially Chapters 4 and 5.

to define an agent's beliefs and desires. For either view, we might think of decision theory as precisifying the way we interpret others' mental states on the basis of their behavior. It is important that the formal principle that links mental states and preferences is a normative principle. This is because aiming at the relevant norm—preferring the means to your ends or preferring consistently—is supposed by the interpretive theorist to be a constitutive principle of action or preferences.

It should be clear how representation theorems are useful to interpretive theorists. If an agent's preferences obey the axioms of the correct theory, then the interpretive theorist can start with the agent's (observable) preferences and derive the probability function and utility function that represent him. It should also be clear why it is important that the theorems result in *unique* probability and utility functions. If there were multiple <*p*, *u*> pairs that each could represent the agent, we would not know which way of representing the agent accurately captures "his" beliefs and desires. (Note that for all the representation theorems under consideration here, the utility function is only unique up to positive affine transformation. Therefore, only the facts that are common to all of the utility functions—for example, the relative size of the utility intervals between outcomes—can be rightly called facts about the agent's utilities.)

What does the interpretive theorist do if the agent's preferences do not satisfy the axioms necessary for representation? The interpretive theorist has some leeway in interpreting the agent's preferences. If the agent's preferences approximate preferences that obey the axioms—the preferences of his "rational counterpart"—then the theorist can interpret him as having the beliefs and desires that those preferences would entail, but as making errors in cases in which his preferences do not line up with those entailed by the representation. She can do so because the interpretive assumption is that the agent is aiming at preferring that which it is rational for him to prefer, not that he is successfully doing so. Perhaps the agent suffers from weakness of will or thoughtlessness when making the choices in which his preferences deviate from the represented ones, or perhaps some of the choices are simply too mathematically complex for him to make well. The interpretive theorist is also not constrained by the agent's own interpretation of his preferences: for example, if the agent claims to prefer vanilla ice cream but always chooses chocolate, then it may be permissible for the theorist to interpret the agent as actually preferring chocolate, though the theorist will be guided by a principle of charity that says that an interpretation is better insofar as it is closer to how the agent interprets himself.[4] One particularly important possibility for interpretive leeway—namely, how the agent conceives of the outcomes of the choices he is faced with—will be discussed in detail in the next chapter.

---

[4] See, for example, Lewis (1974). Aside from interpreting an agent as he interprets himself, there are several other criteria that will favor one potential interpretation over another. These might include, as Maher (1993, p. 18) points out, approximating an agent's disposition to choose, interpreting an agent as having the preferences that people normally have in similar situations, and interpreting the agent as honestly reporting his preferences.

There may, however, be cases in which an agent's preferences do not even approximate preferences that conform to the axioms. If this is the case, then what the interpretive theorist will say depends on whether she is a constructivist or a non-constructive realist. The realist can say that the agent has beliefs and desires, but that we are in a poor position when it comes to figuring out what they are via preferences. The constructivist, on the other hand, will say that the agent does not even have beliefs and desires, since having preferences that (approximately) obey the axioms is constitutive of having beliefs and desires.

Interpretive decision theory bears some similarity to descriptive decision theory, so it is important to consider the relationship between the two. It is also important to explain why, given this similarity, interpretive decision theory incorporates a normative model rather than a descriptive model. Both interpretive and descriptive decision theorists are interested in actual agents rather than in their ideal counterparts. But these theorists differ in their goals. Interpretive theorists are generally interested in using decision theory to discover mental states and to explain an individual's preferences in terms of these. Because rationality is the constitutive link between these mental states and preferences—what the agent does in preferring f to g is to take f to be better at satisfying his aims given his beliefs—an interpretation of an agent is better the closer it comes to interpreting him as rational, as preferring that which in fact is a better means to his ends, given his beliefs and desires. Descriptive theorists are generally interested in using decision theory to describe behavioral regularities and to predict behavior. Because decision theory on this view is a kind of empirical scientific theory, a description of an agent is better the more it explains the behavior of a broad class of individuals. Interpretive theorists are thus more concerned with rationality, descriptive theorists with parsimony. I should note that descriptive decision theory can inform the interpretive project insofar as it tells us how individuals generally deviate from rationality: how we can expect their preferences to deviate from those of their ideal counterparts.

We can see that representation theorems are crucial to decision theory on either normative use, so any alternative to EU theory needs a representation theorem if it can hope to serve the purposes to which EU theory is traditionally put. As I will shortly demonstrate, REU theory does have a representation theorem, so we can point to a set of axioms such that the following holds: if a decision-maker's preferences obey these axioms, we will be able to determine a unique probability function, a unique risk function, and a utility function that is unique up to positive affine transformation such that he maximizes risk-weighted expected utility relative to these three functions. In the next section I will explain these axioms and present the theorem, though I leave the proof to an appendix. In the third section of this chapter I will explain the differences between the axioms of the REU theorem and the stronger axioms of the analogous EU theorem. This will help us frame the debate about whether globally sensitive agents are rational around the question of whether they ought to obey the axioms of EU theory or only the weaker axioms of REU theory. In the final section of this chapter I will respond to an important concern that the theorem raises about the interpretation of the functions it constructs.

The bulk of the work that I will draw on for the theorem here has been done by Veronika Köbberling and Peter Wakker (hereafter KW) and by Mark Machina and David Schmeidler (hereafter MS).[5] Köbberling and Wakker prove a representation theorem for another rank-dependent theory: Choquet expected utility (CEU), discussed in Section 1.4. Recall that CEU, like REU, applies to acts rather than lotteries; however, CEU does not represent the agent as assigning *additive probabilities* to events, and thus the representation theorem for CEU does not provide us with a way of determining the agent's degrees of belief from his preferences. Machina and Schmeidler provide conditions under which an agent can be represented as probabilistically sophisticated—as having a unique probability function and preferring in accordance with it—and as maximizing *some* value function, but their conditions do not allow us to determine the values of outcomes aside from the gambles in which they are embedded. I combine these two results to provide conditions under which we can represent an agent as a probabilistically sophisticated decision-maker maximizing the specific function that this book is concerned with: conditions under which we can extract from an agent's preferences a probability function, a utility function, and a *function that represents how he structures the possible realization of his aims in the face of risk*. Thus the set of axioms in the REU representation theorem combines Köbberling and Wakker's axioms with Machina and Schmeidler's, and is strictly stronger than either set of axioms.

3.2   Representation Theorem for REU Maximizers

In this section I will present a set of axioms such that any agent whose preferences obey them can be represented as a risk-weighted expected utility maximizer with a unique probability function p, a unique risk function r, and a utility function u that is unique up to positive affine transformation. I will explain the technical machinery and state the theorem, but postpone its proof to the appendices. As mentioned above, most of the substantial mathematical work has been done by Köbberling and Wakker and by Machina and Schmeidler.[6]

---

[5]   Machina and Schmeidler (1992), Köbberling and Wakker (2003).

[6]   Since proving this theorem in Buchak (2009), it has come to my attention that Nakamura (1995) has proven a representation theorem for what he refers to as CEU with an additive state probability space, which is formally equivalent to what I call REU theory. The theorem yields (u, φ, π), equivalent to my (u, r, p). He also makes use of Machina and Schmeidler (1992). However, his A2, the axiom that is a weaker version of an axiom that EU maximizers obey, is very different from my A6, which plays a similar role. Since I think it is easier to understand the axiom I use, and to see how it corresponds to caring about structural properties of gambles, I will confine my discussion to it and not discuss Nakamura's result further. Gilboa's (1985) also gives necessary and sufficient conditions for the weighting function w in CEU to be interpreted as a distortion function of probabilities of states; however, these conditions are not conditions on preferences but rather conditions on w (in the first half of his paper) or conditions on a qualitative probability relation that is meant to correspond to w (in the second half of his paper). There are two other results worth mentioning. One is due to Schmeidler (1989), who axiomatizes a version of CEU over horse lotteries (acts involving both

3.2.1 Preliminaries

I start by explaining the spaces and relations we are dealing with.[7] The **state space** is a set of states $\mathscr{S} = \{\ldots, s, \ldots\}$, whose subsets are called events. The **event space**, $\mathscr{E}$, is the set of all subsets of $\mathscr{S}$. Since we want to represent agents who have preferences over not just monetary outcomes but discrete goods and, indeed, over outcomes described to include every feature of the world that the agent cares about, it is important that the outcome space be general. Thus, the **outcome space** is a set of outcomes $\mathscr{X} = \{\ldots, x, \ldots\}$. I follow Savage (1954/1972) in defining the entities an agent has preferences over as "acts" that yield some particular outcome in each state. The **act space** $\mathscr{A} = \{\ldots, f(.), g(.), \ldots\}$ is thus the set of all finite-valued functions from $\mathscr{S}$ to $\mathscr{X}$, where the inverse of each outcome $f^{-1}(x)$ is the set of states that yields that outcome, so $f^{-1}(x) \in \mathscr{E}$. So for any act $f \in \mathscr{A}$, there is some partition of the state space $\mathscr{S}$ into $\{E_1, \ldots E_n\}$ and some finite set of outcomes $Y \subseteq \mathscr{X}$ such that f can be thought of as a member of Y^n.[8] And as long as $f(s)$ is the same for all $s \in E_i$, we can write $f(E_i)$ as shorthand for $f(s)$ such that $s \in E_i$. For any fixed finite partition of events $M = \{E_1, \ldots, E_n\}$, all the acts on those events will form a subset $A_M \subseteq \mathscr{A}$. Thus, A_M is defined to contain all the acts that each yield for each event in the partition, the same outcome for all states in that event: $A_M = \{f \in \mathscr{A} \mid (\forall E_i \in M)(\exists x \in \mathscr{X})(\forall s \in E_i)(f(s) = x)\}$. Note that both the act space and the state and event spaces are infinite, but that each act in the act space is only associated with a finite number of possible outcomes; however, for any outcome and any event, there will be an act that yields that outcome in that event. Furthermore, since we are ultimately interested in deriving the probability of every event in $\mathscr{E}$—not just events in a particular partition—the axioms will concern all finite-valued acts, not only those belonging to a particular partition.

The **preference relation** $\geq$ is a two-place relation over the act space. This gives rise to the indifference relation and the strict preference relation: $f \sim g$ iff $f \geq g$ and $g \geq f$; and $f > g$ iff $f \geq g$ and $\neg(g \geq f)$.

unknown and known probabilities), and in particular includes an axiom which he calls the Comonotonic Independence Axiom. Schmeider derives a weighting function w of states, and then, like Gilboa, derives conditions under which w can be interpreted as a distortion function of probabilities (see remark 4.2.1); however, the application of Schmeidler's result to the present discussion is complicated by the fact that Schmeidler builds objective probabilities into his model. Finally, Wakker (1990) shows that if a CEU maximizer has preferences that respect stochastic dominance in what he calls the "intermediate setup," then he is representable as an RDU maximizer; however, stochastic dominance is not directly a condition on preferences, so for our purposes, we cannot simply assume it. Wakker (2010, p. 287) also argues that one can use qualitative probability axioms, rather than probabilistic sophistication, to determine that there exists a probability function of events for a CEU maximizer such that the weighting function is a transformation of the probability function, and cites Chateauneuf (1985) for these conditions; however, to my knowledge, these conditions are the conditions under which a probability function exists, not under which a unique probability function exists.

[7] In the denotation of the spaces, I follow Machina and Schmeidler (1992).

[8] The act set does not include the St Petersburg gamble, in which an infinite number of different outcomes are possible. The salient aspect of the St Petersburg gamble is that its outcomes are unbounded, and unbounded outcomes for a particular act is ruled out because restricting our act set to finite-valued acts, in combination with the ordering axiom that we will introduce, implies that every gamble will have a best outcome and a worst outcome.

For all $x \in \mathcal{X}$, $\underline{x}$ denotes the constant act $\{f(s) = x$ for all $s \in \mathcal{S}\}$. The relata of the preference relation must be acts, but it will be useful to talk about preferences between outcomes. Thus, we will define an auxiliary preference relation over outcomes:

$$x \geq y \text{ iff } \underline{x} \geq \underline{y} \text{ (for x, } y \in \mathcal{X})$$

where indifference and strict preferences are defined as above. It will be useful to talk about preferences between outcomes of particular acts, so, following the above definition, $f(s) \geq g(s)$ holds iff $\underline{f(s)} \geq \underline{g(s)}$, the constant act that yields $f(s)$ in every state is weakly preferred to the constant act that yields $g(s)$ in every state. Taking "$\underline{x} \geq \underline{y}$" to carry the intuitive meaning that the outcome x is weakly preferred to the outcome y, as we do here, carries with it a substantive commitment to how we are to interpret the spaces. In particular, we must assume *state neutrality*: that the outcomes and states are individuated in such a way that there are no interaction effects between outcomes and states. To use Savage's example:[9] if the outcomes are "possession of a bathing suit" and "possession of a tennis racket," and the events are "picnic near water" and "picnic near tennis courts," then the individual's preference between the act that yields the tennis racket in every state and the act that yields a bathing suit in every state will not just depend on whether the bare outcome "tennis racket" is preferred to the bare outcome "bathing suit." As Savage points out, the outcomes must be things like "a refreshing swim with friends," "holding a tennis racket alone while friends swim," and so forth. Savage guaranteed state neutrality by introducing an axiom that is only compelling if we take it for granted that there are no interaction effects between states and outcomes. In Savage's theory, this axiom is his (P3), and it will be entailed by my (A1) and (A2).[10] As we will see, then, the axioms of REU theory, like Savage's axioms, are only compelling if we take it for granted that there are no interaction eff ects between states and outcomes. They are also only compelling if the acts are independent of how likely the states are to obtain: like Savage's axiomatization, the axiomatization here is causal rather than evidential.[11]

Next, $x_E f$ denotes the act that agrees with f on all states not contained in E, and yields x on any state contained in E: $x_E f(s) = \{x$ if $s \in E$; $f(s)$ if $s \notin E\}$. Likewise, for disjoint E_1 and E_2 in $\mathcal{E}$, $x_{E1} y_{E2} f$ is the act that agrees with f on all states not contained in E_1 and E_2, and yields x on E_1 and y on E_2: $x_{E1} y_{E2} f(s) = \{x$ if $s \in E_1$, y if $s \in E_2$, $f(s)$ if $s \notin E_1 \cup E_2\}$. Similarly, $g_E f$ is the act that agrees with g on all states contained in E and agrees with f on all states not contained in E: $g_E f(s) = \{g(s)$ if $s \in E$; $f(s)$ if $s \notin E\}$. We say that an event E is **null** on $F \subseteq \mathcal{A}$ just in case the agent is indifferent between any pair of acts which differ only on E: $g_E f \sim f$ for all $fg_E f \in F$.[12] Although "null" will eventually come to mean, in the presence

[9] Savage (1972, p. 25).
[10] See Appendix A. Savage's (P3) is equivalent to what I list in Appendix A as (A2′)—an axiom which appears in Machina and Schmeidler (1992).
[11] Unlike in the theories which go by the name "causal decision theory," both Savage's axiomatization and the axiomatization here build into the framework, rather than into the decision rule, the assumption needed to rule out the effects of evidential correlation between acts and states on a decision.
[12] Machina and Schmeidler (1992: 749).

of the other axioms, that the agent assigns E zero probability, the basic interpretation is that the agent does not care what happens on that event.

Several concepts are important in Köbberling and Wakker's result. The first, comonotonicity, was introduced by Schmeidler (1989). Two acts f and g are **como-notonic** if there are no states $s_1, s_2 \in \mathcal{S}$ such that $f(s_1) > f(s_2)$ and $g(s_1) < g(s_2)$. This is equivalent to the claim that for any partition A_M of acts such that $f, g \in A_M$, there are no events $E_1, E_2 \in M$ such that $f(E_1) > f(E_2)$ and $g(E_1) < g(E_2)$. The acts f and g order the states (and, consequently, the events) in the same way: if s_1 leads to a strictly preferred outcome to that of s_2 for act f, then s_1 leads to a weakly preferred outcome to that of s_2 for act g. We say that a subset C of some A_M is a **comoncone** if all the acts in C order the events in the same way: for example, the set of all acts on coin-flips in which the heads outcome is as good as or better than the tails outcome forms a comoncone. Formally, as Köbberling and Wakker define it, take any fixed partition of events $M = \{E_1, \ldots, E_n\}$. A permutation ρ from $\{1, \ldots, n\}$ to $\{1, \ldots, n\}$ is a *rank-ordering* permutation of f if $f(E_{\rho(1)}) \geq \ldots \geq f(E_{\rho(n)})$. So a comoncone is a subset C_ρ of A_M that is rank-ordered by a given permutation: $C_\rho = \{f \in A_M \mid f(E_{\rho(1)}) \geq \ldots \geq f(E_{\rho(n)})\}$ for some ρ. For each fixed partition of events of size n, there are n! comoncones.[13]

Here is an example to illustrate the idea of a comoncone. The act {HEADS, $50; TAILS, $0} is comonotonic with the act {HEADS, $100; TAILS, $99}: in either case, the outcome in heads is strictly preferred (and thus weakly preferred) to the outcome in tails. The act {HEADS, $0; TAILS, $50} is not comonotonic with either act, since the outcome in tails is strictly preferred to the outcome in heads. The act {HEADS, $70; TAILS, $70} is comonotonic with all the acts mentioned so far: the heads outcome is weakly preferred to the tails outcome, so it is comonotonic with the first two acts mentioned, and the tails outcome is weakly preferred to the heads outcome, so it is comonotonic with the third act. The first two acts and this act together form (part of) a comoncone, the comoncone in which heads is weakly preferred to tails; and the third act and this act form (part of) a different comoncone, the comoncone in which tails is weakly preferred to heads. As we see, an act can be contained in more than one comoncone.

We say that outcomes $x^1, x^2, \ldots$ form a **standard sequence** on $F \subseteq \mathcal{S}$ if there exist an act $f \in F$, events $E_i \neq E_j$ that are non-null on F, and outcomes y, z with $\neg(y \sim z)$ such that for all k, $(x^{k+1})_{E_i}(y)_{E_j}f \sim (x^k)_{E_i}(z)_{E_j}f$, with all acts $(x^k)_{E_i}(y)_{E_j}, (x^k)_{E_i}(z)_{E_j}f \in F$.[14] The intended interpretation is that the set of outcomes $x^1, x^2, x^3, \ldots$, will be "equally spaced." Since the agent is indifferent for each pair of gambles, and since each pair of gambles differs only in that the "left-hand" gamble offers y rather than z if E_j obtains, and offers x^{k+1} rather than x^k if E_i obtains, the latter tradeoff must exactly make up for the former. And since the possibility of x^{k+1} rather than x^k (if E_i) makes up for y rather than z (if E_j) for each k,

---

[13] Köbberling and Wakker (2003: 400). On p. 403, Köbberling and Wakker (2003) point out that we can also define a comoncone on an infinite state space, though this is not necessary for our purposes.

[14] Köbberling and Wakker (2003: 398). The concept of a standard sequence, however, does not originate with them.

the difference between each x^{k+1} and x^k must be constant. Note that a standard sequence can be increasing or decreasing, and will be increasing if $z > y$ and decreasing if $y > z$. A standard sequence is bounded if there exist outcomes v and w such that $\forall i(v \geq x^i \geq w)$.

We are now in a position to define a relation that is important for Köbberling and Wakker's result and that also makes use of the idea that one tradeoff exactly makes up for another. For each partition M, we define the relation $\sim^*(F)$ for $F \subseteq A_M$ and outcomes x, y, z, w $\in \mathscr{X}$ as follows:

xy $\sim^*(F)$ zw iff $\exists f,g \in F$ and $\exists E \in \mathscr{E}$ that is non-null on F such that $x_E f \sim y_E g$ and $z_E f \sim w_E g$, where all four acts are contained in F.[15]

Köbberling and Wakker explain the relation $\sim^*(F)$ as follows: "The interpretation is that receiving x instead of y apparently does the same as receiving z instead of w; i.e., it exactly offsets the receipt of the [f's] instead of the [g's] contingent on [¬E]."[16] The idea here is that if one gamble offers f if Ē obtains, whereas another gamble offers g if Ē obtains, then this is a point in favor of (let us say) the first gamble. So in order for an agent to be indifferent between the two gambles, there has to be some compensating point in favor of the second gamble: it has to offer a better outcome if E obtains. And it has to offer an outcome that is better by the right amount to exactly offset this point. Now let us assume that offering y rather than x (on E), and offering w rather than z (on E) both have this feature: they both exactly offset the fact that a gamble offers f rather than g (on ¬E). That is, if one gamble offers f if Ē, and a second gamble offers g if Ē, then this positive feature of the first gamble would be exactly offset if the first offered x if E and the second offered y if E—and it would be exactly offset if instead the first offered z if E and the second offered w if E. If this is the case, then there is some important relationship between x and y on the one hand and z and w on the other: there is a situation in which having the first member of each pair rather than the second both play **the same compensatory role**. This relationship is called $\sim^*$ or **tradeoff equality**. We write xy $\sim^*(C)$ zw if there exists a comoncone $F \subseteq A_M$ such that xy $\sim^*(F)$ zw: that is, if x and y play the same compensatory role as z and w in some gambles f and g where all of the modified gambles after x, y, z, and w have been substituted in are in the same comoncone.

The relation $\sim^*(F)$, and particularly $\sim^*(C)$, will feature centrally in the representation theorem, because one important axiom will place restrictions on when it can hold: on when pairs of outcomes can play the same compensatory role. This relation will also play a crucial role in determining the cardinal utility difference between outcomes using ordinal preferences. I will explain this more fully in the next section.

---

[15]   Köbberling and Wakker (2003: 396–7).

[16]   Köbberling and Wakker (2003: 397). Note the similarity to the four-place relation "=" in Ramsey's (1926) axiomatization of EU theory. In Ramsey's axiomatization, "xy = zw" holds when the agent is indifferent between {E, x; Ē, w} and {E, y; Ē, z} for any "ethically neutral" proposition E believed to degree 0.5.

Next, we can give the conditions under which a function that assigns a numerical value to each event in the event space counts as a finitely additive probability function. We say that p: $\mathscr{E} \to [0, 1]$ is a **finitely additive probability function** iff:

(1) $p(\varnothing) = 0$.
(2) $p(\mathscr{S}) = 1$.
(3) p is additive for any finite sequence of disjoint events.

We say that a probability function is non-atomic when each event E (set of states) contains a subset E′ such that $0 < p(E') < p(E)$. Given that we will be interested in the probability that a particular act yields a particular outcome, we will eventually be interested in thinking of an act as a probability distribution over outcomes. Therefore, it is useful to point out that each act f gives rise to a **probability distribution of outcomes** P: $\mathscr{X} \to [0, 1]$ such that $\sum_{x \in X} P(x) = 1$ and for all $x \in \mathscr{X}$, $P(x) = p(f^{-1}(x))$. Since acts are finitely valued, these probability distributions assign non-zero probability to only a finite number of outcomes:[17] they can be represented as finite-valued lotteries $\{(x_1, P_1; \ldots ; x_m, P_m)\}$

Finally, I will say that r: $[0, 1] \to [0, 1]$ is a **risk function** iff $r(0) = 0$, $r(1) = 1$, and r is increasing. In Chapter 2 I left it as an open question whether r must be increasing, or whether it would be enough if r were non-decreasing; here, however, I take a stand that r must be increasing—we will see why the axioms imply this shortly. I will not build into the definition of r that r must be continuous.

Before turning to the axioms, I want to say something about the setup. Like Savage, I distinguish the sets of outcomes, states, and acts. There are three assumptions at work in doing this that one might object to. The first is that we can carve up the states in such a way that there are no "interaction effects" between acts and states: the probability the agent assigns to a state is independent of which act she chooses. As mentioned, this makes REU theory a causal decision theory. I will not spend much time on this worry, other than to note it and to add that nothing in the *philosophical* foundations of REU theory requires this assumption, so those who accept the philosophical view argued for in this work, but who are uncomfortable with this assumption, can work on extending the mathematical foundations of the theory to do away with it.

The second assumption is that we can carve up the states in such a way that there are no interaction effects between outcomes and states: the agent is indifferent between getting an outcome in one state and getting that same outcome in another. This is the assumption of state neutrality, and in conjunction with the assumption implicit in the definition of the act space that for each outcome there is a constant act that results in that outcome in every state, this leads to what Peter Fishburn calls the "constant act problem."[18] As Fishburn points out, in most realistic problems, some outcomes and states will be incompatible with each other; for example, the outcome "carry an

---

[17] Machina and Schmeidler (1992: 753).   [18] Fishburn (1981: 162–3).

umbrella on a sunny day" is incompatible with the state in which it rains. However, the act that yields "carry an umbrella on a sunny day" if it rains or it shines must be an object of preference; so must the act that yields and "carry an umbrella and get wet" if it rains or it shines. Therefore, there will be many acts that can never be the object of an actual choice but that must figure into an agent's preference ordering nonetheless: the agent must have, in John Broome's terminology, many "non-practical preferences."

There are two separate worries about these non-practical preferences. One is a metaphysical worry about whether acts involving outcome/state pairs like those mentioned are even coherent, and the other is a conceptual or epistemological worry about whether anyone has preferences about these acts or could know what they are if she does. I will not address this issue in detail.[19] But I want to briefly suggest that neither worry is serious. Certainly we can imagine what these gambles would be, even if they cannot be actual. And an agent can abstract away from the impossibility of a gamble in order to evaluate it, particularly since she can determine the probabilities she assigns to states on the basis of her more practical preferences: for example, she might ask herself, "would I rather have the outcome 'carry an umbrella and get wet' in the event of rain and 'carry an umbrella on a sunny day' otherwise, or 'carry an umbrella on a sunny day' in the event of rain and 'carry an umbrella and get wet' otherwise?" and reason, "the latter, because I think rain is really likely and I would rather carry an umbrella on a sunny day."

There is another worry about the assumption of state neutrality. Mark Schervish, Teddy Seidenfeld, and Joseph Kadane (1990) show that on standard approaches that assume state neutrality (including Savage's) the uniqueness of the probability function is relative to what the set of constant acts is, which in turn depends on which prizes get counted as outcomes. In their example, if we let the events be possible exchange rates between dollars and yen, then we will get a different (and incompatible) probability distribution on events if we assume that outcomes in the outcome set are dollar amounts than if we assume that the outcomes in the outcome set are yen amounts.[20] This worry prompts the authors to consider how we might elicit probabilities for state-dependent utilities. But we might draw a different conclusion from their result: namely, that the assumption of state neutrality makes little sense without the assumption of a set of privileged outcomes.

This brings us to the final—and most philosophically loaded—assumption underlying the tripartite approach of separating outcomes, states, and acts: that we can isolate a privileged set of final outcomes. One might worry that any supposed outcome is itself a gamble: for example, receiving $30 is really a gamble over various states of the world: the value of a dollar might go up or down, one might or might not have the opportunity to purchase various goods, these goods might or might not turn out to bring one as much pleasure as one thought they would, and so forth. The idea that there are "final"

---

[19] See Broome (1993) and Dreier (1996) for further discussion of this issue.
[20] Schervish, Seidenfeld, and Kadane (1990: 843–4).

outcomes—that it is not risk all the way down, so to speak—will be important to my project in particular: although Savage assumes a separation between acts and outcomes, his theory is more amenable to allowing outcomes to themselves count as gambles, since for EU theory the value of an act is not altered by replacing an outcome with a gamble of equivalent value.

Here is a defense of the idea that there really are final outcomes—outcomes whose value to the agent does not depend on any additional assumptions about the world. Although many of the things we might ordinarily call outcomes, such as getting money or carrying an umbrella in the rain, are divisible further, there has to be a level at which this bottoms out. If there are not some ultimate values underlying our preferences over more complicated outcomes, it is hard to see what these preferences can be based on in the first place.[21] Granted, we ordinarily do not talk at the level of these ultimate outcomes. But that just means that our ordinary talk is not always the level at which to apply the theory. Indeed, it will be an interesting question when REU maximization in what Savage calls a "small-world" decision problem, a decision problem that artificially confines attention to certain salient options and states, will approximate REU maximization in the "grand world" decision problem—the decision problem that takes account of everything that actually matters to the agent and the decision problem that decision theory is "really" about. I will return briefly to this question in Chapter 7.

No doubt some will be concerned with these issues surrounding the Savage framework, or will want the components of the theorem to be more general: for preferences to range over infinitely valued acts; for the axioms to imply a countably additive rather than a finitely additive probability function; or for the "technical" axioms discussed in the next section to be weaker. However, I urge the reader as far as is possible to separate these technical issues, some of which may be amenable to further treatment by refining the theorem, from the basic point about risk-attitudes. My main goal is to defend a weakening of the axioms of EU theory that allows global sensitivity.

3.2.2 Axioms

With the preliminaries out of the way, I can now present the axioms of REU theory. Ultimately I will argue that these axioms, rather than the axioms of subjective expected utility theory, are the appropriate restrictions on rational preference. However, I will postpone discussion of the differences between REU theory and EU theory to the next section, and the debate about which captures the requirements of rationality to the second half of this book.

---

[21] McClennen (1990) offers a similar defense of the distinction between outcomes and gambles. He writes that "the concept of a terminal outcome seems rather to be a natural and inevitable component of any evaluative procedure" (249). He argues that even if there is no bedrock level of the world at which there are no further risks and uncertainties involved, the agent involved in deliberation must assume one. For further discussion see McClennen (1990), Sections 4.7 and 14.6.

The first axiom is the ordering axiom, and it dictates that the preference relation $\geq$ be a complete ordering:

(A1) **Ordering** (MS P1 and KW 396[22]): $\geq$ is complete (f $\geq$ g or g $\geq$ f), reflexive (f$\geq$f), and transitive (f$\geq$g & g$\geq$h $\Rightarrow$ f$\geq$h).

This axiom is standard and fairly straightforward. No one rejects reflexivity, and very few reject transitivity as a normative constraint.[23] In any case, I will not consider arguments against transitivity here. Completeness is more controversial, because it is not clear that all goods are comparable. I must confess that I am torn about this. On the one hand, it is true that many outcomes are intuitively incomparable because they are attractive for very different reasons that are difficult to weigh against one another. For example, it may be hard to say what one's preference is between a week relaxing at a familiar vacation spot with friends and a week exploring new lines of academic research in an exotic locale, because there are genuine goods to be had in either circumstance. On the other hand, in practice one does make a choice, and not just arbitrarily. Despite feeling torn, I will not examine the issue here further and I will assume that rational preferences are complete. There is one further upshot of assuming completeness: since the act space is the set of *all* finite-valued functions, an agent must have preferences over all possible functions from states to outcomes, even if some of the outcomes could never in principle appear in those states: one must have some non-practical preferences. This will become important in the next chapter.

The first axiom imposes a restriction on preferences between acts given other preferences between acts. The second axiom imposes a restriction on preferences between acts given preferences concerning the outcomes they are composed of. In particular, it dictates that if the outcome of an act is weakly preferred in every state, then that act must be weakly preferred full stop. If an act is weakly preferred in every state, and is strictly preferred in some (non-null) states, then it must be strictly preferred full stop:[24]

(A2) **State-Wise Dominance**: If f(s) $\geq$ g(s) for all s$\in\mathscr{S}$, then f $\geq$ g. If f(s) $\geq$ g(s) for all s$\in\mathscr{S}$ and if f(s) > g(s) for all s$\in$E$\subseteq\mathscr{S}$, where E is some non-null event on $\mathscr{A}$, then f > g.

Recall the betterness-for-reasons principle, mentioned in Section 2.4: one act can only be strictly preferred to another if it is strictly preferred in some state. That is to say, if an act is at least as good as another in every state, then it cannot be dispreferred. When we add that if such an act is also better in at least one state then it must also be strictly preferred, we get the State-Wise Dominance axiom. Plausibly,

---

[22] Note that Köbberling and Wakker (2003, p. 396) only holds that $\geq$ is complete and transitive; however, completeness implies reflexivity. I list both conditions here for clarity.

[23] For a helpful discussion of the considerations in favor of and against transitivity, see Maher (1993).

[24] This axiom in this form is not explicitly adopted by either Köbberling and Wakker (2003) or Machina and Schmeidler (1992), but it implies KW's Weak Monotonicity, and in the presence of A1, it implies MS's Event-Wise Monotonicity. See Appendix A.

this is a condition that an agent must satisfy in order to count as preferring the means to his ends.

This axiom rules out maximin, maximax, and the Hurwicz criteria, discussed in Section 2.3. Given that our goal is to derive a unique probability function from an agent's preferences, it is unsurprising that we need to rule these out: the maximini-mizer, for example, will be indifferent between any two acts with the same worst outcome, as long as that outcome is on a non-null event. So for the maximinimizer, we will only be able to tell the difference between events that are null and events that are non-null; we will not be able to make finer gradations among non-null events. Perhaps ruling out these extreme strategies places requirements on rationality that are too strong. But this axiom does have strong intuitive pull. Again I will note that there might be some disagreement, but move on.

Recall the point that we must properly separate the state, outcome, and act spaces if the axioms are to be convincing. We can see how the interpretation I just gave of this axiom depends on delineating a set of outcomes whose values are state-independent. Again, "$x \geq y$," the preference relation between outcomes, is defined within the frame-work of the theory as $\underline{x} \geq \underline{y}$. But if the values of the outcomes are not independent of the states, then $x \geq y$ cannot be naturally interpreted as "outcome x is weakly preferred to outcome y," and so "$f(s) \geq g(s)$," the preference relation that holds when the constant act that yields $f(s)$ in every state is preferred to the constant act that yields $g(s)$ in every state, cannot be naturally interpreted as "act f in state s is preferred to act g in state s." A similar point holds for delineating a set of events whose likelihoods are independent of the act: that f is preferred to g in every state will not be a convincing reason to prefer f to g unless the choice has no effect on which state occurs.

The next three axioms are what we might call "technical axioms." Their main pur-pose is not to fix how agents can respond to various features of acts, but rather to ensure that the sets of outcomes and acts are rich enough that preferences will reveal unique p, r, and (family of) u functions. The first of these guarantees that the agent's preferences make fine enough distinctions among outcomes:

(A3) **Preference Richness** ((i)MS P5 Nondegeneracy, (ii)KW 398, Solvability):

(i)   There exist outcomes x and y such that $x > y$.
(ii) For any fixed partition of events $\{E_1, \ldots, E_n\}$, and for all acts $f(E_1, \ldots, E_n)$, $g(E_1, \ldots, E_n)$ on those events, outcomes x, y, and events E_i with $x_{E_i}f > g > y_{E_i}f$, there exists an "intermediate" outcome z such that $z_{E_i}f \sim g$.

Part (i) of this axiom states that a decision-maker cannot be indifferent over all pos-sible outcomes. It is clear why this is necessary for a representation theorem: if an agent does not care which outcome results from an act, then no act will be better than any other. In particular, no act will be better than another in virtue of the fact that it has a higher probability of yielding a better outcome, so we will not have any way to determine the probability the agent assigns to any event. As for its plausibility as a restriction on rational preferences, the axiom seems to state a necessary condition for *having* ends. If an agent does not care about what happens, he cannot be meaningfully said to have ends; consequently, he cannot be meaningfully said to structure his preferences coherently in service of attaining these ends. Part (ii) of this axiom ensures that for any two outcomes, there is an outcome of intermediate value. But it does so for a particular purpose: to ensure that additional outcomes can be added to an increasing standard sequence as long as there is a sufficiently good outcome, and that additional outcomes can be added to a decreasing standard sequence as long as there is a sufficiently bad outcome.[25]

The next axiom, Small Event Continuity, ensures that the events can be partitioned finely enough: specifically, if we have an act that is preferred to another act, then the events can be partitioned finely enough that altering either of the acts to yield some different outcome in some event will not reverse the preference.[26]

(A4) **Small Event Continuity** (MS P6): For all acts $f > g$ and any outcome x, there exists a finite partition of events $\{E_1, \ldots, E_n\}$ such that for all i, $f > x_{E_i}g$ and $x_{E_i}f > g$.

This axiom also says something about the values of outcomes: namely, that there is no outcome whose presence swamps what is happening in the rest of the gamble, provided that outcome occurs on a "small enough" event.

The final technical axiom is the Comonotonic Archimedian Axiom. Recall that a standard sequence is to be interpreted as a sequence of outcomes whose value differences are equally spaced. If we can find an outcome that is at least as good as every member of the sequence, and an outcome that is at most as good as every member of the sequence, then the sequence is bounded. Now, if a standard sequence is infinite and bounded, then the values of the members will span a range unbounded by any finite value but bounded by the value attaching to some outcome. Therefore, there will be an outcome whose value is infinite (positive or negative). The Comonotonic Archimedian Axiom says that preferences cannot give rise to value that is structured in this way.

(A5) **Comonotonic Archimedean Axiom** (KW 398, 400): For each comoncone $F \subseteq A_M \subseteq \mathscr{A}$, every bounded standard sequence on F is finite.

Why is this axiom restricted to comoncones? Because, as it will turn out, a standard sequence can only be interpreted as a sequence of outcomes with equally spaced value differences if all the members of the standard sequence lie within a comoncone. Therefore, unbounded infinite standard sequences that do not lie within a comoncone do not entail that some outcome has infinite value.

These three technical axioms have the weakest claim to being rational constraints on preferences; however, no representation theorem can avoid using some technical axioms. I will not argue extensively that any agent whose preferences fail to obey these axioms should count as irrational, but I will mention some of the patterns of preference they rule out (in the presence of the other axioms). One example of such a pattern is the preferences of the person who is not willing to accept any chance of

---

[25] Köbberling and Wakker (2003: 398).   [26] Machina and Schmeidler (1992: 751).

death, however small, for some particular amount of money. Another example is the pattern of preferences needed to make Pascal's wager valid: an agent strictly prefers any act that has a chance of eternal bliss to any act that does not. Another pattern of preference they rule out is the following: an agent strictly prefers outcome x to outcome y, but there is no outcome that is strictly preferred to y and dispreferred to x. To the extent that we think these preferences are irrational we should find these axioms compelling. So if the reader wishes to object to these axioms, defending some of these preferences is a good place to start. Alternatively, we might think of the technical axioms as simply delineating the kinds of agents and situations we can represent: agents with rich enough preferences, who make fine enough distinctions between events and between outcomes, and who do not value any one outcome infinitely.

The next axiom, Comonotonic Tradeoff Consistency, is the axiom that will be largely responsible for turning the ordinal preference scale into a unique cardinal utility scale. Recall that the relationship $\sim^*(C)$ holds between xy and zw if receiving x rather than y plays the same compensatory role as receiving z rather than w in some event in some pair of acts where every act is within a comoncone. We are eventually going to want it to be the case that when this relationship holds between xy and zw, then the utility difference between x and y is the same as that between z and w. Given this, in order for "utility difference" to be a well-defined quantity, we need to place a restriction on when two pairs of outcomes play the same compensatory role. That is precisely what Comonotonic Tradeoff Consistency does.

In order to explain this restriction, allow me to start with a stronger axiom, Unrestricted Tradeoff Consistency, which REU theory does not endorse but EU theory does. Consider two pairs of outcomes such that $xy \sim^*(A_M) zw$: that is, two pairs of outcomes that play the same compensatory role in gambles not necessarily within the same comoncone. There will be some acts f and g and a non-null event E such that $x_E f \sim y_E g$ and $z_E f \sim w_E g$. Now consider some outcome $y' > y$. We would conclude that for a rational person $y_E g < y'_E g$, since $y'_E g$ is at least as good as $y_E g$ in each state of the world, and better in some non-null state of the world. Therefore, $x_E f < y'_E g$: so x rather than y' will not be an equivalent tradeoff for z rather than w in this particular act. But we might conclude further that x rather than y' ought not be an equivalent tradeoff for z rather than w in *any* act: this would be to say that z rather than w has a *fixed* compensatory role, one that lines up with x rather than y, and therefore that cannot line up with x rather than y'. This is what Unrestricted Tradeoff Consistency says:

Unrestricted Tradeoff Consistency (KW 397): For all $A_M \subseteq \mathscr{A}$, improving an outcome in any $\sim^*(\mathscr{A})$ relationship breaks that relationship. In other words, $xy \sim^*(A_M) zw$ and $y' > y$ entails $\neg(xy' \sim^*(A_M) zw)$.

Comonotonic Tradeoff Consistency restricts this principle to acts within the same comoncone. Recall that a comoncone is a set of acts that agree on a weak ordering of events from best to worst. CTC says that z rather than w has a *fixed* compensatory role, one that lines up with x rather than y, and therefore that cannot line up with x

rather than y' *as long as the acts in which the outcomes are playing a compensatory role are all in the same comoncone; that is, as long as they order the events in the same way*:

(A6) **Comonotonic Tradeoff Consistency** (KW 397, 400): Improving an outcome in any $\sim^*(C)$ relationship breaks that relationship. In other words, xy $\sim^*(C)$ zw and $y' > y$ entails $\neg(xy' \sim^*(C)$ zw).

That is, if there exists a comoncone $C_1 \subseteq A_M \subseteq \mathscr{A}$ such that xy $\sim^*(C_1)$ zw, and if $y' > y$, then there is no comoncone $C_2 \subseteq A_M \subseteq \mathscr{A}$ such that xy$' \sim^*(C_2)$ zw.

This axiom will be extremely important in the discussion that follows. Indeed, the crux of the disagreement I have with the EU theorist is that he thinks rational preferences ought to obey Unrestricted Tradeoff Consistency, and I think they need only obey Comonotonic Tradeoff Consistency plus a final axiom that guarantees stable probabilities. Thus, I will postpone the bulk of the discussion of Comonotonic Tradeoff Consistency to the next section.

The final axiom ensures that the agent assigns a stable probability to each event: that the likelihood he attaches to an event does not depend on the choices under consideration. Let us assume that an agent strictly prefers x' to x and weakly prefers $x'_{E1}x_{E2}g$ to $x_{E1}x'_{E2}g$. Since a rational agent would rather have a higher chance of getting the better outcome x', all else equal, this implies that he believes E_1 to be at least as likely as E_2 when he is considering these two acts. If his beliefs are stable, then he must also believe E_1 to be at least as likely at E_2 when he is considering other acts. So, for example, if he is choosing between $y'_{E1}y_{E2}g$ and $y_{E1}y'_{E2}g$, he must think that the former gives at least as high a chance of y' as the latter. And if he strictly prefers y' to y, he must therefore weakly prefer $y'_{E1}y_{E2}g$ to $y_{E1}y'_{E2}g$. This is the thought behind the final axiom:

(A7) **Strong Comparative Probability** (MS P4*): For all pairs of disjoint events E_1 and E_2, all outcomes $x' > x$ and $y' > y$, and all acts g,h$\in \mathscr{A}$, $x'_{E1}x_{E2}g \geq x_{E1}x'_{E2}g \Rightarrow$ $y'_{E1}y_{E2}h \geq y_{E1}y'_{E2}h$

Conforming to this axiom amounts to (i) having an opinion about the relative probability of every pair of events (E_1 is more probable than, less probable than, or equiprobable to E_2) and (ii) preferring a higher probability of a better outcome. Clearly (ii) is a rational constraint, but what about (i)? Is it really a requirement of rationality that for any two events we have an opinion about which is more likely? Actually, all the axiom requires is that if we treat an event as more likely in one act comparison, we are committed to doing so in a different comparison: it does not matter how we adjudicate between events, as long as we do so consistently. But even so, it is not clear that rational people should do this: for example, the Ellsberg paradox presents a situation in which it seems reasonable to many people that they should behave in a way that violates the axiom.[27] This discussion is beyond the scope of this work. At the very least, however, it is clear that there is an important notion of rationality that requires obedience to this axiom:

---

[27] See the discussion in Ellsberg (2001).

indeed, it is this notion of rationality that those working with sharp degrees of belief—that is, probabilists—assume.

3.2.3 Theorem

We can now state the theorem:

Theorem (Representation): If the relation $\geq$ satisfies (A1) through (A7), then there exist:

(i)   a unique finitely additive, non-atomic probability function p: $\mathscr{E} \rightarrow [0, 1]$
(ii) a unique risk function r: $[0, 1] \rightarrow [0, 1]$
(iii) a utility function unique up to positive affine transformation

such that for any $f \in \mathscr{A}$, each of which we can write as $\{F_1, O_1; \ldots; F_n, O_n\}$ where for all i, $f(s) = O_i$ for all $s \in F_i \subseteq \mathscr{S}$, and $O_1 \leq O_2 \leq \ldots \leq O_n$,

$$\text{REU}(f) = u(O_1) + r\left(\sum_{i=2}^{n} p(F_i)\right)(u(O_2) - u(O_1)) + r\left(\sum_{i=3}^{n} p(F_i)\right)(u(O_3) - u(O_2))$$
$$+ \ldots + r(p(F_n))(u(O_n) - u(O_{n-1}))$$

represents the preference relation $\geq$ on $\mathscr{A}$.

That is, there exists a unique probability function p, a unique risk function r, and a utility function u unique up to positive affine transformation such that for all outcomes $x_1, \ldots, x_n, y_1, \ldots, y_m \in \mathscr{X}$ and events $E_1, \ldots, E_n, G_1, \ldots, G_m \in \mathscr{E}$,

$$\{E_1, x_1; \ldots; E_n, x_n\} \geq \{G_1, y_1; \ldots; G_m, y_m\} \text{ iff}$$
$$u(O_1) + r\left(\sum_{i=2}^{n} p(F_i)\right)(u(O_2) - u(O_1)) + r\left(\sum_{i=3}^{n} p(F_i)\right)(u(O_3) - u(O_2)) + \ldots$$
$$+ r(p(F_n))(u(O_n) - u(O_{n-1}))$$
$$\geq$$
$$u(Q_1) + r\left(\sum_{i=2}^{m} p(H_i)\right)(u(Q_2) - u(Q_1)) + r\left(\sum_{i=3}^{m} p(H_i)\right)(u(Q_3) - u(Q_2)) + \ldots$$
$$+ r(p(H_m))(u(Q_m) - u(Q_{m-1}))$$

for some rank-ordering permutations Δ and Ψ such that $x_{\Delta(1)} \leq \ldots \leq x_{\Delta(n)}$, $O_i = x_{\Delta(i)}$, and $F_i = E_{\Delta(i)}$, and $y_{\Psi(1)} \leq \ldots \leq y_{\Psi(n)}$, $Q_i = y_{\Psi(i)}$, and $H_i = G_{\Psi(i)}$.

If there are three such functions so that REU(f) represents the preference relation, we say that REU holds. Furthermore, in the presence of (A3), if REU holds with a continuous r-function, then the remaining axioms are satisfied. Therefore, if we assume Preference Richness (A3), we have:

(A1), (A2), (A4), (A5), (A6), (A7) are sufficient conditions for REU.
(A1), (A2), (A4), (A5), (A6), (A7) are necessary conditions for REU with continuous r-function.

The proof of this theorem, with references to details found in Köbberling and Wakker (2003) and Machina and Schmeidler (1992), can be found in Appendix A.

3.3 Comonotonicity and Global Properties

In the remainder of this chapter we will see how the difference between the axioms of REU theory and the stronger axioms of EU theory amounts to the difference between allowing agents to care about structural features of acts and prohibiting them from doing so. To understand, it will be helpful to see the axioms of REU theory side by side with those of the analogous representation theorem for EU theory,[28] as follows.

EXPECTED UTILITY THEORY

A1. Ordering: $\geq$ is complete, reflexive, and transitive.

A2. State-Wise Dominance: If $f(s) \geq g(s)$ for all $s \in \mathcal{S}$, then $f \geq g$. If $f(s) \geq g(s)$ for all $s \in \mathcal{S}$ and $f(s) > g(s)$ for all $s \in E \subseteq \mathcal{S}$, where E is some non-null event on $\mathcal{A}$, then $f > g$.

A3. Preference Richness: (i) There exist outcomes x and y such that $x > y$. (ii) For any fixed partition of events $\{E_1, \ldots, E_n\}$, and for all acts $f(E_1, \ldots, E_n), g(E_1, \ldots, E_n)$ on those events, outcomes x, y, and events E_i with $x_{E_i}f > g > y_{E_i}f$, there exists an "intermediate" outcome z such that $z_{E_i}f \sim g$.

A4. Small Event Continuity: For all acts $f > g$ and any outcome x, there exists a finite partition of events $\{E_1, \ldots, E_n\}$ such that for all i, $f > x_{E_i}g$ and $x_{E_i}f > g$.

B5. Archimedean Axiom (KW 398): Every bounded standard sequence on $\mathcal{A}$ is finite.

B6. Unrestricted Tradeoff Consistency (KW 397): For all $A_M \subseteq \mathcal{A}$, improving an outcome in any $\sim^*(A_M)$ relationship breaks that relationship. In other words, $xy \sim^*(A_M)$ zw and $y' > y$ entails $\neg(xy' \sim^*(A_M)$ zw).

RISK-WEIGHTED EXPECTED UTILITY

A1. Ordering: $\geq$ is complete, reflexive, and transitive.

A2. State-Wise Dominance: If $f(s) \geq g(s)$ for all $s \in \mathcal{S}$, then $f \geq g$. If $f(s) \geq g(s)$ for all $s \in \mathcal{S}$ and $f(s) > g(s)$ for all $s \in E \subseteq \mathcal{S}$, where E is some non-null event on $\mathcal{A}$, then $f > g$.

A3. Preference Richness: (i) There exist outcomes x and y such that $x > y$. (ii) For any fixed partition of events $\{E_1, \ldots, E_n\}$, and for all acts $f(E_1, \ldots, E_n), g(E_1, \ldots, E_n)$ on those events, outcomes x, y, and events E_i with $x_{E_i}f > g > y_{E_i}f$, there exists an "intermediate" outcome z such that $z_{E_i}f \sim g$.

A4. Small Event Continuity: For all acts $f > g$ and any outcome x, there exists a finite partition of events $\{E_1, \ldots, E_n\}$ such that for all i, $f > x_{E_i}g$ and $x_{E_i}f > g$.

A5. Comonotonic Archimedean Axiom: For each comoncone $F \subseteq A_M \subseteq \mathcal{A}$, every bounded standard sequence on F is finite.

A6. Comonotonic Tradeoff Consistency: Improving an outcome in any $\sim^*(C)$ relationship breaks that relationship. In other words, $xy \sim^*(C)$ zw and $y' > y$ entails $\neg(xy' \sim^*(C)$ zw).

A7. Strong Comparative Probability: For all pairs of disjoint events E_1 and E_2, all outcomes $x' > x$ and $y' > y$, and all acts $g, h \in \mathcal{A}$, $x'_{E_1}x_{E_2}g \geq x_{E_1}x'_{E_2}g \Rightarrow y'_{E_1}y_{E_2}h \geq y_{E_1}y'_{E_2}h$.

---

[28] Mostly following Köbberling and Wakker (2003). I alter their axioms slightly, to make the comparison clear. See Appendix B.

Any agent whose preferences obey the axioms in the left-hand column maximizes expected utility relative to a unique probability function and a utility function unique up to positive affine transformation. Furthermore, in the presence of (A3), any agent who maximizes expected utility will satisfy the remaining axioms.[29]

Thus, we can see that the disagreement I have with the EU theorist is about whether agents are required to conform their preferences to (B5) and (B6) or only to the weaker (A5), (A6), and (A7). And since (A5) and (B5) serve primarily to ensure that utility values range over real numbers,[30] the substantial disagreement between us is whether rationality requires Unrestricted Tradeoff Consistency or only the combination of Comonotonic Tradeoff Consistency and Strong Comparative Probability.

To understand the difference between Unrestricted Tradeoff Consistency and Comonotonic Tradeoff Consistency, it is helpful to understand the general structure of representation theorems. The axioms must restrict the ordinal preference relation in such a way that we can derive a stable family of cardinal utility functions. Recall that utility difference ratios are the only "real fact" about utility functions, since utility functions are equivalent up to positive affine transformation. Thus, the axioms must guarantee that utility difference ratios are fixed across different choices. To locate axioms that will do this, we can isolate when choices should reveal something about utility difference ratios between outcomes apart from the gambles in which these outcomes are embedded, and we can guarantee that whatever is revealed is stable across all choices. Similarly, as we will see in the next section, to figure out axioms that will restrict ordinal preferences in such a way that we can derive a stable probability function, we can isolate when choices should reveal something about which of two states an agent treats as more likely, and again we can guarantee that whatever is revealed is stable across all choices.

In axiomatizations of EU theory, there are at least two different ways to ensure that agents view value differences between outcomes in a stable way, and in a way that allows us to represent an agent as an EU maximizer. The first involves using an axiom like Unrestricted Tradeoff Consistency.[31] The second involves using an axiom like the one introduced by Savage (1954/1972), which has come to be known as the Sure-Thing Principle. REU maximizers only obey restricted versions of these axioms. The goal in this section is to explain how accepting restricted versions of these axioms allows agents to care about global properties in the way outlined in the first two chapters. In each case, the REU axiom will be restricted to acts that are comonotonic. Let me remind the reader what this means. Acts f and g are comonotonic if there are no events E_1 and E_2 such that $f(E_1) > f(E_2)$ and $g(E_1) < g(E_2)$: if E_1 leads to a better outcome than E_2 on f, then E_1 leads to at least as good an outcome as E_2 on g. Again, a comoncone is a set

---

[29]   See Appendix B, which relies on Theorem 5 in Köbberling and Wakker (2003).

[30]   (A5) is weaker than (B5) because the remaining EU axioms imply that standard sequences have equally spaced utility values, and the remaining REU axioms only imply that standard sequences *on each comoncone* have equally spaced utility values.

[31]   Ramsey (1926) also took this kind of approach.

of acts that are all comonotonic: all the acts in a comoncone weakly order the events in the same way. For each comoncone, then, we can order the events so that for each act in the comoncone, the agent weakly prefers events that are "higher" in the ordering. We can thus think of a comoncone as corresponding to a weak preference ordering over events. For example, the acts <{HEADS, $50; TAILS, $0}, {HEADS, $100; TAILS, $99}, {HEADS, $70; TAILS, $70}> are contained in the comoncone in which HEADS is weakly preferred to TAILS, and the acts <{HEADS, $0; TAILS, $50}, {HEADS, $70; TAILS, $70}> are contained in the comoncone in which TAILS is weakly preferred to HEADS.

We now turn to the first way to ensure that value differences between outcomes are stable: tradeoff consistency.

3.3.1 Tradeoff consistency

Recall the idea of tradeoff equality. The relation $\sim^*(F)$ holds of (xy, zw) when there are two acts f and g contained in F (recall: a set of acts on some finite event-partition) and an event E such that the agent is indifferent between the act that agrees with f on $\neg E$ but yields x on E and the act that agrees with g on $\neg E$ but yields y on E; and the agent is indifferent between the act that agrees with f on $\neg E$ but yields z on E and the act that agrees with g on $\neg E$ but yields w on E. That is, $x_E f \sim y_E g$ and $z_E f \sim w_E g$. Each of these four acts must be contained in F, and E must be non-null. See Table 3.1.

Again, the idea behind tradeoff equality is that receiving x rather than y in E plays the same role as receiving z rather than w in E: they both exactly compensate for getting f rather than g in the remaining states.

What we are ultimately interested in is the utility contribution each outcome makes to each act it is part of: this will help us determine the utility values of outcomes. More precisely, since utility *difference ratios* are what matter, we are interested in the utility contribution that x rather than y makes to each act, relative to some other pair. And tradeoff equality gives us a way to begin to determine this: if getting x rather than y in event E and getting z rather than w in event E both exactly compensate for getting f rather than g in event Ě, then they make the same utility difference contribution in event E in those gamble pairs. In order to get from the utility difference contribution two pairs make in a particular event in a particular gamble to their utility difference ratio full stop, we need to fix when two pairs making the same difference in utility contribution means that they have the same difference in utility. And to do this, we will identify the conditions under which if two pairs have the same difference in utility

Table 3.1. Tradeoff equality.

	Event E	Event Ě			Event E	Event Ě
Act A	x	f		Act C	z	f
Act B	y	g		Act D	w	g

$xy \sim^*(F)$ zw holds, provided E is non-null, if Act A $\sim$ Act B and Act C $\sim$ Act D.

(full stop), they must make the same difference in utility contribution, and constrain the rational agent to treat each pair consistently in these situations—to consistently make tradeoffs.

Tradeoff consistency axioms provide such a constraint. Recall these axioms, identified by Köbberling and Wakker, from above:

> **Unrestricted Tradeoff Consistency (UTC):** For all $A_M \subseteq \mathscr{A}$, improving an outcome in any $\sim^*(A_M)$ relationship breaks that relationship. In other words, $xy \sim^*(A_M) zw$ and $y' > y$ entails $\neg(xy' \sim^*(A_M) zw)$.
>
> **Comonotonic Tradeoff Consistency (CTC):** Improving an outcome in any $\sim^*(C)$ relationship breaks that relationship. In other words, $xy \sim^*(C) zw$ and $y' > y$ entails $\neg(xy' \sim^*(C) zw)$.

The difference between $\sim^*(A_M)$ and $\sim^*(C)$ is that the former places no restrictions on the "modified" acts within a particular event-partition (e.g. $x_E f$) aside from that they satisfy the indifference relation; but the latter holds only when there exist modified acts in the event-partition that satisfy the indifference relation *and* are contained within a single comoncone. So the difference between the two axioms is that UTC says that if two tradeoffs are equal, they must be equal irrespective of the acts they are embedded in and the events they are substituted in for; but CTC says that they need only remain equal if they are substituted in for events in such a way that the resulting acts are comonotonic with each other. Note that CTC is stronger than the idea that UTC must hold on every comoncone: it is stronger because if $xy \sim^*(C_1) zw$ holds for some comoncone $C_1 \subseteq A_M$, then CTC entails that for any comoncone $C_2 \subseteq A_M$, $xy' \sim^*(C_2) zw$ cannot hold. CTC follows from UTC, but not *vice versa*. Furthermore, each serves to fix utility difference ratios in the presence of the other axioms: for REU maximizers (as for CEU maximizers), $xy \sim^*(C) zw$ holds just in case $u(x) - u(y) = u(z) - u(w)$, and for EU maximizers, $xy \sim^*(A_M) zw$ holds just in case $u(x) - u(y) = u(z) - u(w)$.[32] So in each theory, the relevant type of tradeoff equality holds when utility differences are equivalent.[33]

According to UTC, whether x-rather-than-y-in-some-event plays the same compensatory role as z-rather-than-w-in-that-event does not depend on the structure of the gambles involved. But according to CTC, it can so depend: it can depend on whether each outcome is in the same structural position in the gamble. Why would not staying within a comoncone make a difference to the utility contribution that y-in-some-event rather than x-in-that-event makes? To make things concrete, let us examine a set of preferences that satisfies Comonotonic Tradeoff Consistency, but not Unrestricted Tradeoff Consistency. Assume the agent is indifferent between these two gambles:

$\{\$10, \textsc{Heads}; \$150, \textsc{Tails}\}$
$\{\$0, \textsc{Heads}; \$170, \textsc{Tails}\}$

---

[32] See Appendix C.
[33] As discussed in fn. 16, this is similar to Ramsey's (1926) approach, in which the relation "$xy = zw$" is central, and whenever $xy = zw$ holds, $u(x) - u(y) = u(z) - u(w)$.

Then $10 rather than $0 in HEADS is an appropriate tradeoff for $150 rather than $170 in TAILS. The advantage in the HEADS state ($10 rather than $0) exactly compensates for the disadvantage in the TAILS state ($150 rather than $170). Now let us assume that the agent is also indifferent between these two gambles:

{$110, HEADS; $150, TAILS}
{$100, HEADS; $170, TAILS}

Then $110 rather than $100 in HEADS is also an appropriate tradeoff for $150 rather than $170 in TAILS. UTC says, therefore, that whenever $10 rather than $0 in some event is an appropriate tradeoff for whatever happens if that event does not occur, then $110 rather than $100 must also be an appropriate tradeoff in that event for what happens if the event does not occur.[34]

So, let us assume the agent has the above preferences, and let us also assume the agent is indifferent between these gambles:

{$10, HEADS; $50, TAILS}
{$0, HEADS; $70, TAILS}

Again, $10 rather than $0 in HEADS is an appropriate tradeoff for $50 rather than $70 in TAILS. Therefore, UTC implies that the agent must also be indifferent between the following two gambles:

{$110, HEADS; $50, TAILS}
{$100, HEADS, $70, TAILS}

CTC does not have this implication, because this final pair of gambles and the previous pair are not in the same comoncone.

Violating UTC, according to the EU theorist, is supposed to amount to not evaluating outcomes consistently: to allowing the value difference between a pair of outcomes to vary depending on the circumstances. But what UTC neglects is that an agent might evaluate outcomes consistently, but allow that an outcome makes a different contribution to the value of a gamble when it occurs in a different structural part of that gamble. An agent might care about where in the structure of the gamble a tradeoff occurs. For example, we can give a rationale for an agent's having the following four preferences, which I have just said UTC rules out:[35]

{$10, HEADS; $150, TAILS} ~ {$0, HEADS; $170, TAILS}
{$110, HEADS; $150, TAILS} ~ {$100, HEADS; $170, TAILS}

---

[34] Strictly speaking, UTC says that <some amount of money that is preferred to $110> rather than $100 cannot be an appropriate tradeoff in that event for what happens if the event does not occur, but the difference does not matter here.

[35] Strictly speaking, what is ruled out is the first three indifferences in combination with {HEADS, $x; TAILS, $50} ~ {HEADS, $100; TAILS, $70}, where $x > $110. But since the rationale is the same, and in the presence of the other axioms these preferences imply the above preferences, I use the above preferences for ease of exposition.

{$10, HEADS; $50, TAILS} ~ {$0, HEADS; $70, TAILS}
{$110, HEADS; $50, TAILS} < {$100, HEADS, $70, TAILS}

Here is the rationale. For small amounts of money, making the HEADS state better by $10 might exactly compensate for making the TAILS state worse by $20 *when the HEADS state is the worst state*. When the TAILS state is the worst state, making the HEADS state better by $10 might not compensate for making the TAILS state worse by $20. As an analogy: we might think that giving $10 to one person and taking $20 from another preserves the overall value of a social distribution only if we are giving the $10 to the worst off person, since we might think it okay to take more from the top in order to give something to the bottom, but not *vice versa*.

If which tradeoffs an agent is willing to accept is sensitive to where in the structure of the act these tradeoffs occur (in the worst event or the best event, for example), then facts about which tradeoffs an agent considers appropriate will only reveal utility differences when we are dealing with acts that order the events in the same way. This is exactly what the Comonotonic Tradeoff Consistency Axiom says. Two tradeoffs might be equal either because of local considerations about the difference between outcomes or because of global considerations about where the tradeoffs occur. Therefore, Comonotonic Tradeoff Consistency limits the situations in which we can infer utility differences from which tradeoffs an agent is willing to accept to those situations in which the only differences between acts are local differences.[36]

Why might it make a difference which structural part of the gamble a tradeoff occurs in? For example, why does $10 rather than $0 in HEADS play the same compensatory role as $110 rather than $100 in HEADS when HEADS is the worst state in both cases, but $10 rather than $0 in HEADS when HEADS is the worst state does not play the same compensatory role as $110 rather than $100 in HEADS when HEADS is the best state? There are two possibilities. The first is that the agent considers HEADS more likely when it has a worse outcome associated with it, and less likely when it has a better outcome associated with it. She cares more about what happens in the worst possible state because the worst possible state is more likely. In this case, the agent would not have a fixed view of the likelihood of events but would instead be pessimistic: she would consider an event more likely simply because its obtaining would be bad for her. But the fact that the agent is represented as having a stable probability distribution over events rules this interpretation out. At least, it rules it out once we are convinced that p really does represent beliefs: this will be argued for in the next section.[37]

The second possibility is that what happens in E matters more to the agent when E is lower in the structural ordering not because she considers E itself more likely, but

---

[36] For those who think that even REU theory is too restrictive in how decision-makers can take global properties into account, this is the place to consider modifying the theory: limit even further the situations in which tradeoffs reveal utility differences.

[37] One additional possibility that I will not consider is that the agent has stable beliefs but they are not probabilities. This is also ruled out by the existence of a stable probability distribution that represents beliefs.

because this feature of the overall gamble plays a larger role in the agent's considerations. If an agent is more concerned with guaranteeing herself a higher minimum, for example, then tradeoffs that raise or lower the minimum are going to matter more than tradeoffs that raise or lower the maximum. I stressed that one thing an agent must determine in instrumental reasoning is the extent to which she is willing to trade off a guarantee of realizing some minimum value against the possibility of getting something of much higher value: the extent to which she is willing to trade raising the minimum against raising the maximum. So we can now see that restricting Tradeoff Consistency to gambles with the same structural properties—gambles that order the events in the same way—captures the idea that agents who are globally sensitive structure their goals differently than EU maximizers. Unrestricted Tradeoff Consistency says that substituting one outcome for another must make the same value difference to a gamble regardless of how these outcomes feature into the structural properties of the gamble. But Comonotonic Tradeoff Consistency says that the difference a substitution makes depends not just on the difference in value between the outcomes in the particular state, but on where in the structure of the gamble this substitution occurs. If the agent cares about these structural properties then she will only obey the comonotonic version of the axiom.

What does Comonotonic Tradeoff Consistency rule out, then? Recall our example from above. Comonotonic Tradeoff Consistency allowed that $110 rather than $100 in HEADS when HEADS is the best event plays a different compensatory role than $110 rather than $100 in HEADS when HEADS is the worst event. But in all of the gambles in which HEADS is the worst event, $110 rather than $100 in HEADS must make the same difference as $10 rather than $0 in HEADS; and similarly for all of the gambles in which HEADS is the best event; and similarly for gambles in which these outcomes occur on TAILS and TAILS is the worst event; and so forth. *More generally, the relative value of tradeoffs must be stable when the tradeoffs occur in the same structural part of the gamble: that is, when there are no global considerations at issue.* This means that while an agent may decide whether raising the minimum is more important than raising the maximum and how much more important, or in general which structural portions of a gamble are most important and how important they are, she must have a stable view about this for all acts.

So the proponent of UTC and the proponent of the weaker CTC have different views about what it is to consistently value outcomes. According to the proponent of UTC, an agent consistently values outcomes if the relative value each outcome contributes to an act is the same for all acts. According to the proponent of CTC, an agent consistently values outcomes if the relative value each outcome contributes to an act is the same for all acts in which the outcome occupies the same structural position. If preferences obey UTC, then the contribution of each outcome to the value of an act is *separable*: it does not depend on which other outcomes the act contains. If preferences obey CTC, then the contribution of each outcome to the value of an act is *semi-separable*: it does not depend on which other outcomes the act contains, unless which other outcomes an act contains affects the relative ranking it occupies in a gamble.

3.3.2 The Sure-Thing Principle

For historical reasons, the debate about whether it is rationally permissible to care about global properties has not focused around axioms like Tradeoff Consistency, but rather around a better known axiom from Savage's representation theorem for EU theory, which is also meant to ensure that value differences between outcomes are stable across different choices. This axiom is known as the Sure-Thing Principle:[38]

Savage's Sure-Thing Principle: For all $f,g,h,j \in \mathscr{A}$ and $E \in \mathscr{E}$, $f_E h \geq g_E h \Leftrightarrow f_E j \geq g_E j$

Here is a slightly different version of this principle, which concerns gambles that agree on one particular outcome rather than on all outcomes of a sub-act:[39]

Sure-Thing Principle (STP): For all $f,g \in \mathscr{A}$, $x,y \in \mathscr{X}$, and $E \in \mathscr{E}$, $f_E x \geq g_E x \Leftrightarrow f_E y \geq g_E y$

It is this second formulation that I will refer to as the Sure-Thing Principle. Both versions capture the idea that if an agent would weakly prefer to replace the part of an act that occurs on E with f rather than with g, then for *any* act, an agent must weakly prefer to replace the part of that act that occurs on E with f rather than with g. Since $f_E x$ and $g_E x$ agree on what results in $\bar{E}$, the only relevant consideration in deciding between them is what results in E. So if $f_E x$ is weakly preferred to $g_E x$, then it must be either because E is null on the relevant A_M or because f-in-E is weakly preferred to g-in-E. If E is null, then $f_E y \sim g_E y$ for all y. If f-in-E is weakly preferred to g-in-E, then $f_E y$ must be weakly preferred to $g_E y$, since, again, the only relevant consideration in deciding between these acts is what happens in E. STP also has the upshot that $f_E x > g_E x \Leftrightarrow f_E y > g_E y$: the only relevant consideration in deciding between $f_E x$ and $g_E x$ is what results in E, and so it must be that f-in-E is strictly preferred to g-in-E; therefore $f_E y$ must be strictly preferred to $g_E y$. Note that the same things can be said of what I have called Savage's Sure-thing Principle, using "h" and "j" in place of "x" and "y."

Again, this principle has a comonotonic version:[40]

Comonotonic Sure-thing Principle (CSTP): For all $f,g \in \mathscr{A}$, $x,y \in \mathscr{X}$, and $E \in \mathscr{E}$, $f_E x \geq g_E x \Leftrightarrow f_E y \geq g_E y$ if all four acts are comonotonic.

---

[38] Savage himself used the term "sure-thing principle" as a general principle that comprised several of his axioms. Nowadays, however, the term is used to refer only to his P2 (Savage 1954/1972: 23), which is what I have called "Savage's Sure-Thing Principle."

[39] Chew and Wakker (1996, p. 8) claim that this is equivalent to Savage's Sure-Thing Principle. Since there is some dispute over what exactly "Savage's Sure-Thing principle" refers to, I do not want to claim that what I have called Savage's Sure-Thing Principle is equivalent to the principle I have called STP, but the latter at least follows from the former, so agents who violate this principle, which I will continue to call STP, will also violate the (possibly stronger) principle listed.

[40] Chew and Wakker (1996).

Table 3.2. Sure-thing principle.

Event	E	Ē	Event	E	Ē
Deal A	f	x	Deal C	f	y
Deal B	g	x	Deal D	g	y

Deal A ≥ Deal B iff Deal C ≥ Deal D

CSPT states that the Sure-thing Principle need only hold when the gambles whose relationships it restricts order the events in the same way.[41]

We might represent these principles schematically (Table 3.2), keeping in mind that f and g represent subgambles rather than final outcomes. STP says that if I weakly prefer deal A to deal B, I must weakly prefer deal C to deal D, and *vice versa*. CSTP says that this is true as long as deals A, B, C, and D are comonotonic.

REU maximizers do not necessarily obey STP. For example, as I will discuss shortly, the Allais preferences directly violate STP, but can be captured by REU theory. But REU maximizers do obey CSTP.[42]

So another way to state the difference between the standard view and my view is that the EU theorist claims that the preferences of rational agents conform to STP, whereas I claim they need only conform to STP when all four acts order the events in the same way. And the disagreement again comes down to a claim about what it means to value outcomes consistently. The defender of STP thinks that consistently valuing outcomes requires that including one sub-act rather than another on a particular event contributes the same value (or, really, the same valence of value: positive, negative, or neutral) to an act regardless of what happens on the rest of the act. Again, this will imply that the value an outcome contributes to the value of an act cannot depend on which other outcomes might result from the act: it will imply that the value that an outcome contributes is *separable* from what happens in the rest of the act. But I claim that this need only be true when the sub-act in question plays the same structural role in the larger act, so again, the contribution of an outcome will be only *semi-separable* from what happens in the rest of the act.

Again, the difference between STP and its comonotonic counterpart corresponds to caring about structural properties in the ways suggested in earlier chapters. (I should note that I think the correspondence is clearer in the case of UTC and CTC; but most

[41] Chew and Wakker (1996) use this principle to prove a representation theorem for a rank-dependent theory with a more general weighting function than that of CEU, one in which the utility of an outcome depends on the state in which the agent receives that outcome. However, we should be able to add conditions to Chew's and Wakker's axioms to create another representation for CEU since CEU is a special case of the theory Chew and Wakker discuss. (Recall that Köbberling and Wakker's (2003) axioms for CEU form one part of the REU representation theorem.)

[42] We can see this by noting that REU is a special case of the rank-dependent theory that Chew and Wakker discuss, since REU is a special case of CEU and CEU is a special case of the theory Chew and Wakker discuss. See also Lemma 1 (Chew and Wakker 1996, p. 8).

Table 3.3. Allais' decision problem.

Ticket	1	2–11	12–100	Ticket	1	2–11	12–100
L_1	$0	$5M	$0	L_3	$0	$5M	$1M
L_2	$1M	$1M	$0	L_4	$1M	$1M	$1M

of the philosophical discussion about whether conforming to the axioms of EU theory is rationally required has focused on the Sure-Thing Principle, so STP will be more of a focus in the arguments about rationality than UTC). The preference pattern that STP rules out but that CSTP allows is one in which an agent weakly prefers $f_E x$ to $g_E x$ but also strictly prefers $g_E y$ to $f_E y$, and in which these four acts are not comonotonic. For example, the standard Allais preferences are like this, if (as Savage suggested) the prizes are determined by drawing one of 100 equiprobable tickets as follows:

L_1: $0 if ticket 1 is drawn, $5M if ticket 2–11 is drawn, $0 if ticket 12–100 is drawn.
L_2: $1M if ticket 1–11 is drawn, $0 if ticket 12–100 is drawn.
L_3: $0 if ticket 1 is drawn, $5M if ticket 2–11 is drawn, $1M if ticket 12–100 is drawn.
L_4: $1M if ticket 1–100 is drawn.

This is represented schematically in Table 3.3.

Recall that most people prefer L_1 to L_2 and prefer L_4 to L_3. If we let E be the event in which ticket 1–11 is drawn, f_E be the sub-act that yields $0 if ticket 1 is drawn and $5M if ticket 2–11 is drawn, and g_E be the sub-act that yields $1M if ticket 1–11 is drawn, then it is easy to see that this pattern of preferences violates STP. However, it does not violate CSTP, because L_1, L_2, L_3, and L_4 are not comonotonic.[43]

Recall the earlier explanation for the Allais preferences: L_1 and L_2 have the same minimum value, but L_1 yields much higher winnings at only slightly lower odds, so L_1 is preferred; and while L_3 also yields much higher winnings at only slightly lower odds than L_4, L_4 has a much higher minimum than L_3, and so L_4 is preferred. There are two "local" considerations in each choice: that the first member of each pair offers $5M rather than $1M if ticket 2–11 is drawn, and that the first member of each pair offers $0 rather than $1M if ticket 1 is drawn. The first consideration outweighs the second in the choice between L_1 and L_2, but not in the choice between L_3 and L_4. And this is because the weight that each consideration gets depends on where in the structure of the act the relevant outcomes appear. Again, considerations about outcomes that are "higher up" in the order of outcomes get less weight for the person who is more concerned with securing a higher minimum than with securing some possibility of a much better outcome; and these considerations get more weight for the person who trades off these concerns in the opposite manner. And the local considerations

---

[43] And, indeed, we could not set up the outcomes over events differently to make gambles with the Allais probabilities simultaneously comonotonic and fit the STP schema.

will be about different parts of the structure when and only when the acts are not comonotonic.

3.4 Separating Beliefs from Risk-Attitudes

This section is concerned with how to understand the three functions u, p, and r that result from the theorem. In particular, I will show that we ought to interpret p as a reflection of the agent's beliefs and r as a reflection of how she structures the potential realization of her aims. In the previous section we were able to isolate the preference structures that determine u, apart from p and r. In particular, for decision-makers who obey the REU axioms, utility difference ratios are determined by which tradeoffs play the same compensatory role in comonotonic acts. So if two decision-makers have the same ordinal preferences over outcomes but disagree about u, they disagree about which outcome "swaps" play the same compensatory role, when we remove considerations of likelihood (because the swaps occur on the same event) and considerations of where in the structural ordering of an act the outcomes fall. Now we can isolate the preference structures that determine p and r. But first let me say why it is particularly important to understand precisely how each of these functions reflects preferences.

As I noted, the REU representation theorem combines two results. The first result, due to Köbberling and Wakker (2003), shows that if a decision-maker's preferences satisfy a subset of the axioms, then there will be a unique (not-necessarily-additive) weighting function of events, W, and a unique (up to positive affine transformation)[44] utility function of outcomes, u, such that preferences can be represented by:[45]

CEU: $f \mapsto \sum_{j=1}^{n} \pi_{\Phi(j)} u(f(E_{\Phi(j)}))$, where $\pi_{\Phi(j)} = W(E_{\Phi(1)} \cup \ldots \cup E_{\Phi(j)}) - W(E_{\Phi(1)} \cup \ldots \cup E_{\Phi(j-1)})$ for all j and for some rank-ordering permutation Φ on $\{1, \ldots, n\}$ that orders the events of f from best to worst.

The second result, due to Machina and Schmeidler (1992), shows that if a decision-maker's preferences satisfy a different subset of the axioms, then there will be a unique probability function of events, p, and a value function V of probability distributions over outcomes that respects both strict and weak stochastic dominance.[46]

The REU theorem combines these two results to yield a utility, probability, and risk function such that preferences can be represented as maximizing risk-weighted expected utility. It combines them by showing that provided the decision-maker satisfies both sets of axioms, KW's weighting function W can be equated to a transformation of MS's probability function p, and KW's utility function u will be compatible with

---

[44] For readability, in the rest of this section I will describe the utility function that results from the representation theorems as "unique," and this should be read as meaning "unique up to positive affine transformation."

[45] Köbberling and Wakker (2003, pp. 399–400, Theorem 8). See Part one of Appendix A.

[46] Machina and Schmeidler (1992, p. 766, Theorem 2). See Part two of Appendix A.

MS's value function V. In particular, I define $r(c) = W(A)$ for any A such that $p(A) = c$, and show that r is well-defined.

Given this construction, there is an issue about how we should understand u, p, and r. We have derived two "weighting" functions of events, p and W, the latter which is equivalent to r applied to a specific p-value. Thus, each event has two numbers associated with it, its p-value and its W-(or r-) value. I have called the former function a probability function, and the latter a weighting (or risk) function, but I have not yet shown that p corresponds to the agent's beliefs and W (or r) corresponds to his risk attitudes. I have not ruled out, for example, that W corresponds to his degrees of belief which turn out to be non-additive, as CEU is often understood. I also have not ruled out that π (defined from W, and so related to r) reflects his beliefs, and that he is pessimistic: his beliefs depend on which states of the world are good for him. Each of these possibilities would be a way of holding that r is the function in REU theory that reflects beliefs.

The way to show that it is p that represents beliefs is to examine the differences between the ways in which p and r depend on an agent's preferences. Let us start with p. Notice that a particular preference structure plays a role in Axiom (A7): preferences about pairs of the form $(x_{E_1}x'_{E_2}g, x'_{E_1}x_{E_2}g)$: pairs that differ only in which of two outcomes E_1 results in, where E_2 results in the other. Call these MS pairs, after Machina and Schmeidler. Notice further that because REU preferences respect stochastic dominance, $p(E_1) \geq p(E_2)$ iff $(x > x' \Leftrightarrow x_{E_1}x'_{E_2}g \geq x'_{E_1}x_{E_2}g)$. Therefore, p takes at least as high a value for one event than another just in case the agent would always weakly prefer to put a better outcome on the first event than the second, holding fixed what happens in the rest of the gamble. So if two decision-makers agree about p, they agree about which event they want the preferred outcome on; and if they disagree about p, they disagree about which event they want the preferred outcome on. Take two agents who obey the REU axioms and have the same ordinal preferences over outcomes. For a given $E_1, E_1 \in \mathscr{E}$, if their probability functions agree about the relative likelihood of these events, then the agent's preferences agree about all associated MS pairs. Let p_1 and p_2 be the probability functions of the two agents, and $>_1$ and $>_2$ be their preference relations. If $p_1(E_1)$ and $p_2(E_1)$ are each greater than, each less than, or each equal to $p_1(E_2)$ and $p_2(E_2)$, respectively, then: for all outcomes x, x', either $(x_{E_1}x'_{E_2}g >_1 x'_{E_1}x_{E_2}g)$ and $(x_{E_1}x'_{E_2}g >_2 x'_{E_1}x_{E_2}g)$; or $(x_{E_1}x'_{E_2}g <_1 x'_{E_1}x_{E_2}g)$ and $(x_{E_1}x'_{E_2}g <_2 x'_{E_1}x_{E_2}g)$; or $(x_{E_1}x'_{E_2}g =_1 x'_{E_1}x_{E_2}g)$ and $(x_{E_1}x'_{E_2}g =_2 x'_{E_1}x_{E_2}g)$. Alternatively, if their probability functions disagree about the relative ordering of these events, then their preferences disagree about all associated MS pairs: for all x, x', if $(x_{E_1}x'_{E_2}g >_1 x'_{E_1}x_{E_2}g)$ then $\neg(x_{E_1}x'_{E_2}g >_2 x'_{E_1}x_{E_2}g)$, and so forth.

So, a disagreement about which of two events has a higher p reflects a disagreement about *which event to bet on*. Assuming that decision-makers care only about getting the best outcomes, this is grounds for thinking that a disagreement about p is a disagreement about what the world is like: about which state is more likely to obtain or more plausible given the evidence. p is intended to "fit the world": it is the function that corresponds to beliefs. A disagreement about p reflects a disagreement about which of two states the agent cares more about what happens in, when all else is equal in the rest of the act and the only outcome considerations are ordinal comparisons which they agree about.

Next let us focus on r. The preference structure that plays a role in determining r is which act indifferences *make* the relation xy $\sim^*$(C) zw hold for a particular x, y, z, w. To see this, consider two agents with the same utility function and probability function. Since they have the same u, and xy $\sim^*$(C) zw holds just in case u(x) − u(y) = u(z) − u(w), they agree about which tuples satisfy xy $\sim^*$(C) zw. Recall that this relation holds just in case there are acts f and g and an event E such that $x_E f \sim y_E g$ and $z_E f \sim w_E g$, and all four modified acts are comonotonic. The intuitive idea underlying these indifferences is that receiving x rather than y if E exactly makes up for receiving f rather than g if ⌐E. Which acts f and g play this role for a given event and comoncone depends on how much weight E gets in an agent's deliberations: for example, if it gets a lot of weight, then f and g must be events that differ significantly on ⌐E in order to balance out the difference on E. Recall that r is determined from the function W, and W reflects how much weight an event E gets in comoncones when E is the best event (since $\pi_{\Phi(1)} = W(E_{\Phi(1)})$. So, two agents with different r functions but the same u and p functions will disagree about which f and g make the relation xy $\sim^*$(C) zw hold: an agent who assigns a higher r to a given event E when E is the best event will require a larger utility difference in the rest of the gamble to make up for what happens on E; and an agent who assigns a lower r to this E will require a smaller utility difference in the rest of the gamble to make up for what happens on E. The two agents will disagree about how much worse they are willing to make the rest of the gamble in order for something better to happen on the best event. More generally, in each particular ordering of events, π (again, which r is fixed by) represents the weight that each event gets in that ordering, and therefore reflects the size of the tradeoffs that are needed to compensate for a particular utility difference on each event.

If two agents with the same u and p disagree about r, they agree about which events they want the better outcomes on but disagree about how important what happens on E is for a given ordering of events. Furthermore, a given agent might think that for a given ordering of events, what happens on E is more important than what happens on Ē—the utility tradeoff might need to be bigger on Ē to compensate for a smaller utility tradeoff on E—even if in a choice between where to put the better outcome he would rather have the better outcome on Ē. How important what happens on E is will be relative to its structural position, whereas which outcome one would rather have on E is only relative to how good the outcomes are. Finally, all the events with a given p and a given structural position will get the same weight as each other in deliberation: the compensation for a particular utility difference on that event will have to be the same in each case. Thus, r does not seem to reflect what the world is like, but rather to reflect how much weight to give to a particular structural position once one has settled on what the world is like. Plausibly, it reflects how an agent structures the possible realization of his aims in response to the world: that is, which tradeoffs to accept.

This discussion also brings out an interesting point about the structure of representation theorems for EU theory with Savage acts. Again, the REU theorem derives two functions of events: a function p that measures how the agent compares them in deciding where to put the better outcome, and a function $r \circ p$ that measures how the agent weights what happens in them. But the REU axioms are strictly weaker than the corresponding EU axioms. It might initially seem surprising that weaker axioms allow us to derive more facts about an agent's preferences: the REU axioms reveal u, p, and r (or W) rather than just u and p. But what is actually the case is that the stronger axioms of EU theory also allow us to derive these three functions, but the sense in which they are stronger is that they entail that $W = p$: that is, that $r(p) = p$. And thus, in EU theory, the two questions that the agent faces—which events to bet on and which events to weight more heavily in a given act—must necessarily be given the same answer. EU theory has the resources to derive separately both probabilities and decision weights, but the axioms are so strong that they entail that these two things coincide: in EU theory, decision weights *are* probabilities.

In this chapter I have shown how the difference between the axiomatization of REU theory and that of EU theory maps onto caring about structural properties of gambles. I have also shown how the utility function, the probability function, and the risk function correspond at the level of preferences to the three elements of instrumental reasoning. Now that we have seen the difference between what EU theory requires of agents and what our more permissive theory requires of them, we can properly address the question of which theory captures the requirements of instrumental rationality: whether rational decision-makers can be globally sensitive or instead must be globally neutral. But before we turn to that debate, there is one final avenue the EU theorist has for accommodating globally sensitive preferences on his theory: redefine the notion of an outcome so that EU theory already takes global properties into account. Whether this avenue can be successful is the topic of the next chapter.

4

Redescription

4.1 The Role of Rationality in Decision Theory

I have explained risk-weighted expected utility theory, how it corresponds to taking structural properties of gambles into account, and how it captures preferences that many people have but that seem to violate expected utility theory. I have argued in particular that expected utility theory has ignored a third subjective component of instrumental rationality, the extent to which a decision-maker is willing to trade a high probability of something good for a lower probability of something better, and that this component is captured by REU theory, as seen in its axiomatic foundations. So it appears that if a decision theorist wants to capture the preferences in the counter-examples I have presented, she must reject EU theory. However, there is one strategy that I have not yet considered that may allow the EU theorist to accommodate these preferences after all: redescribing the choice problems a decision-maker faces by individuating the outcomes more finely, so that the preferences in question are actually instances of EU maximization. That strategy will be the focus of this chapter. Understanding the strategy and when it can be employed relies on understanding the role of rationality in decision theory, so I will begin by explaining what that role is, though I will postpone the question of what rationality amounts to more substantively to the next chapter.

In the previous chapter I distinguished two ways in which normative decision theory is used. When decision theory is used prescriptively, the theorist judges whether the agent has the preferences he ought to have, or the agent determines which preferences he ought to adopt in light of the ones he currently has. When decision theory is used to interpret agents, the theorist takes the agent's preferences as data and uses them to determine his beliefs and desires (and, in the case of REU theory, his risk attitudes). Rationality plays a different role in each use of decision theory.[1] For prescriptive decision theorists, rationality is a norm: one ought to have preferences that are rational. For interpretive theorists, on the other hand, rationality is a guiding assumption for interpretation.

These two senses of rationality are connected, as we can see by looking more closely at what sort of norm prescriptive decision theory is supposed to embody, and what sort

---

[1] For an extensive discussion of the relationship between rationality and the uses of decision theory, see Bermùdez (2009). See also Buchak (2013).

of assumption interpretive decision theory is supposed to make. Prescriptive decision theory enjoins agents to have consistent ends and to consistently prefer the means to their ends. David Velleman has a slightly different but congenial take: according to Velleman, the norm embodied in decision theory is that of intelligibility, and the axioms of the theory direct an agent to "coordinate [his] preferences in such a way that they will make sense."[2] We might add that he must coordinate his preferences so that they make sense as embodying well-structured goals and aiming at their fulfillment. Interpretive decision theory enjoins the theorist to ascribe to the agent beliefs and desires that provide good reasons for his behavior: for example, if an agent raises his arm at a particular time, we, as interpreters, ought to ascribe to him beliefs and desires according to which raising his arm is a way of aiming at the fulfillment of his desires given his beliefs.[3] As Bermùdez puts it, "we assume, in working backwards from behavior to psychological profile, that the beliefs and desires we attribute must rationalize the behavior we are trying to explain."[4] Thus, interpretive decision theory says to *interpret* the agent as having well-structured goals and aiming at their fulfillment.

It is an interesting question how the same principle can serve both as a guiding assumption in discovering an agent's beliefs and desires and as a norm.[5] I cannot treat it in detail here, but I tentatively propose that the answer lies in the fact that the interpretive theorist need not look for a set of beliefs and desires that rationalizes *all* of the agent's preferences. Rather, she looks for an interpretation that comes as close as she can: she infers beliefs and desires from the preferences of the ideally rational agent that is "closest" to the agent in question. She then interprets the deviations of the actual agent from the preferences of his ideal counterpart as instances of irrationality (weakness of will, thoughtlessness, and so forth). Given this interpretive principle, an interpretation will be closest to the actual agent insofar as it involves attributing fewer mistakes to him, though in certain cases the choice between interpretations might depend on one's views about human nature: for example, is it better to interpret an agent as acting against his desires or against his beliefs? So the assumption of rationality in interpretive decision theory is not that the agent acts rationally in every instance, but that the agent acts approximately rationally: his actions can in broad strokes be seen as aiming at the fulfillment of his particular goals. We can see how this naturally complements prescriptive decision theory: the directive from prescriptive decision theory is to transform one's preferences into those of one's ideally rational counterpart, and the agent is assessed by how closely he comes to that ideal.

[2] Velleman (2000, p. 162).

[3] Example from Lewis (1974, p. 337).

[4] Bermùdez (2009, p. 18).

[5] Bermùdez thinks the same theory cannot play both roles: see his arguments in Bermùdez (2009). I am optimistic about the possibility of decision theory playing both roles. However, the main thrust of my project is to undermine and replace a tenet that is at the heart of decision theory in both its prescriptive and interpretive use: its view of rationality. (It may be that ultimately interpretive theory has to reject the assumption that agents are rational, but insofar as it does not, my project will be important for interpretive theorists.) So I will set these foundational questions about decision theory in general aside.

Even though the interpretive theorist can interpret the agent as acting irrationally in particular instances, the guiding assumption is a principle of charity. She will aim to interpret the agent as having beliefs and desires that rationalize his actual preferences, especially when the agent clings to these preferences upon reflection. However, when encountering a preference that does not seem to fit with her interpretation, there is another option besides calling it irrational: she might instead conclude that the agent is conceiving of the outcomes differently than she had assumed. After all, what the agent believes and desires is what she is trying to determine, and that includes what the agent believes about the choices he faces.

For example, consider an agent with an avowed preference for attending to his friend's needs rather than attending to his own, so that in general, if he and his friend are equally hungry and there is only one cookie available, he prefers that she have it. However, this agent is observed on some occasion to snatch a cookie out of his hungry friend's hands. At first glance, he may appear to have inconsistent preferences, or to choose inconsistently with what he prefers. However, the theorist might discover that in this choice of "I eat a cookie" over "friend eats a cookie," the cookie is (unbeknownst to the friend) a peanut butter cookie, and the friend is allergic to peanuts. In this case, the theorist can interpret the agent as facing a different decision problem than the theorist initially thought, because the theorist did not take into account everything the agent cares about in the setup of the choice problem: the theorist can interpret the outcomes not as "I eat a cookie" and "friend eats a cookie" but rather as "I eat a peanut butter cookie" and "friend eats peanut butter cookie." This is an explicit (if somewhat pedantic) description of a kind of reasoning we routinely do in interpreting each other. If there is a way to describe the options so that the agent is decision-theoretically rational, the interpretive theorist is permitted to describe them as such. Within reason, anyway: and just what counts as within reason will be the subject of this chapter.

This suggests a strategy for responding to the counterexamples to EU theory that I have presented in this book: redescribing the choice problems in the examples by individuating outcomes more finely, so that EU theory can accommodate the stated preferences after all. In the next section I will explain this strategy (the "individuation strategy") in more detail by showing how it can be used to respond to a variety of so-called counterexamples aside from those involving risk. I will then explain how it might be used to respond to the counterexamples in this book. The remainder of the chapter is devoted to arguing that while this response may succeed against many of the non-risk-related counterexamples, it does not succeed against the counterexamples that motivate REU theory.

Whether this strategy can succeed is an especially important question for the interpretive EU theorist: if it cannot, and if I am correct that the "counterexample" preferences are widespread, then the task of interpreting actual people under the assumption of EU theory will be very difficult. For if violations of EU theory are not isolated events, then for most people, the "closest EU approximation" will not be very close; indeed, there might not be a fact of the matter about which of several not-too-close approximations is correct.[6] But this strategy is also important for the prescriptive theorist. If the prescriptive EU theorist can handle the counterexamples using the individuation strategy, then he need not argue that the "counterexample" preferences are irrational. If the strategy does not succeed, then the question of which theory to accept will turn on whether the EU theorist has a good argument against the preferences of globally sensitive agents.

4.2 The Individuation Strategy

We can see how the individuation strategy responds to potential counterexamples to EU theory (or, indeed, to any decision theory) by examining two well-known examples. In each example there is a purported violation of the theory, an explanation for why the preferences in question make sense, and a new description of the available options on the basis of this explanation to show that the theory can accommodate these preferences.

The first example is a purported violation of transitivity, and is described by Philip Pettit.[7] A decision-maker is given a choice between two pieces of fruit: one will go to him, the other to his dining companion. Imagine that when the choice is between a large apple and an orange, he chooses the large apple, and when the choice is between an orange and a small apple, he chooses the orange. However, when the choice is between a large apple and a small apple, he prefers to take the small apple and offer the large apple to his companion, in order to be polite. This is an apparent violation of transitivity, since the decision-maker seems to prefer the large apple to the orange to the small apple to the large apple.

We can see that the agent's preferences are sensible: taking a large apple and giving your companion a small apple is worse (for you) than taking a large apple and giving him an orange, because it is impolite. But since taking a large apple is better or worse depending on what the other choices are, it seems that the option "taking a large apple" should be carved up in a more fine-grained way. Thus, the defender of standard decision theory notes that there are not really three choices on the table, but six: taking

---

[6] One might wonder whether the existence of violations that REU theory does not take into account, like those discovered by Kahneman and Tversky (1979) and discussed in Section 2.4, implies that the same thing can be said about REU theory. I offer a tentative reply. People do not cling to preferences that violate other EU axioms in the way that they cling to preferences that violate STP. Patrick Maher notes that people do not usually change their preferences when told they violate STP, but they do when told they violate transitivity. For the former claim, he cites studies by MacCrimmon (1968), Slovic and Tversky (1974), and MacCrimmon and Larsson (1979); for the latter claim, he cites MacCrimmon (1968). Maher (1993, pp. 65, 34). So there is a case for thinking that there is a fact of the matter about the person's closest "considered" REU-counterpart, and this is the counterpart whose preferences will reveal our agent's beliefs and desires. This highlights one reason that it is important for the interpretive theorist to have the correct theory of *rationality* (the correct prescriptive theory).

[7] Pettit (1991). Pettit notes that the example is not his, but that he does not know where it comes from. Similar examples appear in Sen (1993, pp. 501–2).

a large apple and leaving one's companion a small apple; taking a large apple and leaving one's companion an orange; taking an orange and leaving one's companion a small apple; and so forth. This more fine-grained individuation of the alternatives the agent has to choose from is perfectly natural; and the pattern of preferences mentioned above, thus described, does not violate transitivity.[8]

The second example, due to Peter Diamond, concerns a choice between giving a prize to one or the other of two equally deserving people.[9] We have a good that cannot be divided, such as a new car; we are going to give it either to John or to Mary. We are indifferent about who gets the car. Let us say we can choose to allocate it by way of one of four coin-flip lotteries:

M_1: Give the car to Mary if the coin lands heads, give the car to John if the coin lands tails.

M_2: Give the car to John if the coin lands heads, give the car to Mary if the coin lands tails.

M_3: Give the car to Mary if the coin lands heads or tails.

M_4: Give the car to John if the coin lands heads or tails.

M_1 and M_2 each seem better than M_3 and M_4, because flipping a coin is a fair way to distribute the car. However, these preferences violate the Sure-Thing Principle (STP), an axiom of Savage's theory discussed in the previous section.[10] Since we prefer M_1 to M_3, and since these gambles only differ in what happens when the coin lands tails, it must be (by STP) that we prefer giving the car to John if tails comes up. And since we prefer M_2 to M_3, we prefer giving the car to John if heads comes up. So we should prefer M_4 to all three gambles; but, of course, we do not.

Again, the pattern of preferences seems reasonable: M_1 is better than M_3 even if the coin lands heads: that is, even if the result would be Mary getting the car either way. If the coin lands heads, then under M_3 we think that John was treated unfairly, but under M_1 we do not. Enter the individuation strategy.[11] All the possible outcomes appear to either be "Mary gets the car" or "John gets the car." However, we can individuate them as "Mary gets the car and John is treated unfairly," "Mary gets the car and John is not treated unfairly," and so forth, so that the options the agent is actually deciding between are:

---

[8] Note that this type of example does not depend on the rejected alternatives going to someone else. Broome mentions a case with the same structure: Maurice would choose to stay home rather than go sightseeing in Rome, and would choose to go sight-seeing rather than go mountaineering; however, he would choose to go mountaineering rather than stay home, because passing up a mountaineering trip in favor of staying home would be cowardly. In Broome (1993, p. 70).

[9] Pettit (1991). Derived from Peter Diamond (1967). Dreier (1996) and Machina (1989) also discuss an example of this form. The prize that is to be divided varies in presentations of this example.

[10] Note that these preferences also violate the weaker CSTP, and so violate REU theory as well as EU theory.

[11] John Broome shows how this strategy can be employed for examples like this in Broome (1991).

M_1': car to Mary if the coin lands heads, car to John if the coin lands tails.

M_2': car to John if the coin lands heads, car to Mary if the coin lands tails.

M_3': car to Mary and John is treated unfairly if the coin lands heads or tails.

M_4': car to John and Mary is treated unfairly if the coin lands heads or tails.

A preference for M_1' and M_2' each over M_3' and M_4' does not violate the Sure-Thing Principle, because M_1' and M_2' do not have outcomes in common with M_3' and M_4'.

Since the set of acts is the set of all arbitrary finite-valued functions from states to outcomes, individuating the outcomes more finely will give rise to additional acts, some of which could never be objects of choice in principle, or could never be the objects of some pair-wise choices. For example, "car to Mary if the coin lands heads, car to John and Mary is treated unfairly if the coin lands tails" must be an object of choice; and the agent must have a preference between "large apple while leaving a small apple for my companion" and "large apple while leaving an orange for my companion." Preferences between options than an agent can never in principle face a choice between are called *non-practical preferences*.[12] As discussed in Section 3.2, I do not think there is a problem with attributing these preferences to agents. However, how we come to know what the agent's non-practical preferences are—and in particular whether it is up to the agent or up to the theorist to determine them—will become important later in this chapter.

We are now in a position to see how the EU theorist might use the individuation strategy to respond to the counterexamples in Chapter 1, to claim that EU theory really can accommodate them.[13] Recall that Jeff prefers Deal 2 to Deal 1 (Table 4.1):

Table 4.1. Jeff's decision problem.

	HH	HT	TH	TT
Deal 1	Elvis stamp	Elvis stamp and gloves	Nothing	Gloves
Deal 2	Elvis stamp	Elvis stamp	Gloves	Gloves

[12] Terminology Broome (1991).

[13] To my knowledge, the earliest use of this strategy to respond to the Allais paradox is in Raiffa (1968, p. 85). Weirich (1986) explains in mathematical detail a way to formalize this strategy to respond to how decision-makers take risk into account in general. One of Weirich's main points is that EU theory cannot accommodate agents' risk-attitudes in the absence of this strategy—a position with which I agree—and his other point is that the EU theory supplemented with the individuation strategy can accommodate them. I disagree with this latter position, though it is worth saying that Weirich does not try to show that the strategy could accommodate agents who adhere to the particular non-expected utility theory proposed in this book. In Weirich (1987), Weirich takes up the problem of representing another particular non-expected utility theory, namely what he calls mean-risk decision analysis, a theory which treats global properties as valuable in themselves. My conclusions here do not refute his specific conclusions in that article. However, if I am right that global properties are not to be thought of as valuable in themselves but as dictating the way in which local properties contribute to the value of a gamble, then mean-risk analysis is not the correct analysis of rational risk-aversion, and so his argument does not show that the individuation strategy solves the general problem for EU theory.

Table 4.2. Jeff's decision problem—with regret.

	HH	HT	TH	TT
Deal 1A	*Elvis stamp*	*Elvis stamp and gloves*	***Regret***	*Gloves*
Deal 2A	*Elvis stamp*	*Elvis stamp*	*Gloves*	*Gloves*

With respect to the initial description of the outcomes, under the assumption that Jeff values the goods independently, this preference violates expected utility theory.[14]

However, the defender of expected utility theory could argue that the reason that Jeff has the preferences he has is that if he chooses Deal 1 and TH comes up, he will regret his choice. It is relevant to the value of not receiving any prize that Jeff might have acquired something had he chosen differently, because the regret he would feel itself has negative value: "no prize and regret" is worse than "no prize."[15] Thus, the correct description of the outcomes is more fine-grained than initially presented in the problem; the real choice is shown in Table 4.2.

The outcome in TH is not simply the status quo, so Jeff's preference for Deal 2A over Deal 1A does not violate expected utility theory.[16]

Alternatively, if this does not seem to describe Jeff's preferences, I have said that Jeff prefers Deal 2 to Deal 1 because he is sure to win a prize. The EU theorist could say that this is because the fact of a getting a prize for certain adds value to the entire deal: that is, to each outcome in Deal 2. In Table 4.3 we could describe the outcomes to take this into account.

Again, Jeff's preference for Deal 2 over Deal 1 no longer violates expected utility theory.[17]

Table 4.3. Jeff's decision problem—with surety.

	HH	HT	TH	TT
Deal 1B	*Elvis stamp*	*Elvis stamp and gloves*	*Nothing*	*Gloves*
Deal 2B	*Elvis stamp **and surety***	*Elvis stamp **and surety***	*Gloves **and surety***	*Gloves **and surety***

---

[14] The constructivist EU theorist may question that Jeff does value the goods independently. If he is worried about this, he should note two things. First, if I am correct that Jeff is an REU maximizer with respect to the initial description of the outcomes, then there will be some preference that violates EU theory in conjunction with his other preferences. And second, as we will see, everything I say here about the "Jeff" example can be said about the Allais paradox, which EU theory cannot handle without the individuation strategy, regardless of whether we take decision theory to be constructivist or realist.

[15] Alternatively, Jeff might regret that the "losing" state came up; I will discuss this in the next section.

[16] $u(\text{deal } 1) = {}^1/_4 u(\text{stamp and gloves}) + {}^1/_4 u(\text{stamp}) + {}^1/_4 u(\text{gloves}) + {}^1/_4 u(\text{regret})$. The conditions that the goods are independent is that $u(\text{stamp and gloves}) - u(\text{gloves}) = u(\text{stamp}) - u(\text{neither})$, and since the term "u(regret)" does not appear in this equation or the equation for the value of u(deal 2), there is no contradiction.

[17] $u(\text{deal } 2) = {}^1/_2 u(\text{stamp and surety}) + {}^1/_2 u(\text{gloves and surety})$; again, neither of these terms appear in the equation for independence or in the equation for the value of u(deal 1).

There may be other individuations that will make the preferences acceptable, but they will all be of two general forms, each corresponding to a type of feature that the theorist claims is mistakenly left out of the outcome description. On the one hand, they might claim that the agent cares about a feature that is intuitively a feature of the outcome itself: a feature that matters to the agent even once the gamble has been "resolved"—once the risky event occurs and one outcome has been selected. This gives rise to what we might call "local" individuation. Redescribing the choice problem as one between Deal 1A and Deal 2A uses local individuation: regret makes an outcome worse because regret is an unpleasant emotion. In general, individuations that do not relabel all of the outcomes of some gamble will count as local individuations. But some individuations that relabel all of the outcomes might also count as local individuations. Redescribing the problem as one between Deal 1B and Deal 2B, if "surety" is cashed out as a psychological response to taking a gamble that guarantees a prize (such as pleasurable anticipation or a lack of anxiety), counts as a local individuation because it is the fact that one undergoes the psychological response that is desirable or undesirable in itself. The agent cares about taking a gamble with a particular minimum because he would prefer to experience the pleasant feelings associated with knowing he will get a prize. Th e motivation for any particular local individuation is the thought that we have not described every feature, of the possible outcomes, that the agent cares about.

Local individuation contrasts with what we might call "global" individuation. Theorists using global individuation redescribe the choice problem so that the outcomes of each gamble include features of the gamble itself, but features that cease to play a role once the gamble has been resolved. Redescribing the problem as a choice between 1B and 2B uses global individuation if we think of "surety" as a feature that makes the gamble better but not because it makes any particular outcome better—a feature that the agent values independently of any benefit (psychological or otherwise) it confers on any of the particular outcomes. The agent cares about taking a gamble with a particular minimum not because of any feelings associated with doing so, but because he thinks a higher minimum is a positive feature of a gamble, independently of what actually happens and the feelings he experiences before the gamble is resolved. The motivation for any particular global individuation is that we have not described everything that the agent cares about full stop.

We might also put the distinction in the following way. All individuations label the outcomes in a more fine-grained way than initially specified in the problem. Individuations that are local redescibe outcomes on the basis of facts that are not essentially linked to which gamble the outcome is part of, though these facts may hold contingently because of the gambles involved. For example, anxiety may be induced by a gamble with a low minimum, but anxiety is an unpleasant emotion regardless of how it was induced. Individuations that are global redescribe outcomes on the basis of facts that essentially depend on which gamble the outcome results from: for example, having a particular minimum is a feature of the gamble itself. Local individuation applies if a low minimum is the cause of some bad feature of the gamble; global individuation if a low minimum is the bad feature.

In the apple/orange example we individuated the apple outcome into "taking a large apple and leaving one's companion a small apple" and "taking a large apple and leaving one's companion an orange" because the former makes one's choice impolite. This seems most naturally read as a local individuation: the impoliteness is an undesirable feature of the state in which the agent gives the small apple to his companion. Indeed, in cases of decision-making under certainty, it is hard to imagine what a global individuation would look like, since there is no feature that ceases to matter once the state of the world is known (the state of the world is already known), and it is unclear how someone could care about something full stop without caring about it as part of an outcome. In the Mary/John example, if the unfairness is bad in each world once the coin is flipped, then individuating on the basis of unfairness is a local individuation; if it is a bad-making feature of the gamble that does not show up in any world, then it is a global individuation. It seems to me that authors making this move in this example intend to make the point that unfairness is bad even once we know who gets the car, so this use of the individuation strategy is most naturally read as a local individuation.[18]

The EU theorist can respond to the Allais paradox in a way similar as to the Jeff example—and indeed, this is a very standard move.[19] The theorist points out that it is relevant to the value of receiving $0 in L_3 that you might have received $1m had you chosen differently, because you feel regret, which itself has negative value. Thus, the correct description of deal L_3 is "$1M with probability 0.89, $5M with probability 0.1, $0 *and regret* with probability 0.01." And if this is the correct description of L_3, then the typical preferences no longer violate expected utility theory.[20] And as in the Jeff example, we might instead individuate globally: for example, L_4 might be "$1M when the minimum is $1M, with probability 1."

This strategy can also be employed for Linda's and John's preferences, as well as for the preferences in the Rabin example. However, it will be more complex, since in these examples it is very clear that there is not just one offending preference against the background of many EU-maximizing preferences. Since my remarks are parallel for all five examples, I will confine my discussion to the Jeff and Allais examples for brevity; everything I say applies in parallel to the other three.

[18]   See, for example, Broome (1991, pp. 111–16). Those who want to challenge the claim that decision theory can handle this example might want to deny that it is a case of local individuation, and adapt my arguments against global individuation from those in the risk case (Section 4.4). I do not want to take a firm stance in this example: the example is complicated by the fact that the preference depends on the betterness relations of both individuals and how to take inequality into account when aggregating facts about these relations. But since this example is a standard example and orthogonal to the discussion of risk here, it is important to discuss how it might be handled via individuation, and how this differs from how the risk examples might be handled via individuation.

[19]   See, for example, Raiffa (1968), Schick (1991), Broome (1991), and Bermúdez (2009).

[20]   Expected utility theory can now capture the preference for L_1 over L_2 and L_4 over L_3: there is no contradiction between the following two equations:

$$0.1(u(\$5m)) + 0.9(u(\$0)) > 0.11(u(\$1m)) + 0.89(u(\$0))$$
$$u(\$1m) > 0.89(u(\$1m)) + 0.1(u(\$5m)) + 0.01(u(\$0 \text{ and regret}))$$

On the contrary, it is easy to find utility functions that satisfy both equations.

The individuation move is *prima facie* convincing. However, I will argue that an agent can prefer Deal 2 to Deal 1, or prefer L_1 to L_2 and L_4 to L_3, without any of the newly individuated choices being legitimate descriptions of the choice problem he takes himself to face. And, I will show, this implies that expected utility theory cannot accommodate these preferences: Jeff and the Allais agent are not interpretable as EU maximizers. I will argue first that local individuations do not solve the problem because they rest on incorrect assumptions about the agents' reasons for having the preferences in question, and I will then argue that global individuations do not solve the problem because they cannot capture the agents' preferences without individuating overly finely.

4.3   Local Individuation

Both interpretive and prescriptive decision theorists take decision theory to spell out the idea that rational agents are consistent, even though the former takes this to be a guiding assumption for interpreting agents and the latter a norm. Given this, it is clear why the individuation move might be employed. It is a way to respond to the charge that an agent is being inconsistent, by pointing out how we can conceive of the choices facing the agent so that he is choosing consistently. It is a way of pointing out that the agent's actions are intelligible. And so it is a way to avoid mislabeling as irrational preferences that seem perfectly justified, like the preferences in the apple/orange example. But it is also clear that there needs to be a restriction on when two outcomes can be distinguished. I illustrate this by way of an example.

Consider an agent who has frequently been offered a choice between chicken and steak, and has always chosen chicken, in a variety of circumstances: at his favorite fancy restaurant, at mediocre restaurants, when cooking at home, and so forth. As it turns out, during all of these occasions there just happened to be a high tide in Alaska. Now assume the agent is offered a choice between chicken and steak at his favorite fancy restaurant when the Alaskan tide is low, and he chooses steak.

As interpretive theorists we want to discover the agent's beliefs and desires, and interpret him, if we can, as having consistent preferences. One way to interpret him is to say that he prefers steak to chicken when the tide is high in Alaska, and chicken to steak when it is not. This interpretation makes him consistent, but if he does not have any knowledge of the Alaskan tide and we cannot see why it would make a difference to him (perhaps he is even causally cut off from the tides), then this interpretation will not help us get at his actual beliefs and desires, because it will not help us make sense of what he is doing. It will not make his actions intelligible as attempts to take the means to his actual ends. This is not to say we can only individuate on the basis of features an agent is consciously aware of; on the contrary, the best way of making sense of an agent may rely on citing features he is unaware of. For example, it might be that our agent generally prefers wine to beer, but on one occasion, when he has just been playing basketball, chooses beer over wine. Unbeknownst to him, beer has particular properties that make it taste better after physical exertion. This seems to be a case in which we want to allow individuation of outcomes into "beer after physical exertion" and "beer not after physical exertion," even though the agent might not know the reason for his preference. Unlike facts about the Alaskan tides, the fact that he has just physically exerted himself is causally connected to his preference and we can see why it would make a difference. If we are interested in decision theory as a framework for discovering an agent's beliefs and desires, we want to rule out interpretations of the agent's beliefs and desires that do not correctly explain what motivates him, while allowing interpretations that do explain what motivates him.

As prescriptive theorists we try to judge whether the agent is rational. Again, we could make him consistent by saying that the outcomes involved in the above example really are "steak when the tide is high," "chicken when the tide is high," and so on. But if we think that he ought not or does not care about the tides in his food preferences, then this interpretation will not actually make him instrumentally rational in the sense of having consistent ends and taking the means to them. (The distinction between thinking he ought not care and thinking he does not care will become important later in this section, but I will leave the disjunction for now.) Furthermore, if the agent is using decision theory to guide his actions, and if he does not in fact care about the tides, then if he notices the seeming inconsistency in his steak/chicken preferences, individuating on the basis of the tides will not save him from having to alter some of his preferences: he will either have to alter his preferences or admit that he does care about the tides or find some other distinction that he does care about.

Whether we take decision theory prescriptively or interpretively, therefore, we need constraints on when the individuation move can be made.[21] Once we have these constraints in place, we can see whether the individuation strategy can be employed in the risk cases. In the remainder of this section I will consider three principles for restricting individuation, and argue that none of the principles will allow the EU theorist to appeal to local individuation to successfully respond to the risk-related counterexamples. I will then give reasons for thinking that regardless of the specifics of the restriction principle we adopt, no local individuation will allow the EU theorist to accommodate these examples.

4.3.1 Individuation by justifiers

One candidate constraint on individuation is due to John Broome. He introduces a principle he calls the Principle of Individuation by Justifiers:[22]

(PIJ) Outcomes should be distinguished as different if and only if they differ in a way that makes it rational to have a preference between them.

---

[21] In the previous chapter I mentioned the distinction between *interpretive* and *descriptive* decision theory. The individuation strategy is not central in descriptive decision theory, since descriptive decision theorists are more interested in parsimonious and universal models, and in predicting behavior. Therefore, the need to interpret outcomes in a very fine-grained way will be a strike against a descriptive decision theory, particularly if the interpretation of outcomes is very different for different agents. Insofar as there is some distinction that most decision-makers make, the descriptive decision theorist will be apt to make it, but because of the nature of her project, she will be inclined to fix the outcomes ahead of time.

[22] Broome (1991, p. 103).

Of course, "rational" here means "rationally permissible." So "chicken when the Alaskan tide is high" and "chicken when the Alaskan tide is low" are the same outcome if it is not rationally permissible to have a preference between them. Broome thinks that strictly speaking the theorist ought to be able to individuate *any* two outcomes, but that rationality requires an agent to be indifferent between some of outcomes. But as he points out, (PIJ) implies a rational requirement of indifference: unless two outcomes differ in a way that makes it rational to have a preference between them, an agent must be indifferent between them. So, unless chicken-at-high-tide and chicken-at-low-tide differ in a way that makes it rational to prefer one to the other, the agent must be indifferent between them, and therefore they must be interchangeable in the agent's preferences: they must be functionally identical. Requiring the agent to be indifferent between them and requiring the theorist to count them as the same outcome thus have the same upshot: a single utility value must be assigned to them both. Since the difference does not matter for our discussion, we will follow Broome in using (PIJ) rather than a principle about indifference, which he himself does for expository reasons.

Recall that one way to state the difference between EU theory and REU theory is that the former includes the Sure-Thing Principle as a rational requirement. We have not yet given an explicit analysis of what it is for a preference between two outcomes to be rational. However, Broome has an ingenious argument that regardless of the content we give to the concept of rationality, no rational agent can violate the Sure-Thing Principle: that any intuitive counterexample, if it has any pull at all, is not really a counterexample. And since we only need decision theory to accommodate Jeff's preferences, and those of the Allais agent, if these preferences are rational, Broome's argument (if successful) will be enough to answer the challenge that risk-related counterexamples pose to EU theory. We will see how this argument is supposed to show that the Allais agent cannot violate STP while remaining rational, and then generalize it.

Broome writes:

All the [rationalizations of the Allais preferences] work in the same way. They make a distinction between outcomes that are given the same label in [the initial presentation of the options], and treat them as different outcomes that it is rational to have a preference between. And what is the argument that Allais' preferences are inconsistent with the sure-thing principle? It is that all the outcomes given the same label [initially] are in fact the same outcome. If they are not . . . [the decision problem] will have nothing to do with the sure-thing principle. Plainly, therefore, the case against the sure-thing principle is absurd. It depends on making a distinction on the one hand and denying it on the other. (Broome 107)

Broome points out that in order to use the Allais example—or the Jeff example or any other example—to show that rational agents violate EU theory, one needs to show both that the preferences involved are rationally permissible, and that they violate the theory. In order to show that they violate the theory, one must show that the outcomes that appear the same in the original choice problem should not be individuated more finely.

That is, we need to show that there is *no rational difference between them*. However, if the preferences are rationally permissible, claims Broome, it must be true that there *is* a difference, a difference the agent is permitted to care about, between some of the outcomes that appear the same. So there can be no rational preferences that genuinely violate EU theory.

Broome's argument is most naturally read, I think, as an argument about local individuations,[23] so I will discuss it in detail in this section, but I will briefly come back to it in the section about global individuation. When I say that his argument is about local individuation, I mean that we should interpret him as claiming that whenever someone has the Allais preferences, the *outcomes themselves* differ in a way that the agent cares about. That is, he has a preference between outcomes initially given the same label because of some positive or negative feature of the world in which they obtain: for example, he would rather have "nothing" in the L_1 gamble than "nothing" in the L_3 gamble because regret is unpleasant. And so, if this preference is rational, the theorist can individuate the outcomes; and if it is not, it does not matter to decision theory.

This argument can be applied to the non-risk-related violations of EU theory described in the previous section. If the agent can give a reason for a purported violation, then (by Broome's line of reasoning) it will make reference to local differences among some of the outcomes that initially appear the same; but then the decision theorist will point out that the preferences involving the newly described outcomes do not actually violate the theory. And this seems right in those examples. In the apple/orange example, one can only have the 'intransitive' preferences if one has a preference about which fruit to give one's companion. Either is it rational to have a preference about which fruit one gives one's companion or it is not. If it is, then the 'intransitive' preference is rational, but the theorist can distinguish between taking the large apple while leaving one's companion the orange and taking the large apple while leaving one's companion the small apple—and thus the 'intransitive' preference is not intransitive after all. And if it is not rational to have a preference about which fruit one gives one's companion, then decision theory need not accommodate the intransitive preference. Similarly for the Mary/John example: we can only have the pattern of preferences described if, in the event that Mary gets the car, we care whether John would have gotten it, had the coin landed differently.[24] And if this is a rational pattern of preferences to have, it does not violate EU theory. In these cases, since having the preference that seems to violate EU theory depends on having a preference between outcomes that initially appear the same, the rational permissibility of having the former preference depends on the rational permissibility of the latter. Therefore,

---

[23]   Broome (1991, p. 98) claims that "all the rationalizations of Allais' preferences point out a good or bad feeling you may experience."

[24]   Perhaps the reader is not convinced by this claim, and consequently is not convinced that the standard theory can handle this example by local individuation. Again, I do not challenge the standard responses to these examples here, although nothing I say hangs on their being good responses.

the rationality of having preferences that seem to violate EU theory depends on their not actually violating the theory at all! In these examples, Broome's line of reasoning is vindicated.

But now assume that Jeff and the Allais agent have their preferences for the reasons explained in the first three chapters: they take structural properties of gambles into account in decision-making, and in particular they weight the minimum value they might receive more heavily than a standard expected utility maximizer does. More succinctly, we might say that Jeff prefers Deal 2, and the Allais agent prefers L_4, because these options have a higher minimum, and (average values being equal, at least) these agents prefer to guarantee themselves as much as they can guarantee: while this may be oversimplifying their reasons, it will do for our purposes. *This does not in any obvious way depend on distinguishing between two outcomes that initially appear identical—as the preferences in the other examples do—but rather on distinguishing between how two identical outcomes contribute to the overall value of different gambles.* This is because for globally sensitive agents the utility *contribution* of an outcome to a particular gamble depends on its structural position in the gamble, even while the utility *value* of the outcome is fixed.

Unlike in the examples in Section 4.2, Jeff's reasons for preferring Deal 2 to Deal 1 need not be accompanied by reasons for preferring one of the "gloves" outcomes to the other, or for preferring "nothing" in the context of Deal 1 to "nothing" more generally (to the status quo). They *might* be accompanied by these reasons, but they might instead be accompanied by different sorts of reasons. To put the point another way, if Jeff is indifferent between, say, receiving nothing when he might have received a prize and receiving nothing more generally, his reasons for indifference need not give rise to indifference between Deal 1 and Deal 2. Jeff might be indifferent between receiving nothing and receiving nothing when he might have received a prize because he does not care about what might have been had he taken a different gamble or had the gamble he took turned out differently. He might not care about these non-actualized possibilities because the fact that he could have received certain amounts of money or prizes, had the world turned out differently, does not affect the value of his property in the actual world. To put it more concretely, if an agent prefers x to y, then there is some amount of money he is willing to pay to have x rather than y (or some amount he would be willing to pay if that were possible). But Jeff might not be willing to pay to eliminate possibilities that were never realized. For example, he might not pay any amount of money to trade in "nothing when I might have had gloves" for "nothing when I could not have had gloves" (if this were possible). And yet he might still prefer Deal 2 to Deal 1 because he thinks he will do better for himself by taking the deal with the higher minimum. Note that in the Allais case the amount of money the agent would pay to eliminate regret would have to be particularly high if the disvalue of regret is to justify the common preferences, since people tend to have a very strong preference for L_4 over L_3, and "regret" only adds 0.01 times its utility disvalue to L_4. *The amount of money one would have to be willing to pay must have a utility value that is 100 times* *the utility difference between L_1 and L_2, plus 100 times the utility difference between L_4 and L_3.*[25]

The role that particular possibilities play in evaluating a gamble when they are definitively non-realized is different from their role when the results of a gamble are not yet known. An agent might weight outcomes in a particular way when they are still possible—that is, when the results of a gamble are yet unknown—and yet not care at all about them when he learns they are not realized. In particular, an agent might weight possible outcomes heavily in part because these outcomes have a property that depends on their relationship to other outcomes (for example, the property of being the minimum) without thereby caring about these other outcomes once they become non-actualized. Jeff might consider the fact that Deal 1 has a low minimum to be a strike against that deal—where the fact that some particular outcome is the minimum depends on what the other outcomes are—without thereby caring what the other outcomes were once he receives some particular outcome. In short: disliking risk while all the possibilities are still on the table need not entail experiencing regret in some of these possible occurrences.

Broome's argument, considered as an argument about local individuation, makes an assumption that turns out to be false: that any reason for preferring Deal 2 to Deal 1, or for preferring L_1 to L_2 and L_4 to L_3, relies on making a distinction, in the local sense, between outcomes that are initially given the same label. In the examples in Section 4.2 the reasons an agent might have for the "counterexample" preferences are tied to the reasons he might have for a preference between outcomes initially given the same label. In the risk cases, however, these potential reasons come apart: one might have reasons for preferences that appear to violate expected utility theory without having reasons for preferences between outcomes initially labeled the same. Therefore, Broome's general argument fails.

We might instead try to use Broome's principle to save expected utility theory by arguing for a theory of rationality that explicitly allows for a rational preference between the outcomes that initially appear the same in Jeff's decision problem. After all, Broome's principle allows the theorist to distinguish between any outcomes that differ in a way that makes it rational to have a preference between them, not only between outcomes that the agent in fact has a preference between. If it is rational to have a preference between "gloves when . . ." and "gloves when . . ." then the theorist can treat them as different, regardless of whether the agent treats them as different. But we can quickly see that this will not help accommodate the examples: even if the theorist can treat the outcomes as different, he cannot assign them different utility values unless the agent himself has a preference between them, or else the utility function will not

---

[25] If L_1 is better than L_2 by b utils and L_4 is better than L_3 by c utils then the following two equations hold:

$$0.1(u(\$5m)) + 0.9(u(\$0)) = 0.11(u(\$1m)) + 0.89(u(\$0)) + b$$
$$u(\$1m) = 0.89(u(\$1m)) + 0.1(u(\$5m)) + 0.01(u(\$0 \text{ and regret})) + c.$$

These jointly imply $u(\$0) - u(\$0 \text{ and regret}) = 100(b + c)$.

represent the agent's preferences. For example, it will interpret the Allais agent as being willing to pay a lot of money to eliminate regret, when she would not in fact be willing to do this. Whether expected utility theory can accurately capture an agent's preferences using individuation depends on the agent's own reasons for those preferences.

4.3.2 Individuation by actual preferences

Broome's principle is an external constraint on interpretation: it makes the possibility of distinguishing outcomes dependent on some objective feature of the agent's situation: namely, whether having a preference between the outcomes is rational. It might be seen as a principle of charity for interpretation: we should interpret an agent as making a distinction only if it is rational to make that distinction. However, it restricts preferences beyond what the agent himself values. It restricts preferences relative to a substantive theory of rationality that rules out particular preferences on the basis of their content, regardless of what the agent in fact views as better. As Broome himself notes (Broome 1993), this is against the spirit of "Humeanism" in decision theory, which will be discussed in the next chapter. For these reasons, we might favor a principle that makes the possibility of distinguishing outcomes dependent on the agent's internal state instead. I turn now to two such principles.

The first of these principles is proposed by Dreier (1996), and it states that we should look to the agent's actual preferences as a guide for how to interpret her:[26]

> **(PIA)** Outcomes should be distinguished as different if and only if the agent actually has a preference between them.

This principle allows the substantive facts about an agent's preferences to be up to her. And if it is possible for the agent to know her preference between any two outcomes, then this principle is easy to apply. If we restrict individuation according to this principle, then Jeff and the Allais agent cannot be interpreted as EU maximizers, given what I have said about their reasons for their preferences. They take themselves to be indifferent between the outcomes initially labeled the same, but those outcomes make different value contributions to the gambles in which they are embedded.

However, the EU theorist might protest that an agent does not have access to her non-practical preferences, or at least does not have access to them in the relevant cases. On the contrary, whether an agent has a preference between two outcomes must depend on her choice behavior with respect to acts that can in principle be the objects of actual choice, or at least must depend on other features of her psychology besides her say-so. I do not see any reason why an agent should not have access to these. However, since the debate seems impassible here, I will move on to the next principle, which is also an internalist principle but restricts individuation on the basis of other psychological features besides the agent's preferences themselves.

---

[26] Dreier (1996, p. 260).

4.3.3 Individuation by desirable properties

In "Decision Theory and Folk Psychology," Philip Pettit takes issue with the claim that the basic units of desire are what he calls prospects.[27] Prospects are sets of possible worlds, which correspond in my terminology to gambles, or to outcomes in the limiting case. Pettit argues that the basic units of desire are properties, not prospects: that is, that agents have preferences over properties, and agents desire prospects because of the properties they instantiate.[28] He calls this the "desiderative structure." In the course of this argument, Pettit formulates an individuation principle which respects this observation about the basis of prospect-desires which we might call the Principle of Individuation by Properties:[29]

> (PIP) Outcomes should be distinguished as different if and only if they differ in regard to properties that are desired or undesired by the agent.

Assuming preferences really are over properties, this principle has the attractive feature that it does not place substantive limits on what an agent can value. Pettit points out that his assumption of the desiderative structure is itself meant to be a constraint of consistency between an agent's desires for prospects and this same agent's desires for properties.[30] His principle places limits on which outcomes the theorist can interpret as different and thus on which outcomes an agent can have preferences among; however, these are not additional limits beyond the limits that the axioms of transitivity, completeness, and so forth place on preferences. They are rather, I presume, a delineation of when these conditions apply: they apply only when we are dealing with gambles that contain outcomes that are genuinely the same.

   Pettit's principle provides a way of spelling out when two outcomes are the same. They are the same when the agent counts them the same: when they do not differ in regard to properties that *the agent* cares about. But unlike (PIA), (PIP) does not give the agent the final word about which outcomes count as the same for him. Whether an agent counts two outcomes the same is determined by the agent's other preferences. It is determined by whether his other preferences reveal that he does indeed care, or not care, about those properties. Thus, (PIP) is in the same spirit as (PIA), but rests the question of outcome distinction on something other than the agent's preferences about the outcomes themselves. Like (PIA), (PIP) places no additional constraints on preferences—or the interpretation of preferences—outside of what the agent himself values. Thus, it preserves the relationship between an agent's reasons for his preferences on the one hand and the outcomes that can be distinguished by the theorist on the other.

---

[27] Pettit (1991).

[28] Pettit's position is compatible with the formal apparatus of decision theory as it is normally conceived, since he assumes that agents do have preferences over prospects (gambles), even if these are not the "basic" units of desire. He thinks that the formal apparatus of decision theory should be *supplemented* with an appropriate picture of how desires about prospects relate to desires about properties.

[29] Pettit (1991, p. 212).

[30] Pettit (1991, p. 201).

Pettit's principle gives the right answer in the examples in Section 4.2, as he points out. Leaving a small apple rather than an orange makes taking the large apple impolite, so if an agent cares about politeness, then the two situations in which the agent takes the large apple should be distinguished. Having given John an equal chance of winning the car (rather than no chance at all) makes giving Mary the car fair, so if we care about fairness, then the two situations in which Mary receives the car should be distinguished.

There is a way to test whether the above properties really are what the agent cares about when making the choices in the examples, and thus to determine whether the individuation is legitimate. For each example, we can construct a case that is similar but in which the options lack the property that the agent supposedly cares about, and we will find that the intuitive preferences switch. For example, we might provide the standard apple/orange choices (large apple or orange, orange or small apple, large apple or small apple, where the remaining fruit goes to one's dining companion), but this time stipulate that your dining companion has a small appetite and is thus indifferent between a large apple and a small apple. Or we might add that when the dining companion is given a similar choice between the large apple and the small apple, he always keeps the large apple for himself, and so stipulate that this is not an impolite thing to do in your circles. Or that the dining companion will not know that the choice is up to you—he will not know how it came about that each person got the fruit he got (if it is only the appearance of impoliteness that you care about). All of these scenarios are ways of giving you the same initial outcomes and alternatives, but removing impoliteness (or the appearance thereof) from the choice of a large apple when the small apple is the alternative. And in the first two scenarios, and possibly the third, it seems that you would now choose the large apple over the small apple. If you do not, your preferences are closer to looking incoherent, because it becomes hard to see what the reason for your original preferences could be. Similar scenarios could be constructed to show that fair treatment really is the property we care about in the Mary/John case, if indeed the local individuation works in this example.

I will take it as a general rule that if the theorist wants to accommodate an agent's preferences by distinguishing between two outcomes and stating that one has a desirable (or undesirable) property that the other lacks, then *when we present an alternative scenario in which the outcomes are the same except for that property, the agent's preferences should switch:* the preferences in the alternative scenario should not violate the theory. (Pettit himself points out that if the agent desires a property, then, all things being equal, this property will make a difference to the value of a prospect.) This test will only make sense when dealing with local individuations, since we will not be able to describe a scenario in which a gamble has all the same outcomes but different global properties.

Let us now examine what Pettit's principle has to say about the candidate local individuations in the risk cases. According to (PIP), we can distinguish "getting nothing" in Deal 1 from "getting nothing" in general—or "gloves" in Deal 1 from "gloves" in

Deal 2—if one of these outcomes instantiates a property that the agent cares about but the other does not. For example, we can distinguish "gloves and delightful anticipation" from "gloves without delightful anticipation" if the agent cares about anticipating some prize. So, we want to know whether someone who prefers Deal 2 to Deal 1 must have a preference for some property such that (PIP) permits us to interpret him as an EU maximizer. I will argue that this need not be the case: an agent can have a preference for Deal 2 over Deal 1 without any of the outcomes differently instantiating local properties that he cares about.

To show this, I will proceed as follows. I will consider the different properties that one "nothing" outcome instantiates but the other does not (or one "gloves" outcome instantiates but the other does not), and see whether someone must care about one of these properties in order to coherently prefer Deal 2 to Deal 1. I will rely on both the test mentioned above and on general considerations of how certain properties should function in decision-making. If an agent must care about one of these properties in order to prefer Deal 2 to Deal 1, then the decision theorist will be licensed to distinguish the outcomes by (PIP), because the outcomes will genuinely differently instantiate a property that the agent cares about. On the other hand, *if an agent can hold that Deal 2 has properties that make it more desirable than Deal 1, without any of the outcomes that appear the same actually differently instantiating desirable properties, then—if we restrict individuation using (PIP)—EU theory cannot accommodate these preferences.* Again, everything in the discussion that follows applies to the Allais preferences, as well as the preferences in my other examples.

As mentioned above, one property that might be differently instantiated in outcomes that appear the same is regret. There are two things that a decision-maker might regret if TH comes up and he chose Deal 1: that TH came up, or that he chose Deal 1. In other words, the agent might hold either feature of the situation fixed, and regret the other. We might call this first possibility "state" regret (Table 4.4): regret that one received nothing because, had a different state come up, one would have received something.[31]

Now consider the following scenario: the choice is exactly the same—between Deal 1 and Deal 2—but immediately after you make the decision, you will forget that you were ever offered a deal at all. Call these Deals 1* and 2*. Whatever prize you receive from Deal 1* or Deal 2* will be given to you simply as a gift—or you will just happen to

Table 4.4. Jeff's decision problem, incorporating state-regret.

	HH	HT	TH	TT
Deal 1A'	*Elvis stamp*	*Elvis stamp and gloves*	*Regret that TH came up*	*Gloves*
Deal 2A'	*Elvis stamp*	*Elvis stamp*	*Gloves*	*Gloves*

---

[31] This is the general motivation behind the theory found in Loomes and Sugden (1986).

acquire it—and if you do not receive a prize, you will never know that you had a chance at one. So the outcome of "nothing" in the TH state of Deal 1* cannot possibly come with regret, since you will not know the facts that might lead you to feel regret. (If memory erasure sounds too weird, think of choosing between the deals for a friend who will never know she was in a position to receive a prize.) It is still coherent to prefer Deal 2* to Deal 1*, because it is coherent to think that by taking Deal 2* instead of Deal 1*, you are leaving your future self (or your friend) in a better position. Indeed, this is exactly what the risk-avoidant agent thinks: he thinks that Deal 2* is a better means to his ends than Deal 1*, because he thinks that the best way to get as good a prize as he can is to take a gamble with a good chance of a moderate payoff, rather than a gamble with a smaller chance of a high payoff. More crucially, it is coherent to prefer Deal 2* to Deal 1* for the exact same reason that one might initially prefer Deal 2 to Deal 1: the way the outcomes in Deal 2* are arranged across the possibility space is preferable to the way the outcomes in Deal 1* are arranged.

As mentioned above, another way to individuate outcomes so that the preference for Deal 2 over Deal 1 no longer violates standard decision theory is to individuate the outcomes in Deal 2 to include peace of mind about getting some prize; we might also individuate the outcomes in Deal 1 to include experiencing anxiety about winding up with nothing (or we might do both). Again, we can use the preceding test to show that the agent need not be responding to these properties: forgetting you are involved in a gamble removes the peace of mind or the anxiety (and choosing for a friend without her knowledge of the gamble removes the possibility that her peace of mind or anxiety plays a role in your choice), but knowing you will forget does not undermine a preference for Deal 2 over Deal 1 that is based on thinking Deal 2 is a better means to one's ends. It does not undermine a preference that is based not on the *feeling* of certainty as one undergoes the gamble, but rather on the conviction that having a higher minimum is a favorable property of a gamble. Again, in thinking about Deal 1* and Deal 2*, we have eliminated the psychological benefits of certainty from the outcomes, but we have not altered the way in which the outcomes are arranged across the possibility space.

Let us now turn to the other way regret might enter into one of the outcomes: a decision-maker might regret the deal he chose, given which state came up. Call this "choice" regret[32] (Table 4.5). If TH comes up, you might regret that you chose Deal 1

---

[32] This is the motivation behind the theory found in Bell (1982) and Bell (1983), discussed in Chapter 1, fn. 51. Weber (1998) has an argument, different from the argument in this book, that individuating the outcomes of the Allais paradox to include regret does not succeed. His argument relies primarily on the psychology and function of various types of regret: Weber claims that there is no negative feeling that could function in the way regret must function in order to make the Allais preferences capturable by expected utility theory. What I call "state regret" corresponds to what Weber calls "disappointment" (102), and what I call "choice regret" corresponds to what Weber calls "regret," though he makes a further distinction between "outcome regret," or regret that one chose what one chose, given how things turned out (that is, which state came up); and "decision-making regret," or regret that one chose what one chose, given what one knew at the time (that is, regret that one did not choose the rational option). As I say later in this section, I think that choice-regret should, in the decision-making of rational agents, primarily function in the latter sense.

Table 4.5. Jeff's decision problem, incorporating choice-regret.

	HH	HT	TH	TT
Deal 1A″	*Elvis stamp*	*Elvis stamp and gloves*	*Regret that you did not choose 2A″*	*Gloves*
Deal 2A″	*Elvis stamp*	*Elvis stamp*	*Gloves*	*Gloves*

rather than Deal 2, and, if so—the individuation story goes—this will be part of the outcome in that state.

Again, if regret about which deal one chose is genuinely an outcome-property that makes the outcome worse for the agent, this individuation will be legitimate. One way to set up a situation in which the agent will not regret his choice is to stipulate that one of the deals is simply assigned to him, and ask which would come as better news to him—the news that he holds Deal 1 or the news that he holds Deal 2. This takes away any feeling that it was within the agent's control to bring about a better outcome; thus, if TH occurs, he will not "kick himself" for having made the wrong choice. However, in this case, he still might regret his *holding*: given that TH comes up, he regrets that he holds Deal 1 rather than Deal 2. So, noting his preferences in this scenario is not enough to show that the individuation fails.

Constructing a deal in which none of the options instantiates regret about the choice one made involves setting up a situation in which the agent has no other options; but, of course, we cannot evaluate the utility of a deal on its own, without knowing where it stands in an agent's preference ordering, since utility is derived from pairwise preferences. So I will need a different response to this proposed individuation in the Jeff case.

One thing to point out is that if an agent experiences choice-regret in the TH state of Deal 1—if he regrets that he might have had a pair of gloves, rather than nothing—then he should also experience choice-regret in the HT state of Deal 2: he should regret that he might have had an Elvis stamp and a pair of gloves rather than just an Elvis stamp. Indeed, he has the same cause for regret, since in both states the value difference between what he could have had if he had chosen differently and what he actually has is (the value of) a pair of gloves. So the utility of the two deals should still average out to exactly the same value.[33]

What this highlights is the way in which choice-regret ought to function as a consideration in decision-making for a rational agent. When someone thinks "If I make

---

[33] If u(stamp) − u(stamp and regret) = u(nothing) − u(nothing and regret), then the difference in expected utility values between the two individuated deals will be the same as the difference in expected utility values between the two original deals: namely, zero. One might press this response further by pointing out that the regret involved in the TH state of deal 1 is not just about the utility difference between what you have and what you might have gotten, but about getting *nothing* as opposed to getting something. But it seems to me that this sentiment should be interpreted either as state-regret ("I had the opportunity to win a prize, and I came up empty-handed!") or as valuing winning for its own sake, both of which can be shown to be inadequate to respond to the counterexamples using the test mentioned previously.

this choice, then if a particular state comes up, I will kick myself for making it," this fact itself should not add disvalue to a particular outcome, but rather it is a way of drawing attention to value that is already present.[34] The fact that you might regret a choice is a reminder of the value difference between the gambles in the state in which you will feel regret. This value difference will already be taken into account in your evaluation of the gambles. Alternatively, anticipating regret might be a sign that it is not the rational choice to make. But as Michael Weber points out, regret that a choice of *g* rather than *f* would be irrational cannot ever justify a preference for *f* over *g*, since it requires a judgment that *f* is a more rational choice than *g*, independent of the regret that one might feel.[35]

We have seen that none of the proposed local properties of the outcomes of Deal 1 and Deal 2 is a property that an agent who prefers Deal 2 to Deal 1 must care about; and so none of them is a good candidate for use in individuating outcomes to save EU theory. Of course, some individuals might in fact have the preferences for one of the reasons listed, and EU theory can accommodate the preferences of these individuals. But the point is that individuals with the counterexample preferences *need not* care about the properties on the list: their preferences are perfectly understandable without positing that they care about these properties. In particular, risk-avoidant agents can have the counterexample preferences without caring about any of the properties on the list. And so, by (PIP), we cannot individuate on the basis of these properties: we cannot interpret *our* agent by pointing out that *some* agent could have those preferences and remain an EU maximizer. Doing so would not interpret the agent as consistently taking the means to his own ends.

Furthermore, we have reason to think that no other local property one can hypothesize will save EU theory when it comes to risk-avoidant agents who have the counterexample preferences. If an agent evaluates a risky gamble in a manner different from averaging the values in all of the states, the search for a *local* property that he cares about but that is not initially labeled is not likely to succeed, because caring about structural properties need not correspond to caring about any properties of *outcomes* besides their stated features. If we adopt (PIP), then local individuation corresponds to interpreting the agent as actually caring about local properties not listed in the initial setup. This is a reason to think that local individuation cannot save EU theory in these cases regardless of which individuation principle we employ. Our utility assignment must be sensitive to agents' actual preferences, and if an agent is genuinely globally sensitive then we will not find outcomes that the agent actually has a preference between that make his preferences conform to EU theory. If any individuation is going

---

[34] Of course, regret *could* add disvalue to a particular outcome for some agent, but if it does, he ought to bemoan the fact that this is true of him. This is not to say that this kind of regret is irrational in the decision-theoretic sense, but it is unfortunate in the same sense that it is unfortunate to find oneself with a preference for items of food that happen to be very expensive. It seems like the way that the possibility of regret is *meant* to function in rational decision-making is as a (possibly defeasible) guide to what to choose.

[35] Weber (1998, p. 108).

to work to accommodate the preferences of these agents, it will have to be a global one. I now turn to the question of whether global individuation can save EU theory.

4.4 Global Individuation

I have so far been focusing on individuations that describe differences that matter to the agent apart from the gamble in which the outcomes are embedded (even though their being embedded in the gamble might be the cause of the differences). I have argued that all individuations of this type fail to make sense of the risk-avoidant agent's preferences because they get his reasons for his preferences wrong. But another kind of individuation takes the reasons that I myself cite for the decision-makers' preferences—considerations about global properties of gambles—and uses these to redescribe the outcomes. These are considerations that necessarily depend on the particular gamble in which the outcome is embedded, but the agents in question do genuinely care about them, so (says this response) the EU theorist should be able to take them into account as part of the outcomes.

In the Jeff example I have said that Jeff cares about the minimum value of each gamble. Therefore, the EU theorist using global individuation can claim that each outcome includes not just the prize received, but the fact that the agent took that particular gamble. For example, "gloves" in the two deals is really "gloves as part of a deal that guarantees something at least as good as gloves" and "gloves as part of a deal that guarantees something at least as good as the status quo"; "Elvis stamp" is really "Elvis stamp as part of . . ." and so forth (Table 4.6).

It is easy to see that by including which deal an agent choses as part of each outcome, EU theory can accommodate agents who aggregate values in a way other than averaging.[36] It is also clear that agents like Jeff do care about the properties in question, so it is easy to see that (PIP), interpreted as a principle that ranges over both local and global

Table 4.6. Jeff's decision problem, global individuation.

	HH	HT	TH	TT
Deal 1C	Elvis stamp from a deal that guarantees nothing	Elvis stamp and gloves, from a deal that guarantees nothing	Nothing from a deal that guarantees nothing	Gloves from a deal that guarantees nothing
Deal 2C	Elvis stamp from a deal that guarantees at least gloves	Elvis stamp from a deal that guarantees at least gloves	Gloves from a deal that guarantees at least gloves	Gloves from a deal that guarantees at least gloves

---

[36] Weirich (1986) suggests a strategy like this to accommodate agents who are described by "mean-risk" decision rules.

properties, licenses this individuation. Likewise, (PIA), interpreted as allowing distinctions between outcomes when the agent has a preference between gambles which include them, licenses this individuation. Additionally, if (PIJ) is interpreted to apply to global individuation—if it allows the theorist to make a distinction between outcomes if it is rational for the agent to care about the differences in the gambles they result from—then as long as these preferences are rational (and it will be important to my project not to deny this claim), (PIJ) licenses this individuation as well.

However, there are three problems with this approach. The first problem is that outcomes that we might have initially wanted to count as equivalent will be differentiated. For example, the outcomes under HH initially appeared the same across deals, but according to the new presentation of the problem, they must be different in a way the agent cares about. So once the agent knows that the coins have landed HH, he must still care whether he holds Deal 1 or Deal 2. And as I noted in the previous section, this seems counterintuitive.

The EU theorist can reply by pointing out that the agent does care, because it makes a difference to him which deal he takes. Consider an analogy. We could evaluate the option "$1 as the result of someone's untimely death" in two ways: either we could evaluate the badness of receiving a "tainted" dollar, or we could evaluate the badness of getting $1 *and* someone dying: that is, the badness of the entire state of affairs. And while one may or may not think that a dollar that results from someone's untimely death is worse than an ordinary dollar (holding fixed the fact that this person died), it is certainly the case that the state of affairs in which someone dies and you get a dollar is worse than the state of affairs in which no one dies and you get a dollar. Analogously, while the value of an Elvis stamp to our stamp-collector might not depend on where it came from, the EU theorist can claim that the state of affairs in which one takes a deal one disprefers and gets an Elvis stamp is worse than the state of affairs in which one take a deal one prefers and gets an Elvis stamp. Given that the agent cares about making good choices, and that he thinks that Deal 2 is a better choice, he does care whether he takes Deal 1 or Deal 2, even in the situation in which he ends up with the same prize either way.

There is something unsettling about this response, though: there is an odd double-counting going on. If this response is correct, then it appears that the agent starts with a preference ordering based purely on his evaluation of the gambles themselves (call this value a gamble's "basic value"), and then in any particular choice situation "bumps up" the values in the best deal, since the fact of taking that deal rather than another is something he cares about. Depending on the size of this "bump," an agent might prefer an outcome with a lower basic value that is best in some particular choice situation, to a deal with a higher basic value that is worse in some particular choice situation. For example, an agent might prefer "a guaranteed $1 when the other options are much worse than a guaranteed $1" to "a guaranteed $2 when the other options are much better than a guaranteed $2." Again, this might not be so bad, because it might be that the agent so values being rational that he would rather make a rational choice that makes him monetarily worse off than an irrational choice that makes him monetarily better off.

However, this seems to me the wrong way to think about making rational choices. Picking the rational option—the gamble you prefer, given the values of the outcomes and the likelihoods of the states—is not valuable in itself. Rather, it is *instrumentally* valuable: it does a better job of getting you the things you do value in themselves. This is similar to the point against taking choice-regret into account in the outcomes. It is also worth noting that building into decision theory that agents assign *utility* to picking the best gamble threatens to make decision theory hopelessly unwieldy, and, unless we have two separate utility functions, circular.

The second problem with global individuation is that what an agent chooses in one decision scenario will tell us little or nothing about what he will or should choose in any other scenario. How an agent values an Elvis stamp when he has it as the result of such-and-such gamble need not have any specific relationship to how he values an Elvis stamp in a different gamble, or as a stand-alone outcome (in the constant 'gamble'). And there will be nothing to constrain his preferences about Elvis stamps as the result of (even slightly) different gambles. Consider, for example, the gamble that is identical to Deal 2 except that in the TH and TT states, the agent gets an additional dollar: the possible outcomes of this gamble are "Elvis stamp from a deal that guarantees at least $1 and gloves" and "$1 and gloves from a deal that guarantees at least $1 and gloves." For all the agent has revealed to us so far, we have *no idea* how he values the outcome "Elvis stamp from a deal that guarantees at least $1 and gloves." This outcome could be astronomically better (or worse) than "Elvis stamp from a deal that guarantees at least gloves": there is nothing in the agent's preferences so far that fixes its value.[37]

Velleman states what is troubling about this in a particularly clear way. Recall Velleman's claim that the norm embodied in prescriptive decision theory is intelligibility. He points out that the more we allow that the outcomes of a decision-maker's various choices are different from each other, the less intelligible the decision-maker becomes. Velleman adds that you "violate the spirit of the axioms when you redescribe your existing options as having nothing in common with one another, even if you simultaneously invent a larger range of choices for them to have something in common with" because "making sense of your preferences requires you to see them as manifesting some constant, underlying posture toward the options."[38] If decision theory does not rule out that an Elvis stamp might have a different value in every context in which it appears, then there is no pressure from prescriptive decision theory to take a unified stance on the stamp's value. And things seem even worse for the interpretive theorist, since facts he learns about the agent in one context will tell him nothing about the agent in other contexts.

These problems seem bad to me. But let us grant that they are not enough to dissuade the EU theorist. He may be happy to take on board the idea that preferences are extremely complex, and allow decision theory to be correspondingly complex even if

---

[37] We might add additional constraints on how preferences over redescribed acts (the preferences to which decision theory applies) are related to preferences over "simpler" outcomes. For example, if the value of a "total" outcome is decomposable into an outcome part and a value-of-risk part, as Weirich (1986) suggests, then the agent's preferences about the Elvis stamp in these two deals will be constrained.

[38] Velleman (2000, p. 163).

the cost is making values extremely context sensitive. However, there is a final and more serious problem for global individuation. We have so far been talking loosely as if the only global property that Jeff cares about is a gamble's minimum. In fact, if some agents really are REU maximizers, as I have proposed, then this is too simplistic. Indeed, the agent will care about many global features of gambles. More precisely, there will be many global features that will make the agent's preferences different from those of the standard EU maximizer, and the EU theorist will have to take all of these into account when individuating outcomes. And I claim that as a result, redescriptions of outcomes will either be too coarse-grained to allow REU maximizers to be interpreted as EU maximizers or else so fine-grained that they allow them to be interpreted in *too many* ways. To explain this point, let me first give a more precise account of what the EU theorist needs the individuation strategy to accomplish.

Let us assume we have an agent who maximizes REU relative to a set $\mathcal{A}$ of acts on an outcome set $\mathcal{X}$. The EU theorist seeks to transform the outcome set into a new set of outcomes such that the agent's transformed preferences over the set of new acts on the new outcomes can be interpreted as maximizing expected utility. So, given $\mathcal{X}$ and $\mathcal{A}$, the theorist produces a set $\mathcal{Y}$ of "relabeled" outcomes. This gives rise to an act space $\mathcal{A}''$, the set of all finite-valued functions from $\mathcal{X}$ to $\mathcal{Y}$. The theorist also produces a "relabeling" function σ from $\mathcal{X} \times \mathcal{A}$ to $\mathcal{Y}$ such that each "old" gamble $f = \{E_1, x_1; \ldots E_n, x_n\}$ has a "new" counterpart $f^* = \{E_1, \sigma(x_1, f); \ldots E_n, \sigma(x_n, f)\}$. For example, {HEADS, chocolate; TAILS, strawberry} may be relabeled as {HEADS, chocolate as part of a gamble one of whose outcomes is strawberry; TAILS, strawberry as part of a gamble one of whose outcomes is strawberry}; or as {HEADS, chocolate when chocolate is the worst outcome; TAILS, strawberry when strawberry is the best outcome}; or even as {HEADS, chocolate as part of the {chocolate, HEADS; strawberry, TAILS} gamble; TAILS, strawberry as part . . . }. Next, the theorist interprets the agent as preferring f^* to g^* just in case he prefers f to g. The "counterpart space" $\mathcal{A}^*$ of acts in the agent's original preference ordering is $\mathcal{A}^* = \{f^* \in \mathcal{A}'' \mid (\exists f \in \mathcal{A} \mid f = \{E_1, x_1; \ldots E_n, x_n\}$ & $f^* = \{E_1, \sigma(x_1, f); \ldots E_n, \sigma(x_n, f)\}\}$. $\mathcal{A}^*$ will be a proper subset of $\mathcal{A}''$. There will be some new acts not in $\mathcal{A}^*$: in our example above, one such act is {HEADS, chocolate as part of a gamble one of whose outcomes is strawberry; TAILS, chocolate as part of a gamble one of whose outcomes is strawberry}. These will be in $\mathcal{A}'' \backslash \mathcal{A}^*$, the set of non-practical acts, and the theorist can determine the agent's preferences involving acts in $\mathcal{A}'' \backslash \mathcal{A}^*$ in any way he wishes.[39] The theorist then shows that there

---

[39] There are two things worth noting in this setup. First, I am allowing that the theorist can determine all of the agent's preferences involving the newly invented gambles. Some might object to this assumption on the grounds that the agent does have access to some of his non-practical preferences. But this objection cannot help the EU theorist, since it only adds more constraints on interpretation, constraints that, if an agent really is an REU maximizer, will not be friendly to interpreting the agent as an EU maximizer. The second thing worth noting is that I am only considering individuations on the basis of the properties of an act itself. I am not considering individuation on the basis of the alternative choices offered, as in the apple/orange example. But I am not clear how individuation on the basis of alternatives could help, since the issue here is whether EU theory can account for an aggregation method that allows the value of a gamble to depend on its global properties, not on the alternatives under consideration.

is some probability function of events p* and some utility function of new outcomes u* such that REU(f) ≥ REU(g) if and only if EU(f*) ≥ EU(g*): that is, if and only if $\sum_x p^*(f^{-1}(x))u^*(\sigma(x,f)) \geq \sum_x p^*(g^{-1}(x))u^*(\sigma(x,g))$.

The interesting question is when two of the relabeled outcomes count as the same as each other: that is, when $\sigma(x, f) = \sigma(x, g)$. On what we might call the maximally fine-grained individuation, new outcomes never count as the same if they are part of different (old) gambles: $\sigma(x, f) = \sigma(x, g)$ iff f = g. On this individuation, it is easy to see that an REU maximizer can count as an EU maximizer: for example, we can set $u^*(\sigma(x, f)) = REU(f)$ and $p^*(E) = p(E)$.[40] We can then calculate the EU of the non-practical acts, and set the agent's non-practical preferences so that he prefers the act with the higher EU. But this individuation has two problems.

The first problem is that the agent will be representable as following many other decision rules. For example, we can represent the agent as a maximinimizer or a maximaximizer using $u^*(\sigma(x, f)) = REU(f)$. Indeed, we can represent the agent as following nearly any aggregation rule we can think of. Since each new outcome appears in only one old act (that is, only one act in $\mathcal{A}^*$), we have a lot of freedom in setting the utility function of outcomes. And so we can simply put the new acts in the order the agent prefers them, assign cardinal values to the acts in this order, pick the rule we want to read him as using to get from outcomes to acts, and assign values to outcomes such that they yield the values of the acts via the rule. Given this fact, the claim that the agent is an expected utility maximizer is hollow: she is no more an expected utility maximizer than an anything-else maximizer. The other two problems are that the agent can be represented as an EU maximizer relative to many very different utility functions, and relative to *any* probability function. To see the former, note that each new outcome appears in only one constraint equation if we set EU(f*) = REU(f). To see the latter, note that relative to u^* defined earlier and any probability function q, EU(f*) = $\sum_x q(f^{-1}(x))u^*(\sigma(x,f)) = \sum_x q(f^{-1}(x))[REU(f)] = REU(f)$. We might call these the problems of rule proliferation, desire proliferation, and belief proliferation.[41]

The EU theorist should not be satisfied with the maximal individuation anyway. After all, if he knows that an individual is an REU maximizer (relative to the old set of acts), then he is going to think that there are some connections between outcomes in various acts, since only particular global features make a difference to the value of an act for an REU maximizer. Sometimes (old) outcomes contribute the same value to different (old) acts, and the EU maximizer is going to want to capture this feature of the REU maximizer's preferences. Indeed, if he grants that an agent is an REU maximizer, then he knows precisely what the connections between the same outcome in different acts are: outcomes contribute the same value to acts that are comonotonic.

---

[40] $EU(f^*) = \sum_x p^*(f^{-1}(x))u^*(\sigma(x,f)) = \sum_x p^*(f^{-1}(x))REU(f) = REU(f)$

[41] Zynda (2000) raises the following problem: for a given set of preferences, there are many pairs of "value" and "belief" functions that represent the preferences, each relative to a particular decision rule, if the belief functions are not assumed ahead of time to be probability functions. This is different from the problems I note here, which are problems even under the assumption that beliefs are represented by a probability function.

So the thought is that the EU theorist should be able to impose some constraints, to avoid the proliferation problems but still capture the preferences of REU maximizers, by holding that new outcomes are the same when they occupy the same structural position in comonotonic old acts: $\sigma(x, f) = \sigma(x, g)$ if $f^{-1}(x) = g^{-1}(x)$ and f and g are comonotonic.[42] Call this the "comonotonic individuation." Recall that in REU theory, the value that each outcome contributes to REU(f)—the term associated with an outcome x in the REU equation—is $\pi_{\Phi(j)} \cdot u(x)$, where Φ is a rank-ordering permutation that orders the events in f from best to worst, $E_{\Phi(j)} = f^{-1}(x)$, and $\pi_{\Phi(j)} = r(p(E_{\Phi(1)} \cup \ldots \cup E_{\Phi(j)})) - r(p(E_{\Phi(1)} \cup \ldots \cup E_{\Phi(j-1)}))$. By contrast, the value that each new outcome will contribute to EU(f^*)—the term associated with an outcome $\sigma(x, f)$ in the EU equation—will be $p^*(E)u^*(\sigma(x, f))$, where $E = f^{-1}(x)$. Given this, it seems that the EU theorist can define u^* and p^* so that each new outcome $\sigma(x, f)$ makes the same contribution to EU(f^*) that x makes to REU(f):[43]

$$p^*(E) = p(E)$$

$$u^*(\sigma(x, f)) = \pi_{\Phi(j)} \cdot u(x)/p(E_{\Phi(j)}),$$

where Φ is a rank-ordering permutation that orders the events in f from best to worst,

$$E_{\Phi(j)} = f^{-1}(x),$$

and

$$\pi_{\Phi(j)} = r(p(E_{\Phi(1)} \cup \ldots \cup E_{\Phi(j)})) - r(p(E_{\Phi(1)} \cup \ldots \cup E_{\Phi(j-1)})).$$

With this definition in place, we can show that the EU of a new act is equivalent to the REU of an old act, and therefore that EU(f^*) $\geq$ EU(g^*) iff REU(f) $\geq$ REU(g).[44]

---

[42] This need not be a necessary condition. For example, we might want the stronger condition that $\sigma(x, f) = \sigma(x, g)$ if $f^{-1}(x) \subseteq g^{-1}(x)$ & f and g are comonotonic. Alternatively, we might want the stronger condition that $\sigma(x, f) = \sigma(x, g)$ if f and g are "probability comonotonic;" that is, if there is some gamble h with the same probability distribution of outcomes (according to p) as g such that f and h are comonotonic and $f^{-1}(x) = h^{-1}(x)$. The condition above is only a necessary condition for equivalence, and my point will be that even it is too strong. Also note that throughout this discussion, "comonotonic" means comonotonic with respect to the old acts.

[43] This possibility was suggested by Jim Joyce (personal correspondence). I preserve the notation of the hardback edition, but note that a confusion might arise, since it might appear from the definition of $\pi_{\Phi(j)}$ that $\pi_{\Phi(j)}$ is a function of $\Phi(j)$ (or more generally that π_x is a function of x, so that if x = y then $\pi_x = \pi_y$). $\pi_{\Phi(j)}$ is in fact a function of both Φ and j, so it would be clearer to write $\pi(\Phi, j)$ or $\pi_\Phi(j)$ instead of $\pi_{\Phi(j)}$.

[44] EU(f^*) $= \sum_j p^*(f^{-1}(x_j))u^*(\sigma(x_j, f))$
    $= \sum_j p^*(E_{\Phi(j)})u^*(\sigma(f(E_{\Phi(j)}), f))$
    $= \sum_j p(E_{\Phi(j)})(\pi_{\Phi(j)} \cdot u(f(E_{\Phi(j)})))/p(E_{\Phi(j)})$
    $= \sum_j \pi_{\Phi(j)} \cdot u(f(E_{\Phi(j)}))$
    $=$ REU(f).

For example, if we are talking about gambles over two events, {HEADS, TAILS}, and if f = {HEADS, $0; TAILS, $50}, then $E_1 =$ TAILS, $E_2 =$ HEADS, $\sigma($0, f)$ represents "$0 and receiving the worst outcome," and $\sigma($50, f)$ represents "$50 and receiving the best outcome." Now assume the agent assigns u($0) = 2, u($50) = 8, p(E_1) = p(E_2) = 0.5, r(0.5) = 0.25. Then:
    u*($\sigma($50, f)) = (0.25)(8)/(0.5) = 4$
    u*($\sigma($0, f)) = (0.75)(2)/(0.5) = 3$
    EU(f^*) = (0.5)(4) + (0.5)(3) = 3.5
    REU(f) = 2 + (0.25)(6) = 3.5

Furthermore, we will not expect to run into the problem of rule proliferation, since there will be many constraints on the values of outcomes, because each outcome will appear in many acts.

Although this appears at first to represent the agent as an EU maximizer, u^* turns out not to be well-defined, and for an interesting reason.[45] The problem is that some acts can be ordered by more than one permutation, if two events yield outcomes of the same utility. If $u(f(E_i)) = u(f(E_j))$, then there will be two rank-ordering permutations Φ and Ψ that are identical except that $\Phi(k) = i$ and $\Phi(k+1) = j$, while $\Psi(k) = j$ and $\Psi(k+1) = i$. And so we will have (assuming $E_i = f^{-1}(x)$):

$$u^*(\sigma(x, f)) = \pi_{\Phi(k)} \cdot u(x)/p(E_i)$$
$$u^*(\sigma(x, f)) = \pi_{\Psi(k+1)} \cdot u(x)/p(E_i)$$

There is no guarantee that these two expressions are equivalent. In particular, they will be different for the risk-avoidant agent with strictly convex r.[46]

Of course, the u^* and p^* assignments mentioned above are not the only possible way for the EU theorist to assign values on the comonotonic individuation. But the problem generalizes. We tried to define u^* and p^* so that the utility* contribution that $\sigma(x, f)$ makes to $EU(f^*)$ is the same as the utility contribution that x makes to $EU(f)$. As it turns out, though, "the utility contribution that x makes to the risk-weighted expected utility of the act it is embedded in" is not well-defined when there are multiple outcomes with the same utility value. For example, consider the act $g = \{E_1, \text{chocolate}; E_2, \text{vanilla}\}$, where $E_1 = \bar{E}_2$, and where the agent is indifferent between chocolate and vanilla; for example, $u(\text{chocolate}) = u(\text{vanilla}) = 2$. There are two ways of calculating $REU(g)$, since $\Phi = \{(1, 1), (2, 2)\}$ and $\Psi = \{(1, 2), (2, 1)\}$ both order the outcomes from best to worst. Using Φ, we can calculate $REU(g) = r(p(E_1))u(\text{chocolate}) + (1 - r(p(E_1))u(\text{vanilla}) = 2$. And using Ψ, we can calculate $REU(g) = r(p(E_2))u(\text{vanilla}) + (1 - r(p(E_2))u(\text{chocolate}) = 2$. In the first calculation, "chocolate" contributes a utility value of $r(p(E_1))(2)$, and in the second, a utility value of $(1 - r(p(E_2)))(2)$. Thus, there is no such thing as a utility value a particular (old) outcome contributes to an act, because there are different ways of conceiving of the value an outcome contributes, based on conceiving of the act as belonging to different comoncones.

---

[45] There will be an additional complication for the EU theorist, because u is just one member of a family of utility functions that represents the agent, and the resulting u^*'s (defined for each u in this family) will not be positive affine transformations of each other. For each x, $u(x)$ will be multiplied by some different factor, so utility functions that are constant multiples of each other will result in u^*'s that are constant multiples of each other, but utility functions that are shifted by a constant will not be positive affine transformations of each other. In any case, there is a more basic problem with this definition of u^*, so I will set this problem aside.

[46] The two equations above yield:

$$r(p(E_{\Phi(1)} \cup \ldots \cup E_{\Phi(k)})) - r(p(E_{\Phi(1)} \cup \ldots \cup E_{\Phi(k-1)})) = r(p(E_{\Psi(1)} \cup \ldots \cup E_{\Psi(k+1)})) - r(p(E_{\Psi(1)} \cup \ldots \cup E_{\Psi(k)})).$$

If we let B stand for $(E_{\Phi(1)} \cup \ldots \cup E_{\Phi(k-1)})$, this equation holds only when $r(p(B \cup E_i)) - r(p(B)) = r(p(B \cup E_j \cup E_i) - r(p(B \cup E_j))$. There is no guarantee this will hold in general, and it definitively does not hold when r is strictly convex.

Here is another way to think about the problem. When the outcomes of a given utility are all grouped together (because there is only one distinct outcome with that utility, say), then they get the same π coefficient in the REU equation. Call this coefficient π_c. When the outcomes of a given utility are split into two groups, one of which is thought of structurally as higher than the other, then outcomes in the two groups get different π coefficients, whose weighted average is equal to π_c. And when the other group of outcomes is thought of as structurally higher, then they again get different π coefficients— different both from each other and from the coefficients when considering the outcomes under the first structuring—whose weighted average is again equal to π_c. REU needs to be evaluable, and equivalent, relative to each of these structurings, because many acts can appear in more than one comoncone.

That many acts can be conceived as belonging to multiple comoncones poses no problem for calculating the *REU* of an act in a well-defined way: the total value of the act under either ordering is the same, since the other outcomes of the same utility make up the difference. In the example above, whatever value "chocolate" contributes, "vanilla" contributes the remaining value to the total: it contributes $(1 - r(p(E_1)))(2)$ or $r(p(E_2))(2)$, respectively. The quantity that is well-defined is the total contribution that *all outcomes of a particular utility value* make to the REU of an act. So the EU theorist might take this into account in his individuation. He might assign utility* values such that if a utility* value is assigned to some outcome, then utility* values must be assigned to the other outcomes of the same utility value in a way that makes the total utility* contribution of these outcomes to the EU equation equivalent to the total utility contribution of these outcomes to the REU equation. (This is a weaker condition than the condition that each individual outcome must make the equivalent value contribution.) In general, if x and y are both possible outcomes of f, and if $u(x) = u(y) = c$ for some real number c and no other outcomes have utility value c, then the EU theorist must assign utility* such that $p^*(f^{-1}(x))u^*(\sigma(x, f)) + p^*(f^{-1}(y))u^*(\sigma(y, f)) = (\pi_{\Phi(k)} + \pi_{\Phi(k+1)})u(x)$ for some rank-ordering permutation Φ such that $E_{\Phi(k)} = f^{-1}(x)$ and $E_{\Phi(k+1)} = f^{-1}(y)$.

However, this will be problematic when we consider that two acts can each be comonotonic with a third act without being comonotonic with each other. For assume we have two outcomes x and y such that $u(x) = u(y) = c \neq 0$,[47] and let f, g, and h be such that: x and y are outcomes of f but f has no other outcomes of utility c; f is comonotonic with g under Φ; $f^{-1}(x) = g^{-1}(x) = E_1$; g has no other outcomes of utility c besides x; f is comonotonic with h under Ψ; $f^{-1}(y) = h^{-1}(y) = E_2$; h has no other outcomes of utility c besides y; and g and h are not comonotonic with each other because $g(E_1) < g(E_2)$ but $h(E_1) > h(E_2)$. To simplify the proof, we will also assume that Φ and Ψ agree on events in $\neg(E_1 \cup E_2)$, so $\Phi(1) = \Psi(2)$ and $\Phi(2) = \Psi(1)$ (Table 4.7).

Then, on the comonotonic individuation, it must be that $\sigma(x, f) = \sigma(x, g)$ and $\sigma(y, f) = \sigma(y, h)$, by definition of the comonotonic individuation. Furthermore, using

---

[47] Recall from fn. 45 that the choice of scale matters, which is why we need a particular assumption about a utility value rather than a utility difference ratio.

Table 4.7. A problem for the comonotonic individuation.

	...	E_1	E_2	...
f	...	x	y	...
g	...	x	z (> x)	...
h	...	w (> y)	y	...

the previous proposal, the value contribution of each set of outcomes with utility c to the value of each act will be fixed by the value contribution this set of outcomes has to the REU of the act. So we will have:

$p^*(E_1)u^*(\sigma(x, f)) = \pi_{\Phi(1)}(c)$ (from the contribution x makes to g)
$p^*(E_2)u^*(\sigma(y, f)) = \pi_{\Psi(2)}(c)$ (from the contribution y makes to h)
$p^*(E_1)u^*(\sigma(x, f)) + p^*(E_2)u^*(\sigma(y, f)) = (\pi_{\Phi(1)} + \pi_{\Phi(2)})(c)$ (from the contribution $\{x, y\}$ makes to f)

These hold jointly only when $\pi_{\Phi(1)} + \pi_{\Psi(2)} = \pi_{\Phi(1)} + \pi_{\Phi(2)}$—that is, when $\pi_{\Psi(2)} = \pi_{\Phi(2)}$—but this will not in general be true: we know that $\Phi(1) = \Psi(2)$ and so $\pi_{\Psi(2)} = \pi_{\Phi(1)}$, but of course $\Phi(1) \neq \Phi(2)$, and so it can be the case that $\pi_{\Phi(2)} \neq \pi_{\Phi(1)}$, and thus that $\pi_{\Psi(2)} \neq \pi_{\Phi(2)}$.

Could we define u^* and p^* so that the utility* contributions of a group of outcomes to EU(f) need not always be the utility contribution of these outcomes to REU(f*)? I do not have a general proof that we cannot, but I think we have good reasons to doubt that we will be able to do this. Doing this requires assigning utility* in a way that is not connected to the utility contributions of outcomes, while simultaneously respecting the agent's preferences and the connections between outcomes in comonotonic acts. It is a precarious matter whether there will be enough outcomes unconstrained by preferences so that the EU theorist has freedom to assign value to them, and when we add that the EU theorist only succeeds if he can do this for *all* sets of REU preferences, the task seems hopeless. In addition, if the utility* value assignment is so unconnected to the role the outcomes play in acts for the REU-maximizer, then it will not seem to genuinely illuminate the agent's preferences as a case of EU maximization: how his values determine his preferences will be unclear. Nevertheless, I concede that this is an avenue of exploration technically still open to the EU theorist who wants to use the comonotonic individuation.

The problem with setting $\sigma(x, f) = \sigma(x, g)$ whenever f and g are comonotonic and x is on the same event is that comonotonicity is not transitive—g and h might each be comonotonic with f without being comonotonic with each other—and so the same outcome will appear in non-comonotonic acts. And this will mean we cannot always consistently assign value to outcomes by thinking about the contribution that an outcome makes to REU when considered as part of a particular comoncone. So the maximal individuation runs into the proliferation problem, and the comonotonic individuation cannot capture the preferences of REU maximizers at all because this individuation leads to contradiction. And there seems to be no non-*ad hoc* option between the maximal individuation and the comonotonic individuation that will not face the proliferation problem.

Let me close this discussion by considering how bad the proliferation problem is for the constructivist EU theorist and the non-constructivist realist EU theorist, in turn. Rule proliferation is particularly problematic for the constructivist EU theorist because she does not think there are independent facts about utility anyway. So for her the upshot of rule proliferation is that representing the agent using the EU equation and whatever utility function(s) represent the agent's preferences has nothing to formally recommend it over representing the agent using a number of other equations and their corresponding utility function(s). A similar point holds for desire proliferation. The non-constructivist realist EU theorist has a stronger leg to stand on: she can claim that there is a privileged utility function (of new outcomes) and that it is a function relative to which the agent is an EU maximizer, rather than a maximizer of some other quantity. But the realist should be more skeptical of global individuation from the start: it is implausible that the real entities an agent has preferences over are the incredibly complex ones the theorist has to postulate.

What about belief proliferation for the realist and the constructivist about credence? (I note that one can be a constructivist about utility without being a constructivist about credence, and *vice versa*.) Again, belief proliferation is particularly problematic for the constructivist about credence, since no single credence function will formally recommend itself over others. And again, it is less of a problem for the realist about credence since she can say that one of the probability functions represents the agent's actual beliefs. However, unless the agent is able to introspect his precise credences, a serious epistemic problem arises: many probability functions are compatible with each set of preferences, so we will not be able to determine the agent's actual beliefs from his preferences.

Global individuation was initially promising because one might have thought that the question about whether to incorporate global properties into the aggregation method or instead incorporate them into the description of the outcomes is a question of choosing between formalisms with identical upshots. But we have seen that REU theory is not merely a notational variant or a special case of EU theory: incorporating the global properties that the globally sensitive agent cares about into the outcomes cannot rescue EU theory without causing a proliferation problem.

4.5 The Failure of the Individuation Strategy

A decision theorist need not accept counterexamples to her theory at face value: there may be more to the outcomes than is stated in the initial choice problem. We can often specify outcomes more finely, so that the preferences in a purported counterexample no longer violate the theory. However, individuation of outcomes is licensed only under certain circumstances. On some plausible ways of restricting these circumstances, while individuation works to dismiss certain purported counterexamples to EU theory, it does not work against them all: in particular, it is not enough to allow the EU theorist to accommodate the preferences in the risk-related examples.

I considered two ways one might individuate outcomes. The first involved individuating locally: individuating on the basis of features of an outcome that still matter to an agent once a gamble has been resolved. Local individuation successfully accommodated the apple/orange example and (perhaps more arguably) Diamond's example. Local individuation is successful insofar as the properties that are used to individuate are properties that have value (or disvalue) in themselves: the agent in the apple/orange example cares about what piece of fruit his dining companion gets, and we care not just about who gets a car but about whether each person is treated fairly.

Local individuation, however, cannot accommodate risk-avoidance, because risk-avoidant preferences do not actually stem from attaching additional value or disvalue to an outcome when it is part of a gamble with different global properties. Unlike in the other examples, after the gamble has been resolved, and a risk-avoidant agent is left with his prize, he need not care which gamble it resulted from, or that he might have received something else. His preferences stem from the fact that identical outcomes make different value contributions to different gambles—value contributions that depend on where in the structure of the gamble the outcome falls. Properties that contribute to a gamble's riskiness—a low minimum, for example—have only *instrumental* value or disvalue: they are important to an agent insofar as they play a role in the agent's obtaining the things he wants (the things that are non-instrumentally valuable), but they contribute no value once the gamble has been resolved.

The second way of individuating outcomes involved individuating globally: individuating on the basis of any features of a gamble that the agent cares about, irrespective of whether these features appear to be properly features of the outcomes themselves. There were three problems with this approach. The first was that global individuation forces the theorist to differentiate outcomes that we might have wanted to count as equivalent, and that seem equivalent in that agents will profess to have no preference between them. The second problem was that global individuation breaks the connection between what an agent chooses in one decision scenario and what he will or should choose in other, very similar scenarios: this robs decision theory of some of its interpretive and prescriptive power. Finally, global individuation runs into the proliferation problems: if enough is left open to allow EU theory to capture the preferences of (apparent) REU maximizers, this also allows that these preferences can be captured by any probability function under EU maximization, by many different utility functions under EU maximization, and by many different decision rules.

Decision theorists started with the idea that there are two components in interpreting an agent or in evaluating his rationality: his beliefs and his desires, or his beliefs and his local reasons. I argued in the first three chapters that there is an additional component: his norm for translating these into preferences over acts whose outcomes are not certain, or his method for weighing local considerations. Earlier-discussed attempts to account for this third component argued that it is reducible to desire or the role of local considerations; for example, by postulating that money has diminishing marginal utility. The individuation strategy follows the observation that there is another kind of "moving piece" in interpretation: how the agent conceives of the outcomes presented to him. And the attempt in this chapter to account for globally sensitive preferences argued that they are reducible to how the agent conceives of the outcomes. But this did not succeed: we saw again that all four components are independent and crucial parts of instrumental rationality.

One lesson of this chapter is that how the agent conceives of outcomes is not something that can be fixed ahead of time by the theory: we do not know what the agent cares about until we consult him. And, indeed, individuating outcomes to explain, interpret, and justify an agent's preferences is sometimes licensed: it is the right thing to say about the apple/orange case, for example. But another lesson is that the theorist is not always free to individuate the outcomes as finely as she wishes. If individuation is to accommodate the preferences in question without causing problems for the theory, it must be based on a feature of an outcome that the agent cares about for not—purely—instrumental reasons.

What I have shown in the first four chapters of this book is that there are patterns of preference that are pervasive; that are systematically explainable as attempts by agents with consistent ends to choose the means to their ends; and that expected utility theory cannot accommodate. However, if they are not in the end *rational* preferences, then *normative* decision theory need not accommodate them anyway. In order to argue that we must replace EU theory with REU theory as our theory of instrumental rationality, I must argue that the preferences of REU maximizers are in fact rational. It is to this task that the remainder of the book is devoted.

5

Consistency

5.1 Decision-Theoretic Rationality

In the previous chapter I discussed how rationality plays a role in both prescriptive and interpretive decision theory: rationality is a guiding assumption in interpretive decision theory, and a standard of evaluation in prescriptive decision theory. The goal of Chapters 5, 6, and 7 is to show that global sensitivity is rationally permissible. Rational agents maximize risk-weighted expected utility, and they need not confine themselves to a linear risk function: rational agents may, but need not, maximize expected utility. But first I need to say more about which of the many concepts of rationality decision theorists take themselves to be working with. The sense of rationality that decision theory analyzes is usually identified in one of two ways: as *instrumental rationality* or as *consistency*.

To understand the idea of decision theory as elucidating instrumental rationality, it is helpful to understand that decision theorists often take themselves to be formalizing a view about motivation that is generally attributed to Hume. (I take no view about how well what is nowadays called the "Humean" theory of motivation maps onto Hume's original picture.[1]) Recall that the basic elements on which decision theory proposes constraints are preferences over acts, and notice that according to folk psychology such preferences involve both desires about outcomes and beliefs about what the world is like. On the Humean view, desires are not subject to rational scrutiny: as Hume famously said, it is not irrational to prefer the destruction of the whole world to the scratching of one's little finger.[2] However, the Humean thinks there are two failings for which we can criticize an individual: we can criticize her for having irrational beliefs, and we can criticize her for choosing "means insufficient for her ends"—for choosing acts that from her own point of view will not result in the things she desires.

---

[1] For a clear example of the Humean view outside of decision theory, see Smith (1987). Similarly, Hampton (1995) outlines what she calls the "instrumental theory of reason," which is the theory to which modern-day "Humeans" subscribe, but she argues that this theory is not in fact in the spirit of Hume's position. She takes the instrumental theory to include three theses: "(1) An action is rational to the extent that an agent believes (reasonably) that it furthers the attainment of an end; and (2) [Instrumental] reasoning involves the determination of means to achieve ends, in a way described by the theory; and (3) These ends are in no way fixed by reason operating non-instrumentally; i.e. what makes them our ends is something other than reason." (57)

[2] Hume (1739/1978, p. 416, Book 2, Part 3, Section 3).

This picture recognizes three elements that could be subject to scrutiny: desires or preferences about outcomes, beliefs about the world, and preferences over acts in light of these. The Humean view appears to be that whereas desires about outcomes are not subject to rational scrutiny, the other components are: one's beliefs must be rational, as must one's acts—the means one chooses—in light of what one believes and desires. The stance of modern decision theory is close to this, but there are two complications. The first is that although there are no substantive constraints on preferences over outcomes, sets of preferences are subject to constraints. Decision-theoretic rationality does allow one to prefer the destruction of the world to the scratching of one's little finger, but it does not allow one to also simultaneously prefer the scratching of one's little finger to the destruction of the world. Does this mean that decision theory, contra the Humean view, does subject desires to rational scrutiny? One might argue that the formal consistency which decision theory requires for outcome-preferences is not a necessary condition for desires to count as rational so much as a necessary condition for an individual to count as having a clear desire at all, though it is more difficult to make this case when we consider the more complex requirements imposed on outcome-preferences, such as transitivity. I will not take up the question further.

The second complication concerns the constraints on beliefs. The Humean picture allows that beliefs can be criticized as irrational. Regardless of what the Humean means by this, it is important to note that in decision theory, beliefs can be criticized as irrational only if they are inconsistent. The only constraint that beliefs are subject to on decision theory is that an agent must have coherent degrees of belief: her degrees of belief must conform to the probability calculus.[3] It is a bit odd to think of this as a requirement of instrumental rationality: that one should have coherent credences is more naturally a requirement of epistemic rationality. A similar point holds, perhaps, in the case of desires. It is not clear that having consistent desires is properly part of instrumental rationality, since instrumental rationality is concerned with taking the means to one's ends, not with the ends themselves. However, we might think of having coherent credences and desires as necessary preconditions to being able to take the means one believes will lead to one's ends: if credences or desires are incoherent, one will get conflicting recommendations about which means to take to one's ends.

To summarize, decision-theoretic rationality appears to be broadly consonant with the Humean idea that "ultimate" desires do not answer to beliefs and are not subject to criticism on the basis of their substance, although decision-theoretic rationality imposes the additional constraint that these desires must be consistent with each other. It also appears to be broadly consonant with the idea that beliefs are subject to criticism; however, the only criticism it subjects them to is inconsistency. Finally, one can

---

[3] At least on the decision theories that are the subject of this book. Some authors have considered whether rational agents might instead have "non-sharp" or "imprecise" credences (see Levi (1974), Gärdenfors and Sahlin (1982), White (2009), Elga (2010), Joyce (2010)). The constraints imposed by the alternative proposals are still consistency constraints rather than substantive constraints.

run afoul of decision-theoretic rationality by choosing acts that do not further one's ends, given what one believes and desires. I should note that talk of "taking" and "choosing" the means to one's ends makes it appear as if the main concern of decision theory is actions over which the agent has control. However, the main concern of decision theory is in fact preferences—preferences over a particular type of entity. While this entity is called an "act," and can be an action of the agent, it need not be: it could be an action of another individual ("my husband makes me an omelette"), or a way the world could be ("gas prices increase"), as long as these descriptions specify what ultimate outcome the individual gets in each state of the world.

What is it to prefer an act that from one's own point of view will not result in what one desires? When an individual knows exactly what the world is like—when she is making a choice under *certainty*—this criticism applies when an individual prefers x to y and believes that act f will bring about x and act g will bring about y, but prefers g instead of f. In the situations that are the concern of this book—namely, decisions in which the agent is unsure about what the world is like—it is less clear what this criticism amounts to. Recall the discussion in Section 1.3. Preferences about acts involve both desires about outcomes and beliefs about the outcomes that will result from various acts. Since it is beyond an individual's power to simply pick the act that will lead to the most preferred outcome when choosing under risk, preferences over acts also involve a method (not necessarily explicit) for ranking acts given the beliefs and desires involved. Since decision-making under risk necessarily involves such a method, it will be a substantial question what choosing means insufficient to one's ends, in light of what one believes and desires, amounts to. Indeed, this question will occupy much of this and the next two chapters.

The Savage framework fits well with the above picture of action. Recall from Chapter 3 that the framework assumes a distinction between acts and outcomes, and that outcomes are basic in the sense that one's preferences for them do not depend on any further facts about how the world might turn out. Furthermore, one's preference for one act rather than another is solely a matter of which outcomes result from that act in each possible state. So preferences over acts are instrumental in the sense that they are based on which basic outcomes they lead to in what circumstances, and on the value of these outcomes or the reasons in favor of them. As mentioned, we might support the distinction between acts that are only instrumentally valuable and outcomes that are valuable in themselves as follows. While many choices can be supported by pointing out that they are means to some further end, this process of giving reasons cannot continue indefinitely: it cannot be means "all the way down." One might invest in a particular company in order to get more money, and one might want more money in order to buy a house, and one might want a house in order to keep one's family warm at night, and so forth, but in the end we will have to come either to some ultimate justification or to a desire in the Humean sense that cannot and need not admit of further explanation.

The distinction between the "final" value of an outcome and the "instrumental" value of an act, therefore, is well-grounded. An outcome's final value is the extent to which one values it in itself, and an act's instrumental value is its value as a means of obtaining the things that are of final value. Decision theory provides a way to evaluate, for a particular agent, whether the utility value of outcomes can be represented by a cardinal structure, whether degrees of belief are coherent, and whether the agent's assessment of instrumental value is appropriate. If we *assume* that degrees of belief ought to be coherent and that outcome values ought to be representable cardinally (because, for example, utility corresponds to strength of desires, which is cardinal), then the general question of how the instrumental value of an act should be related to the final values of its possible outcomes, given a set of credences, will be answered in decision theory with a rule about what quantity ought to be maximized. However, the general question may also be answered without making these assumptions about the structure of utility and degrees of belief from the outset. One could instead assume that the agent has non-instrumental reasons for outcome-preferences and, on the basis of these, also has instrumental reasons for act-preferences. One could then take the general question to be about what rules govern the relationship between these kinds of preferences. The general question is then a question about which axioms preferences ought to obey.

In addition to being described as an account of instrumental rationality, decision theory is also sometimes described as an account of *consistency*. Discovering the requirements of consistency is not unrelated to discovering the requirements of instrumental rationality, but for those who emphasize consistency rather than instrumental rationality, the basic entity under consideration is a single type of entity: preferences over acts. Instrumental rationality is concerned with three types of entity —desires, beliefs, and preferences over acts—and their interrelationships. But when one is concerned with decision theory as a theory of consistency, one is generally concerned with the relationship that act-preferences bear to each other. If to have rational preferences is to have consistent preferences, then this is to say, again, that it is not the content of preferences that renders them irrational, but rather their logical form. No act-preference is ruled out on its own, but rather certain patterns of preference are ruled out.[4] On this picture, decision theory provides a way to evaluate whether an agent meets the constraints of consistency in her act-preferences. Since the relationship among preferences is central, the general question of whether an agent is consistent will be answered in decision theory by citing a set of axioms which these preferences must obey.

The question of which decision theory is correct can therefore be thought of in one of two ways: as the question of which maximization norm governs the way the value of acts relates to the value of their possible outcomes or as the question of which axiom norm governs the relationship of preferences to each other. Representation theorems

---

[4] I should note that there is some dissent about whether, and in what sense, it is possible for decision theory to impose constraints on preferences that are merely consistency constraints. For example, Broome (1993) thinks that the constraint we adopt on individuation must be substantive (we examined his constraint in the previous chapter).

show us that an answer to either question has a mathematical equivalent in an answer to the other, so one cannot be committed to an answer to one without being committed to an answer to the other. However, the questions and their answers are conceptually distinct, and which question is prior depends on how one is thinking about decision-theoretic rationality. If one thinks of decision-theoretic rationality as instrumental rationality, one might consider either question to be prior, depending on how one views the utility function. If one thinks of decision-theoretic rationality as consistency, one will consider the question about the axiom norm to be prior.

What is the relationship between instrumental rationality and consistency? There are several possible answers. One might hold that the importance of consistency in act-preferences is that it reduces to consistency in the three kinds of entity with which instrumental rationality is concerned.[5] Alternatively, one might think that instrumental rationality requires consistency in act-preferences, because one cannot act on inconsistent preferences, and therefore inconsistent preferences prevent one from taking the means to one's ends. Finally, one might think that consistency and instrumental rationality are about two different subjects—instrumental rationality is about the relationship of preferences to ends and consistency in act-preferences is about the relationship of preferences to each other—and they are related only in that they are both important to decision theory.[6] My sense is that the two notions are so tied together in arguments within decision theory that they cannot be separated cleanly. Luckily, I do not need to take a stand on whether instrumental rationality and consistency are in the end equivalent, or, if they are not, whether decision theory is a theory of instrumental rationality or of consistency or of their conjunction. This is, first, because decision theorists generally agree on the conditions a theory of rationality has to satisfy (these will be the subject of the next section) and second, because the discussion will be largely defensive. Certain principles have, by different authors, been taken to form the basis of decision theoretic rationality. Some of these principles may be endorsed on both conceptions of rationality, others on only one. I will show that *none* of these principles support global neutrality as a requirement. So it does not matter to my arguments which notion we endorse, in the end. However, to respect both notions I will use as a slogan that **to be decision-theoretically rational is to have consistent preferences, and to prefer the means to one's ends given one's beliefs and desires**.

There is a worry one might have about decision-theoretic rationality as just outlined. One might object that our commonsense notion of rationality is substantial rather than formal. Consider the case of beliefs and desires. We may call a person's beliefs irrational even though they are consistent, for example, if she holds to a conspiracy theory. Failing to proportion one's degrees of belief to the actual evidence is often deemed irrational, even if an agent proportion her degrees of belief to the

---

[5] This is suggested, for example, by David Christensen's (1991) argument that what is objectionable about being Dutch-bookable is that it reveals that one has inconsistent beliefs.

[6] This is suggested by Hammond's (1988a) distinction between consistency and consequentialism as separate conditions in decision theory.

evidence as she sees it, thereby believing consistently. And we may call a person's desires irrational: contrary to the Humean maxim, we might think it really is irrational to prefer the destruction of the world to the scratching of one's finger.

What this brings out is that there are two senses of rationality as applied to preferences: *consistency* or *instrumental rationality*, and *reasonableness*. The former imposes structural restrictions on preferences, whereas the latter restricts the content of preferences. Therefore, they come apart quite readily: we can separate structural restrictions (those suggested by decision theory) from substantial restrictions (those suggested by various theories of what is good or desirable or justified). We might think that both consistency and reasonableness are necessary conditions for rationality; we might want agents who are consistent but not reasonable to count as rational; or we might think that consistency only matters because the norms of consistency derive from norms governing reasonableness.[7] I will not take a stand on the relationship between formal and substantive rationality here. At the very least, formal rationality is important for our understanding of rationality in full, and it is formal rationality that decision theory analyzes. So we will use the term "rational" to mean "decision-theoretically rational"—that is, consistent and instrumentally rational—without taking a stand on whether rationality "in full" might additionally impose substantive constraints.

To understand this point, it is helpful to consider the related idea that logic analyzes what it is to have consistent binary beliefs. There are two important standards at work in binary belief. First, an agent ought (roughly) to believe what is reasonable to believe, given her evidence. This is a requirement about the substance of her beliefs, or about the content of her beliefs *vis-à-vis* her evidence or what the world is like. Second, an agent's beliefs ought to be consistent with one another in the sense elucidated by logic. For example, she ought not simultaneously believe *p*, *if p then q*, and *not-q*. This is a requirement about the structure of her beliefs, or about the content of her beliefs *vis-à-vis* the content of her other beliefs. This is not to say that agents must be logically perfect or omniscient, or that there is a single objective standard of adherence to the evidence. It also is not to say anything about how structural requirements and substantial requirements are related to each other,[8] or about what we ought to do all-things-considered if these two kinds of requirements can conflict. The point is that these are two different kinds of norm, and we can separately ask the questions of whether a believer conforms to each. We can also separately ask the questions of what specific conditions spell out each norm.

Similarly, in evaluating preferences over acts, there are two questions we might ask: whether an agent's preferences are reasonable, and whether they are consistent (or instrumentally rational). Here, the axioms of decision theory are supposed to play a parallel role that the axioms of logic play in belief: without regard to the content of an agent's preferences, we can tell whether they obey the axioms. Just as the axioms

---

[7] As regards this final view, see, for example, the parallel view in Kolodny (2007).

[8] For two different perspectives about the relationship between reasons and rationality, see Broome (2007) and Kolodny (2007).

of logic are supposed to spell out what it is to have consistent binary beliefs, so too are the axioms of decision theory supposed to spell out what it is to have consistent preferences. And we can ask the question of what specific conditions spell out the requirements of consistency, separately from considering the question of what it is reasonable to prefer in a particular situation.

However, there is at least one important difference between logical consistency and decision-theoretic consistency. Logical consistency is consistency of a single kind of entity: belief. And although the axioms of decision theory only impose constraints on preferences over acts, decision-theoretic consistency may be thought of as an amalgamation of consistency in three kinds of entity, as we saw in the previous discussion. Therefore, although the formal conditions of decision theory apply only to one kind of entity, the justification of these conditions might be more pluralistic. Similarly, the question of reasonableness can be asked of all three entities: beliefs, desires, and aggregation norms. We already know what the reasonableness discussion looks like for the first two, and in the conclusion of the book I will return to the reasonableness of the latter—specifically, reasonableness as applied to risk functions. I turn now to the kinds of justification for the formal conditions of decision theory.

5.2 Coherent Consequentialist Preferences

To be decision-theoretically rational is to have consistent preferences, and to prefer the means to one's ends given one's beliefs and desires. The arguments about which theory is the correct one will center around which theory spells out the specific requirements of this kind of rationality. We can distinguish several different kinds of conditions that decision-theoretic rationality involves. Settling on the correct decision theory will then largely be a matter of determining what follows from these conditions. Those who endorse the idea that decision theory is only a theory of consistency or only a theory of instrumental rationality may accept the conditions for different reasons, but they are all conditions that play a central role in arguments about the correct decision theory.

The first condition is that an agent have **stable beliefs and desires**. This will translate into the requirement that the agent have a well-defined probability function and well-defined utility function, each of which is stable across all of the choices the agent faces. An agent will violate this requirement if, for example, her degrees of belief about events outside of her control vary with the gambles she is being offered. Thus, if importance coefficients—the weight that each outcome gets in each particular gamble—correspond to beliefs, then REU maximizers will violate this requirement. On the other hand, if, as I have argued, the p function corresponds to beliefs, then REU maximizers will not violate this requirement. An agent will also violate this requirement if the utility function is meant to correspond to desires and the agent does not have a stable utility function, or if she does not have stable preferences over outcomes. For example, Schick (1991) presents an example of a doctor treating a patient who is also a murderer: the doctor prefers that the patient live rather than die, but prefers that the murderer die rather than live, even though he recognizes that the patient and the murderer are the same person. Given that the representation theorem for REU theory yields a stable utility function as well as a stable probability function, globally sensitive agents meet this first condition of rationality.

The second condition is that one's preferences about acts must be consistent with each other in the sense that they could give rise to a plan to act that is not incoherent. Call this **means–means consistency** or **coherence**. This is spelled out in part by the minimal condition of consistency, introduced in Section 2.4:

(MCC) For all f, g, h, and j, if f and h are (known to be) the same gamble, and if g and j are (known to be) the same gamble, then f is preferred to g if and only if h is preferred to j, for both strict and weak preference.

This condition is violated by agents under the influence of framing effects, as outlined by Kahneman and Tversky's prospect theory. If one does not obey (MCC), then one cannot even act in accordance with one's preferences in the choice between the two options $f(h)$ and $g(j)$, since one cannot both choose f over g and fail to choose h over j. One's preferences are not jointly satisfiable, and this is solely because of their logical form. But it is not an inability to bring about what you want *per se* that is the problem: after all, there is nothing irrational about preferring an act that is unavailable to you. Rather, the problem is that there is no way to formulate a plan of action because of the way you have structured your preferences: you are of two minds about the value of an act. This kind of requirement is one motivation for the Ordering Axiom (A1), which is the only axiom that does not mention outcomes or events but rather restricts the relationship between preferences about acts independently of which outcomes compose those acts. So, for example, we might think the requirement that preferences over acts be transitive arises from the fact that having transitive preferences is a necessary condition for having a coherent strategy for realizing one's aims.

The third condition necessary for decision-theoretic rationality is that one's preferences over acts must be related to one's preferences over outcomes in an appropriate way: one's preferences about means must be consistent, in light of what one believes about which ends those means might realize, with one's preferences about ends. Call this **means–ends consistency** or **consequentialism**.[9] A motto of decision theory is that "acts are valued by their consequences."[10] Decision theory, therefore, requires that one's preferences over acts must be based *only* on considerations about the consequences of those acts: one's preferences about acts can take account only of one's preferences about outcomes and one's beliefs about which acts might realize them. We have already seen

---

[9] The meaning of term "consequentialism" in decision theory differs somewhat from the meaning of this term in moral theory.

[10] Hammond (1988a, p. 25). Quoted in Levi (1991). Hammond uses "consistency" to mean what I call coherence and "consequentialism" to mean what I also call consequentialism. I do not use his terminology because most authors these days use "consistency" to encompass both conditions.

one example of a requirement of consequentialism: the betterness-for-reasons condition, introduced in Section 2.4:

(BFR) An act is strictly preferred to another only if it is strictly preferred in some state of the world.

The motivation for this condition is that the only reason an act can be preferred to another is if at least one of its consequences is preferred.

Consequentialism is to be distinguished from the possibility that evaluation of an act can include features of the act itself, aside from the outcomes to which it leads. This is not to say that good or bad features of the acts themselves cannot matter to the agent: it is just that the ways in which they matter must be considered part of the outcomes. For example, if I do not want to get $100 by stealing it from someone, then for this preference to count as consequentialist, the undesirability of this act would have to be traced to the fact that the *outcome* "I get $100 by stealing" is undesirable.[11] Given this, it is easy to see that whether a preference ordering is consequentialist can depend on how we describe the outcomes. For example, the preference ordering partially determined by the norm that says, "pick the act that results in the highest amount of money, if doing so does not involve stealing, but choose $0 over any amount of money that involves stealing" is not consequentialist if outcomes are merely sums of money, but it may be consequentialist if outcomes are sums of money acquired in a particular manner. As we saw in the previous chapter, the correct description of the outcomes is sometimes open to dispute. Nonetheless, let us assume we have settled on the correct description of a set of outcomes. Then a decision-maker's preferences satisfy consequentialism only if the value of an act can be determined from the values of its outcomes and the probabilities of their obtaining.[12] Thus the requirement that two gambles with the same probability distribution of outcomes be evaluated in the same way—that the mechanism for determining the outcome of a gamble does not matter—is a necessary condition of consequentialism.

I do not mean to imply that the three conditions—stable beliefs and desires, coherence, and consequentialism—are totally separate. For example, one way in which inconsistent beliefs or desires could manifest themselves is in giving rise to act-preferences that are not coherent. Rather, each type of consistency underlies some requirements that we might impose on rational agents, and many of the arguments that have been put forward in support of global neutrality (that is, in support of EU

---

[11] It is important to note that Axiom 4 (Small-Event Continuity) does exclude as irrational the preference ordering which *prohibits* particular types of acts no matter what, if any act that involves the *possibility* of violating the prohibition is worse than any act that does not.

[12] I do not dispute with the EU theorist that the rational agent has sharp probabilities over events, so I am formulating this condition in terms of probabilities rather than events. However, it is an interesting question how we might formulate consequentialism if the agent's credences are not sharp. Furthermore, here I am assuming that which *event* an outcome occurs on does not matter, or, more precisely, that if it does then this is already taken into account in the description of the outcomes. See also Levi (1991) for a discussion of the variety of ways to cash out the consequentialist assumption in decision theory.

theory) can be seen as arising from a consistency requirement of one type or another. Since the representation theorem in Chapter 3 shows that globally sensitive agents can have stable beliefs and desires, the remainder of this book will address arguments to the effect that globally sensitive agents fail to be coherent or consequentialist.

There are two strategies for arguing for the requirement of global neutrality. The first is to argue that the axioms of EU theory that REU theory rejects are themselves coherence or consequentialist constraints. A proponent of this kind of argument holds that once we understand the axioms, we must accept that they are constraints on coherent consequentialist preferences. (Notice that this was the kind of justification I gave in Chapter 3 for some of the axioms that EU theory and REU theory share.) The remainder of this chapter will consider arguments to this effect.

The second strategy is to argue that for those who violate the disputed axioms, there will be particular situations in which they will violate some particular coherence or consequentialist constraint. Chapter 6 is devoted to arguments of this type—in particular, as regards coherence and consequentialism over time. These arguments purport to show that there are situations in which globally sensitive agents make plans that they cannot follow through on, violating coherence, or they pick acts that are worse in every state of the world than other acts available to them, violating consequentialism. Chapter 7 considers an argument that globally sensitive agents are subject to sure loss at the hands of clever bookmakers—as we will see, another way of bringing out the idea that an agent's preferences are incoherent—and an argument that the globally neutral agent better satisfies her aims over the long-run than the globally sensitive agent. I will, unsurprisingly, conclude that none of these arguments succeed in showing that globally sensitive agents are irrational. But I will also show exactly what the dispute hangs on: what one must give up by allowing global sensitivity, and what one must give up by prohibiting it.

5.3 The Sure-Thing Principle and the Independence Axiom

Recall that the primary axiomatic difference between EU theory and REU theory, as I have presented their axiomatizations, is that the former is committed to Unrestricted Tradeoff Consistency whereas the latter is committed only to the weaker combination of Comonotonic Tradeoff Consistency and Strong Comparative Probability. Comonotonic Tradeoff Consistency allows the compensation needed for receiving one outcome rather than another in a particular event—and therefore the weight that the outcome in that event receives—to depend on where in the structure of a gamble the event occurs; whereas Unrestricted Tradeoff Consistency entails that the weight an outcome receives cannot depend on its structural position. The comonotonic version of the principle, then, allows that global properties of a gamble are relevant to its overall value.

When considering arguments for global neutrality, then, it would make sense to focus on arguments that rational preferences must obey Unrestricted Tradeoff

Consistency rather than the weaker principle. However, for historical reasons the debate about whether caring about global properties is rationally permissible has focused around each one of two other axioms that each play the same role in their respective representation theorems for EU theory as Unrestricted Tradeoff Consistency does: they fix utility difference ratios, and they do so by guaranteeing that the value an outcome contributes to the overall value of the gamble in which it is embedded cannot depend on the other possible outcomes of the gamble.

The first of these two axioms was discussed in Chapter 3. It is the Sure-Thing Principle:[13]

Sure-thing Principle (STP): For all $f,g \in \mathscr{A}$, $x,y \in \mathscr{X}$, and $E \in \mathscr{E}$,
$$f_E x \geq g_E x \Leftrightarrow f_E y \geq g_E y$$

And as mentioned, this principle has a comonotonic version, which REU maximizers satisfy:[14]

Comonotonic Sure-thing Principle (CSTP): For all $f,g \in \mathscr{A}$, $x,y \in \mathscr{X}$, and $E \in \mathscr{E}$,
$$f_E x \geq g_E x \Leftrightarrow f_E y \geq g_E y \text{ if all four acts are comonotonic.}$$

REU maximizers do not necessarily obey STP, but REU maximizers do obey CSPT.

Like Unrestricted Tradeoff Consistency, STP implies that the value an outcome contributes to the value of an act cannot depend on which other outcomes might result from the act: it implies that the value that an outcome contributes in an event is *separable* from what happens in the rest of the act. But the comonotonic versions of each principle hold that the value contribution of an outcome need only be fixed for a given ordering of events. Thus, the value contribution depends both on what happens in the relevant event and on where in the ordering the event is: the value contribution is only *semi-separable* from what happens in the rest of the act.

As discussed in Chapter 3, there are two possible reasons why an agent could violate UTC and STP while adhering to their comonotonic counterparts. One reason is that the agent does not have a stable probability distribution over events. There could in turn be several reasons why an agent lacks a stable probability distribution. She might be pessimistic and believe that an event is more likely if it results in a bad outcome. Or she might have stable beliefs that do not behave like probabilities. The second reason that the value contribution of an outcome might depend on its structural position in the gamble is that even though the agent has stable probabilities and chooses according to them—chooses gambles that stochastically dominate with respect to them—she weights events more or less heavily than their probability values in her deliberations, depending on where they fall in the rank-ordering. She cares proportionally more about what happens in the worst-case scenario than in the best-case scenario, or *vice versa*. As I have shown, globally sensitive agents do choose according to a stable

---

[13]   Originally Savage (1954/1972). The formulation here comes from Chew and Wakker (1996).
[14]   Chew and Wakker (1996).

probability distribution, and so their reason for preferences that violate UTC or STP will be the latter.

Given that the requirement of a stable probability distribution is not in question, there is a third way to frame the axiomatic dispute between global neutrality and global sensitivity. Notice that the Tradeoff Consistency Axioms and the Sure-Thing Principles apply to decision-making when the probabilities are not given or assumed, and these are the primary situations with which this book is concerned. However, there is a closely related axiom that underlies objective EU theory (EU theory assuming objective probabilities)—an axiom which applies to preferences between lotteries. It is usually attributed to von Neumann and Morgenstern (1944), and is known as the Independence Axiom:[15]

Independence Axiom (IA): For all lotteries L_1, L_2, L_3 and all $0 < p \leq 1$,
$$L_1 \geq L_2 \Leftrightarrow \{L_1, p; L_3, 1-p\} \geq \{L_2, p; L_3, 1-p\}$$

This axiom requires that if an agent weakly prefers one lottery to another, then she also weakly prefers a p chance of the first lottery to a p chance of the second lottery, when the alternative with a $1 - p$ chance is the same either way.[16]

We saw in Section 3.3 that STP rules out the Allais preferences. Independence rules them out for a similar reason. Recall that most people prefer L_1 to L_2 and L_4 to L_3:

L_1: $5M with probability 0.1, $0 with probability 0.9.
L_2: $1M with probability 0.11, $0 with probability 0.89.
L_3: $5M with probability 0.1, $1M with probability 0.89, $0 with probability 0.01.
L_4: $1M with probability 1.

If we let A = {$5,000,000, 10/11; $0, 1/11} and B = {$1,000,000, 1}, and accept that a compound lottery can be reduced to a single lottery with the same probability of each outcome, we can see that the lotteries in the Allais problem are equivalent to:

$L_1 = \{A, 0.11; \$0, 0.89\}$
$L_2 = \{B, 0.11; \$0, 0.89\}$
$L_3 = \{A, 0.11; \$1M, 0.89\}$
$L_4 = \{B, 0.11; \$1M, 0.89\}$

The preference for L_1 over L_2 and L_4 over L_3 will clearly violate Independence. For if $L_1 > L_2$, then by Independence, A > B, and then again by Independence, $L_3 > L_4$; but $L_4 > L_3$.

---

[15] Formulation in Machina (1982, p. 278). Other formulations can be found in Samuelson (1952, p. 672) and Marschak (1950, p. 120). Machina points out that von Neumann and Morgenstern did not explicitly use this axiom in their axiomatization of objective EU theory, but that Malinvaud (1952) showed that it was implicit in their mathematical setup.

[16] One might ask whether this principle has a corresponding comonotonic version. The closest principle that appears in the literature, to my knowledge, is an axiom that Chateauneuf and Wakker (1999) use to axiomatize cumulative prospect theory. This axiom, which they refer to as "tradeoff consistency" in that paper, is an objective probabilities version of what is called comonotonic tradeoff consistency in this book (and in other papers by Wakker); however, it is less clear how this relates to Independence.

We can see that Independence is supposed to capture the same intuitive idea as the Sure-Thing Principle: when making a decision between two lotteries, you need to compare them only in the respects in which they are different. Like the Sure-Thing Principle, the Independence Axiom ensures that including some particular sub-lottery rather than another is always positive, always negative, or always neutral, regardless of what happens in the rest of the lottery. And indeed, if our decision-maker under uncertainty has a probability distribution over events, then the Independence Axiom entails the Sure-Thing Principle.[17] Since globally sensitive decision-makers choose according to a stable probability distribution, then a successful argument that either principle is a rational requirement will show that global sensitivity is irrational. Both conditions, like Unrestricted Tradeoff Consistency, imply that one cannot care about structural properties in the way globally sensitive decision-makers do.

The debate about whether to allow global sensitivity is about what the prescription to value outcomes consistently and to prefer the means to one's ends entails about how one must rank the various acts which have some chance of resulting in these outcomes. The defender of the thesis that we ought to be globally neutral endorses Unrestricted Tradeoff Consistency, the Sure-Thing Principle, and the Independence Axiom, each of which provides a way of ensuring that an outcome contributes the same value to the value of a gamble regardless of what will happen if this outcome does not occur. Importantly, each ensures that an outcome contributes the same value regardless of that outcome's structural position in the gamble. Contrary to this, the defender of global sensitivity holds that the value contribution of an outcome can depend on its position in the rank-ordering, so that agents can value acts in a way that reflects sensitivity to their global features.

5.4 The Argument from Dominance and No Interaction Effects

One thought about the Sure-Thing Principle and the Independence Axiom is that they are self-evident constraints of consequentialism once they are properly understood.

---

[17] It is slightly tricky to formulate Independence in our Savage-style framework, because Independence uses variables that on the left-hand side denote lotteries and on the right-hand side denote sub-lotteries, but in our framework acts cannot strictly speaking also be sub-acts. But here are two ways to argue that a suitably formulated version of Independence implies the Sure-Thing Principle. Here is the first way. Assume $f_E x \geq g_E x$. Then the agent weakly prefers a $p(E)$ chance of f-in-E and a $1-p(E)$ chance of x-in-Ē to a $p(E)$ chance of g-in-E and a $1-p(E)$ chance of x-in-Ē. If we can suitably formulate f-in-E and g-in-E as acts in themselves, then the agent must weakly prefer the former to the latter, by Independence. Again by Independence, she must weakly prefer a $p(E)$ chance of f-in-E and a $1-p(E)$ chance of y-in-Ē to a $p(E)$ chance of g-in-E and a $1-p(E)$ chance of y-in-Ē. Therefore, $f_E y \geq g_E y$, and so STP holds. The other way to argue that Independence implies STP is as follows. Note that in the lotteries framework it follows from the Independence Axiom that for all lotteries L_1, L_2, L_3, L_4, and all $0 \leq p \leq 1$, $\{L_1, p; L_3, 1-p\} \geq \{L_2, p; L_3, 1-p\} \Leftrightarrow \{L_1, p; L_4, 1-p\} \geq \{L_2, p; L_4, 1-p\}$. Assuming the agent has a fixed probability distribution over events, then this is equivalent to STP when we plug in f-if-E for L_1, g-if-E for L_2, x-if-Ē for L_3, y-if-Ē for L_4, and $p(E)$ for p.

Savage, for example, reports that he initially found the Allais preferences appealing, but upon reflection about the reasoning behind STP, his preferences reversed.[18] That others do the same is not quite borne out by experimental evidence.[19] Nonetheless, it is worth considering why some have thought that STP and Independence need no further justification.

Let me start by spelling out the intuition that the Sure-Thing Principle is supposed to formalize. Suppose I am deciding between two options, say, driving on the highway and driving on the parkway; and I am uncertain about whether it will rain. I might then consult my preferences among the options in the event of rain, and in the event of no rain. Suppose I realize that if it rains I am indifferent between the two options, since rain will prevent me from enjoying the scenery regardless—on either route, the outcome is "a 2-hour drive without nice scenery." Then I can simplify my decision by only consulting my preference about what will happen if it does not rain, and letting this preference determine my overall preference. In general, if I have to make a decision and I do not know what will happen, one way to simplify my decision is to ignore all eventualities that result in the same outcome no matter what I choose. We might call this *sure-thing reasoning*: if two gambles agree on what happens if one event obtains, then my preference between them must depend only on my preference between what they yield if this event does not obtain (if it rains, the outcome they agree on is a "sure-thing" in the sense that I will get it regardless of what I choose).

The Sure-Thing Principle is supposed to formalize an upshot of sure-thing reasoning: given that I need only consider what happens in states that differ, it does not matter what exactly happens in the state in which the acts are the same. For example, it does not matter if the "rain" outcome in either case is "a 2-hour drive without nice scenery" or "a 5-hour drive in heavy traffic" or "trip canceled." Table 5.1 is a schematic representation of the Sure-Thing Principle, where W and Z represent f restricted to E and g restricted to E, respectively (we will be able to talk intuitively, but not within the formal theory, about a preference between W and Z):

Table 5.1. Sure-Thing Principle.

Event	E	Ē	Event	E	Ē
Act A	W	x	Act C	W	y
Act B	Z	x	Act D	Z	y

Again, STP says that if you weakly prefer Act A to Act B, you must weakly prefer Act C to Act D, and *vice versa*. The idea is that you have some stable preference between W and Z. If you weakly prefer W to Z, then you weakly prefer a gamble that yields W in

[18] Savage (1954/1972, pp. 101–3).
[19] As detailed in Chapter 4, fn. 6, Patrick Maher (1993) cites studies to the effect that people do not usually change their preferences when told they violate STP.

some states to one that yields Z in those states, as long as the gambles agree on what happens otherwise.

Why exactly do you need only consider which act you prefer where the options differ? There are two possible justifications here. The first is that STP is a straightforward application of the principle that if an act is at least as good no matter what, then you should prefer it. Think back to the decision about which route to take. One could reason as follows: if I prefer the scenery on the highway to the scenery on the parkway, *I will do at least as well by taking the highway as by taking the parkway, regardless of the weather* (and *vice versa* if I prefer the scenery on the parkway). And this is true no matter which outcomes we plug into the "rain" event, if we plug in the same outcome for both acts. Furthermore, this reasoning is independent of the particular example: it depends only on the example fitting the schema. In general, if choosing one act rather than another will result in an outcome that is weakly preferred, regardless of which state obtains, then I should weakly prefer the former act to the latter. Furthermore, if choosing the former act does in some state result in an outcome that is strictly preferred, and I assign this state some probability (it is non-null), then I should strictly prefer the former.[20]

Indeed, this is the reasoning that John Harsanyi gives in support of the Sure-Thing Principle in response to Watkins' (1977) criticisms of expected utility theory:

> [The sure-thing principle] is essentially a restatement, in lottery-ticket language, of the *dominance principle* . . . The dominance principle says, If one strategy yields a better outcome than another does under *some* conditions, and never yields a worse outcome under *any* conditions, then always choose the first strategy, in preference over the second. On the other hand, the sure-thing principle essentially says, If one lottery ticket yields a better outcome under *some* conditions than another does, and never yields a worse outcome under *any* conditions, then always choose the first lottery ticket. Surely, the two principles express the very same rationality criterion! (Harsanyi 1977, p. 384)

What Harsanyi and the hypothetical reasoning above have in common is that they defend STP on the grounds that it follows from a principle that says to prefer act f over act g if f is not worse, and might be better, than g. In other words, it seems to follow from betterness-for-reasons and a consequentialist principle that is a sort of dual to betterness-for-reasons, which we might call **reasons-for-betterness**:

> **(RFB)** If an act is weakly preferred to another act in every possible state of the world and is also strictly preferred to that act in some non-zero-probability state of the world then it is strictly preferred to that act all-things-considered.

An agent cannot violate STP in the driving example without violating RFB (if one strictly prefers the scenery on one route) or BFR (if one is indifferent). However, reasons-for-betterness does not apply in all cases in which STP yields a verdict, and so STP cannot follow from it. Here is why. In the example, we plugged in (non-risky) outcomes for x, y, Z, and W; but in STP, Z and W range not only over outcomes but also

---

[20] If $f_E x > g_E x$ for some x, then by STP $f_E x > g_E x$ for all x. And if $f_E x > g_E x$ for some x, then this is intuitively because E has some probability of obtaining and f-in-E is strictly preferred to g-in-E.

over *gambles*. More precisely, Z and W range over sub-acts: that is, parts of acts that can themselves have more than one possible outcome. And when sub-acts are plugged in for these variables in the STP schema, it is not always the case that one act is better in every state, so we cannot always apply RFB.[21] For example, consider again (in Table 5.2) the choice which the Allais agent faces:

Table 5.2. Allais' decision problem.

Ticket	1	2-11	12-100	Ticket	1	2-11	12-100
L_1	$0	$5m	$0	L_3	$0	$5m	$1m
L_2	$1m	$1m	$0	L_4	$1m	$1m	$1m

In order for STP to be satisfied, an agent's preference between deal L_1 and deal L_2 must be the same as that between deal L_3 and deal L_4. Importantly, though, for neither of the choices—the choice between L_1 and L_2 or the choice between L_3 and L_4—is it the case that she can do better no matter what by taking one gamble rather than the other. If ticket 1 is drawn, L_2 and L_4 are better, and if one of tickets 2-11 is drawn, L_1 and L_3 are better. It is not the case that she prefers L_1 to L_2 or L_2 to L_1 in *every* state of the world: if ticket 1 is drawn, she prefers L_2, and if one of tickets 2-11 is drawn, she prefers L_1. And similarly for L_3 and L_4.

Recall the distinction between local and global considerations: the former is a consideration about what happens in a gamble in some particular state of the world, and the latter is a consideration about structural properties of a gamble. RFB only applies when *all* the local considerations favor one gamble over the other: what RFB says is that if an agent prefers W to Z in every state of the world then she must prefer that W rather than Z be a sub-act of any act that she takes. In other words, RFB says that if all the local considerations favor one sub-act over another, then when these sub-acts are part of two larger acts that are themselves identical with respect to every other local consideration, local and global considerations combined cannot possibly tell in favor of the gamble that includes Z rather than the gamble that includes W. And this seems right: any structural feature one could possibly care about from the point of view of taking the gamble that best realizes one's aims must tell in favor of the gamble that better realizes one's aims *no matter what*. But STP requires something stronger: that if the local considerations in favor of W against Z *merely outweigh* those in favor of Z rather than W, then when these are part of larger gambles, local and global considerations combined cannot tell in favor of the gamble that includes Z over the gamble that includes W, even when there are considerations that tell either way. This is to say that structural properties of gambles can *never* make a difference to how considerations are weighed.

---

[21] Edward McClennen makes a similar point in McClennen (1983, pp. 176–8) and McClennen (1990, pp. 77–81).

One reason, I suspect, that STP initially sounds so intuitive is because the applications we immediately call to mind are those in which the variables range over outcomes. This seems to fit with how Harsanyi phrases it. However, in restricting our attention to these applications, we are actually considering the much weaker State-Wise Dominance Principle (Axiom 2). Indeed, it is SWD that is equivalent to the conjunction of reasons-for-betterness and betterness-for-reasons.[22] STP does not follow from these principles, because these principles apply only when local considerations unanimously favor one of the gambles over the other—but there are some applications of STP in which neither option is such that the agent will do at least as well in every state by taking that option as by taking the other.[23]

RFB applies if there is a *pro tanto* reason to prefer W to Z, and *no pro tanto* reason to prefer Z to W, and its conclusion is that one must prefer W to Z all things considered. But what the Sure-Thing Principle requires is that if I *all-things-considered* prefer W to Z, I must prefer that W rather than Z be a sub-act of any act I choose. And to prefer something all things considered is not to think that all the reasons tell in its favor; rather, it is to think that the considerations in its favor outweigh the considerations against it: for example, the *pro tanto* reasons in favor of W rather than Z outweigh the *pro tanto* reasons in favor of Z rather than W. Since the dominance argument does not apply in the case where there are reasons on either side, it cannot support STP.

I will return to the question of weighing reasons shortly. First I want to briefly outline the analogous argument for Independence and an analogous response. One might initially support Independence by calling to mind the following kind of example. If one is deciding between two restaurants (each requiring equal hassle to get to, say), and each has the same chance of being closed, then even if the circumstances under which each will be closed are different, the only relevant consideration is which restaurant one would prefer to dine at if it is open. And this is because if one prefers restaurant *A* when open to restaurant *B* when open, then by choosing the lottery involving a

---

[22] In the presence of the Ordering Axiom.

[23] STP in fact follows from a stronger dominance principle, if we assume the relation "is weakly preferred in an event" is complete:

> (EWD) Event-Wise Dominance: If there is some partition of states into events such that f is weakly preferred to g in all events, then f is weakly preferred to g. If, additionally, f is strictly preferred in at least one non-null event, then f is strictly preferred to g.

This principle is stronger than the State-Wise Dominance Principle. However, it is far from an obvious consistency constraint. (EWD is false in cases with unbounded values—see Chalmers (2002)—but these cases are importantly different from the cases I consider here.) McClennen (1990) notes that Savage's motivation for accepting EWD is the thought that what counts as a "final outcome" is relative to a particular description of the decision problem—there is no privileged set of outcomes that count as "final"—and so there is no important difference between SWD and EWD. However, McClennen (1990, pp. 77–81) also notes that this thought might instead prompt a worry about SWD, or about whether there is really no privileged final outcome set. In any case, since arguments for EWD are easily recast as arguments for STP, I will concentrate on arguments for STP. Should those of us who reject EWD also worry about SWD in the case of gambles whose outcomes are monetary values? Savage (1954/1972, p. 99) provides a reply on our behalf. He points out (though does not follow through on the line of argument) that a larger sum of money state-wise dominates a smaller sum, since money can always be thrown away, transforming the larger sum into the smaller sum.

chance of A rather than that involving the same chance of B one gives oneself at least as good a chance of obtaining a certain level in one's preference ranking. This might lead us to believe that Independence is merely a restatement of the principle that if for any given outcome, one has at least as high a chance of obtaining something at least that good by picking one lottery rather than another, then one should weakly prefer the former to the latter; if one also has a higher chance of obtaining some particular out-come or better then one should strictly prefer it. This is the Stochastic Dominance Principle. But Stochastic Dominance, which globally sensitive agents do adhere to, is actually weaker than Independence. The Independence Axiom says that if local con-siderations about the chance of attaining a particular outcome on balance favor one lottery over another, then when these are sub-lotteries of two larger lotteries that are themselves identical with respect to other local considerations, then local considera-tions on balance cannot possibly tell in favor of the of the latter. Again, Stochastic Dominance applies when local considerations unanimously favor one lottery, but Independence applies also when there are considerations on both sides.

This brings us to the second argument in favor of STP and Independence—in favor of the idea that it should not matter what is in the "shared" column Ē or in the "shared" outcome with probability $1 - p$. It begins with the observation that what happens in Ē cannot affect the value of what happens in E. Samuelson (1952) draws our attention to a version of the Independence Axiom which states that if L_1 is preferred to L_2 and K_1 is preferred to K_2, then $\{L_1, 0.5; K_1, 0.5\}$ is preferred to $\{L_2, 0.5; K_2, 0.5\}$, where "preference" can be read throughout the whole statement as weak preference or strict preference.[24] He considers that the result of each compound lottery is determined by a coin-flip and writes: "Either heads *or* tails must come up: if one comes up, the other cannot; so there is no reason why the choice between $[L_1]$ and $[L_2]$ should be 'contaminated' by the choice between $[K_1]$ and $[K_2]$."[25] He goes on to point out that this is different from the case in which an agent is choosing between receiving both L_1 *and* K_1 together as a bun-dle and receiving both L_2 and K_2 together as a bundle. In the latter choice, there may be interaction effects that mean we cannot determine my preferences about the bundles by looking at my preferences between each member of the pair. For example, I may rather have a hat than a left-hand glove and rather have a hat than a right-hand glove, but I may rather have the pair of gloves than two hats. But in the choice to which the Independence Axiom applies, receiving L_1 and receiving K_1 are mutually exclusive out-comes, as are receiving L_2 and K_2, so there can be no interaction effects. Since the pref-erence between L_1 and L_2 and that between K_1 and K_2 cannot be altered by the presence of the other choice in a state that cannot be simultaneously realized, the choice between the two compound lotteries will follow the preference between each sub-lottery. Samuelson's example and reasoning about Independence also applies as a defense of STP, and Broome interprets the Sure-Thing Principle in a similar way. He writes, "And

---

[24] According to Samuelson (1952, p. 672, ff.2), this differs trivially from the formulation used in the previ-ous section.

[25] Samuelson (1952, pp. 672–3).

this is the essence of the sure-thing principle: what happens in one state can be evaluated separately from what happens in the others."[26]

I do not dispute that the value of an outcome in a state cannot be affected by what happens in states that cannot be realized simultaneously with that state. Or, more precisely, I agree that if what happens in a non-simultaneously-realizable state affects the value of an outcome in a different state, that outcome must be described so as to take that fact into account. But there are two ways one outcome in a gamble might be affected by the presence of another: its value might depend on whether the other is included in the gamble, or the value contribution it makes to the gamble might depend on whether the other is included in the gamble. So there are two ways that a preference about which sub-gamble should be part of a gamble might be affected by what the rest of the gamble is like. Samuelson and Broome rightly point out that, assuming an outcome is described so as to take into account all of its relevant features, what happens in a different state cannot make a difference to the value of that outcome. However, they miss the possibility that a non-simultaneously-realizable outcome can affect the value *contribution* of an outcome to the gamble as a whole, and therefore that what happens in a non-simultaneously-realizable state can affect a preference about which sub-gamble to include in the gamble. It is for this second reason that globally sensitive agents fail to adhere to the Sure-Thing Principle and the Independence Axiom.

What Samuelson and Broome miss is that the local considerations about what happens in a particular state could remain the same in the presence of various outcomes in the other states—the desirability of each outcome could remain the same—but that these local considerations could be *weighed* differently in the presence of the other outcomes. They could be weighed differently because how important each of these considerations is depends on where in the rank-ordering the outcome is in the gamble, which depends on which other outcomes appear in the gamble. For example, let W be a 10/11 chance of receiving $5m, determined by drawing one of tickets 1–11, and let Z be receiving $1m for certain. An agent might all-things-considered prefer Z to W because although W has features to recommend it over Z (for example, $5m rather than $1M if one of tickets 2–11 is drawn), the considerations that recommend Z over W (for example, $1m rather than $0 if ticket 1 is drawn) are more compelling, since they concern the worst state. However, when W and Z are embedded in gambles which yield $0 if one of tickets 12–100 is drawn, to form gambles L_1 and L_2, the considerations that recommend W might be more compelling, given that the considerations that recommend Z no longer concern the worst state of L_2. It might be more instrumentally valuable to include W rather than Z in one gamble, and more instrumentally valuable to include Z rather than W in a different gamble, because of how each contributes to the properties that help determine instrumental value. What happens in Ē does not introduce additional considerations about how things go in E; rather, it changes how the considerations in favor of one sub-gamble are weighed against the considerations in favor of the other.

---

[26] Broome (1991, p. 96).

Recall the discussion of independence of *goods* in Section 1.2. The terminological similarity is no accident. To say that two goods are independent is to say that the value contribution of one good to the entire "bundle" does not depend on the presence or absence of the other: it does not depend on some other parts of the outcome. To say that preferences satisfy the Independence Axiom is to say that the value contribution of one outcome to the entire gamble does not depend on what happens in other states: it does not depend on some other part of the gamble. The move from expected monetary value maximization to expected utility maximization followed the realization that amounts of money are not valued independently. Similarly, I am proposing the move to REU maximization, on the grounds that the utility contribution that an outcome makes to a gamble is not independent of where in the structural ordering that outcome falls, and so not independent of what other outcomes compose the gamble.

Let us examine in more detail Broome's justification of STP in terms of weighing reasons, taking on board the consequentialist idea that a reason to prefer one gamble to another must derive from a reason to prefer it in some state. Taking A, B, C, and D to be the gambles in the sure-thing schema,[27] he writes:

Any reason for preferring A to B will also be a reason for preferring C to D. And any reason for preferring B to A will also be a reason for preferring D to C. So the reasons for preferring A to B will, on balance, be at least as strong as the reasons for preferring B to A if and only if the reasons for preferring C to D are, on balance, at least as strong as the reasons for preferring D to C. Consequently, rationality requires you to prefer A to B, or be indifferent between them, if and only if you prefer C to D, or are indifferent between them. That is the sure-thing principle.[28]

The only reasons for preferring A to B will be reasons that favor W over Z, since A and B agree about what happens in the rest of the gamble (Ē). Broome concludes that if the reasons in favor of W rather than Z outweigh the reasons in favor of Z rather than W in the choice between A and B, then this should hold true in the choice between C and D, because what happens in Ē is irrelevant to reasons for W or Z. So if an individual prefers W to Z all-things-considered, then she ought to prefer that W rather than Z be a sub-gamble of any gamble.

As we have just seen, we can respond to this argument without denying that the only reasons to prefer one gamble to another must concern what happens in some state. Once we know what the reasons are in favor of one gamble over another and *vice versa*, we still have to decide how to weigh these competing reasons. And while what happens in Ē does not affect what happens in E—the reasons to prefer one sub-act in each state of E and the reasons to prefer the other remain unchanged—it can affect how these reasons are weighed, because it can affect which states get priority. To use an analogy: consider two scenarios, one which is better for some group of people and one which is better for a different group of people. There are reasons, reasons concerning what

---

[27] He actually uses the more complicated schema, where what happens in Ē could be a gamble, but the argument is unchanged.

[28] Broome (1991, pp. 95–6).

happens to each individual person, in favor of both scenarios. When choosing which scenario is better *tout court*, we have to weigh the reasons concerning each person who is benefited by the first scenario against the reasons concerning each person who is benefited by the second. One thing that might determine how these reasons are weighed is which people are the worst-off in each scenario: reasons concerning their well-being might count for more. Now let us introduce a third group of people, each of whom are benefited equally by both scenarios. How things go for individuals in this third group does not change the reasons concerning the individuals in the first two groups, but it might differently affect how relatively well-off the members of each group are in each scenario: it might change which individuals are the worst-off and therefore which reasons should be weighed more heavily in determining which situation is better overall. Similarly, if we consider two gambles, one which is better in some states in E and one which is better in other states in E, what happens in Ē does not change the reasons in favor of each gamble in each state, but it might change how important these reasons are in the overall evaluation of the two gambles.

So the "global reasons" that favor one gamble over another—such as a high minimum—are not separate reasons to be weighed against the local reasons concerning what happens in each state. Rather, they only enter into the calculus about which gamble is better because they help determine how to tally the local reasons.

We have looked at two intuitive arguments for STP (and Independence), both of which tried to show that if an agent prefers W to Z, then her reasons for preferring W to Z should carry over in such a way that she prefers Deal A to Deal B and Deal C to Deal D. The first argument said that if an agent prefers W to Z, then Deal A (C) must be better in every state than Deal B (D), but this is only the case if W and Z are final outcomes, so this argument only supports the weaker State-Wise Dominance (and Stochastic Dominance). The second argument pointed out that—assuming reasons for preference can only concern what happens in some particular state—outcomes in event Ē cannot alter the agent's reasons for preferring W to Z or for preferring Z to W in each state in event E, and therefore that the reasons that led her to choose W over Z and reasons against that choice must be the same as the reasons in favor of including W over Z as a sub-act. However, it does not follow from the fact that the reasons must be the same that they must be weighed the same when W and Z are sub-acts of different acts. *Global properties of acts make a difference to globally sensitive agents not by affecting the local considerations but by affecting how the local considerations are weighed to arrive at an all-things-considered preference.*

Recall that globally sensitive agents do obey the *Comonotonic* Sure-Thing Principle (CSPT), which is intermediate between the State-Wise Dominance Principle and the Sure-Thing Principle. State-Wise Dominance implies that if there are reasons that recommend W over Z and none that recommend Z over W, then an agent is being inconsistent by choosing Deal B or Deal D. STP implies that if the reasons in favor of W over Z outweigh the reasons in favor of Z over W when deciding between Deal A and Deal B, then they also have to outweigh them in the choice between Deal C and Deal D: if an agent is coherently structuring the realization of his aims, what happens in Ē is irrelevant to how these reasons weigh against each other. CSTP says that if the reasons that favor W over Z outweigh the reasons that favor Z over W in the choice between Deal A and Deal B, then they must also outweigh them in the choice between Deal C and Deal D *unless these gambles differ in structural properties as a result.* Specifically, they must outweigh them unless the gambles differ in where in the structural ordering the states (the states that the reasons concern) occur. That is, CSPT says that in order to coherently structure the realization of his aims, the agent must weigh the reasons that recommend W over Z against those that recommend Z over W in the same way as long as they are reasons that concern the same structural parts of gambles.

The axioms of decision theory are supposed to spell out what it means to consistently value ends, and to consistently prefer the means to one's ends. The defender of global neutrality claims that this kind of consistency requires that preferences obey the Sure-Thing Principle. Although this principle initially appears to be an innocuous dominance principle, upon closer inspection, it requires something much stronger. It requires that if I *all-things-considered* prefer W to Z, I must prefer that W rather than Z be a sub-act of any act I take. Both the defender of global sensitivity and those who hold that we ought to be globally neutral think that the only reasons to favor one act rather than another must arise from what happens in some state. What is at issue between the two positions is whether rational agents are required to weigh reasons about what happens in each state in the same way even when gambles differ in structural properties. Although the Sure-Thing Principle seems to be a clear requirement of consequentialism when restricted to situations in which all of the considerations about what happens in some state tell in favor of one gamble, the claim that violating the full principle is anti-consequentialist requires further argument. I turn now to an examination of such arguments: each tries to capture what is correct about sure-thing reasoning by showing that those who violate STP are unable to formulate coherent plans.

6

Diachronic Choice

6.1 Three Diachronic Arguments

In the previous chapter we noted that the debate about whether global sensitivity is rational turns on whether the Independence Axiom and the Sure-Thing Principle are rational requirements. We considered two arguments that each principle itself spells out what it is to consistently prefer the means to one's ends. Each of these arguments tried to show the following. If an individual, who values outcomes consistently, prefers one gamble W to another gamble Z, and if she is choosing between two gambles that differ only in that one includes W as a sub-act where the other includes Z (or that one includes W with a particular probability where the other includes Z), she must prefer the gamble that includes W. The first argument was based on the supposition that if she prefers W to Z, then there must be no local considerations at all in favor of the gamble that includes Z; but this supposition turned out to be false. The second argument was based on the supposition that if she prefers W to Z, then the local considerations in favor and against choosing the gamble that includes W must be the same as those in favor of and against choosing W itself. While this supposition is true, it does not imply that the agent should pick the gamble including W over the gamble including Z, because global features of the larger gamble might provide reason to weigh the local considerations differently than in the choice between W and Z.

To allow STP violation is to allow that a rational individual can prefer Z to W considered as sub-gambles while preferring W to Z considered on their own. What this means is that for the relevant acts f and g that contain Z and W as sub-gambles, there will be some way of carving up the world into two events such that g is preferred to f conditional on each of these events (strictly preferred on at least one of them), but f is preferred to g overall. Diachronic arguments try to show that this pattern of preferences leads to inconsistency over time, by considering what happens to an agent's preferences when she learns which of the events obtains. In this section I will briefly explain three ways of drawing out the supposed inconsistency. Understanding how to respond to these arguments will require thinking about what it is to have a coherent, consequentialist method for choice over time, and I will discuss this question in the Section 6.2. In Section 6.3 I will spell out the three arguments in more detail and consider how the defender of global sensitivity should respond to them. The fourth section will examine the question of whether, even if the globally sensitive agent can choose consistently over time, the need to adopt a particular method to do so reveals that her underlying preferences are inconsistent. Throughout this discussion I will assume that our globally sensitive agent does have a coherent credence function, so that Independence and STP amount to the same thing and can thus be used interchangeably. (This is useful, because some authors have framed their diachronic arguments as arguments for Independence, others as arguments for STP.)

To examine the arguments, it is helpful to keep an example of STP violation in mind. We will once again use the Allais example because many authors have formulated their arguments in terms of the Allais preference. The standard preferences in the Allais paradox violate the Independence Axiom as stated, and violate the Sure-Thing Principle when we interpret the probabilities involved as subjective and pick appropriate events. Again (in Table 6.1), if we let prizes be determined by drawing one of 100 equiprobable tickets, the Allais agent prefers L_1 to L_2 and L_4 to L_3:

Table 6.1. Allais' decision problem.

Ticket	1	2–11	12–100	Ticket	1	2–11	12–100
L_1	$0	$5M	$0	L_3	$0	$5M	$1M
L_2	$1M	$1M	$0	L_4	$1M	$1M	$1M

Now (in Table 6.2) let E be the event in which ticket 1–11 is drawn, A be the sub-gamble that yields $0 if ticket 1 is drawn and $5M if ticket 2–11 is drawn, and B be the sub-gamble that yields $1M if ticket 1–11 is drawn:

Table 6.2. Sub-gambles in Allais' decision problem.

Ticket	1	2–11	
A	$0	$5M	= $5,000,000 with probability 10/11, $0 otherwise.
B	$1M	$1M	= $1,000,000 with probability 1.

Let us assume that our agent strictly prefers A to B. Given that she has the standard Allais preferences, if she is choosing between L_3 and L_4, she will strictly prefer L_4: she will choose L_4 and reject L_3. However, if she were told ahead of time that event E obtained, she would prefer the lottery that offers A in this event to the lottery that offers B in this event: she would prefer L_3 to L_4. On the other hand, if she were told ahead of time that event Ē obtained, she would be indifferent between L_3 and L_4. So if she makes her choice after she learns the truth-value of E, she will be happy to choose L_3 (she will either strictly or weakly prefer it).[1] If, contra our initial supposition, the agent strictly prefers B to A, then there will be a parallel incongruity in the choice between L_1 and L_2:

---

[1] Learning the truth-value of E means learning whether "E" is true or false.

she strictly prefers L_1, but conditional on learning the truth-value of E strictly or weakly prefers L_2. If the agent is indifferent between A and B, then in either pair she will have a strict preference when she does not know the truth-value of E but be indifferent when she does. Thus, regardless of her preference between A and B, if the agent makes her choice before she knows the truth-value of E, she will choose (and prefer) differently than she will if she makes her choice after she knows the truth-value of E.[2] And there will be some proposition like this for any violation of STP.

Throughout the rest of this discussion we will assume for definiteness that the agent prefers A to B.[3] We will also assume that all of the strict preferences in all of the examples to follow are robust enough that adding a dollar to the dispreferred option or subtracting a dollar from the preferred option does not change the preference (for example, $A > B + \$1; A - \$1 > B$). So we have an agent who strictly prefers L_3-if-E to L_4-if-E and weakly prefers L_3-if-Ē to L_4-if-Ē, but strictly prefers L_4 to L_3. There are three classic ways to bring out how these preferences purportedly lead to diachronic inconsistency. The first is to claim that our STP violator will be unable to make a plan and stick to it.[4] Assume our agent finds herself in the following situation. At time t_1, she faces the prospect of a choice between L_3 and L_4, a choice which she will not make until time t_2, after she learns the truth-value of E. She plans to pick L_4, but in the event that she learns that E, she will be unable to stick to the plan, since she prefers L_3-if-E to L_4-if-E. If she finds out Ē, she will pick what amounts to the same thing either way. She will therefore plan to pick L_4, but end up with something extensionally equivalent to L_3.

The second way of bringing out what is wrong with our agent's preferences makes the phenomenon just mentioned particularly troubling by making the agent pay for changing her plans.[5] For this scenario, let us introduce a mild sweetening of L_3 by adding a dollar to tickets 12–100: L_{3+} = {\$0, ticket 1; \$5M, ticket 2–11; \$1M+\$1, ticket 12–100}. L_{3+} has the property that it is *strictly* preferred to L_4 conditional both on E and on Ē: it is strictly preferred conditional on E because A is strictly preferred to B, and it is strictly preferred conditional on Ē because it is better by a dollar in every state. However, L_4 is strictly preferred to L_{3+} full stop. Now assume that our agent makes a choice between L_{3+} and L_4 at time t_1. She knows that after she makes her choice, she will learn the truth-value of E, and then at t_2 a clever bookmaker will allow her to pay \$1 to switch her choice. Our agent will at time t_1 choose L_4, but she knows ahead of time that she will be willing to accept the bookmaker's offer, leaving her with L_{3+} and down a

---

[2]   That decision-makers do sometimes prefer *g* to *f* on the supposition that E and *g* to *f* on the supposition that Ē but nonetheless prefer *f* to *g* full-stop is a known psychological phenomenon: see Tversky and Shafir (1992) for examples. The primary explanation they give for their examples involving risk is loss aversion.

[3]   We could run parallel arguments to the arguments I discuss if we instead assume B > A or assume A = B. Any preference between A and B is compatible with REU theory, and I think A > B brings out what might seem objectionable about the Allais preferences most strongly.

[4]   Machina (1989, pp. 1636–7). Machina also cites Markowitz (1959) and Raiffa (1968).

[5]   Machina (1989, pp. 1637–8). Machina traces this argument to several authors, the earliest of which is Raiffa (1968). This can be considered a kind of "money pump" argument. I will discuss money pump arguments in more detail in the next chapter.

dollar.[6] So she pays a dollar for something she could have had for free, and does so foreseeably.

This second argument allows the agent at t_2 to pay to "undo" an earlier choice, with the result that she will be worse off than she could have been. A third argument allows the agent at t_1 to pay to guard against future choice, again with the result that she will be worse off than she could have been.[7] She again at t_1 faces the prospect of a choice between L_3 and L_4, a choice which she will make at t_2, but this time she can either be told the truth-value of E before she makes the choice, or pay not to know the truth-value of E. Given that she prefers L_4 but knows she will choose L_3 once she finds out the truth-value of E, she is willing to pay to avoid the information, even though the information will be factually correct.

Each of these arguments rests on a particular assumption about choices at a time in light of preferences over time, or, if one does not want to separate choice from preference, about preferences at a time in light of past and future preferences. Before we evaluate these arguments, we must say something about what principles hold of individuals with coherent consequentialist preferences.

6.2 Diachronic Choice under Certainty

Decisions over time can be represented in **extensive form** by decision trees. A decision tree represents all the possible sequences of choices by the agent and all the relevant possible "moves" by nature. At each choice point, the agent's options are represented by lines emanating from the square **choice node**, and at each chance point, when the agent is made aware of whether some event obtains or not, the information the agent learns is represented by a line emanating from the circular **choice node**. For example, consider the following decision problem. An individual has just missed the bus he normally takes to work, and he needs to decide whether to drive or to wait for the next bus. He might encounter traffic if he drives, and if he does encounter traffic he can either continue on his regular route or take an alternative toll route. Fig. 6.1 is an extensive form representation of his decision problem.

In these problems, what happens at a chance node is independent of what the agent does. A complete plan will tell a decision-maker what to do at each decision node in the tree, even if the decision-maker never reaches that node.[8] In this problem, there are four plans: [drive, alternative route], [drive, regular route], [bus, alternative route], and [bus, regular route]. The latter two plans will always, in fact, result in the same outcome, but they count as different plans nonetheless. If the agent is to choose the entire plan at the outset, we could represent this problem (in Table 6.3) as we have been representing our synchronic problems, in **normal form**.

---

[6] If she finds out that E, she will strictly prefer to accept the offer. If she finds out that Ē, then keeping L_4 results in the same outcome as paying a dollar to switch to L_3, so she will be indifferent.

[7] Machina (1989, p. 1638). See also Wakker (1988).

[8] Rabinowicz (1995) uses the term "strategy" for what I call "plan."

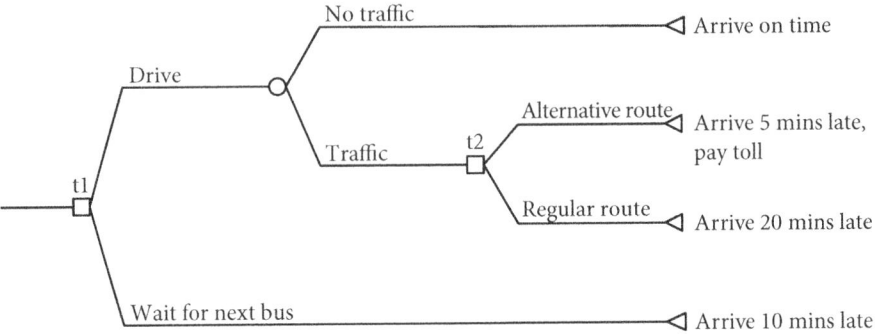

Fig. 6.1. Sample decision tree.

Table 6.3. Normal form representation of decision problem.

	No Traffic	Traffic
Drive at t_1; Alternative route at t_2	Arrive on time	Arrive 5 mins late, pay toll
Drive at t_1; Regular route at t_2	Arrive on time	Arrive 20 mins late
Bus at t_1; Alternative route at t_2	Arrive 10 mins late	Arrive 10 mins late
Bus at t_1; Regular route at t_2	Arrive 10 mins late	Arrive 10 mins late

All the diachronic arguments in this chapter turn on what consistency requires of preferences over time. There are actually two separate issues here. To understand them, notice that there are two relevant option sets over which the agent has preferences at each time. The first is the set of plans available to her at that time. (I will say more about what constitutes an available plan shortly.) Therefore, the first issue about consistency over time is whether the agent's preferences at each time-slice over the available plans are attuned only to the consequences of each plan; and whether there is a plan with the property that she weakly prefers it at each time. In other words, are her preferences at each time consequentialist, and do the preferences of the time-slices of the agent taken together form a coherent plan? The second set of options over which the agent has preferences is the set of plans available to her at all of the times taken together. One might ask whether, say, the agent at t_1 orders [drive, regular route] and [drive, alternative route] in the same way that the agent at t_2 orders these options, even though they are available only to the agent at t_2. The second issue about consistency across time, then, is whether the agent's preferences at each time are the same—whether they cohere with each other. In other words, does the agent have coherent diachronic preferences?

The first issue concerns whether an agent can make plans and what they are like, and the second concerns the preferences at each time upon which the plans are based. Therefore, there is a sense in which the second issue is more fundamental. However,

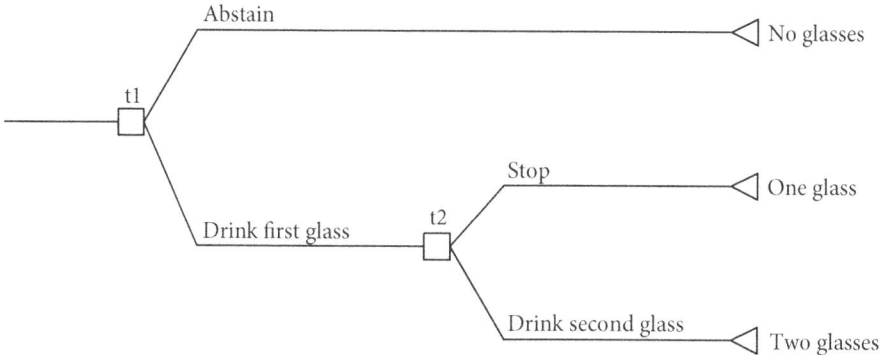

Fig. 6.2. The weak-willed wine-drinker.

I will postpone the discussion of coherent diachronic preferences to Section 6.4, and focus in this section and the next on coherent, consequentialist plans. It is instructive to start with an example of what coherent and consequentialist plan-making requires in the case of decision-making under certainty—when chance is not involved at all— before we address the question for decision-making under uncertainty and risk. To separate the issue of plan-making from that of coherent diachronic preferences, we will concentrate on an example in which the underlying preferences are clearly dia-chronically incoherent because there is no single preference ordering that the agent adopts at every time.[9]

Consider a decision-maker facing a two-stage decision involving some activity about which he is weak-willed—let us say, drinking wine (see Fig. 6.2). At time t_1 he will decide whether to drink a glass of wine, and if he drinks, at time t_2 he will decide whether to have a second glass of wine. At t_1 he prefers having one glass of wine to hav-ing none, and having none to having two (because he knows that having two glasses of wine induces a bad hangover); but he knows that once he has had one glass of wine, he will be unable to resist the second one. At t_1 his preference ordering over outcomes is [one > none > two], and at t_2 his preference ordering over outcomes is [two > one > none], and, moreover, he is aware of all of this. There are four possible plans: [abstain, stop] and [abstain, second glass] both result in no glasses; [first glass, stop] results in one glass; and [first glass, second glass] results in two glasses.

Given how the agent ranks the consequences, how does he at each time rank the plans available to him at that time? There are several methods the agent might use to form preferences over plans at a given time, given his preferences over outcomes. (I will state these methods in terms of *choice*, but I remind the reader that we are assum-ing that the agent chooses what he prefers, with one possible caveat that I will mention shortly.) One of these methods is **naïve choice**: at each time the agent prefers the plan that results in the best outcome given his preferences at that time, and he thus chooses

⁹ Example similar to that in Hammond (1988a).

the action that is part of that plan. The agent guided by this choice method will prefer [first glass, stop] at t_1 to every other plan, and will prefer [first glass, second glass] to [first glass, stop] at t_2, and so he will end up drinking at both choice points. Since there is no plan with the property that he prefers it at every time, he will be unable to execute his intended t_1 plan. He therefore fails to have a coherent plan.

One might think that the naïve agent's mistake is to assume at t_1 that the plan [first glass, stop] is available to him, given that he knows that he will prefer to drink once he reaches t_2. This suggests a different choice method, known as **sophisticated choice**:[10] the agent anticipates what his preferences will be at each final choice node, assumes he will choose in line with those preferences, and treats each of those nodes as having the outcome that results from those future choices. He then works backward using the same method to assign outcomes to each earlier choice node.[11] This mirrors the method of backward induction in game theory. In the above problem the agent will at t_2 choose to continue drinking, since he prefers [first glass, second glass] to [first glass, stop] at that node, and since those are the options available to him. The agent will at t_1 thus take his t_1 choice to be between [first glass, second glass] and [abstain, second glass]; at time t_1 he prefers the second plan and will therefore choose to abstain. The idea behind this choice method is that the agent realizes that his available options at t_1 are constrained by what he expects he will do at t_2. After all, the t_2 agent is constrained in what is available to him by what happened at t_1, so why should not the t_1 agent be constrained by what will happen at t_2? This method produces a unified plan with the property that at each time the agent will prefer it to his other available options, by definition of an available option. The agent treats as available only those plans which include what he prefers—and actually does—at other times.[12]

Finally, an agent might choose according to a method that Edward McClennen calls **resolute choice**:[13] he might at t_1 choose a single strategy and adhere to it regardless of his preferences at future times. In this problem, for example, he might decide at t_1 to have one glass and then stop; and then at t_2 he will carry through on his initial decision to not have a second glass. This is different from *binding* himself at t_1 to abstain from drinking at t_2 by removing the choice at t_2, for example, by pouring the rest of the bottle down the sink before drinking the first glass. Binding is a way of changing the decision problem, not a separate method of choice for a given problem. Resolute choice need not always involve only taking account of one's earlier preferences; on the contrary, one might strike a balance among one's preferences at different times. We might conceive of the resolute chooser as trying to strike a balance among the preferences of his

---

[10] Hammond (1988a, p. 6).

[11] Note that this only makes sense if there is a known endpoint. It is an interesting question how to interpret sophisticated choice when the agent does not know what his last choice will be, but a question that is beyond the scope of this work.

[12] I have not said what to do in the case of indifference. This is a tricky issue and is treated in McClennen (1990).

[13] An exposition and thorough defense of this choice method appears in McClennen (1990). See also the discussion in Gauthier (1997) and McClennen (1997).

different time slices in a similar way that one might try to strike a balance in group decision-making among the preferences of different individuals, and perhaps resolute choice ought to result in decisions that obey classic group decision desiderata such as Pareto optimality.[14]

How should we describe this strategy in terms of choice and preference? One way to describe it is that the resolute chooser has a choice to make at t_2 and chooses *against* his preferences at that time. A different way to describe it is that the resolute chooser at t_2 prefers a different option than he would prefer at that node considered in isolation of how he arrived at it. Gauthier seems to favor the former characterization, McClennen the latter.[15] So as to avoid severing the connection between preference and choice, and to be able to continue formulating the issue as one about what consistency requires of preferences, I will describe the agent as having different preferences than he would have had if he had not made the resolution. So "what the agent chooses" will continue to be equivalent to "what the agent (all things considered) prefers." However, I see nothing wrong in principle with formulating resolute choice as choosing against preferences, when supplemented by a suitable theory of the relationship between preferences and choice. Like the sophisticated chooser, the resolute chooser will have a coherent plan, a plan that at each time will be preferred to all other available plans, in this case because the agent's preferences by definition depend on what the plan is.[16] And for both choosers, the question of what one prefers (or chooses) given the sequential problem one's choices are embedded in is separate from the question of what one would prefer in the absence of past or future preferences. This is why the issue of coherent plan-making—the issue of whether there is a single plan one implements over time—is separate from the issue of coherent preferences—the issue of whether there is a single preference ordering on which all the time-slices agree.

Unlike naïve choice, then, both sophisticated choice and resolute choice give rise to coherent plans: an agent's preferences at each time agree on a plan. Which of the three choice methods give rise to consequentialist plans? According to Peter Hammond, none of them do.[17] Hammond claims that consequentialism requires that preferences over available plans obey at least two principles. The first principle states that which plan an agent chooses in a decision problem must not depend on the structure of the decision tree. All that matters are the logically possible consequences. Let us call this principle Only Logical Consequences:

---

[14] See McClennen (1990, pp. 211–12).

[15] Gauthier (1997) writes: "McClennen supposes that the resolute chooser develops endogenous preferences for plans (and so choices) that do not correspond to her evaluations of prospects. I would characterize a resolute chooser rather as adopting a mode of deliberation about plans (and so choices) that does not depend directly on her evaluations of prospects. What distinguishes the resolute from the sophisticated chooser is not to be found at the level of preferences, but at the level of procedures—they deliberate in different ways" (24).

[16] If we state resolute choice in terms of choosing against one's preferences, the issue of coherence will be whether an agent *follows through* on a plan that she chooses at each time, and so the resolute chooser will similarly be coherent by definition.

[17] Hammond (1988a).

Only Logical Consequences (OLC): If two decision problems have the same logically possible consequences, and the plan the agent chooses in one problem results in consequence *c*, then the plan he chooses in the other problem must also result in consequence *c*.

If our wine-drinker faces the choice problem that just involves selecting one glass, two glasses, or no glasses of wine from the outset (at t_1), he will choose [one glass]. This choice problem has the same consequences as the sequential problem involving a choice at t_1 and at t_2, and so any strategy that results in a different outcome in the sequential problem will violate OLC. Thus, according to Hammond, neither naïve nor sophisticated choice can count as consequentialist, since they result in the agent drinking two glasses and zero glasses of wine, respectively.

In the statement of OLC, for decision-making under certainty, a consequence is just an outcome; however, for decision-making under risk, a consequence can be a *lottery*, and for decision-making under uncertainty, an *act*. This rules out the possibility that two acts count as having different consequences simply because the world turns out differently: consequences include a specification of what happens in all the ways the world could go that are not up to the agent. Recall from Section 5.1 that one requirement of consequentialism is that two gambles with the same probability distribution of outcomes be evaluated in the same way. It follows from that requirement that the order of chance nodes in an extensive form decision problem should not matter: if a gamble is to be resolved by the flip of a coin and the roll of a dice, it does not matter in which order these events happen. OLC implies this requirement, and also implies a sort of dual to this requirement: that the order of choice nodes should not matter. It should not matter if I am first offered a choice between no glasses of wine and at least one, and then a choice between one and two; or if I am first a choice between two glasses of wine and fewer than two, and then a choice between one and none (this might consist of a choice about whether to pour most of the bottle down the sink, followed by a choice about whether to drink one glass). We will see when we move to discussion of decision-making under risk and uncertainty that OLC implies a further requirement that the relative order of choice nodes and chance nodes should not matter. The justification for OLC is that if the agent chooses differently in two decision problems with the same consequences, then he cares about something other than the consequences.

The second principle that preferences over available plans must obey in order to count as consequentialist for Hammond is often referred to as *Separability*.[18] However, I want to distinguish this principle from the idea discussed in Section 3.3, that the contribution each outcome makes to the value of an act is separable from what happens in other states, since I reject that idea but may be willing to accept this following principle. So I will call this principle Only Future:

---

[18] See, for example, Machina (1989) and McClennen (1990).

Only Future (OF): If a portion of a decision problem that starts at choice node n and proceeds forward in time is identical to another complete decision problem, then the plan the agent chooses at n is identical to the plan he chooses in the complete decision problem.

According to OF, which plan an agent prefers at a choice node, of the plans still available, cannot depend on what happened prior to that node: at each choice node a consequentialist choice method must recommend that the agent behave as he would if the choice problem had started with that node. OF guarantees that at any choice node we can "snip off" the portion of the tree that came before the choice node and treat the agent as facing a *de novo* choice at that node. Resolute choice tells our wine-drinker to violate this principle, since the agent upon finding himself at t_2 without having encountered the earlier choice would pick [second glass] rather than [stop], whereas the resolute agent picks [first glass, stop] rather than [first glass, second glass].

It should be clear from the discussion about which principle each choice method rejects that sophisticated choice and resolute choice are not "mirror images" of each other. Sophisticated choice involves acknowledging that the outcomes of one's current choices may not be what they would be in the absence of future choices. The *acts* are different than you thought they were, says sophisticated choice: you would be facing a choice between some acts f and g if there were no future choice to be made, but you are instead facing a choice between acts with different consequences. Resolute choice involves acknowledging that one's *preferences* may not be what they would be in the absence of past choices: you still face a choice between f and g, but your preferences between the gambles are different than they would be if you had not made the resolution in the past. (In the way of thinking about resolute choice that involves choosing against preferences, resolute choice involves acknowledging that one's *choices* may not be what they would be in the absence of past choices.)

Does this mean that we ought to distinguish, for the resolute chooser, f-when-a-resolution-was-made and f-when-a-resolution-was-not-made as different acts, since the agent's preference depends on whether a resolution was made? No, because resolutions can affect preferences without thereby appropriately being included in the content of those preferences. I do not want to take a stand on the exact mechanism of resolutions.[19] However, to illustrate the distinction between an event in an agent's history bringing about a preference and the event being part of the content of that preference, consider the following example from David Lewis.[20] Imagine a coffee-drinker who is put among tea-drinkers and comes to prefer tea, not because he wants to fit in but because he has been exposed to their preferences and genuinely comes to prefer tea. It is not that he prefers coffee-if-others-drink-coffee to coffee-if-others-drink-tea (or prefers coffee-*and*-others-drink-coffee to coffee-*and*-others-drink-tea): he is indifferent

---

[19] See McClennen (1990 and 1997) and Gauthier (1997).
[20] Lewis (1969, p. 119).

between these two, because he does not care what others drink. Rather, his unconditional preference change is explained by the fact that he was around tea-drinkers. Similarly, because of the resolution, the agent prefers f to g when he would otherwise have preferred g to f, but he also, having made the resolution, prefers f-when-a-resolution-was-not-made to g-when-a-resolution-was-not-made.

The resolute agent's new preferences are explained by his resolution without taking the resolution as part of their content. This is partly why resolute choice is different from binding: it does not transform the decision problem into one with different options. Resolving is a way of altering your future preferences, not of changing the decision problem you face. Given this, one might worry that there is no method of resolving that can be effective for a rational agent. One might reject resolute choice on the grounds that it is impossible to allow a past resolution to affect your current preferences if the reason that your past self had for those preferences is no longer a reason for you.[21] So the reader should keep in mind that there may be a motivational difficulty here, and whether agents can actually act on this strategy will be a consideration in whether we can accept it.

Are OLC and OF really requirements of consequentialist preferences? I submit that whether consequentialism requires each of these principles depends on what agency over time is like. There are two competing views about this. To the extent that we are drawn to the one view we ought to reject OLC, and to the extent that we are drawn to the other we ought to reject OF. Therefore, while each of these principles has some claim to being a requirement of consequentialism, there is no unified view which makes them both requirements: either sophisticated choice will be a consequentialist choice strategy, or resolute choice will be.

Let us start with OLC and the idea that the order of choice nodes should not matter if an individual's preferences are attuned only to which act produces the best consequences—best from his own point of view. The presumed justification for OLC—that if the agent cares only about consequences he should end up with the same result in two decision problems with the same logically possible consequences—depends on the assumption that the order or number of choice nodes does not change the available consequences of a decision problem. It depends on the assumption that every logically possible consequence is available to the agent. But it is natural to think that having one glass of wine is not an available consequence for the agent at t_1 in our original problem.[22] Indeed, one might think that the backward-looking method of sophisticated choice proceeds exactly by eliminating the consequences that are not available: are not available because of the agent's future preferences. Furthermore, in a dynamic context, we cannot always talk about the consequences that are best for the agent considered as a single entity over time, since we are leaving open so far that the agent might value the consequences differently at different times. Therefore, we must restrict our discussion

---

[21] See Kavka's (1983) discussion surrounding his "toxin puzzle."

[22] This is argued by Levi (1991).

to the consequences that are best for a time-slice. And the sophisticated chooser does choose at each time the consequences that are best for him given his preferences at that time, of the options that he can reasonably consider available. Therefore, the defense goes, sophisticated choice is a consequentialist choice method.

This defense rests on the view of an agent as a series of time-slices, each of which makes decisions given its preferences formed in isolation of what the other time-slices prefer. The only continuity between the preferences of each time-slice is psychological or historical. On this view, one stands in a similar relationship to one's future time-slices that one stands to other people: their actions may affect yours, and your actions may affect theirs, and you might have mutual concern for each other's preference satisfaction, but you are not related to them in a more direct way: you cannot decide *for* them. You can influence the actions of your future self only in the ways you can influence the actions of others: by giving them incentives to do particular things or by acting on the world in a way that changes their mental states. Like other individuals, your future self may in fact care about your preferences, and take them into account for that reason, but you cannot directly control whether he does. On this view of agency, sophisticated choice really is a consequentialist decision strategy, because it never asks the agent to choose or prefer something with worse consequences for him than some other available option. There is no agent with a unified will that rejects some consequence that is from his point of view better and available to him, because there is no agent to whom temporally extended acts are available: there is only a temporal extension of time-slices to whom acts-as-a-time are available.

Consequentialism is compatible with rejecting OLC if one adopts a "time-slice" view of agency. However, consequentialism requires OLC if one thinks that there is a single agent to whom every logically possible plan is available.

Let us turn to OF, which seems to capture the intuitive idea that for an agent who cares only about consequences, all that matters is the choices that are available to her now, not what she has done in the past.[23] After all, the "sunk-cost fallacy," treating what one has given up to arrive at a choice node as relevant to what one ought to choose now, is considered a *fallacy*. Allowing one's current preferences to depend on the plans one made in the past rather than on what one desires now is straightforwardly an instance of not taking the currently available means to one's currently desired ends.

McClennen (1990) argues that OF is not a requirement of consequentialism, and indeed that consequentialist rationality may sometimes require individuals to violate OF. In particular, he points out that the agent who violates OF because she employs resolute choice opens up possibilities for better consequences than the agent who does not.[24] Crucially, "consequences" here means consequences from the point of view of

---

[23] See Machina (1989).

[24] McClennen (1990, pp. 200–18). Machina (1989) also argues against the claim that OF is a rational requirement, but only by arguing for a rejection of consequentialism. Since I want to maintain that sophisticated choice is a consequentialist strategy, at least if one adopts a particular view of agency, I cannot make use of his argument.

the agent as a whole rather than from the point of view of each time-slice. He writes in McClennen (1997):

> Being resolute can involve being able to say "no" to what, from a separable perspective, one judges to be the option with the most preferred outcome at a given choice point, and to coordinate what one does there with what one does at other choice points as well, with a view to realizing an even better outcome than can be realized by choosing in accordance with [OF]. The key, in each case, then, is that deliberation takes place against a broader, or, as I am inclined to say, a more holistic view of the decision problem.[25]

Thus, if one adopts an "holistic" view of agency, on which an agent is a temporally extended entity with control over temporally extended acts or over choices (and preferences) across time, consequentialism is compatible with violating OF, and may even sometimes require violating it.

I will not take a stand on which view of agency is correct. The important point is that for those who reject sophisticated choice, the natural reason to reject it is to hold that limiting the possibilities that count as available based on the choices of one's future self fails to account for the way in which agents are unified over time. But insofar as we reject sophisticated choice on these grounds, we are pushed in the direction of accepting resolute choice and rejecting OF. Insofar as we think that one's future preferences cannot limit the options because they are *one's own* preferences and thus one ought to be able to exert control over them, we should also think that one ought to let one's at-a-time choices or preferences be controlled to some degree by one's past preferences. If at-a-time agency requires coordination with one's future self (rather than merely treating one's future self as a part of nature), it seems to also require coordination with one's past self. In short: either it makes sense to speak of a unified locus of control over temporally extended actions or it does not. If it does, then resolute choice is consequentialist because it allows the agent to choose temporally extended acts with better consequences. If it does not, then sophisticated choice is consequentialist because the only entity with choices to make does in fact pick, of the options available to her, the option with the best consequences.

Sophisticated choice makes sense if consequentialist plan-making must only be forward-looking. If one's preferences do not matter when they are in the past, one has no recourse except to predict how one will act in the future, and choose the best option now, holding one's future actions fixed. The actions available to one really are only those actions that are consistent with what one's future self will do: OLC ought to be rejected, because there are extra-logical constraints on which temporally extended actions are available to the at-a-time agent. And so the sophisticated chooser chooses, at each time, the actions that are best, from the point of view of their consequences considered at that time: sophisticated choice is consequentialist. But if consequentialist plan-making need not be only forward looking, then OF can be rejected, and resolute choice is a consequentialist choice method. The resolute chooser chooses,

---

[25] McClennen (1997, p. 235).

over time, the actions that are best, from the point of view of their consequences considered over time. One can only maintain that both OLC and OF are requirements of consequentialism if one thinks that a rational agent must ignore the past in forming preferences at a time, but that temporally extended acts rather than acts at a time are the appropriate unit of evaluation.

I conclude that at least one of sophisticated choice and resolute choice is consequentialist.[26] But the very need for these strategies might worry us. When these strategies do not coincide with naïve choice, we have reason to worry that the underlying preferences are inconsistent. The fact that the agent's preferences necessitate treating certain options as impossible, or necessitate resolving to act otherwise than she would if facing the choice *de novo* gives us *prima facie* evidence that the agent is of two minds about which consequences are preferable. Indeed, as I said at the outset, the case of the wine-drinker is a straightforward case of diachronically incoherent preferences. The agent at t_1 prefers [first glass, stop] to [first glass, second glass] and therefore would prefer [stop] to [second glass] if this were the choice facing him, since these latter options have the same consequences as the former. At t_2 he prefers [second glass] to [stop], and so the t_1 agent and the t_2 agent have different preferences between these two options.

The worry is that although rejecting OLC or rejecting OF can be consequentialist, the fact that one of these needs to be rejected will always reveal incoherent diachronic preferences. For the sophisticated wine-drinker, the reason that the outcome "one glass" is not available to her is that at t_1 her future preferences thwart her ability to end up with what she wants. The resolute wine-drinker is similarly handicapped at t_2 by her past preferences. Using a non-naïve choice method to determine preferences over plans is not itself irrational—it results in choices and preferences that are coherent and consequentialist—but it may be a symptom of irrationality. The *underlying* at-each-time preferences—the preferences in absence of consideration of other time-slices—may be incoherent. Indeed, in the case of choice under certainty, it seems that the need for a non-naïve choice method will only arise when the underlying preferences are inconsistent, for the following reason. Since the consequences of particular action sequences do not change at all between t_1 and t_2, the agent's preference ordering at t_1 of all plans with a fixed t_1 component is equivalent to his preference ordering at t_2 of this same set (where t_2 is the choice node arrived at by making the specified t_1 choice). And sophisticated and resolute choice disagree with naïve choice just in case, considering the agent's preference among all of the logically possible plans, the plan the agent prefers at t_1 includes a different t_2 component than the plan the agent would prefer at t_2 if given the choice *de novo*. More generally, whenever the agent does not learn anything new or forget anything between choice nodes, sophisticated and

---

[26] Rabinowicz (1995) introduces a dynamic choice method he calls *wise choice*, which is a sort of hybrid of sophisticated and resolute choice: he rejects both OF and a condition that holds if OLC holds: namely, reduction to normal form. I will not comment on the merits of wise choice. However, if the reader thinks that neither OF nor OLC is necessary for consistent consequentialist plans—or thinks that each is appropriate in different circumstances—then she may be interested in this third option.

resolute choice agree with naïve choice if preferences are diachronically coherent: if the time-slices of the agent share a preference ordering. Therefore, if the order of choice nodes relative to each other matters, then we may conclude that the underlying preferences are diachronically incoherent, even if there are coherent, consequentialist ways to make plans given this underlying inconsistency.

We have so far been talking about the requirements of coherence and consequentialism when outcomes are certain. But the situations in which we are interested are situations in which the agent cannot be guaranteed an outcome on the basis of his choice. So what are the requirements of coherence and consequentialism in decision-making under risk? If we accept both OLC and OF, where "consequence" in these principles is understood to mean a lottery, and we accept some other assumptions I will not dispute, then Hammond shows that preferences must obey the Independence Axiom.[27] As I said previously, I think consequentialists can reject one of these two assumptions, so his proof as stated need not worry us. However, in the case of decision-making under certainty, the need to reject one of these assumptions only comes up in the case of diachronically incoherent preferences. So the burden is on the defender of global sensitivity to show that this is not the case when dealing with decision-making under risk. Before turning to what diachronic coherence amounts to in decision-making under risk, let us examine in detail the three arguments at the beginning of this chapter. In the next section we will see that those who endorse sophisticated choice have a response to all of them, as do those who endorse resolute choice. So the problem of plan-making on the basis of globally sensitive preferences will be resolved: we will see that globally sensitive agents can make coherent, consequentialist plans. In Section 6.4 we will then consider whether the underlying preferences are incoherent. Finally, in Section 6.5 we will explore more generally what the lessons are for risk and dynamic choice.

6.3   Diachronic Choice under Risk

In decision-making under certainty, OLC implies that the order of choice nodes does not matter. In decision-making under risk (or uncertainty), OLC implies that the order of choice nodes and chance nodes relative to each other does not matter. We can now see how the extensive form version of the Allais example violates this dictum. Consider on the one hand the choice between L_3 and L_4 before the agent learns whether ticket 1–11 has been drawn, and on the other hand the choice between L_3 and L_4 after she learns whether ticket 1–11 has been drawn (Fig. 6.3).

In the first choice problem, the agent will strictly prefer L_4 to L_3, but in the second problem she will (strictly or weakly) prefer each part of L_3 over each part of L_4: she will prefer L_4 at t_{2A}, and she will be indifferent at t_{2B}. These two problems have the same possible consequences, L_3 or L_4, but in one the agent will end up with L_4 and in the other with L_3, because of the structure of the decision tree.

---

[27]   Hammond (1988a).

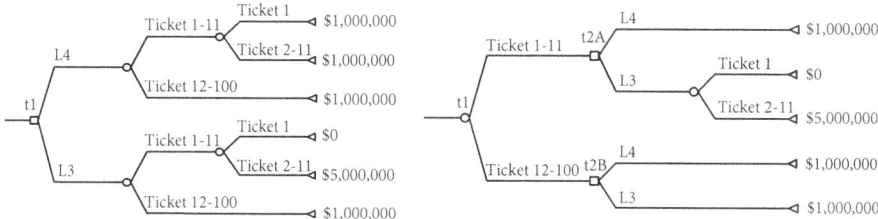

Fig. 6.3. Allais preferences in extensive form.

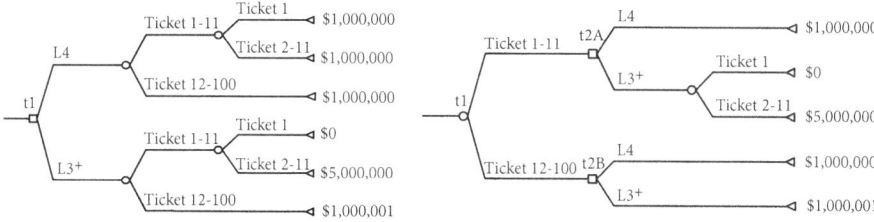

Fig. 6.4. Modified Allais preferences in extensive form.

Now, we have to be careful about two things. First, one might worry that some of the work is being done by the fact that the agent will be merely indifferent at node t_{2B}: she will be happy to choose L_3, but she will also be happy to choose L_4. Presumably, a reversal from a strict preference to a weak one reveals the same potential problems that a reversal to the opposite strict preference reveals. But regardless, this worry is easily dismissed. For if the agent strictly prefers L_4 to L_3, we can consider the mild sweetening of L_3, $L_{3+} = \{\$0$, ticket 1; $\$5M$, ticket 2–11; $\$1M + \$1$, ticket 12–100$\}$. The agent strictly prefers L_4 to L_{3+} when the choice node comes first, and strictly prefers L_{3+} to L_4 when the chance node comes first (Fig. 6.4).

The second thing that we have to be careful about is this. Implicit in the claim that the two problems have the same possible consequences, but that the order of chance and choice nodes will result in the agent choosing a different consequence in each choice problem, are two assumptions. The first is that lotteries themselves count as consequences. In the weakness-of-will example there were three consequences: one glass, two glasses, and none. In the example under consideration now, L_3 and L_4 must each count as consequences. So the notion of consequence is not just restricted to what I call outcomes. Since principles about outcomes do not always generalize to principles about lotteries—I argued, for example, that a dominance principle concerning outcomes is a requirement of rationality but a dominance principle concerning lotteries is not—we need to keep this distinction clear. So we will distinguish between "lottery-consequences" and "outcome-consequences." In the left-hand choice problem in Fig. 6.3, the agent chooses between lottery-consequences L_3 and L_4 (L_4 counts as both a lottery-consequence and an outcome-consequence). In the right-hand choice problem the agent who reaches node t_{2A} chooses between lottery consequences A and B,

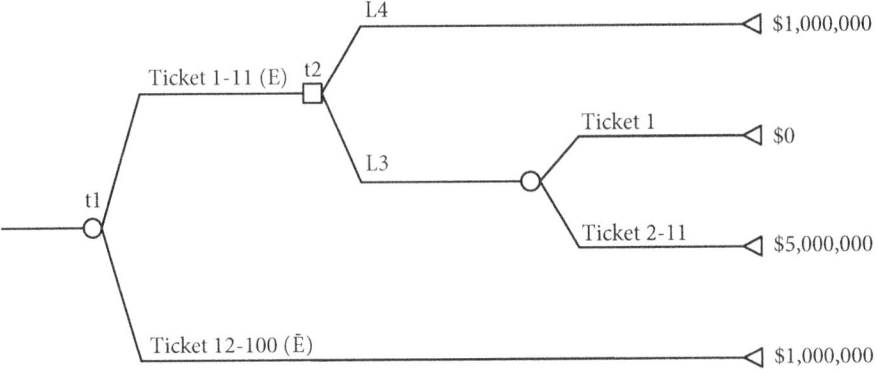

Fig. 6.5. Cannot follow through on plans (first argument).

and there is no sequence of nodes in which she ends up with exactly L_3. Compare: regardless of the structure in the wine-drinking problem, there is always a branch leading to two glasses, to one glass, and to no glasses. L_3 is never directly available to the agent in the right-hand choice problem, although anticipating picking the branch labeled "L_3" at both nodes is extensionally equivalent to picking L_3.

Let us now consider what might be wrong with our agent's preferences. Again, I will discuss whether the agent's plans must be incoherent or non-consequentialist in this section, and postpone the question of whether her diachronic preferences cohere with each other to the next. As we saw in Section 6.1, there are three ways to bring out the agent's supposed inability to make coherent consequentialist plans. The first is to claim that the agent cannot make a plan and stick to it.[28] Consider the following decision problem, where E is the event "one of tickets 1–11 is drawn" (Fig. 6.5). The argument says that if the agent finds herself at t_1 in the diagram she will plan to pick L_4 at t_2, since she prefers L_4 to L_3. But if she finds herself at t_2 she will be unable to adhere to this plan, since she prefers A to B.

The second way to bring out the agent's purported plan inconsistency is to claim that the agent can be put in a situation in which she will pick an option that is statewise dominated: she will foreseeably pick an option that is worse than some other option that is available to her.[29] In this example (Fig. 6.6) the agent must choose between L_{3+} and L_4, and she will then, after learning whether E obtains, be allowed to pay $1 to switch her choice from L_4 to L_{3+}. She will initially prefer L_4, but will then be willing to pay to switch to L_{3+} after finding out the truth-value of E. So she will end up with {–$1, ticket 1; $5M – $1, ticket 2–11; $1M, ticket 12–100}: that is, L_{3+} minus $1. But since she could have had L_{3+} without paying any fee, she chooses a course of action that is dominated by some other course of action: her action is worse in every state of the world by $1.

---

[28] Based on Machina (1989, pp. 1636–7).   [29] Based on Machina (1989, pp. 1637–8).

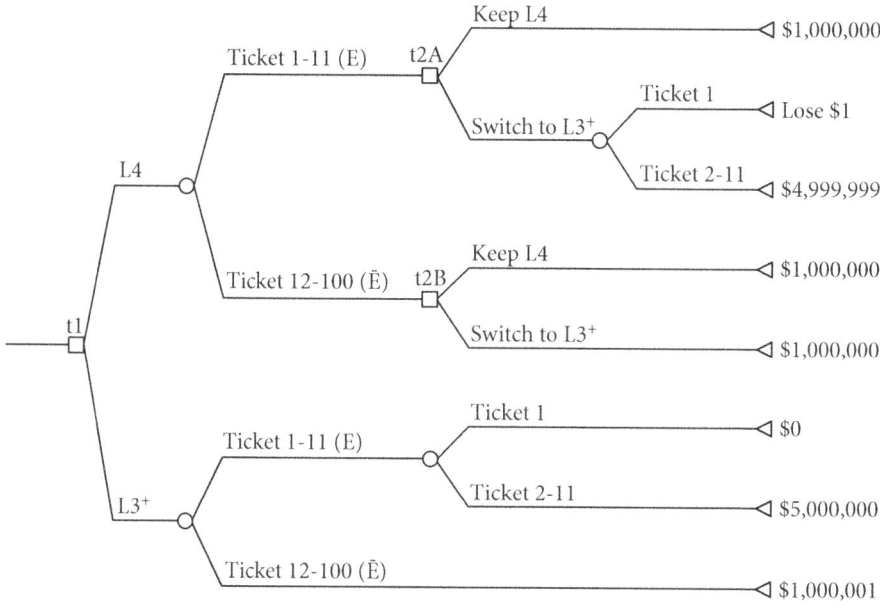

Fig. 6.6. Paying to change one's mind (second argument).

The third argument also puts the agent in a situation in which she will pick a state-wise dominated option, this time by allowing her to pay up front to avoid having a choice after learning whether E obtains.[30] Recall the difference between the left-hand choice problem and the right-hand choice problem in Fig. 6.3: if the agent faces the former she will choose L_4 and if she faces the latter she will choose what is extensionally equivalent to L_3. Furthermore, she knows this. At time t_1 she prefers L_4 to L_3, so she prefers to face the left-hand choice problem rather than the right-hand choice problem; and since her preference is strict, she would be willing to pay to face the former rather than the latter. We can represent *this* decision in Fig. 6.7. The agent will choose to pay to face the left-hand problem, and then at t_{2A} she will choose L_4, so she will end up with L_4 minus \$1. But if she had chosen to face the right-hand problem and then picked L_4 at t_{2B} and t_{2C}, she could have had an outcome that is exactly a dollar better in every state of the world.

All these arguments are ways of bringing out the supposed inconsistency involved in not wanting to learn information prior to making a choice, even though that information does not alter the consequences. The first argument illustrates the fact that acquiring information is bad in the sense that it foreseeably leads the agent to do something that from her earlier point of view she prefers not to do. Both the second and the third argument show how we can penalize the agent for the fact that there is some cost-free information that she prefers to avoid. The second argument makes her pay at

---

[30] Based on Machina (1989, p. 1638).

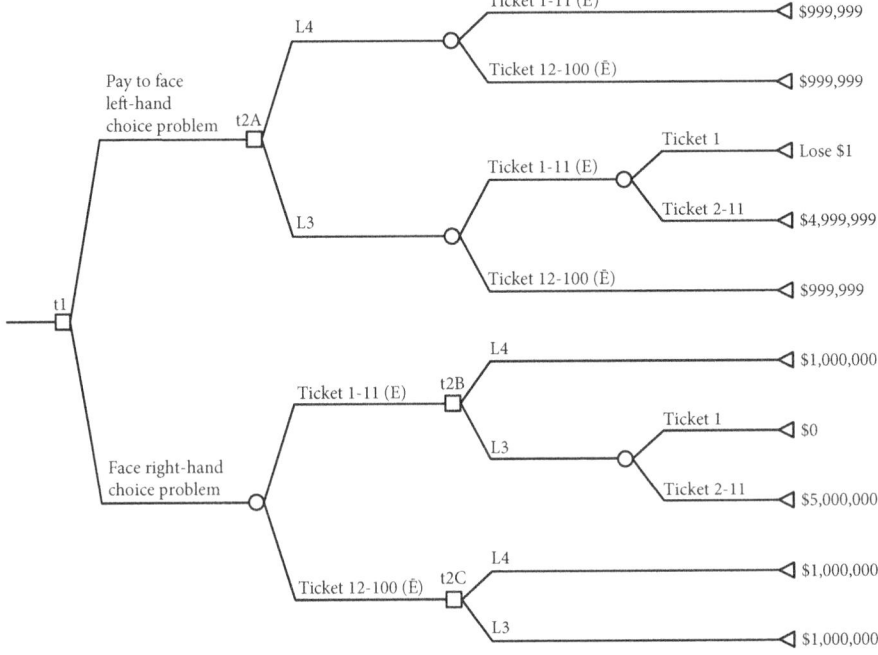

Fig. 6.7. Paying to eliminate a choice (third argument).

the later time for the preference she had before she learned the information. The third argument makes her pay at the earlier time for the preference she will have after she learns the information.

It is worth mentioning that while on Savage's EU theory, cost-free information is always weakly preferred,[31] a modification of the theory that allows for global sensitivity is not the only modification with the upshot that cost-free information is sometimes dispreferred. For example, evidential EU theory, as formulated by Jeffrey (1965), and causal EU theory, as formulated by Skyrms (1980), Lewis (1981), and Sobel (1986), both sometimes recommend against acquiring cost-free information, when acquiring the information is evidence for a state that it has no tendency to cause.[32] Like REU maximizers, causal EU maximizers will sometimes foreseeably prefer a different act at a future choice node than they prefer now.[33] So the importance of the general question

[31] I. J. Good (1967) shows that more information can never have negative value for the EU maximizer.

[32] Adams and Rosenkrantz (1980) show that evidential EU theory has this feature; Maher (1990) shows that causal EU theory has this feature, and that the situations in which acquiring cost-free information is irrational are not the same for the two theories. REU theory, because it uses the Savage framework, is a "causal" theory but takes the acts and states to be separated before application of the decision rule, so there will not be acts the performance of which is evidence for states they do not cause.

[33] Maher (1990, p. 488). Maher claims that evidential EU theory recommends against acquiring cost-free information even when one can now control one's future choices, because acquiring evidence that a bad state obtains can be enough reason not to acquire that evidence; however, if one can now control one's future choices, causal EU theory never recommends against acquiring cost-free evidence (Maher 1990, p. 497).

of how to handle this phenomenon, and whether it reveals irrationality, extends beyond this work.

How can the defender of global sensitivity respond to the three arguments? The first two arguments clearly assume that the agent is naïve. And it should be obvious from the discussion in the previous section that the coherent, consequentialist plan-maker need not choose like this. I have argued that at least one out of sophisticated and resolute leads to both coherent and consequentialist plans. Each of these choice methods provides a response to the first two arguments. The sophisticated chooser can respond to the first argument (Fig. 6.5) by pointing out that her plan at t_1 will be informed by her t_2 preference, and so she will plan to choose L_3, and the resolute chooser can respond to the first argument by pointing out that her action at t_2 will be informed by her plan at t_1, and so she will plan to choose L_4 and then do so. Either way, she will make a plan and stick to it. Similarly, in the second problem (Fig. 6.6), neither the sophisticated agent nor the resolute agent needs to pick the dominated option, L_{3+} minus \$1. The sophisticated chooser realizes that at both t_2 nodes she will at least weakly prefer "switch," and so sees her initial choice as between L_{3+} minus \$1 and L_{3+}, and therefore will select L_{3+} at t_1 and receive L_{3+}. The resolute chooser plans to end up with L_4, and carries through with the plan by selecting to keep L_4 at whichever t_2 node she finds herself. Therefore, neither of these choosers picks a dominated option.

The third argument (Fig. 6.7) actually *assumes* sophisticated choice, since the naïve agent would choose to face the right-hand choice problem at t_1 and choose L_3 at t_{2B}. It is because of arguments like the third argument that Machina and McClennen both think that adopting sophisticated choice is not a viable way to argue for the dynamic consistency of STP/Independence violations.[34] If they are correct that sophisticated choosers can end up with a dominated option, then sophisticated choosers are in trouble. However, the sophisticated chooser can respond to this argument by pointing out that although she ends up with $L_4 - \$1$, L_4 is not actually an available option for the t_1 agent, since at t_1 the agent knows she will not choose L_4 at t_{2B}.[35] The view of agency which makes sophisticated choice attractive in the first place is one on which once our future preferences are fixed, certain logically possible future options are not within our grasp. Granted, the fact that the option is unavailable to the agent at t_1 because of her own future choices might reveal that she has diachronically inconsistent *preferences*, a possibility which I will examine in the following section; but her plan does yield, for each given time-slice, the best consequence available to that time-slice. Finally, the

---

[34] Both defend the rationality of STP/Independence violation, McClennen (1990) on the grounds that consistent consequentialist agents can be resolute choosers and Machina (1989) on the grounds that rational agents need not have preferences that adhere to consequentialism.

[35] McClennen (1990) argues that this option is available to the t_1 agent. The correctness of his argument, as he confirms (p. 198) depends on the claim that resolute choice is feasible; and his argument that resolute choice is feasible depend in part on the claim that consequentialist rationality does not require OF. Therefore, if he is correct, the Independence violator cannot be a sophisticated chooser with consistent consequentialist plans, but she can be a resolute chooser with consistent consequentialist plans. In either case, there will be some diachronic choice method that will allow the agent to violate Independence while having consistent consequentialist plans.

third argument does not create a problem for the resolute chooser, since it is false that she will pay to face the left-hand choice problem: she will face the right-hand choice problem, and select L_4.

Indeed, McClennen shows that both sophisticated and resolute choice can be generalized to stave off potential inconsistency resulting from violations of Independence. He shows that violations of Independence are compatible with accepting the following three restrictions on preference: (1) that an agent will follow through on the plans she makes; (2) that an agent chooses at each point the plan that has the best lottery consequence (evaluated as if at a single time) of the plans available to her; and (3) OF holds: the plan an agent chooses at a node n is equivalent to the plan she would choose in an identical decision problem starting from n. An agent who violates Independence can make consequentialist plans and follow through on them, as long as we are willing to count as unavailable at a given time any plan that the agent will not strictly prefer at each future node. In particular, we must assume that if the agent strictly disprefers k at some future node, then no plan involving k is available at the present node, and if the agent is indifferent between k_1 and k_2 at some future node the set of available plans at the present node can only include plans that require $k_1 \vee k_2$ rather than plans that require k_1 or plans that require k_2.[36] Treating plans that the agent does not strictly prefer as unavailable corresponds to the strategy of sophisticated choice: ruling out any plan that contains a component that she does not know her future self will choose (note that this is slightly stronger than ruling out any plan that contains a component that she knows her future self will not choose). This results in denying OLC, since the structure of the tree determines what counts as available. It may seem odd that sophisticated choice does not provide a simple answer to the question of how to expect one's future self to break ties—that when $k_1 \sim k_2$, it must leave open only plans requiring $k_1 \vee k_2$. For example, one might think that ties should be broken by deferring to the preferences of the past self. But to allow such deference would run contrary to the view of agency on which sophisticated choice is based: if at a time you really are indifferent between two options, there is nothing more to recommend one or the other.

Similarly, McClennen shows that violations of Independence are compatible with accepting the following three restrictions on preference: (1) that an agent will follow

---

[36] McClennen (1990), Proposition 8.2, p. 139, and Proposition 8.4, p. 141. See also pp. 154–6. How the agent plans for nodes at which she will be indifferent is a matter of some importance for the following reason. Seidenfeld (1988a) proves that if a sophisticated chooser (an agent who obeys his "Dynamic Feasibility" condition) who violates Independence accepts that we can at any future choice node substitute options that she is indifferent between without changing the plan she will pick (if she accepts "Dynamic Substitution"), then she will be inconsistent. In response to McClennen's (1988) charge that Dynamic Substitution will not seem intuitively compelling to an opponent of Independence, Seidenfeld (1988b) shows that Dynamic Substitution follows from less controversial assumptions if we also assume a particular view of how the agent anticipates adjudicating between ties in the future. Wlodek Rabinowicz argues that the view in question does not seem to be required by rationality. (On the view that plays a role in McClennen's Proposition 8.4, Seidenfeld's argument does not go through.) See Rabinowicz (1995) and Rabinowicz (1997) for the details of Seidenfeld's argument and of Rabinowicz's response. Thus, the matter of how a rational agent anticipates adjudicating between ties is of some importance to sophisticated choice.

through on the plans she makes; (2) that an agent chooses at each point the plan that has the best lottery consequence (evaluated as if at a single time) of the plans available to her; and (3) that any logically possible plan is available. These restrictions are compatible with Independence violations as long as OF is denied.[37] Denying OF corresponds to the strategy of resolute choice: allowing that one's choices are affected by plans one has made in the past. For both the resolute and the sophisticated chooser, what they prefer at various nodes when involved in a sequential form decision will not be so tightly related to how they would make the 'same' decision in non-sequential form, but this is because they will take themselves to be facing different decision problems.

6.4 Inconsistent Preferences?

For STP violators, as for the weak-willed wine-drinker, there are choice plans which are coherent and which count at each time as taking the means to one's preferred ends given the options available at that time. But also, as in the wine example, the issue of whether there is a plan that is both coherent and consequentialist at each time is not the only issue. In the wine-drinking example, the reason that sophisticated or resolute choice was necessary is that the agent's underlying preferences were unstable across time. The reason that the best option was not available to the sophisticated agent at t_1, or to the resolute agent at t_2, is that the agent is trying to bring two disagreeing selves together into an action plan. And one might worry that something similar may be going on for the STP/Independence violator. One might think: if an agent is of a single mind about the value of acts, then she will not need to employ explicit choice methods or take past and future preferences into account in order to get what she wants—things will run smoothly as a result of her merely choosing in accord with the plan she now prefers. So *are* the Allais agent's underlying preferences diachronically incoherent? Is she of two minds about the value of acts? In this section I will argue that the answer to both questions is "no."

The first thing to notice is that the Allais agent does have fixed "underlying" preferences over outcomes. (Throughout the rest of this section I will use "preferences" to mean an agent's preferences in the absence of past and future preferences, not the all-things-considered preferences or choices that result from the employment of one of the choice methods.) She prefers $5M to $1M to $0, and since we are working under the assumption that she is an REU maximizer, she assigns a fixed utility value to each of these outcomes. Therefore, if a charge of inconsistency can be made against her, it cannot be inconsistency in her *desires for outcomes*: she is not of two minds about the value of outcome-consequences, as the wine-drinker is. Furthermore, she is in a situation in which the consequence of each possible act is not known with certainty. The agent

---

[37] McClennen (1990), Proposition 8.5, p. 142. The reader might wonder how denying OF is compatible with accepting (2). The answer is that at each time, the agent compares whole plans, including what is already happened. Of course her evaluation at t_1 will only be consistent with her evaluation at t_2 if her underlying preferences over lotteries are the same across time: that is, if we are not in a case like the wine-drinking case.

cannot simply choose the means to her preferred end: she cannot choose the act with the best outcome-consequence, since she does not know what the outcome-consequence of her act will be. She must instead choose the act that best balances the realization of her goals. And since our agent is an REU maximizer, she does have a fixed norm for choosing such an act. So the agent also assigns a fixed utility value to lottery-consequences. Therefore, across time, the agent has a single ranking of all of the lottery-consequences involved: at each time she ranks {$0, 1/11; $5M, 10/11} over $1M, and she ranks $1M over {$0, 0.01; $1M, 0.89; $5M, 0.1}.

So the agent does have a fixed preference ranking that all of her time-slices share. This, again, is a crucial difference between the weak-willed wine-drinker and the Allais agent: the wine-drinker at t_1 thinks her t_2 self has preferences that are wrong-headed: she disagrees with her future judgment about the relative value of one glass of wine and two. (And presumably the t_2 self thinks the same about the t_1 self.) However, in the Allais example, the agent *endorses* her t_2 preferences: she thinks that those are the preferences she ought to have, given her current values and norm, and given her future information. But this, then, is the source of the potential inconsistency for the Allais agent. It seems that the same norm leads the agent to endorse a preference for L_4 over L_3 (or over L_{3+}) as leads the agent to endorse the opposite preference conditional on whatever information she receives. This comes uncomfortably close to her being of two minds about what to do at t_2. Therefore, the crucial question is whether this preference ranking—the preference ranking that the t_1 agent and the t_2 agent share—is inconsistent with itself. The issue is: are these preferences inconsistent because they reveal the agent to be of two minds about the best means to her ends?

To understand this issue it is important to understand the role new information generally plays in preference change about gambles. Here is a phenomenon that both globally sensitive agents and globally neutral agents are subject to. If an agent prefers some act *f* to some other act *g*, then as long as *f* does not state-wise dominate *g*, there will be some proposition such that learning it will make the agent change her preferences: there will be some E such that g-if-E is all-things considered preferred to f-if-E. Furthermore, there will be some information that will make the agent change her preference in a way that *turns out worse for her given the actual state of the world*: that is, in a way that results in her getting something she disprefers. For example, it might be that *f* state-wise dominates *g* when, say, EF holds, but that *g* is preferred when E holds but no further information is known (that is, when EF v EF̄ holds). In this case, if EF is the actual state of the world and the agent learns E, she will come to prefer *g*, even though *f* is preferred given the actual state of the world. When this happens, we might call the information that E obtains *misleading*: it leads the agent to prefer something that in fact turns out worse for her by her own lights, that she would not have preferred if she had not learned the information. We think that the agent who acts on the basis of misleading information is in an unfortunate position, even though she is acting rationally. To say the information is misleading is not to say that E is false. Indeed, the information has led the agent to the truth in the matter of E. But if EF is true, learning E does lead the agent away from the truth in the matter of $E\bar{F}$: assuming E is the only thing she learns, she will raise her credence in EF, a true proposition, but she will also raise her credence in $E\bar{F}$, a false proposition. And being farther from the truth on $E\bar{F}$ might be worse for her given the decision she is actually faced with, than being closer to the truth on EF is. In this case, given that the information made her change her preferences, it made her worse off.

For example, let us say that there is always a 0.05 probability of heavy traffic on the bridge on my route to work, which will make me 20 minutes late if I drive, but the probability is small enough that I still prefer to drive rather than take the bus, which will make me 10 minutes late no matter what. Now let us say I learn that there is heavy traffic on one of the two bridges in my city, but I do not learn which one (maybe I catch the end of a traffic broadcast on the radio). I rationally update my credence to p(traffic on the bridge on my route) = 0.5 and p(traffic on the other bridge) = 0.5, and as a result I prefer to take the bus. This is possible on both EU and REU theory. But let us say the actual state of the world is that there is no traffic on my route. Then I have acted rationally given my evidence, but things would have gone better for me if I had not obtained the evidence. My credence in the true proposition (traffic on the other bridge) got closer to 1, but my credence in a false proposition (traffic on the bridge on my route) got farther from 0, and being close to the truth on this latter proposition mattered more to my decision.

For the Allais agent choosing between L_{3+} and L_4, learning that ticket 1–11 has been drawn (E) if the true state of the world is that ticket 1 has been drawn (EF), and therefore moving away from the truth about whether ticket 2–11 has been drawn ($E\bar{F}$), is particularly insidious. Whereas before she had credence $p(E\bar{F}) = 0.1$, she now has $p(E\bar{F})$ $= 0.91$. Granted, she is also closer to the truth in the matter of ticket 1 (the actual state of the world): her credence was p(EF) = 0.01 and is now p(EF) = 0.09. However, it turns out to be worse for her to be farther from the truth in the matter of ticket 2–11, since this is what makes her choose L_{3+}, which in fact turns out much worse for her. So, given that she does not know the actual state of the world, the prospect of finding out the truth-value of E and subsequently switching is risky: it might improve her lot (if she finds out that $\bar{E}$, or if she finds out that E when EF holds), but it also might make it much worse (if she finds out that E when $E\bar{F}$ holds). And for the risk-avoidant agent, the 99% chance of improvement (from \$1M to \$1M + \$1 if $\bar{E}$, and \$1M to \$5M if $E\bar{F}$) is not worth the 1% chance of downgrading from \$1M to nothing (if EF). This is just what it means for her to prefer L_4 to L_{3+}. So while the agent at t_1 thinks there is nothing wrong with her future self at t_2 after learning whether E—she is not being irrational, and she has not changed preferences—the agent does think there is a *chance* of something being wrong with the *information*: namely, that it will (rationally) lead her to do something that is in fact worse for her. And, in particular, at t_1 this information is not worth the risk.

Still, what is odd is that the risk of misleading evidence at t_1 is simply the risk of learning E if EF holds, but the risk of EF is not enough to make the agent at t_2 choose B over A (to not be "led" by the information at all). For the EU maximizer, if the chance of E being misleading in this way is high enough to make the agent not want to learn it, then it is high enough to make her prefer B to A. A related worry is that when the Allais agent is choosing between L_{3+} and L_4, the risk of misleading evidence is high enough to make her not want to learn E, but when she is choosing between L_1 and L_2, it is not, even though the evidence, if it is misleading, is misleading in the exact same states and in the exact same way.[38]

So what is the difference between the possibility of misleading evidence about L_1 and that possibility about L_3? For the globally sensitive agent the disvalue the possibility of misleading evidence contributes to the gamble—the weight that possibility gets when considering if one wants to learn whether E—depends on what happens in the rest of the gamble. The possibility of misleading evidence is *more weighty* in the choice between L_{3+} and L_4 than it is in the choice between L_1 and L_2 because the possibility of getting the misleading evidence and choosing A is much worse than all the possible outcomes of L_4: introducing this possibility drastically decreases the minimum. When deciding between L_1 and L_2, learning that E holds when EF holds and choosing A will result in the agent getting $0 when she might have got $1M if she had not learned the information, but from her point of view at t_1, there is already a possibility that she will get $0; that is, if Ē occurs: introducing the possibility of being "misled" will not lower the minimum value she might receive. Since the agent is sensitive to global properties, the possibility of being misled into doing something that in fact turns out badly lowers the value of the gamble more when doing that badly was not already possible. When faced with the choice between L_{3+} and L_4, the agent thinks of information about the truth-value of E as potentially harmful, since misleading evidence would make her much worse off, but not as extremely helpful, since non-misleading evidence would make her only somewhat better off. And these two facts trade off in such a way that the potential benefit does not outweigh the potential harm, since the potential harm lowers the minimum value of the whole deal: it introduces a risk that was not there before—the risk of getting nothing.

So far, this is just a *description* of how the globally sensitive agent thinks about the risk of misleading evidence, and how it differs from the way the globally neutral agent thinks about this risk: this difference maps on to the difference in how they think about the weight of bad possibilities generally. For the EU maximizer, if the risk of ending up with nothing makes it rational to choose A over B, then it makes it rational to choose

---

[38] Therefore, the agent violates what Maher (1993, p. 73) introduces as the "Synchronic Separability Principle." This principle says that an agent's preferences at t_1 about what to choose at t_2 ought not depend on what happens if she does not reach t_2. The reason that I reject Synchronic Separability is this. How you want to choose at a future choice node is just part of which larger gamble you want to take, and how the sub-gamble at t_2 contributes to the value of this gamble will depend on structural properties of the gamble as a whole, which in turn will depend on what happens if you do not reach t_2. I note that Maher thinks there is empirical evidence that people accept Synchronic Separability, though McClennen disagrees about what the empirical evidence shows; see Maher (1993, pp. 71–3).

an act that has A as a sub-gamble over an act that has B as a sub-gamble but is equivalent otherwise; for the REU maximizer, it need not. For both the globally neutral and globally sensitive agent, more information might *in fact* be worse. For the globally sensitive agent only, the instrumental value of more information might be negative given the agent's current beliefs.

Let us return to the crucial issue about the consistency of the globally sensitive agent's preferences. The globally sensitive agent thinks (at both t_1 and t_2) that the preferences she has at t_2 are the preferences she ought to have, given her norm and her information at t_2. Moreover, she already knows at t_1 the preference she will have at t_2, though she does not know her reason for this preference (she does not know if she will prefer L_{3+} because she will have learned E or because she will have learned Ē). Now she can think one of two things about the information she will receive at t_2: she can think it is good information—better to have this information than not—or she can think it is bad information.[39] If she thinks it is good information, but does not adopt the preferences extensionally equivalent to those she knows she will have at t_2, preferences she recognizes will conform to her norm in conjunction with the information, then there must be something wrong with her norm. (This is to say that a rational norm ought to make the agent conform to a kind of preference version of van Fraassen's "reflection principle":[40] if you know you will rationally have some particular preference in the future, adopt it now.) If she thinks there is something wrong with her information—for example, that is has too high a chance of being misleading—and she is aware of this at t_2 and does not adopt the preferences extensionally equivalent to those she had at t_1, then, again, there must be something wrong with her norm. In short: if she thinks the information is good, then she ought to be willing to act on it whether or not she has received it already, and if she thinks it is bad, then she ought not to be willing to act on it at either time. But she is only willing to act on it after she has received it.

This argument assumes that there is a single perspective to which the agent has access, relative to which the information is good or bad. However, what we really have are two different informational positions, and there is no third-person perspective from which we can say which informational position is better without knowing the whole truth: that is, without knowing whether EF holds. Although the agent has a view about what the best decision is when taking into account the information that E and what the best decision is not taking it into account, the two information states are not necessarily comparable. Granted, her information at t_2 is a superset of her information at t_1, but as I have pointed out, she may be farther away from the truth on a proposition that is really important to her decision (EF): there is no natural sense in which her

---

[39] I am using "good" and "bad" in a purely instrumental sense, given the choice she has; again, we know the information is factual.

[40] van Fraassen's (1984) reflection principle implies, roughly, that if you know you will have some particular credence in the future, you ought to adopt that credence now. (I say "roughly" because the principle is formulated in terms of conditional credence, not knowledge.)

information *about EF* at t_2 is a superset of her information *about EF* at t_1. And granted, on average she will be closer to the truth on EF at t_2, but whether what happens on average is a good guide to what she should do now is precisely what is at issue. The agent at the different times is simply in different positions from which to evaluate the instrumental value of an action. Therefore, my defense of the agent neither adopting her t_2 preferences at t_1 nor adopting her t_1 preferences at t_2 is that the preferences she has at each time are the appropriate ones from her perspective at that time, and while she does not think there is anything amiss in her perspective at the other time, she also does not think it is better than her current perspective. And this is not inconsistent, because there is no fact of the matter about which perspective is better, apart from what is actually the case.

We can see, then, why either sophisticated choice or resolute choice could be necessary without any underlying inconsistency. An agent cannot always judge from a neutral position which of two information states is better given the aim of ending up with what she wants. In each of the three arguments in the previous section, the information states at t_1 and t_2 are incomparable in this way. In order to act, the agent needs to make her preferences about plans compatible with one of these information states—being a resolute chooser corresponds to committing to act on the prior information state and being a sophisticated chooser corresponds to committing to act on the posterior information state—but that does not mean she sees the other as worse, and hence does not mean she sees some of her preferences as failing to cohere. Interestingly, then, when we allow a wider range of choices given one's values and beliefs—when we allow that many norms are permissible—we introduce some indeterminacy about which informational position is better.

Does that mean that the defender of global sensitivity must claim that in general more information does not make an agent better off but instead simply puts her in a different, and incomparable, position? No. Most of the time, receiving more information and then acting on it will be at least weakly preferable from *both* points of view. Let t_1 be the time before the agent has received the information, and t_2 be the time after. The information will be preferable at t_2 because the t_2 agent by hypothesis prefers to do the act that maximizes REU given her current beliefs, which take the information into account. And the information will be preferable at t_1 under most conditions because in general it will allow her to eliminate acts whose main virtues lie in what happens in states she may discover do not obtain.

Can we determine any general restrictions on when, if a globally sensitive agent knows she will prefer f to g at t_2 after learning the truth-value of E, she will prefer f to g at t_1? Recall that in the Allais case, the fact that the agent is ambivalent about whether t_1 or t_2 is a better position to judge from—that is to say, her t_1 and t_2 preferences disagree about this—is explained by the fact that the information stands a high enough chance, from the t_1 perspective, of leading her to choose something at t_2 that turns out much worse for her, by leading her to think L_{3+} (or L_3) is much better than it actually is. More abstractly, it is explained by the fact that the agent runs the risk of being misled to think that the good state of L_3 is more likely than it is without at the same time being led to any similar misapprehensions about L_4. In this sense the potential information about the two gambles is asymmetrical. But consider a situation in which the agent is deciding between two acts and all the information that makes one act seem better also makes the other act seem better: for any state of the world, the information partition under consideration is such that each member of the partition increases the value of one gamble only if it increases the value of the other gamble. In this situation, although there may be misleading evidence about the value of each act—the information might make the agent revise the value of each act so that the new instrumental value is farther away from its actual value—there cannot be misleading evidence about *the choice between* the two acts. And, indeed, this is just what the restricted version of STP, the Comonotonic Sure-thing Principle, formalizes.

STP says that if two gambles agree on $\bar{E}$, then an agent's conditional preferences between the gambles upon learning E must be the same as her unconditional preferences between the gambles. CSTP says this need only be true if learning E has the same "status" for all acts: it makes one of the acts seem better only if it does not make the other act seem worse. For example, if it eliminates the worst outcomes of one act, it must only eliminate the worst outcomes of the other. Dynamically, what CSTP says is this. Reversing the order of the choice and chance nodes cannot have an effect on which lottery-consequence the agent ends up with as long as putting the chance node first does not give the agent asymmetric information about the gambles: as long as some event in the chance node does not eliminate outcomes lower in one act's structural ordering than in the other's. So we can see that the globally sensitive agent's unconditional preferences agree across time with her conditional preferences as long as the information she will receive makes the positions comparable in this sense.

6.5 The Cost of Global Sensitivity

I have examined several ways of arguing that STP or Independence violators are inconsistent over time. These arguments center around the fact that for STP/Independence violators there will be some partition of the world into events $\{E, \bar{E}\}$ such that the agent prefers f to g, but would prefer g to f upon learning E and upon learning $\bar{E}$. I examined whether an individual who violates STP/Independence will be unable to follow through on her plans, and whether she will choose options that are foreseeably worse for her or are dominated by some other option that is available to her. While this may be true for the naïve chooser, both the sophisticated chooser and the resolute chooser are able to follow through on their plans and choose non-dominated options. And at least one of these methods is consequentialist. Therefore, globally sensitive agents can make coherent, consequentialist plans. However, the crucial issue turns out not to be whether there is a choice method that when applied to preferences over time produces such plans. After all, there are choice methods that do this for diachronically incoherent preferences, such as those in the wine-drinking example. The issue is whether preferences that give rise to incoherent plans for the naïve chooser must thereby be inconsistent, as they are in decision-making under certainty: whether employing resolute or sophisticated choice is already a sign of inconsistent underlying values.

There are several respects in which the diachronic preferences resulting from STP/Independence violation are different from the preferences with foreseeable shifts in decision-making under certainty. The first is that in the case of STP/Independence violations by globally sensitive agents, the agent's preferences over outcomes do not change. And the second is that in the case of STP/Independence violations, the agent at the later time is not choosing among the exact same options that she was choosing among at the earlier time: they have been narrowed down on the basis of information received in the interim. Furthermore, the agent at the earlier time endorses the preferences she has at the later time, given the information she will have at that time, in the sense that they are the preferences she would have in that situation given her values, beliefs, and norm. Given these two facts, the globally sensitive agent across time has a single preference ordering over both outcome-consequences and lottery-consequences.

Examining these facts led to finally isolating the crux of the worry about diachronic incoherence. Globally sensitive agents who are going to learn whether E know what their future preferences will be, and endorse them, but do not always adopt them. This phenomenon arises only when the truth-value of E is "asymmetric" news for the acts the agent is choosing between, and in particular when receiving misleading evidence about one of the events contained in E and then acting on it would be particularly bad for the agent. The Comonotonic Sure-Thing Principle ensures that the phenomenon does not arise when the possible information to be learned is partitioned into news that is of a similar nature for both gambles.

Consequentialism requires caring only about the results of one's actions and not about intrinsic features of the acts themselves. An agent facing a decision under risk is in a non-ideal position: she cannot be certain of the results of all of the acts available to her and so cannot simply choose the option with the best consequence. Instead, she must choose the option that best trades off her various aims and the probabilities that each act has of realizing these aims. I have argued that the globally sensitive agent will make choices that depend only on how much she values various outcomes and which strategy she thinks will best realize her aims. REU theory is consequentialist in the strongest sense in which a theory of decision-making under risk can be.

Adhering to consequentialism in the sense of having consistent ends and evaluating acts based only on how likely they are to realize those ends does place some requirements on decision-making over time. It requires that one is indifferent to the relative placement of chance nodes: if the agent has a consistent norm for trading off her aims given how she values consequences, then two adjacent chance nodes can be switched without affecting the agent's choice. It also requires being indifferent to the relative placement of choice nodes: if one consistently values ends, then two adjacent choice nodes can be switched without affecting what the outcome of one's preferred plan is. However, it need not require being indifferent to the placement of choice and chance nodes relative to each other: even if an agent's desires, beliefs, and norm are consistent, a choice node cannot necessarily be "switched" with an adjacent chance node, because this changes the lotteries that her choices at each time are between, and the values of these lotteries may be affected by the information she has at the time of choice. In particular, switching the nodes may differently affect the structural properties of the part of each act that might still be "live" at the time the agent is choosing: for example, some information might entail that the option which contains the minimum of one act will still be live while the option which contains the minimum of the other act will not be. We can only guarantee that a chance node can be moved prior to a choice node when doing so does not open up the possibility of the agent learning news that is good for one gamble but bad for another. This will mean that extensive form decisions cannot always be reduced to normal form decisions: one cannot only consider one's preferences over total plans at the outset but must sometimes consider one's future preferences at each choice point. There is an obvious analog here to the fact that in the synchronic case the globally sensitive agent cares about structural properties of acts. Caring about structural features of acts corresponds to caring about structural features of diachronic choice problems such as when decisions are made relative to information, precisely because when one's information is different, the considerations one must balance are different.

Here is what emerges from the discussion. The globally sensitive agent, in certain situations, faces a dilemma about how to choose over time—a dilemma that threatens the claim that her preferences are rational. She can get out of this dilemma—and choose in accordance with consequentialism—by being either a resolute chooser or a sophisticated chooser. However, there is a cost. Being a sophisticated chooser means that she has to pay attention to which choices she will be offered in the future and that her own future preferences will sometimes limit her options. Being a resolute chooser means that she will sometimes have to defer to her past self and stick with a decision that she no longer endorses. But importantly, the situations in which these costs will be borne will be limited: they will be limited to cases in which the possible information the agent expects to learn is asymmetric in the threat that it poses as misleading evidence to each option she is considering. They will be limited to cases in which the agent does not have an independent view of which informational position is better.

Perhaps it is a somewhat unpalatable upshot that more information is not always better for decision-making, and that we cannot always say which of two informational positions is better even when the information in one is a superset of the information in the other. But I think it is more palatable than the claim that rational agents cannot care at all about the structural properties of the acts they are deciding among, particularly when we notice that the incomparability of informational positions arises from instrumental reasons for preference rather than from the values of the outcomes themselves. So I am willing to accept this upshot. If the reader gets off the boat here, then I have at least made it clear what tradeoffs are involved in choosing between permitting global sensitivity and prohibiting it: the bullet one has to bite in accepting global neutrality as the uniquely rational norm is to reject the reasons for caring about global properties discussed thus far, and the bullet one has to bite in accepting that global sensitivity is permissible is to reject the idea that choices are always better from a position of more information.

7

Bookmaking and Packaging

7.1 Bookmaking Arguments

I have considered several arguments that rational decision-makers must have preferences that conform to the Sure-Thing Principle or the Independence Axiom, on pain of
not having consistent ends or of not consistently preferring the means to their ends. If
preferences must conform to STP or Independence, then if rationality requires REU
maximization, it requires global neutrality, and so REU theory collapses into EU theory. I considered an argument from dominance considerations, an argument from
consequentialism along with diachronic choice methods, and an argument about
how an agent's preferences before learning some information should be related to her
preferences upon learning the information; but none of these, I argued, succeeded in
showing that STP and Independence are requirements of rationality. This chapter will
consider two general arguments that the only rational risk function is the globally
neutral one. In particular, we will consider the argument that we can "make book"
against globally sensitive agents and the argument that globally sensitive agents choose
against their preferences in the long-run. These arguments do not address a particular
axiom but rather REU theory as a whole.

This section and the next concern bookmaking arguments. There are two kinds of
bookmaking argument: money pump arguments and Dutch book arguments. In
money pump arguments, a clever "bookmaker" typically offers the agent a sequence of
trades, each of which he finds favorable but that taken together lead to a sure loss. For
example, here is an argument that an agent with intransitive preferences—an agent
who strictly prefers some item X to some item Y, strictly prefers Y to some further item
Z, and strictly prefers Z to X—can be used as a money pump. Let us assume that the
agent starts with Z. A bookmaker offers her Y in exchange for Z and some small
amount of money; and then offers her X in exchange for Y and some small amount of
money; and then offers her Z in exchange for X and some small amount of money. (If
we do not want to assume that the agent starts with Z, the bookmaker can sell her Z at
the beginning of the process and then buy it back at the same price later.) The agent will
then be in the same position she started in except that she will be a few dollars poorer;
furthermore, the bookmaker can repeat the procedure to use the agent as a "money
pump." In Dutch book arguments, the bookmaker typically offers the agent a package
of bets that each pay off in some state of the world, and that she each finds favorable,

but that taken together lead to a sure loss no matter what state the world is in.[1] The bookmaker can thus make a book against the agent: put her in a position to lose money no matter what happens. Since I will discuss these arguments at length, I will not offer an example here. (The terminological difference is that money pump arguments traditionally involve exchanges of goods whose value does not depend on the state of the world; and Dutch book arguments traditionally involve purchases of bets whose value does depend on the state of the world, but nothing crucial hangs on this distinction.) Recall that the outcomes of a gamble must be described to include everything the agent cares about; therefore, it technically does not make sense to talk about a package of gambles that an agent holds simultaneously. So we will refer to **bets**, which are objects of choice whose outcomes are changes in wealth: functions from states of the world to changes in wealth rather than to fully specified outcomes.

In both money pump and Dutch book arguments, the agent is shown to be irrational by showing that she will assent to sure loss. What exactly is the force of the criticism that a decision-maker has preferences that can make her subject to sure loss in these peculiar circumstances, and how does it show that she is irrational? Certainly the criticism cannot be that the decision-maker is in real danger of losing her money. One is not likely to encounter a bookmaker, and even if one did, the bets he offered might be unattractive on other grounds: some propositions may not be decided within one's lifetime, and thus bets on these propositions may have no chance of paying off when the money would be useful; or one might not want to waste one's time for the small sums involved in the bets. On the contrary, what is bad about being subject to sure loss as a result of one's own preferences is that sure loss is something that one disprefers. Thus, what is bad about vulnerability to bookmaking is that the agent's preferences are inconsistent.[2] The agent simultaneously prefers a set of bets or trades to the status quo, because each bet or trade is individually favorable, but she disprefers that very same set to the status quo, because losing money is dispreferred to not losing money. This vulnerability can therefore be cashed out as a violation of (MCC): described as a set of individual bets, the agent prefers the set to the status quo, but described as a collection taken together, she prefers the status quo.

If we can produce a set of bets that the agent finds favorable considered individually and finds disfavorable considered as a package, this will reveal that she has inconsistent preferences. Similarly, if we can produce a set of bets that the agent finds *disfavorable* considered individually but *favorable* considered as a package, the agent will be inconsistent in exactly the same way: she will prefer f to g under one description but g to f

---

[1] There is no generally accepted view on the origins of the term "Dutch book." In an unpublished paper, Paul Humphreys notes that its first use in the philosophical literature was by Lehman (1955), who claims it is a slang term used by professional bettors in America. Humphreys notes three possibilities for inclusion of the adjective "Dutch": the Dutch were thought of by Americans as being interested in gambling; the adjective "Dutch" was sometimes used by Americans as a derogatory slur; and "Dutch" was sometimes used by Americans to refer to Germans ("Deutsch"). Despite the possible regrettable origin, I will continue to use the term, as it has become standard in the literature.

[2] This point was first made by Ramsey (1926).

under another. Therefore, showing that an agent is subject to "reverse bookmaking"—that she is willing to forgo sure gains—is another way of showing that she is irrational. This will be important in what follows.

One's **betting quotient** for a proposition E is the ratio of the maximum amount of money one is willing to pay for a bet that pays $x if E obtains (and nothing otherwise) to the amount of the payoff. For example, if I am willing to pay $3 but no more for a bet that pays $10 if Tenderfoot wins, then my betting quotient for the proposition that Tenderfoot wins is 3/10. Since one's betting quotient can depend on what $x is, a betting quotient will be relativized to the stakes involved. For the EU maximizer dealing with amounts of money over which his utility function is linear, his betting quotients are his degrees of belief: $BQ(E) = p(E)$. The standard use of Dutch book arguments is to show that unless an agent's degrees of belief obey the probability calculus, there will be a set of bets, each of which the agent each finds favorable, that taken together lead to sure loss. But what the argument shows more precisely is that *betting quotients* must obey the probability calculus, when dealing with amounts of money that are valued linearly. The conclusion that credences must obey the probability calculus comes via the purported link between credences and betting quotients—a link which might be taken to be definitional or alternatively to follow from the claim that rational bettors maximize expected utility and utility is linear in small amounts of money. An argument against global sensitivity cannot, of course, assume this link, since the relationship between credences and betting quotients is precisely what is at issue. But there is a natural way to turn the argument into an argument against global sensitivity. On REU theory, $BQ(E) = r(p(E))$, and p is a probability function. Therefore, since one conclusion of the Dutch book argument is that BQ must be additive, the argument can be used to show that $r(p)$ must be additive and thus that $r(p) = p$.[3]

Here is the argument that betting quotients must be additive—that $BQ(E) + BQ(F) = BQ(E \vee F)$ when E and F are incompatible.[4] Assume that the agent's utility function is linear in small amounts of money. Now consider three bets: a bet that pays $1 if E obtains; a bet that pays $1 if F obtains; and a bet that pays $1 if E v F obtains (Fig. 7.1). $BQ(E) is the agent's fair price for ticket 1, $BQ(F) is the agent's fair price for ticket 2, and $BQ(E v F) is the agent's fair price for ticket 3. Now consider what happens if $BQ(E) + $BQ(F) > $BQ(E v F). A cunning bookmaker can sell the agent ticket 1 for $BQ(E) and ticket 2 for $BQ(F), so that the agent will get $1 from ticket 1 if E and $1 from ticket 2 if F; the bookmaker can then buy from the agent ticket 3 for $BQ(E v F): that is, buy from her an agreement that she must pay him $1 if E v F obtains and nothing otherwise. So the agent will be out some positive amount of money $BQ(E) + $BQ(F)

---

[3] Since r is a non-decreasing transformation of p, the additivity of p on events and the additivity of r on events together imply that r is linear. Formally, $p(E \vee F) = p(E) + p(F)$ and $r(p(E \vee F)) = r(p(E)) + r(p(F))$ on all disjoint events E and F implies that $r(a+b) = r(a) + r(b)$ for all a and b; except in the degenerate case in which for some c and for all E, $p(E) \neq c$, in which case $r(c)$ never corresponds to the betting quotient of any bet. To see this, pick E and F such that $p(E) = a$ and $p(F) = b$. Finally, since $r(0) = 0$ and $r(1) = 1$, we have $r(p) = p$.

[4] Versions of this argument appear in Ramsey (1926), Schick (1986), Resnik (1987), Armendt (1993), and Jeffrey (2004), among others.

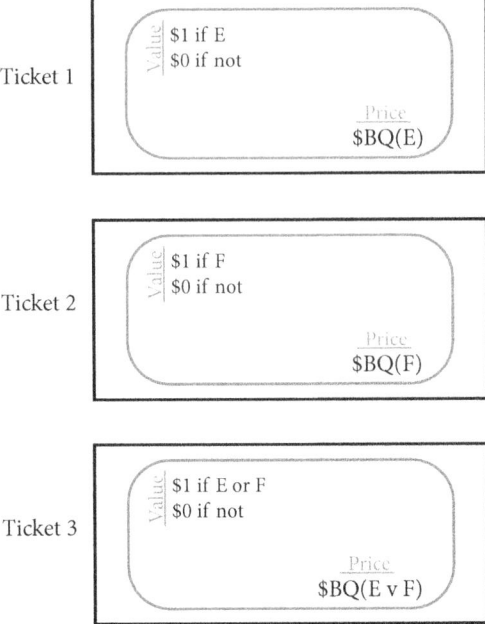

Fig. 7.1. Book-making argument.

− $BQ(E v F) before the bets are paid off. But in every state of the world, the agent's bet pays off if and only if the bookmaker's does, so no money is exchanged. Thus, the agent suffers a sure loss. A similar argument can show that the agent suffers a sure loss if $BQ(E) + $BQ(F) < $BQ(E v F), though in this case the bookmaker buys the first two tickets from the agent and sells her the third. In either case, as Brad Armendt puts it, the bookmaker "sell[s] the agent something at a high price, and buy[s] what is the same thing, or what is in all relevant respects an equivalent thing, back at a low price, and pocket[s] the difference."[5] Consequently, the agent can only avoid sure loss if $BQ(E) + $BQ(F) = $BQ(E v F).

This argument makes an assumption that is not true of a globally sensitive agent. We will see that the assumption is not ultimately crucial to the argument, but it will be helpful to see the role it plays before we eliminate it. The assumption is that the price at which the agent is willing to sell a bet on E (accept money with the understanding that she will pay $1 if E obtains), is the same as the price at which the agent is willing to buy a bet on E (pay money with the understanding that she will get $1 if E obtains: namely $BQ(E)). It assumes that there is a single "fair price" such that the agent is willing to buy a bet on E for this price and willing to sell a bet on E for this price. But this will not be true for the globally sensitive agent. Just to be clear, buying and selling a

_____

[5] Armendt (1993: 6).

bet on E do not mean buying and selling the exact same bet: I am not saying that once an agent purchases a ticket, she will be unwilling to sell it back for the same price, as if a bet is somehow more valuable because it is hers. Rather, the bet that the agent undergoes when she "buys a bet on E" is {E, agent gets $1; Ē, agent gets $0}, and the bet she undergoes when she "sells a bet on E" is {E, agent gets −$1; Ē, agent gets $0}: the inverse of the first bet. For the REU maximizer, the monetary equivalent of the former will be $r(p(E))$, and of the latter will be $\$(r(p(\bar{E})) - 1)$. Thus she will be willing to buy a bet on E for $\$r(p(E))$ and sell its inverse for $\$(1 - r(p(\bar{E})))$. (She will also be willing to sell back or buy back each of these bets for its original purchase price, since she is indifferent between having the purchase price and having the bet.) And while these two expressions will be equivalent when $r(p) = p$, they will not necessarily be equivalent in general. Their equivalence is a consequence of what the Dutch book argument is trying to establish. For the risk-avoidant agent, the buying price of a bet is lower than the selling price of its inverse. Buying a bet amounts to increasing one's maximum and selling a bet to lowering one's minimum. For the same reason, the risk-inclined agent's preferences have the opposite relationship: the buying price of a bet will be higher than the selling price of its inverse.

So, for example, the risk-avoidant agent with $r(p) = p^2$ will be willing to pay 25 cents for a coin-flip that pays her $1 on heads, but she will not be willing to accept 25 cents for a coin-flip in which *she* pays $1 on heads. The minimum amount she would accept for such a bet is 75 cents. So, in the above argument, if E is "the coin lands heads" and F is "the coin lands tails" and the agent believes the coin to be fair, she will pay 25 cents for either of the first two tickets, and sell the third for $1. Or she will sell either of the first two for 75 cents, and buy the third for a dollar. In either case, she will not be subject to sure loss. Interestingly enough, since his buying price is generally higher than his selling price, the risk-inclined agent cannot use this response. A risk-inclined agent with $r(p) = p^{1/2}$, for example, will buy the first ticket for 71 cents and the second ticket for 71 cents, and will sell the third ticket for a dollar. So he *will* be subject to sure loss if the other steps of the argument are correct. Given all this, the most the Dutch book argument can show is that buying prices cannot be higher than selling prices, which is true for the risk-avoidant agent but not the risk-inclined agent.

However, there is also something problematic about this response on behalf of the risk-avoidant agent. If she will pay no more than 25 cents each for the first two tickets, and sell the third for no less than $1, then she will reject the package consisting in buying the first two tickets for 26 cents each and selling the third for $1. In other words, she will not pay 52 cents for a guaranteed dollar; and so she will forgo sure gain. As pointed out above, this is just as bad as being susceptible to sure loss. Given this, and given that the objectionable feature of Dutch-bookable agents is really inconsistent value judgments rather than susceptibility to sure loss, we can recast the argument without the language of buying and selling, but still bring out the worry that the agent is sensitive to how a gamble is described.

Here is the Dutch book argument without the problematic assumption. The agent is willing to pay \$BQ(E) for ticket 1, she is willing to pay \$BQ(F) for ticket 2, and she is willing to pay \$BQ(E v F) for ticket 3. Therefore, she is willing to pay \$BQ(E) + \$BQ(F) for the package consisting of ticket 1 and ticket 2. But this package of tickets pays \$1 in the exact same circumstances in which ticket 3 pays \$1: taking both gamble 1 and gamble 2 is extensionally equivalent to taking gamble 3. Therefore, it had better be the case that \$BQ(E) + \$BQ(F) = \$BQ(E v F). If not, then the agent assigns different value to two acts that are extensionally equivalent. She violates (MCC) and thus values acts inconsistently.

If this argument is sound, then the globally sensitive agent is in bad shape, whether she is risk-avoidant, risk-inclined, or follows any other norm besides the globally neutral norm. In the following section I will show that the argument begs the question against the globally sensitive agent. In particular, the argument assumes that if an agent is willing to pay \$x for one gamble and \$y for another then she is willing to pay \$x + \$y for both, and this assumption is generally false for the globally sensitive agent. Furthermore, we cannot assume there must be a context in which bets are cumulative in this way unless we *start* with the assumption that global sensitivity is irrational.

7.2 The Package Principle

Frederick Schick and Brad Armendt both point out that Dutch book arguments like the above argument rest on the following assumption:[6]

> **Synchronic Package Principle**: The value to an agent of bet A is the same whether or not she thinks bet B is in effect.

This assumption was needed to move from the fact that the agent is willing to pay \$BQ(E) for ticket 1 and is willing to pay \$BQ(F) for ticket 2 to the assertion that she is willing to pay \$BQ(E) + \$BQ(F) for both tickets. Schick also points out that the money pump argument for transitivity relies on an analogous Diachronic Package Principle: namely, that the value of a trade is independent of which trades you have accepted in the past (or will accept in the future).[7]

Why might the Synchronic Package Principle fail? As both Schick and Armendt point out, one reason is that one's beliefs about, for example, E and F (and therefore one's betting quotients for these propositions), might vary with the stakes involved, and another reason is that the utility value of money might not be linear. Schick and Armendt each discuss (though do not necessarily endorse) reasons for thinking that the proponent of the Dutch book argument for betting quotient additivity is not entitled to assume that beliefs are invariant with stakes and that the value of money is linear. However, I do not challenge either of these assumptions, because I do not want the

---

[6] Schick (1986), and Armendt (1993). Formulation Schick's, pp. 113–4. Schick calls this assumption "value-wise independence." Wakker (2010) calls this assumption "additivity of preference."

[7] Maher (1993) makes a similar point.

rationality of global sensitivity to depend on rejecting them: I accept the first as a requirement of rationality, and as for the second, as long as there are some goods or monetary amounts that display value independence—and I will say something in a moment about why we might be entitled to assume there are—we could recast the argument in terms of these.

Alternatively, Schick points out that the Synchronic Package Principle might fail because the agent with non-additive betting quotients recognizes that she had better reject it or she will be in trouble. Schick's suggestion is that Dutch book arguments show that an agent cannot both have non-additive betting quotients and accept the Synchronic Package Principle; and that if an agent becomes aware that her betting quotients are non-additive, she must either change them or not conform to the package principle. Analogously, according to Schick, the money pump argument for transitivity shows that an agent cannot both have intransitive preferences and preferences that conform to the Diachronic Package Principle.

While there is something right in this response, it is not fully satisfying. True, the agent can avoid a Dutch book or money pump by recognizing that it is coming, but unless she has some principled reason for not conforming to the package principles, then it seems like she is avoiding sure loss only by denying her actual preferences. And this does not help show that her actual preferences are consistent. As we saw in the previous chapter, is it perhaps not too difficult to have coherent consequentialist plans given one's preferences, but the need to use sophisticated or resolute choice to do so can sometimes betray diachronically inconsistent preferences. Failure to conform to the Diachronic Package Principle raises a similar worry. Similarly, it is perhaps not too difficult to ensure that one's preferences about packages of bets are consistent, but the need to choose as you otherwise would not on particular bets in these packages—failure to conform to the Synchronic Package Principle—might reveal a problem with the underlying preferences about bets. Furthermore, simply denying one of the package principles does not illuminate what was initially appealing about the bookmaking arguments. What the defender of global sensitivity needs is an explanation both of why we might be drawn to the Synchronic Package Principle, and of why the Synchronic Package Principle does not in fact hold in the Dutch book argument for additivity of betting quotients. Similarly, although I do not defend intransitive preferences, anyone who does defend them needs to explain why the Diachronic Package Principle looks appealing but does not hold in the context of the money pump argument.

The Synchronic Package Principle does not follow from decision theory or its axioms. Indeed, there is a sense in which it is contrary to the technical machinery of decision theory. Recall that an outcome encompasses everything the agent cares about. Ticket 2, "$1 if F, $0 if F̄," is not itself a fully specified act: it is shorthand for {F, status quo plus $1; F̄, status quo plus $0}. But what the status quo is, and whether the status quo should itself be thought of as a gamble itself, depends on which other bets are in effect. So we cannot even state the "full" outcomes of the act of taking a bet without knowing which other bets are in effect. And given that taking concurrent bets will make the act of taking each bet different by definition, restricting preferences so that they do not take concurrent bets into account seems contrary to the Humean idea of allowing decision-makers to have any preferences they want as long as the preferences are internally consistent. Granted, we are currently debating what counts as consistency, but the debate is between REU theory and EU theory, and the Synchronic Package Principle imposes a constraint that is not imposed by either.

However, the Synchronic Package Principle is attractive. Why should this be, given that as far as consistency goes, any change to the world is allowed to affect an agent's preferences? The thought underlying the Synchronic Package Principle, I think, is a view about what human psychology is like: namely, that preferences about incremental changes to the world—receiving goods, say—are relatively stable under changes to the background conditions. For example, if a decision-maker prefers the world he is in plus a candy bar to the world he is in plus an extra \$5, then if we change the world by giving him a brown coat instead of a blue one, then he will (or perhaps should) prefer the new situation plus a candy bar to the new situation plus an extra \$5, even if he has a preference about coat color, as long as his coat color is not relevant to the benefits he can get from the candy bar or \$5. Small changes to the world should not completely unseat preferences about other small changes to the world.

That preferences are stable in this way is an assumption we make when we use preferences to interpret beliefs and desires: when someone selects chicken over steak, we do not only conclude that she prefers the world exactly like ours except that she eats chicken to the world exactly like ours except that she eats steak; rather, we draw the further conclusion that she in general (though not necessarily always) prefers worlds in which she eats chicken to worlds in which she eats steak. Indeed, it is the fact that preferences about small changes are relatively stable that allows us to carry on the non-formal discussion in this book at the level of preferences about changes to the status quo, without having to fix on a particular status quo, instead of at the level of preferences about total situations. We assume that within a limited range of changes to the status quo, it will not matter what else is going on in the world: this is why your preferences in the "Elvis stamp" example will not change when you pick up this book at different times—when your "background" situation looks slightly different. Perhaps more controversially, we also seem to make this assumption in prescriptive decision theory: if your "foreground" preferences do vary when your background situation changes, we think you ought to be able to explain why this change in your total situation is relevant to the foreground choices you face.

In Section 4.3 we examined Pettit's Principle of Individuation by Properties (PIP) and the idea that we ought not distinguish outcomes unless they differ in a property the agent cares about. The point here is an extension of that idea. (PIP) places no restrictions on preferences if the outcomes involved differ in features that the agent cares about. So, if the agent prefers wearing a brown coat to wearing a blue coat, then (PIP) does not say anything about the relationship between his brown-coat-plus-something preferences and his blue-coat-plus-something preferences. But presumably if coat color is something the agent cares about but is not relevant to the feature of the world the agent is making a choice about ($5 or a candy bar, with the color of the coat fixed), then it should not make a difference to that choice. If, say, the agent is indifferent between $5-while-wearing-a-brown-coat and candy-bar-while-wearing-a-brown-coat, then he ought to be indifferent between $5-while-wearing-a-blue-coat and candy-bar-while-wearing-a-blue-coat as long as coat color does not change the desirable features of $5 or the candy bar. This will not directly follow from Pettit's principle, since the blue-coat choices differ from the brown-coat choices in instantiating a property that the agent cares about (coat color), but it is in line with Pettit's point that prospect-desires are based on property-desires.[8] Furthermore, this point explains the intuitive need to locate the difference in the lone steak-rather-than-chicken preference from Chapter 4 in some difference related to those items rather than in some change in the world that the agent cares about but is unrelated.

We can formalize the principle suggested by this point:

Stability Principle: If an agent is indifferent between two gambles f and g whose fully-described outcomes differ only in that f includes some item X where g includes some item Y, then for gambles f' and g' that differ from each other only in that f' includes X where g' includes Y, she is indifferent between f' and g' unless the difference between f and f' or between g and g' is relevant to the choice between X and Y.

Without a principle like this in place, there is nothing to prevent an agent from having wildly different preferences about particular foreground bets against the background of only slightly different fully-described situations. But we think that there are, or should be, strong connections between how an agent evaluates these bets against one background and how she evaluates them against an only slightly different background: foreground preferences ought to be somewhat stable. Compare this proposal to one of the complaints against the "maximal" individuation in Chapter 4: we saw that allowing the theory to individuate maximally finely severs the connection between the value of an outcome in one act and its value in another act. Here I am pointing out that rejecting the Stability Principle severs the connection between the value of a foreground bet against one background and its value against another.

There are three ways to take the Stability Principle. The first is in line with the idea that decision theory places restrictions only on the structure of agents' preferences. On this view, the Stability Principle is taken to *define* what it is for a difference in background to be relevant to a difference in some particular aspect of the world: the difference is relevant just in case it causes a preferences reversal of the sort described in the

---

[8]   Indeed, Pettit himself makes a similar point, in the course of arguing that most of us assume that desires for prospects are based on desires for properties. He points out that we feel some unease about saying that a person who drives across town in order to spend $150 instead of $200, but is not willing to drive across town to spend $15,000 rather than $15,050, is acting rationally, even though her doing so is perfectly consistent with the constraints of decision theory. Pettit (1991, p. 202).

principle above. (Defining relevance in terms of preference is akin to the way independence of goods was defined in terms of utility in Section 1.2.) Taken this way, it cannot have any bite in restricting preferences. The proponent of this interpretation can say one of two things about this. First, he can say that this is unproblematic, because we ought not restrict preferences on the basis of extra-theoretical principles. This response may be fine as far as it goes, though it will make the theory difficult to apply.[9] The other thing a proponent of the first interpretation can say is that the Stability Principle is a kind of defeasible prediction principle: an agent who violates it despite having proclaimed that a particular background difference is irrelevant is not irrational, but behaves in a way that we would not have expected given what we know about human psychology.

The second way to take the Stability Principle is in line with the idea that decision theory places restrictions on the relationship of an agent's preferences to her mental states. On this view, we can use the Stability Principle to restrict preferences, as long as we formulate the notion of relevance in a way that is both subjective and does not mention preferences. Some functionalists may claim, for example, that the role of preferences is more than simply disposing an agent to choose: preferences are also functionally related to the kinds of utterances an agent is disposed to make about what he cares about. For these functionalists, our data about preferences include, for example, that the agent is willing to describe certain features as irrelevant to the value of one another. These functionalists might define relevance, then, as follows: the difference between f and f' is relevant to X if X instantiates a property or occurs in a relation in f' that it does not instantiate in f (or *vice versa*) and the agent cares about this property or relation.

Finally, one might, contra Humeanism, want decision theory to place substantive restrictions on preferences. A proponent of this view can define relevance in terms of some objective standard. Thus, on this third interpretation, the Stability Principle does restrict preferences in a more robust way.

Given the Stability Principle, we can isolate a context in which we need only determine an agent's preferences among various foreground bets in order to determine her preferences among all of the fully described acts. The principle may be thought of as support for Savage's idea that we can solve the problem of what to do in the "grand world" decision problem—the decision problem in which all the potentially relevant factors are distinguished, by tackling simpler decision problems.[10]

The Stability Principle underlies the Synchronic Package Principle: the Synchronic Package Principle holds only if we can, without knowing all of the agent's preferences, isolate a rarified context in which minor changes to the background do not matter. The assumption that the agent's utility function is linear in money (a standard assumption in Dutch book arguments) is a part of isolating such a context: it guarantees that

---

[9] I said that much of the non-formal discussion of preferences in this book assumes this principle. That should not worry decision theorists who reject it, however, since the entire book could be recast with explicit mention of total situations at each turn.

[10] Savage (1954/1972, pp. 15–17 and 82–5).

whether the agent wins or loses on one bet will not make a difference to the utility value of the other bet. There will be no "interaction effects" between the monetary payouts of the bets: for each ticket, the money that that ticket yields (or does not yield) will contribute the same utility value to the total utility value of the *outcome* regardless of whether the other ticket pays off. Therefore, to look at each ticket's utility value contribution in a particular state, we need only look at whether that ticket paid off.

However, there is another kind of interaction effect that the proponents of the argument cannot rule out. This is the interaction effect that results when the money one gets in one state alters the utility value contribution to a *gamble* of the money one gets *in another state*. For globally sensitive agents, altering an outcome in one state of an act can affect the total value of the act via two routes. On the one hand, it can affect the value of the outcome in that state by changing the local properties: it can make that outcome better or worse. On the other hand, it can affect the value contribution of the outcome in that state and the outcomes in other states by changing the structural properties of the act: by raising the minimum, by changing the proportion of outcomes that are above the minimum, and so forth. Given the assumption that u is linear, one's having accepted a bet on E does not change the effect that accepting a bet on F has on the local properties: taking a bet on F makes the outcome in F better by the value of the money one wins if F obtains, and makes all the outcomes worse by the value of the money one pays for the bet. However, having taken a bet on E changes the effect that taking a bet on F has on the structural properties. If the globally sensitive agent does not hold a bet on E (ticket 1), then taking the bet on F (ticket 2) increases the probability of getting \$1 from 0 to $p(F)$; so the ticket will be worth $\$r(p(F))$. However, if she does hold a bet on E, then taking the bet on F increases this probability from $p(E)$ to $p(E \lor F)$. And, as we know, this difference matters to the globally sensitive agent: in general, $r(p(E \lor F)) - r(p(E)) \neq r(p(F)) - r(p(0))$. Increasing the probability of the better outcome makes more of a difference the closer the better outcome already is to certain. Ticket 2 will be worth $\$r(p(E \lor F)) - \$r(p(E))$ if our agent already holds ticket 1, and $\$r(p(F))$ if she does not: and these two values are not the same. In the example above, the value of "\$1 if TAILS" is 25 cents if one does not hold a \$1 bet on heads, and 75 cents if one does. In the context of the general argument, the value of ticket 2 will depend on whether the agent already holds ticket 1, in particular, if she holds ticket 1, then the value of ticket 2 will make up the difference between the value of ticket 3 and that of ticket 1. So tickets 1 and 2 taken together will have the same value as ticket 3, regardless of the shape of the agent's r-function.

To ensure that a "book" is made against agents with non-additive betting quotients, the proponent of the Dutch book argument needs to assume a context in which (1) taking two bets is extensionally equivalent to taking a third *and* (2) in which there are no interaction effects between bets. Satisfying (1) requires that the two bets have a particular relationship to each other: namely, that one bet "fills the gaps" in the states of the other to make the third. One bet must be defined not merely by outcomes on events with particular probabilities, but by outcomes on *particular* events, chosen because they are "troughs" (or "peaks") in the structure of the other bet: they are the events on which the bookmaker does not pay the agent for the other bet, or on which the agent is not forced to pay the bookmaker for the other bet. This means that the context will be one in which there are apt to be the second kind of interaction effects for the globally sensitive agent. The Dutch book arguments assume a rarified context in which the Synchronic Package Principle holds, but for the globally sensitive agent, such a context does not coexist with the bets required for the argument. Therefore, the assumption that there is a context like the one that the argument assumes begs the question against the globally sensitive agent.

For completeness, let me briefly say something about the money pump argument for transitivity. Can the defender of intransitive preferences make a parallel move to the one I have made in defending non-additive betting quotients? He might say that the Diachronic Package Principle is based on a different kind of stability principle: namely, that if one prefers "foreground" item Y to "foreground" item Z against one background, then changing the background in a way that is irrelevant to Y or Z will not unseat this preference. But in the money pump argument, the changes suggested are clearly relevant to the preference: in particular, the future possibility of trading Y for Z is relevant to whether one prefers Y to Z. So the money pump argument seems to beg the question against intransitivity. I do not wish to conclude that intransitivity is rational, however—just that the money pump argument does not bring out the irrationality. The problem with intransitive preferences is not that acting on them leads to doing what one disprefers, but that intransitive preferences cannot even be acted upon, since an agent with intransitive preferences will not be able to pick a "best act" from a set—in this case the set of $\{f + X, f + Y, f + Z\}$. Thus, the intransitive agent cannot coherently prefer the means to his ends, even at a time, because he has inconsistent ends.[11]

The Dutch book argument is supposed to operate in a context in which the Synchronic Package Principle holds of all of the relevant bets. But to assume such a context exists is to assume that agents are not globally sensitive. Moreover, with respect to the bets needed for the Dutch book argument, globally sensitive agents violate the Synchronic Package Principle for non-arbitrary reasons: they violate it because for globally sensitive agents the value of a bet depends on how it affects the risk profile of the entire act to which it contributes. Therefore, Dutch book arguments do not show that global sensitivity is irrational.

7.3 The Hypothetical Long-Run Argument

The final argument I want to consider against the rationality of global sensitivity is the argument that globally neutral agents do better that globally sensitive agents over the

---

[11] Granted, the agent who only ever faces pair-wise choices will never actually be prevented from taking the means to his ends, but neither will the agent who never faces any choice involving any options on which he is inconsistent. Again, it is a theoretical liability to be intransitive, not a practical one, though the liability lies in how the agent would act in hypothetical situations.

long-run. This argument has not been central to justifications of decision rules since the prescription to maximize expected monetary value was replaced by the prescription to maximize expected utility. Nevertheless, the connection between expectation and the long-run is so obvious that many will wonder about whether a long-run case can be make against global sensitivity. Furthermore, responding to this argument will illuminate how globally sensitive agents act when they face repeated bets, and how their expectations about the future bear on how to approach the present choice. There are two ways to formulate the argument that globally neutral agents do better over the long-run, which I will term the *hypothetical long-run argument* and the *motivational long-run argument*. Each argument tries to show, as the Dutch book argument tried to show, that REU theory sometimes gives two conflicting answers about what to prefer.

Let us start with the hypothetical long-run argument. The agent faces a choice between two bets, X and Y, described in terms of changes in utility. Thus she faces a choice between acts $s + X$ and $s + Y$, where s stands for the status quo, which for simplicity we can assume is not itself a gamble. Let us assume that X has a higher expected utility than Y, and so $s + X$ has a higher expected utility than $s + Y$.[12] To see which choice is rational, the argument goes, we must consider what would happen if the agent were to repeatedly face the choice between X and Y, and were to make the same decision each time. We must consider, that is, whether the agent would rather face a series of "X-bets" or a series of "Y-bets," where all of the trials in the series are independent of each other. We know from the Strong Law of Large Numbers that as the number of trials in the series tends to infinity, the average utility value of the members of each series will converge almost surely to $EU(X)$ and $EU(Y)$, respectively.[13] Thus, as long as the number of repeated bets is large enough, taking the X-bets almost surely yields higher utility than taking the Y-bets. Therefore, taking the X-bets in the hypothetical situation is preferred to taking the Y-bets. Given this, says the argument, the agent ought to prefer each instance of X to each instance of Y; in particular, she ought to prefer X to Y in the choice she actually faces. She ought to maximize expected utility.

For example, let X be the coin-flip between 0 utils and 1 util (or between suitable prizes with these incremental values); and let Y be a sure-thing outcome worth 0.4 utils. It is open to the globally sensitive agent to prefer Y: $s + Y$ might have a higher risk-weighted expected utility than $s + X$. However, when considering the choice between n instances of X and n instances of Y, as long as n is sufficiently large, it is almost certain that the former will add close to $0.5n$ utils to the status quo, while the latter will add $0.4n$ utils. So by the agent's own lights, she will prefer the Xs to the Ys. And she should therefore prefer X to Y in the single-shot decision.

---

[12] Technically, we have only defined the expected utility of lotteries and acts, rather than of bets. The expected utility of a bet that is described in terms of the utility change in each state is just a weighted average of the utility changes in each state, each utility change weighted by the probability of that state.

[13] The Strong Law of Large Numbers (SLLN) states that for independent trials {X$_i$} with a common distribution and expectation μ, the average value of the trials tends to μ with probability 1 (converges almost surely). Feller (1966: 233, Theorem 2). The only requirement is that X has finite expectation, which will hold true for all finite-valued bets.

The long-run utility argument rests on two claims: first, that taking the gamble with the higher EU in the hypothetical situation accords with the REU-maximizer's preferences. Second, that the hypothetical situation is a good guide to what the agent ought to choose in the actual, single-shot situation. Let us consider briefly the first claim. Notice that it is actually false for the most extreme risk-avoidant agent, the maximinimizer. If the maximinimizer strictly prefers $s + Y$ to $s + X$, then the maximinimizer will strictly prefer $s + [n$ instances of $Y]$ to $s + [n$ instances of $X]$ even when $s + X$ has higher expected utility, for arbitrarily high n. This is because if Y has a higher minimum than X, then $s + [n$ instances of $Y]$ has a higher minimum than $s + [n$ instances of $X]$, because the X-bets will only be close to $nEU(X)$ with probability less than 1 for any finite n. In the example above there is some chance, vanishingly small but non-zero, that n copies of X will yield 0 utils; however, n copies of Y will yield $0.4n$ utils no matter what. For the maximinimizer, as long as there is still a chance of each X yielding its minimum value, even a vanishingly small chance, she will prefer to take the Y-bets. After all, things could turn out as badly as possible, and all she cares about is the worst-case scenario. In order for her to prefer the X-bets, n would need to be infinite.

In Section 2.3 we explored some reasons for thinking that the maximinimizer may be irrational, so perhaps this gap in the argument is not so bad. Nonetheless, how the maximinimizer evaluates these gambles is instructive, because it gives us insight into how less extreme risk-avoidant REU maximizers—those with continuous r-functions—will evaluate these gambles: in general, the more risk-avoidant an agent is, the higher n will have to be for her to prefer the Xs.[14] Still, as long as r is continuous, there will be some n that will be high enough that the agent will prefer to take n X-bets rather than n Y-bets.[15] So while it is important to temper the claim about the agent's preference for repeated bets—the number of repetitions will need to be very high for the very risk-avoidant agent to prefer the X-bets—the defender of global sensitivity cannot deny that the globally sensitive agent does prefer to repeat the bet with the higher EU (as long as we are dealing with a globally sensitive agent with a continuous r-function). The important question, then, is how the way one chooses in the iterated hypothetical bears on the way one should choose in the single-shot decision.

Before responding to this argument on behalf of the globally sensitive agent, let us examine in more detail what EU theory itself says about the relationship between how

---

[14]   The precise conditions for how fast convergence of a series occurs are beyond the scope of this work.

[15]   Pick $\varepsilon < 0.1$ and $p < 1$ such that $r(p) > 4/(5 - 10\varepsilon)$ (the existence of such a p is guaranteed by the continuity of r). Then, by the SLLN, there exists an N such that for all $n > N$, and $Pr\left(\left| \sum_{i=1}^{n} \{X_i\} - 0.5n \right| < \varepsilon \right) > p$ (where Pr is the objective probability function specified in the SLLN). Assume the agent's subjective probability function agrees with Pr. Then $REU(s + [n$ copies of $X]) > u(s) + r(p)[0.5n - \varepsilon] > u(s) + 0.4n = REU(s + [n$ copies of $Y])$. In general, for a risk-avoidant agent with continuous risk function facing a repeated choice between two utility bets, there will be some n such that n copies of the bet with higher expected utility is preferred to n copies of the bet with lower expected utility. This follows from repeated application of the fact shown in Section 2.2 that as long as r is continuous, as the probability of the most extreme outcome gets arbitrarily close to zero, the value of the gamble gets arbitrarily close to that of the gamble that includes the next-most-extreme outcome in place of that one.

an agent should choose in an iterated decision and a single-shot decision. To do this, consider an argument against EU theory, analogous to the hypothetical long-run argument against REU theory, to the effect that rational agents maximize expected *monetary value* (EMV) rather than expected *utility*: that the utility function of an EU maximizer must be linear in money. This argument is unsound, and it will be instructive to see why. Here is the argument. Consider an agent whose utility function is increasing in money, who faces a choice between two bets X' and Y', described in terms of changes in monetary wealth. Thus she faces a choice between acts $s + X'$ and $s + Y'$. Let us assume that X' has a higher EMV than Y', and so $s + X'$ has a higher expected monetary value than $s + Y'$. Now consider which bet she would prefer to be repeated. Again, as long as the number of trials is large enough, taking the X'-bets almost certainly yields more money than taking the Y'-bets. Therefore, taking the X'-bets each time in the hypothetical situation is preferred to taking the Y'-bets. Given this, the agent ought to prefer taking each instance of X' to taking each instance of Y'; in particular, she ought to prefer taking X' to taking Y' in the choice she actually faces.

To take an example analogous to the one above: let X' be the coin-flip between $0 and $1; and let Y' be a guaranteed $0.40. It is open to the EU maximizer with diminishing marginal utility to prefer Y'. However, when considering the choice between n copies of X' and n copies of Y', as long as n is sufficiently large, the former almost surely will yield close to $0.5n$, while the latter will yield $0.4n$. So by the agent's own lights, she will prefer the X'-bets to the Y'-bets. And she should therefore prefer X' to Y' in the single-shot decision.

The EU theorist will not be fazed by this argument. He will point out that the assumption that when facing repeated copies of a bet, one should choose each time as if one is choosing in the single-shot case, is not justified by EU theory. This is because the EU of repeating a monetary bet need not be directly proportional to the EU of the bet taken only once when utility diminishes marginally. In particular, how the repetitions affect the total EU depends on facts about the distribution of monetary value that make the monetary mean what it is. For example, let $u(\$x) = x^{1/2}$ for amounts of money above the status quo. The first instance of bet X' will be worth 0.5 utils, but the second instance of X' will turn the overall act from the status quo plus bet $\{\$0, 0.5; \$1, 0.5\}$, a bet which has an EU of 0.5, into the status quo plus bet $\{\$0, 0.25; \$1, 0.5; \$2, 0.25\}$, a bet which has an EU of 0.85, and so the second bet will increase the total EU of the package by 0.35. Similarly, the first instance of bet Y' will be worth 0.63 utils, but two instances of Y' will be worth 0.89, so the second bet will only increase the total EU of the package by 0.36 utils. As soon as we get to the third instance of each bet, each instance of X' contributes more to the X'-package than each instance of Y' contributes to the Y'-package. Furthermore, the X'-bets will be worth more than the Y'-bets once there are at least three of each. Since the increase to an outcome's utility value that comes from adding a particular amount of money to a particular outcome depends on how much money is already included in that outcome, we cannot calculate the expected utility of one "instance" of a monetary bet in isolation from the other bets the agent holds.

Therefore, for the EU maximizer, what an agent chooses in a single-shot decision problem need not reveal what she would choose in an iterated version of that problem: the monetary bet an agent would prefer to take once need not be the monetary bet she would prefer to repeat. Therefore, we cannot use a fact about what she ought to choose in the long-run to impugn a single-shot choice. There is no contradiction between a preference for a single-shot Y'-bet rather than a single-shot X'-bet on the one hand and a preference for iterated X'-bets rather than iterated Y'-bets on the other, because EU theory evaluates each member in an iterated series of bets by considering which bets one has already taken. The EU each bet adds to a package depends on which other bets are part of the package.

The REU theorist can apply this same solution to answer the hypothetical long-run argument against global sensitivity. Recall that the argument says that if $REU(s + X) <$ $REU(s + Y)$ but $EU(s + X) > EU(s + Y)$, then REU theory give conflicting recommendations about what to do when facing a decision about repeated iterations of the bets X and Y. On the one hand it will recommend that the agent choose iterations of Y, because taking Y has a higher risk-weighted expected utility. On the other hand it will recommend that the agent choose iterations of X, because this is the choice that, if repeated, will (almost certainly) lead to higher overall utility: $s + [n$ instances of $X]$ has a higher risk-weighted expected utility than $s + [n$ instances of $Y]$. But just as the analogous argument against EU maximization with non-linear utility relied on an assumption that is not faithful to how an EU maximizer evaluates bets, so too does this argument rely on an assumption that is not faithful to how an REU maximizer evaluates bets: it relies on the assumption that when facing repeated copies of a bet, one will choose each time as if one is choosing in the single-shot case. Just as the EU of a package of monetary bets need not be directly proportional to the EU of a single-shot bet, so too the REU of a package of utility bets need not be directly proportional to the REU of a single-shot bet. In the case of REU it need not be directly proportional because how the repetitions affect the total REU depends on the global facts about the distribution of utility value that make the utility mean is what it is. The utility increase to an outcome's utility value that comes from adding a particular utility "amount" to a particular outcome does not depend on how much utility is already included in that outcome (by definition), but the contribution that increase makes depends on the utility and probability profile of the rest of the package, because the weight attached to that increase depends on how much probability is already associated with outcomes of that utility or higher. Therefore, we cannot evaluate the risk-weighted expected utility of one "instance" of a utility bet in isolation from the other bets the agent holds. (See Fig. 7.2.)

There is no contradiction between the globally sensitive agent's preference for a single-shot Y-bet rather than a single-shot X-bet on the one hand and a preference for iterated X-bets rather than iterated Y-bets on the other. There are two ways to think about why multiple copies of one bet might be preferred even though a single copy of the other is preferred. The first is that REU maximizers are sensitive to both the mean and the spread. In the choice between X and Y, the act of taking X has a slightly higher

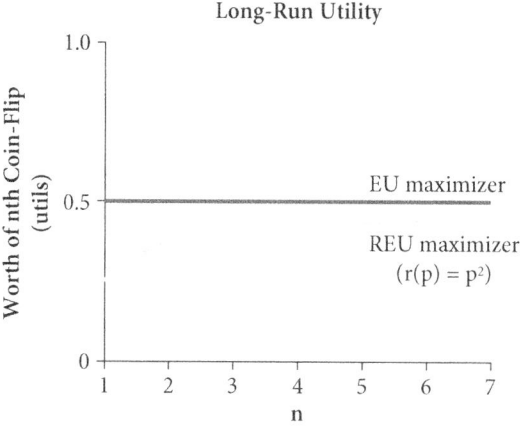

Fig. 7.2. Value of repeated coin-flip.

mean but the outcomes of X are much more spread out. As the number of iterations increases, however, the mean of the act of taking the X-bets becomes much higher than the mean of the act of taking the Y-bets, while the outcomes of the X-package are not *much* more spread out than the outcomes of the Y-package, because the probable outcomes will be concentrated near the mean. So the positive effect of the higher mean swamps the negative effects of the spread. The other way to think about this phenomenon is by considering how each additional bet divides up the possibility space. The first instance of X divides the space into two equally likely possibilities: gaining 0 utils and gaining 1 util. The second instance subdivides each of these possibilities: it divides the former possibility into gaining 0 utils and gaining 1, and the latter into gaining 1 util and gaining 2. In effect, the second instance of the bet eliminates some of the risk, because it makes one event in the worst-case scenario of the first instance less bad.

The hypothetical argument against global sensitivity was framed in terms of bets that each have the same probability of a particular utility increase. However, we could instead consider what would happen when the globally sensitive agent faces a series of bets that are identical in their probabilities of particular monetary outcomes, as we did when considering the EU maximizer's choice between X' and Y'. Interestingly, as long as (1) the agent prefers more money to less, (2) the risk function is continuous, (3) the utility function is not too steep;[16] and (4) the bet will be repeated enough times, both EU theory and REU theory recommend choosing to repeat the bet with the higher expected monetary value, rather than to repeat the bet whose single-shot EU or REU is

---

[16] The exact conditions are beyond the scope of this work. But the rough idea is this: taking an additional bet spreads the probability of the distance between the mean and the actual value outward, but the amount of probability that spreads outward tends to zero, so as long as the utility in each spread is small enough so that each spread makes a smaller overall difference, the increase in mean will eventually compensate for the increase in spread.

higher. Crucially, if these conditions are met, *then maximizing expected monetary value, maximizing expected utility, and maximizing risk-weighted expected utility all tend towards the same recommendation.*

This is why the argument from the hypothetical long-run was doomed from the beginning. Using facts about what an agent should do in a repeated bet in order to show that an agent should not care about risk straightforwardly begs the question. Repeating a bet is a way to minimize risk. Thus, someone who cares about global properties will not behave in the non-repeated situation as she will in the repeated situation. Justifying a single decision by reference to what happens in the long-run obscures the very thing at issue: namely, whether properties of a gamble other than its mean value can matter to a rational agent.

7.4 The Motivational Long-Run Argument

We have just seen that we cannot impugn a single-shot choice by arguing that that choice is not the best one to make repeatedly, since REU theory, like EU theory, can give a different evaluation to an iterated bet than to a single-shot bet. Importantly, both theories are committed to this principle: the instrumental value each bet adds to a package depends on which other bets are part of the package. Nonetheless, there is another way to formulate the worry that REU theory makes conflicting recommendations about the short-term and long-term. The worry is that the recommendation REU theory gives about an iterated sequence considered as a whole conflicts with the recommendation REU theory gives about each iteration. We might call this the motivational long-run argument: "motivational" because, the argument purports to show, following the recommendations of the theory on each individual choice will lead to the agent not following the recommendation of the theory on the package as a whole. Again, a similar worry has arisen for EU theory with a non-linear utility function, and dissolving it will point us to a second principle about choice in the long-run to which the EU theorist is committed, which we can use to help resolve the worry for REU theory with a non-linear risk function. However, as we will see, the worry does not completely dissolve.

Let us begin with the purported worry for EU theory and why it is misplaced. Suppose an agent is facing an actual series of choices between two bets, W' and Z', described in terms of changes in monetary wealth, and is presented with each choice in succession. Suppose further that $EU(s + W') > EU(s + Z')$, but $EV(s + W') < EV(s + Z')$; and that $EU(s + [n \text{ instances of } W'] + [1 \text{ instance of } W']) > EU(s + [n \text{ instances of } W'] + [1 \text{ instance of } Z'])$, so that whenever the agent has n instances of W' she prefers another instance of W'. Since $EV(s + Z')$ is higher than $EV(s + W')$, the iterations of Z' will have a higher EU than the iterations of W' in the limit, and so for some number of iterations she will prefer a package of Z'-bets to a package of W'-bets. However, since given the agent's holdings at any time an additional instance of W' is always preferred to an instance of Z', the agent will make choices that result in her iterating W' rather than iterating Z': *she will make single-shot choices that result in an iterated choice that is dispreferred.* To borrow an example from Paul Samuelson (1963), suppose an individual prefers $0 to a coin-flip between losing $100 and gaining $200. Furthermore, suppose that she prefers 100 such coin-flips to $0.[17] Now suppose she faces a series of choices about whether to take such a coin-flip. When she is offered the first coin-flip, she will reject it. When she is then offered the second coin-flip, she will reject it: since her wealth level is has not changed, she faces the same decision as she faced when deciding about the first coin-flip. And similarly for each successive decision. Thus, since EU theory implies that taking all the coin-flips is better than taking none of them, it seems that following EU theory's recommendations on each decision leads to a choice that EU theory does not recommend.

What is wrong with this argument? John Aloysius points out that it assumes that individuals make choices about bets as if each choice is the only choice they will face: it assumes that agents are **myopic**.[18] By assuming that an agent will reject the first coin-flip in the series, the argument ignores the fact that just as the act of taking a bet cannot be fully described, in the framework of decision theory, without knowing an agent's current holdings—which bets an agent accepted in the past—the act of taking a bet also cannot be fully described without knowing what choices an agent will be offered in the future. How a current bet affects an agent's possible total wealth depends on which bets she expects to take in the future. This, then, is the second principle governing how the EU theorist thinks about the relationship between single-shot and iterated choices: the instrumental value each bet adds to a package depends on which other bets *will be* part of the package. So if an agent expects to take 99 instances of the coin-flip, then taking the initial coin-flip will be worth more—will add more to the instrumental value of the package—than declining it. Thus our agent will not turn down the first coin-flip, as the argument assumes.

We can now consider the analogous motivational long-run argument for REU theory. This argument says that even though REU theory recommends repeating the bet

---

[17] There are utility functions such that this combination of preferences is consistent with EU maximization; see Aloysius (2007) for details.

[18] Term from Bernartzi and Thaler (1999); cited by Aloysius (2007). This is not the same thing as choosing *naively*, as defined in Chapter 6. To choose myopically is to treat the choice at hand as the only one you will be facing. To choose naively is to consider the entire set of choices you will be offered, but to choose in accordance with the plan you prefer now and without regard to your past and future preferences. Historically, the above argument has been the source of some controversy. Samuelson (1963) presented a proof that an EU maximizer cannot prefer to reject the above single-shot coin-flip and at the same time prefer to accept the package consisting of 100 coin-flips. Since it can be shown that there are situations in which EU maximizers prefer to reject a single bet but accept multiple bets—see Aloysius (2007: 64–5) for details—there is a question about where this leaves Samuelson's proof. Aloysius argues that Samuelson's proof assumes that agents are myopic. EU theory with this assumption will yield the same prediction as EU theory without this assumption only if the agent's preferences meet a certain condition, namely that the single-shot coin-flip will be rejected at every wealth level. Therefore, while Samuelson's proof is correct given this assumption, which he makes explicit in his proof, his conclusion does not hold more generally. The erroneous thought that there must be something wrong either with the proof or with preferences that have the above form, according to Aloysius, arose because authors failed to notice the work that the empirical assumption does in justifying the inductive argument in the proof.

that will do better in the long-run, the globally sensitive agent will never end up follow-ing this recommendation if the bets are presented to her in succession. Let Z be a coin-flip between a 100 util loss and a 200 util gain; let W be a guaranteed 0 util gain; and let $r(p) = p^2$, so that $s+W$ is preferred to $s+Z$. Furthermore, for all n, $s + [n$ instances of $W]$ + [1 instance of W] is preferred to $s + [n$ instances of $W] + [1$ instance of $Z]$. To simplify matters, let us say that the prizes are in dollars and the agent has a linear utility func-tion, so that Z and W are just Z' and W' from above. If the choice is to be repeated enough times, the agent will prefer to take Z each time rather than to take W each time, but if she is offered each bet one at a time, then it appears she will always reject Z, since at each time she will start with the status quo and face a choice between −100 utils and 200 utils. As in the analogous argument against EU maximization with a non-linear utility function, this argument is unsound because it relies on the assumption that the agent will reason myopically. The instrumental value each bet adds to a package depends on which other bets *will be* part of the package. Expecting to take a bet in the future changes the value of the act of taking the current bet. So, for example, if the agent is facing the first choice and she expects to take two copies of Z in the future, then she will prefer Z to W in the current choice.[19]

When deciding what to do now, an agent needs to take into account her expecta-tions about the future. If she expects to take two copies of Z in the future, she will prefer Z now, and if she does not, she will prefer W now. But how do her expectations about her future behavior get set, given that her choices in the future also depend on which bets she takes now? Here is how she might reason. By choosing Z now and on the next turn, she will make it rational to choose instances of Z in the future, which gives her an expectation of choosing copies of Z in the future, which supports her choice now and on the next turn. Similar reasoning applies to choosing W. Therefore, either Z or W could be rationalized by future plans. But the plan that leads to the higher overall out-come is the plan that involves choosing Z now and in the future. Therefore, she should choose Z now.

However, this brings up an issue that globally sensitive agents face but globally neutral agents do not. Consider the case in which the globally sensitive agent and the globally neutral agent each face an iterated series of bets—a series of known, finite length—and learn after each trial the result of that bet. If they both use backward induction to reason about their choices, then the choices of the agent with linear r-function but non-linear u-function and those of the agent with non-linear r but linear u will be very different from each other. More strikingly, the choices of the globally sensitive agent will be different than her *ex ante* preferences.

Consider again the choice between the −\$100/\$200 coin-flip and \$0, to be iterated exactly 100 times. On the 100th trial, each agent faces a choice between c_{99} and the gamble $\{c_{99} - \$100, 0.5; c_{99} + \$200, 0.5\}$, where c_{99} is the agent's wealth level after the first

---

[19]   REU(3 instances of Z) = REU($\{-300, 0.125; 0, 0.375; 300, 0.375; 600, 0.125\}$) = 9.375
REU(2 instances of Z + 1 instance of W) = REU($\{-200, 0.25; 100, 0.5; 400, 0.25\}$) = −12.5.

99 trials, and the value of c_{99} is known when the 100th choice is to be made. If the agent with linear r and non-linear u has accepted and won enough of the first 99 coin-flips, then she will have amassed enough wealth to prefer the coin-flip (recall that she prefers the coin-flip at higher wealth levels, which is why she prefers the package). And chances are very high that she will have amassed enough wealth. Thus she knows she will almost certainly choose the coin-flip on the last iteration. The high probability of choosing the coin-flip on the last iteration will, by backward induction, help make rational earlier choices of the coin-flip. Therefore, she can expect to choose the coin-flips, and this is consistent with her *ex ante* preferences.[20] However, when the agent with non-linear r and linear u considers the 100th coin-flip, it does not matter to her how much money she will have amassed, since her rejection of the single-shot bet is based on global, not wealth-level, considerations. Regardless of the value of c_{99}, once she knows what that value is, she will prefer to reject the coin-flip: for every value of c_{99}, the risk-weighted expected utility of $\{c_{99} - \$100, 0.5; c_{99} + \$200, 0.5\}$ is lower than $u(c_{99})$. So if she uses backward induction, she can conclude that she will reject the 100th coin-flip; and so on the 99th decision, she will face a choice between c_{98} and $\{c_{98} - \$100, 0.5; c_{98} + \$200, 0.5\}$. Again, regardless of the value of c_{98}, this gamble has a lower REU than a guaranteed c_{98}. We can work all the way backward to the conclusion that she will not take any of the 100 bets.

It is no surprise that the two different ways to have risk-averse preferences lead to very different behavior in the situation in which the uncertainty is resolved after each turn. The risk-averse preferences of the globally neutral agent with a diminishing marginal utility function are due to the undesirability of smaller amounts of money. Once she reaches a threshold of wealth, or when her expectations about future wealth are suitably high, she reaches a point at which she is willing to take riskier bets. Learning her actual wealth level almost certainly will not make a difference to which bets she is willing to take at that time. The risk-averse preferences of the globally sensitive agent with linear utility function are due to the weight that the worst-case scenario gets in determining instrumental value. Once getting a positive amount from the combined bets reaches a threshold of probability, or when her expectations about future bets mean the current bet will not affect the spread very much, she reaches a point at which she is willing to take riskier bets. But learning her actual utility level will change her probability distribution over utility values in such a way that the current bet does affect the spread, and makes taking a single bet riskier.

The real problem for the globally sensitive agent is that taking the guaranteed $0 each time does not accord with her *ex ante* preference for taking the coin-flip package. We have thus finally isolated a situation in which the globally sensitive agent cannot reason as the globally neutral agent does without being of two minds about the value of a bet. Globally sensitive agents who learn the results of each choice immediately and

---

[20] There is a small chance that she will not have amassed enough wealth at the future iterations, in which case she will reject later coin-flips, but that too is consistent with her *ex ante* preferences, since she has only a conditional *ex ante* preference to accept the later coin-flips.

who use backward induction will do worse than they could, by their own lights, in repeated bets of known finite length.

There are at least three ways in which the defender of global sensitivity can respond. First, she could deny that REU theory recommends taking the coin-flip package in finite, repeated situations of known length. She could argue that the globally sensitive agent simply does not have the option to pick the coin-flip package, as our weak-willed wine-drinker did not have the option to drink one glass of wine. Given that the argument for being of two minds requires backward induction, the proponent of the argument presumably endorses sophisticated choice, and in Section 6.2 we saw that those who endorse sophisticated choice are naturally aligned with the time-slice view of agents, on which it is unsurprising that the agent at one time can thwart the realization of her aims at other times. Alternatively, the defender of global sensitivity could deny that REU theory recommends picking the guaranteed 0 utils in each choice, by endorsing resolute choice. The proponent of resolute choice denies that backward induction is a valid inference pattern, since she denies that each choice will be made in isolation of her previous preferences. Finally, the defender of global sensitivity could point out that the conflict between the recommendations of REU theory, when taken from two different points of view in these kinds of situations, is an instance of a more general phenomenon to which we do not yet have a satisfying response. Consider the similarity between this example and the iterated prisoner's dilemma with a known, finite number of rounds. In such a prisoner's dilemma, if both agents use backward induction then they cannot cooperate on any round, even though in a prisoner's dilemma of unknown length, both agents can cooperate, eliciting a higher payoff for both.[21] More generally, there are situations in which always choosing X is better than always choosing Y, but in which each instance of Y is preferable to each instance of X: interpersonal and intrapersonal situations with the structure of the "tragedy of the commons." Perhaps resolving the general problem will help resolve the problem here. Again, I am interested in illuminating what the tradeoffs are in allowing global sensitivity. That a puzzle arises in finite repeated cases of known length where the results are known at each turn does not seem like too high a price to pay, for reasons articulated in the previous chapter and given the similarity to other puzzling cases.

Let me summarize this section and the last. REU theory faces a worry about how globally sensitive agents will perform over the long-run. This worry mostly dissolves when we keep in mind that in order to fully specify the act of taking a particular bet, we need to know both what bets the agent already holds and which bets she anticipates being offered in the future. We need to know the risk profile of the agent's other holdings, because the probability of any particular final outcome depends on all of the bets in play. When the EU maximizer with non-linear utility function confronts the hypothetical long-run argument, interaction effects between the utility values of outcomes break the link between the instrumental value of one bet and the instrumental value of

---

[21] See Axelrod (1984).

several. When the REU maximizer with non-linear risk function confronts the hypothetical long-run argument, interaction effects between the weights of the probabilities break this link. When each agent is confronted with the motivational long-run argument, we noted that in many cases each agent will be motivated in each particular decision to choose in accord with her *ex ante* preferences. The exception is the globally sensitive agent who faces a known finite number of bets, learns the result of each bet immediately, and uses backward induction to make her choices. Whether the existence of this exception is enough of a strike against the rationality of global sensitivity is up to the reader to decide.

7.5 Insurance

The observations in this chapter to the effect that the value of a bet is lower when that bet introduces a new risk, and higher when that bet offsets the riskiness of a different bet, calls to mind the phenomenon of purchasing insurance. It is worth examining how the globally sensitive agent will feel about purchasing insurance, and in particular the differences between globally sensitive and globally neutral agents. A detailed discussion of insurance behavior is not my aim, since others have covered this topic extensively, including with respect to rank-dependent decision theories.[22] Furthermore, this discussion is not intended to present a decisive argument in favor of either EU or REU theory, since each theory can capture the phenomenon I discuss.[23] Nevertheless, even in very simple examples of insurance purchasing, the analyses are interestingly different; and the two theories do give different recommendations in some situations.

To insure an item is to take a gamble in which one gains money (the payout) if a particular bad event occurs and in which one loses money (the price of the insurance) otherwise, and to sell insurance is to take a gamble in which one loses money (the payout) if the bad event occurs and gains money (the price of the insurance) otherwise. One phenomenon to be explained is that both buyer and seller can find the exchange profitable, even when they agree about the probability of the bad event.

For simplicity, let us assume that if the bad event happens then the agent will pay to replace the item, and that the amount of the insurance is equal to the replacement cost of the item. Let us also assume that the status quo s is not itself a gamble, or that the agent's situation is such that the other risks he faces are either so unlikely or so minor or that the cost of the item if the bad event occurs is so high, that considerations about uncertainties in the status quo are swamped. Finally, let us assume that all utility functions involved are smooth and continuous. For the agent, the act of not buying the insurance is $\{E, s - \$x; \bar{E}, s\}$, where E is the event in which the item is destroyed, and x is the replacement cost of the item. The act of buying the insurance is $\{E, s - \$y; \bar{E}, s - \$y\}$, where y is the cost of the insurance. For the insurance provider, the act of not selling

[22] See Starmer (2000, pp. 364–5), and references therein.
[23] One phenomenon that EU theory cannot capture is the attitude most people have to probabilistic insurance, whereas rank-dependent decision theories can. See Starmer (2000, p. 364).

the insurance is $\{E, t; \bar{E}, t\}$, where t is the status quo for the insurance provider before it has sold the insurance (again, we will make the assumption that the status quo is not itself a gamble). The act of selling the insurance is $\{E, t + \$(y - x); \bar{E}, t + \$y\}$. So we have a situation in which the agent prefers $\{E, s - \$y; \bar{E}, s - \$y\}$ to $\{E, s - \$x; \bar{E}, s\}$, and the insurance provider prefers $\{E, t + \$y - \$x; \bar{E}, t + \$y\}$ to $\{E, t; \bar{E}, t\}$. We can assume that the usual conditions of insurance hold: y is relatively small compared to x, s, and t, $p(E)$ is relatively small, and the expected monetary value of buying the insurance is negative.

Let us start with how EU theory explains the preferences of both the agent and the insurance provider. In order for the preferences of both to be rational, the agent's utility function around her starting wealth level has to have a higher level of marginal diminishment than the insurance provider's utility function around its starting wealth level plus y. There are several ways in which this could be true. One possibility, of course, is that the insurance provider has a utility function with overall less marginal diminishment than the agent does. But there are two interesting possibilities even if the agent and the insurance provider share the same diminishing marginal utility function.

The first possibility is that the insurance provider has a lot more money than the agent and—as seems plausible for many people—the amount of the marginal diminishment is also diminishing. For example, the agent and the insurance provider might each have $u(\$x) = \ln(x)$, where $\$x$ represents total wealth in dollars.[24] If the item to be insured is worth \$10,000 and has a 0.01 probability of being destroyed, then the agent who starts with \$20,000 will be willing pay up to \$138.15 to insure it, and the insurance provider who starts with \$1,000,000 will be willing to sell the insurance for at least \$100.50.[25] The agent will accept the risk of the loss only for a sum of money that is roughly \$38 more than the expected monetary value of accepting that risk, whereas the insurance provider will accept the risk of the loss for a sum of money that is only slightly over the expected monetary value of accepting that risk.

The second way in which the preference of both the agent and the insurance provider would be rational despite a common diminishing marginal utility function is if the insurance provider sells multiple uncorrelated policies. As we saw in the previous section, the EU of a package of identical and independent bets is vanishingly close to the number of bets multiplied by the expected monetary value of each. Therefore, if the insurance provider already possesses a package of such bets—or expects to have the opportunity to take such a package—it will value each additional bet at close to its expected monetary value.

In both of these scenarios, the explanation for the positive value, to both the agent and the insurance provider, of the insurance provider taking on the risk in exchange

---

[24] The function $u(x) = \ln(x)$ is a diminishing marginal utility function: the marginal utility (first derivative) is $1/x$ and the change in marginal utility (second derivative) is $-1/x^2$. The amount by which the marginal utility changes is also diminishing: the third derivative is positive, $2/x^3$.

[25] EU(buy no insurance) = EU($\{10,000, 0.01; 20,000, 0.99\}$), and EU(buy insurance for $\$y$) = EU($20,000 - y$). These are equal when $y \approx 138.15$. For the insurance provider, EU(sell no insurance) $\approx$ EU($1,000,000$), and EU(sell insurance for $\$y$) = EU($\{990,000 + y, 0.01; 1,000,000 + y, 0.99\}$). These are equal when $y \approx 100.50$.

for the agent paying the price of the insurance is that the insurance provider is in a position in which the relevant portion of its utility function is closer to linear than the relevant portion of the agent's utility function, either because of the insurance provider's current wealth level or its expected wealth level based on the other uncorrelated insurance policies it owns. This is to say: the possibility of losing the cost of the item is less of a burden, relative to the price of the insurance, to the insurance provider than it is to the agent.

On REU theory, the explanation for the rationality of insurance is slightly different. While insurance will be rational for both buyer and seller in any of the above scenarios —since EU maximization is a special case of REU maximization—insurance can also be rational for both the agent and the insurance provider even when both have a linear utility function in the relevant interval. This situation is again one in which the insurer owns many uncorrelated policies. A globally sensitive agent with a strictly convex risk function and a linear or concave utility function will always be willing to buy insurance for more than the expected monetary value of not insuring the item: she will prefer $\{E, s - \$y; \bar{E}, s - \$y\}$ to $\{E, s - \$x; \bar{E}, s\}$ for some y greater than $(p(E))(x)$. And an insurance provider will be willing to sell identical uncorrelated insurance policies, each for just slightly more than the monetary mean cost of the damage, under many circumstances: as long as the risk-function is continuous, and the utility function is not too steep, there will be some number of policies such that the insurance provider will prefer selling these policies to not selling them, and will prefer selling an additional policy.

The central explanation on REU theory for why the exchange is favorable for both buyer and seller is not about the impact of particular losses and gains on the wealth level of each. Rather, it is that the possibility of losing the cost of the item is the worst case scenario for the agent, and so she is willing to pay a lot—she is willing to make every other state slightly worse—in order to eliminate this possibility. But the possibility of losing the cost of the item is not the worst-case scenario for the insurance provider, because this possibility is divided into many possibilities, most of which involve the insurance company making money on other policies. (It is true that its worst-case scenario—losing money from every policy—is much worse, but the probability of this is also much lower than that of the worst-case scenario for the uninsured agent and, importantly, the mean is much higher, since it involves a large profit, and this drives up the total REU for all but the maximinimizer.) The reason that buying insurance is rational for the buyer and selling insurance is rational for the seller is that having to pay in the event that the item is damaged is riskier in the global sense for the individual than it is for the insurance provider, since the insurance company holds many uncorrelated insurance policies.

Both EU theory and REU theory explain the rationality of an insurance provider selling many uncorrelated insurance policies (even with the same u and r functions as the agent) by the fact that as long as the policies are sold for more than the mean monetary value of the damage, then the insurance provider will almost certainly make a profit—and as long as the utility of paying off all of the policies is not extremely low, and in the case of REU theory the risk function is continuous around 1, the small chance of losing on every policy will not make a difference. The theories differ, however, on the conditions under which it is rational for an individual to buy insurance for more than the mean monetary value of the damage. On EU theory, this is only rational if utility diminishes marginally in the interval between $s - x$ and s. But on REU theory, insurance can be rational for even the buyer with a linear utility function, when the buyer has a convex risk function. Of course, insurance is also rational for the buyer, on REU theory, if the utility function diminishes marginally, and some combination of facts about the utility and risk function is probably explanatory in many cases.

Here, then, is an important difference about when insurance is rational on the two views. On REU theory it can be rational for an individual to insure an item even if her utility function in the interval between its cost and the status quo is linear. There are some important caveats here. One is that—assuming a risk-avoidant agent—it will only make sense to insure against an event which is "low" in the ordering of events. Low events are weighted by more than their probability value, so losses that happen in these events lower the value of the gamble by more than their mean utility value; but "high" events are weighted by less than their probability value and so impact the gamble by less than their mean utility value. It is worth more than the mean utility value of improving the gamble to raise the troughs in one's utility distribution, but not to raise the peaks. Thus, it is not rational for the individual to insure too many such items. So, relaxing our simplifying assumption that the status quo is not itself a gamble, whether to insure against some particular loss will depend on what the status quo is like. If the status quo is a gamble that includes a high chance of some very bad outcomes, then one will not want to insure against the mildly bad outcomes.

For both EU theory and REU theory, the difference between repeated and non-repeated bets helps explain why it can be rational for an individual to buy insurance and for an insurance provider to sell insurance. REU theory additionally implies that it can be rational to purchase insurance for more than its expected monetary value even for "small ticket" items that cost amounts of money for which the agent's utility function is basically linear, provided the loss of these items is low enough in the agent's ordering of events. It can make sense to pay to "raise the troughs" in the gamble one faces. But even for the risk-avoidant agent, if he has enough of these small ticket items, and their loss is uncorrelated, then paying a premium to purchase insurance on each one is irrational: one ought to just act as one's own insurance provider, so to speak.

7.6 Carving up the World

In examining why the Dutch book argument for additive betting quotients does not work against the globally sensitive agent, we identified a principle that underlies our thinking about how preferences about small changes in the world relate to preferences about fully-specified acts: preferences about small changes should be stable in the face of irrelevant changes to the background. We also highlighted a fact about how globally sensitive agents think about bets: namely, that the value a bet adds to the value of the total package depends on which other bets are in effect. One lesson of Chapters 5 and 6 was that two acts with the same instrumental value need not be interchangeable when considered as parts of other acts: it can be preferable to include one sub-act rather than another in one act, and dispreferable to do so in a different act. The lesson of this chapter is that instrumental value need not be cumulative: the instrumental value of two bets taken together need not be the sum of the instrumental values of each bet, even when taking them together does not alter the utility change in each of their events. Some might think of these upshots as a cost. It does make repeated choice and diachronic choice more complicated. But it seems to me that the question of whether instrumental value really has these properties need not be a pretheoretical question. We cannot know the answer until we settle on the correct theory of instrumental rationality, and we have independent reasons both to allow global sensitivity and to think there are not good pretheoretical arguments that instrumental value should have these properties.

Talk of cumulative bets is natural when we are in what Savage calls a "small-world" decision problem. Strictly speaking, each agent faces only one decision problem (at a particular time): the grand-world decision problem. This is the problem that includes everything that is relevant to a decision: the events are fully individuated with respect to all differences that matter to the agent and all possible future choices that the agent might face, and the outcomes are specified to include all of the features the agent cares about. Small-world decisions are thus grand-world decisions, simplified so that some distinctions between states are neglected and these states are treated as if they have the same outcome. Decision theories are, most precisely, theories about what to prefer in the grand-world problem. Savage points out that there is probably no formal way to scale down decisions so that they are tractable but still take account of everything that is relevant, but we usually make more scaled-down decisions in practice. I have tried to partly illuminate how we can do this by introducing the Stability Principle.

I have argued that how an agent takes risk into account is up to her. It is an important question how this permissiveness in the grand-world decision problem impacts the range of permissible preferences in small-world decisions an individual faces about bets. Insofar as the grand-world decision problem includes a choice about many such bets, the globally sensitive agent's behavior on each will approximate globally neutral behavior. (It is not crucial to this point that the bets are identical, just that they are uncorrelated and have roughly similarly-sized payoffs.) If they face repeated monetary bets and have the same utility function, globally sensitive agents (with continuous r-functions) and globally neutral agents behave almost identically; and, as long as the utility function is not too steep, they behave almost identically to expected monetary value maximizers. REU maximizers, EU maximizers, and EMV maximizers are nearly indistinguishable when they are, for example, engaged in a long game of poker: their norm recommends nearly the same action on each play. Therefore, EU maximization and EMV maximization are generally good heuristics when facing repeated bets. But this is only because the actual norm in the grand-world decision problem is REU maximization.

Where the behavior of the globally sensitive agent and the globally neutral agent diverges is in small-world decisions that are unlikely to be repeated, or are unrepeatable by their nature. For example, they diverge on decisions which a typical person only expects to make once, such as which career to pursue or whom to marry. The epitome of an unrepeatable decision is Pascal's famous wager, whose outcome is determined only once, and at the end of one's life. They also diverge on decisions that are not unrepeatable by nature, but that they know they will not repeat. For example, consider a professional poker player playing his last hand before retiring. Or consider a tourist visiting a city to where he will never return, deciding whether to go to a museum that he knows will be open or a museum that is better but may be closed.

That the behavior of REU maximizers diverges from that of EU maximizers the more exceptional or rare the decision is seems like the right result. The more exceptional a decision, the less intuitive pressure there is to say that what might happen in a repeated long-run scenario bears on how we ought to behave. These one-shot situations are the situations in which we most strongly feel that rationality does not dictate a unique answer, but rather that it is up to the individual herself to decide what to prioritize. It is up to the individual to choose between a small chance of something amazing and a near guarantee of something decent. It does not seem, for example, that there is a unique answer to the question of whether one ought to pursue one's dream career or choose a safer option, even when we know the values and probabilities involved. Because rationality does not dictate a unique answer in these situations—or even dictate a narrow range of acceptable answers—there is less guidance about how we ought to make these decisions.

REU maximization with respect to a single risk function gives different recommendations depending on how often one faces a similar decision. This might be why it seems as if an individual's risk-function is different for different domains. Most people frequently face decisions about money, for example, but most people do not frequently face major decisions about their health.[26]

The frequency with which we face various types of decisions falls on a spectrum. There are certain decisions which are clearly infrequent. As mentioned, there are decisions that shape our entire lives, such as what religion to practice, whom to marry, what career to pursue, and what causes to devote our resources to. And there are other decisions, such as decisions within a poker game, which individuals clearly face many

---

[26] This suggests a possible interpretation of the Rottenstreich and Hsee study, discussed in Section 2.4: the domains about which individuals had a more emotional reaction were those in which decisions tend to be less repeatable, and so the displayed behavior conformed to the decisions that would be made by an individual with a single risk function at a single time, with expectations about what choices she would face in the future.

times. But an important question arises: where on the spectrum do most ordinary decisions fall? Which ordinary decisions should be thought of as part of a larger package? The answer will be crucial to figuring out what REU theory recommends in many cases, and the extent to which REU maximization and EU maximization coincide in our everyday lives: the extent to which EU maximization is a good heuristic for many ordinary decisions. It is easy to see how decisions within a poker game form a package, since they fall within a small time-frame and take place in the context of a single activity. But the various decisions one faces in different contexts about how to spend money might also be thought of as forming a package. For example, we saw that it can be rational to pay a premium to insure against the loss of a single small-ticket item even if one's utility function is linear in the relevant interval, but it is not rational to pay a premium to insure against the loss of many small-ticket items. What about decisions involving different kinds of value: for example, a decision about whether to buy insurance on a particular item and a decision about whether to undergo surgery to address a problem that almost certainly is not bad but may be. Do these form a package?

It is an open question how many of the decisions we actually face should be considered as part of a larger package and how many of them are unique.[27] To pose this question in another way: if we ought to be REU maximizers in the grand-world decision problem, how finely can we carve up the decisions we face into small-world packages, on each of which we ought to let our actions be guided by roughly the same norm that guides us in the grand-world decision problem, but within which the decisions depend on each other; and how many decisions do each of these packages include? This depends on what ultimate value is like. One consideration is whether there is a single value that underlies rational action, such as hedonic pleasure or moral goodness, or whether rational agents aim at many different kinds of values that cannot be subsumed under a single type. Another consideration is the extent to which preference satisfaction in different domains affects well-being independently: if the value of doing well with respect to one's health does not interact with the value of doing well with respect to one's relationships or one's career, then decisions in these different areas will not be part of the same small-world decision package. A final consideration is how underlying value at a time affects the value in an agent's life over time: to the extent that value is the kind of thing that an individual "consumes" but that does not carry over to the value of what happens at other times, the decisions an agent faces will be divided into many separate packages. And the more the decisions an agent faces are divided into separate small-world decision packages, the less her actions need to resemble those which the globally neutral norm recommends.

---

[27] For some empirical results on when individuals tend to in fact consider decisions to be part of a larger package, see Tversky and Kahneman (1981, pp. 456–7).

8

Conclusion

The question of what is instrumentally rational to do is the question of what an agent ought to do, given what she values and what she believes about the world, in order to realize the best consequences. One might have thought that a rational agent's preferences can be determined by knowing two things about her: the extent to which she values various outcomes, or the reasons she has in favor of various outcomes and how these reasons weigh against each other; and how likely she thinks various acts are to realize the outcomes. However, there is a missing ingredient. Since for most choices, one act is preferable in some circumstances and a different act is preferable in other circumstances, we also must know the extent to which the agent is generally willing to accept the risk of something worse in exchange for the possibility of something better: how she structures the potential realization of some of her aims. We have seen that any way of consistently weighing what happens in the worst state against what happens in the best state is representable by a norm which says how much weight the best p-portion of the events get, when aggregating the value of what happens in each event to arrive at a single value for an act. It is representable by risk-weighted expected utility maximization relative to some particular risk function.

The traditional view is that there is only one acceptable norm for rational agents, the globally neutral norm: the weight that the best p-portion of events get is p. At the level of preferences, this means that an individual must make tradeoffs in the same way regardless of where in the event-ordering they occur. When faced with the question of whether making some event better compensates for making some other event worse, the only relevant considerations are what outcomes are being traded off in each event—not where in the ranking the events are. The relative ranking of events cannot matter to which outcome exchanges play the same compensatory role. At the level of value, this means that utility is defined so that the agent cares only about its average value: the only way global properties of an act can matter is if they show up in properties of the utility function itself.

In practice, many people do not follow the globally neutral norm. For many people, whether a tradeoff makes the worst-case scenario better and the best-case scenario worse or *vice versa* makes a difference to whether they are willing to accept that tradeoff, independent of how good the outcomes are in an absolute sense: they care about the relative ranking of events. For these individuals, since their attitudes towards gambles cannot be reduced to their attitudes towards outcomes, there is no utility function whose expected value they prefer to maximize. As a result, many individuals have traditionally been classified as irrational or incoherent. This book has argued that preferences that conform to norms other than the globally neutral norm are rational. Global neutrality requires that an outcome make the same contribution to the instrumental value of different gambles regardless of the structural position it occupies in each gamble. But all that is required for consistent, consequentialist preferences, I have argued, is that an outcome make the same contribution to the instrumental value of different gambles when it occupies the same structural position in those gambles. Thus, rational agents can be globally sensitive. They can have any risk function they want, subject to a few basic constraints. Many common attitudes correspond to natural risk functions. Risk-avoidant agents, those with convex risk functions, care proportionately more about what happens in the worst-case scenario than what happens in the best-case scenario; while risk-inclined agents, those with concave risk functions, have the opposite pattern of concern.

When an individual is generally risk-averse with respect to money or with respect to two goods—when she prefers monetary gambles that are less spread out or prefers to increase the probability of getting at least one good at the expense of lowering the probability of getting both—EU theory must interpret her as valuing outcomes in one of two ways. On the one hand, it can interpret her as having a concave utility function, so that the more money an agent already has, the less additional utility more money adds; or a utility function that displays non-independence, so that once she has one good, the less additional utility the other adds. On the other hand, it can interpret her as treating the outcomes as more complex than they initially appear, so that taking a risk itself has disvalue. Descriptive theories reveal other possibilities: that she lacks sharp degrees of belief, or that she is irrationally pessimistic in that she thinks events that are worse for her are more likely to occur. However, there is an additional possibility open on REU theory. While allowing that the agent has sharp, stable degrees of belief, it can explain her preferences in either of the two ways EU theory explains them, and it can also explain her preferences as a case of sensitivity to the global properties of gambles: the more probability a good outcome already has, the more instrumentally valuable it is to move probability from a worse outcome to that outcome; in other words, the more instrumentally valuable it is to improve things in an event the worse that event is. REU theory allows that a rational agent can have a combination of any attitude towards outcomes and any attitude towards risk, and that these two attitudes, along with her beliefs, determine preferences.

We saw that we can separate the influence of the utility values of outcomes on a particular set of preferences from the influence of risk-attitudes on these preferences, via a representation theorem that yields a separate utility function and risk function. Moreover, we can separate the influence of each of these entities from that of beliefs: since the representation theorem also yields a separate, stable probability function, we need not interpret a globally sensitive agent as irrationally pessimistic or optimistic.

The risk function reflects the weight that an agent places on various structural parts of gambles: the lower r(p) is relative to p, the less weight the agent will place on the best p-portion of the events and hence the more weight she will place on the worst $(1 - p)$-portion of events. The higher r(p) is relative to p, the more weight the agent will place the best p-portion of events. If one is a formalist about the risk function, one could treat it merely as a way to represent preferences, with no psychological correlate. However, for psychological realists, there are several ways of thinking about the psychological feature that the risk function corresponds to. We can think of it as how one trades off two competing values associated with acts: the value of having a good worst-case scenario and the value of having a good best-case scenario. Caring about the former corresponds to the virtue of being prudent and caring about the latter corresponds to the virtue of being venturesome. We can also think of the risk function as corresponding to how, when weighing the interests of one's future possible selves, one takes their comparative well-being into account. Having a particular risk function is like having a policy about the distribution of utility for one's counterparts in different possible worlds.

Decision-theoretic rationality, I have argued, requires having a consistent probability function, a consistent utility function, and a consistent risk function, relative to which the agent maximizes risk-weighted expected utility in all choices. However, there may be other important standards for preferences aside from whether they are rational. Recall the distinction between rationality and reasonableness. The question of whether preferences are reasonable can also be separated into three questions: whether the subjective probability function is reasonable, whether the utility function is reasonable, and whether the risk function is reasonable. The reasonableness question about subjective probability concerns whether the agent is proportioning her beliefs to the evidence. What norms govern this evaluation is a question for epistemology. The reasonableness question about utility concerns whether the agent is tracking what is good, valuable, or choiceworthy, or what will satisfy her, but the exact form this question takes depends on one's view of what the utility function is. For the formalist, the question concerns preferences: do the agent's considerations in favor of one outcome over another correctly identify what is good, valuable, choiceworthy, or will satisfy her? For the psychological realist, the question concerns whether the strengths of the agent's desires in fact track how much various outcomes would satisfy her, or whether they in fact track how good or valuable or choiceworthy the outcomes are. What norms govern these evaluations is a question for ethics or psychology.

Similarly, we can ask which risk functions are reasonable. Is every way of being globally sensitive equally acceptable, or are there some risk functions we want to rule out as betraying the wrong values or principles even though they are consistent? For example, one might argue that some risk functions are overly risk-avoidant or risk-inclined: an agent ought not to be prudent or venturesome at the expense of the other to the degree she is, or an agent ought to not prioritize the interests of some of her future possible selves to the extent she does. Or consider the S-shaped risk function, which allows for both purchasing insurance (paying a premium to avoid a small probability of a large loss) and purchasing lottery tickets (paying a premium for a small probability of a large gain).[1] One might argue, though it is not immediately obvious how such an argument would go, that this combination of attitudes represents an impermissible way of balancing prudence and venturesomeness—or, on the other hand, one might argue that one needs both convex and concave elements to one's risk function in order to balance these goals. At the level of preferences, the question about which risk attitudes are reasonable will be cashed out as whether the individual is making tradeoffs about what happens in the worst state and what happens in the best state (and every state in between) in an appropriate way.

A related question is how one should think about others' risk attitudes. In the case of the utility function, a common position is that I can think your utility function is reasonable without sharing it. You and I might have different preferences or values, and there may be no objective standard that governs these. In the case of the probability function, one way in which I could think your probabilities are reasonable even if I do not share them is if we have different evidence. However, if we do share the same evidence, there may be some tension in my holding that your probability function is reasonable while not adopting it myself, since the only goal of the probability function is to represent the world.[2]

When we note that the risk function represents an individual's way of trading off different virtues, the question of the range of reasonable risk functions might be subsumed under the more general question of how one ought to balance the realization of different virtues. Is there any tension in my thinking the way you trade off the realization of two virtues is reasonable while trading them off in a different way myself? It seems to me that at least within a range of ways to trade them off, there is not any tension, but this is a topic for further discussion.[3]

When we think of the risk function as a measure of distributive justice among our future possible selves, we might consider the parallel question about distributive justice among different people. There may in fact be a unique answer to how we ought to weight the interests of the worst-off in the interpersonal case. Here are two differences, though, between the interpersonal case and the intrapersonal case. First, in the intrapersonal case, only one of my future selves will in fact become actual. Second, in the intrapersonal case, all of the selves in question are *me*; therefore, we might think that it is my choice how to trade off their interests against one another.

The range of attitudes that it is reasonable to have towards risk is fairly wide. Just as it is up to the individual, to a certain extent, which outcomes are worth bringing about, it is up to her, to a certain extent, to take risk into account in whichever way she thinks

---

[1] See Wakker (2010, pp. 205–6).

[2] See the argument in White (2005). It is a contentious question in epistemology whether for a given body of evidence, there is only one rational probability function to hold in response to it: that is, whether the "Uniqueness Thesis" is true: see discussion in White (2005), Feldman (2006), Christensen (2007), van Inwagen (2010), and Kelly (forthcoming).

[3] One might argue, contra my supposition, that there is a unique Aristotelian "golden mean" between these two virtues.

is appropriate for a life well lived. She can be cautious, ensuring that her life will not be filled with many disasters. She can be a romantic, willing to sacrifice everything for a small chance of realizing her highest goals. Or she can strike any number of balances between these two outlooks, including the one which expected utility theory recommends.

Recall the parallel between, on the one hand, William James' point about balancing the two competing goals of knowing truth and avoiding error in forming beliefs and, on the other hand, my point about balancing the two competing goals of being venturesome and being prudent in making choices. Reason, says James, cannot tell us which temperament to have or how to balance the goals of knowing truth and avoiding error, and so we must determine this for ourselves. Analogously, in situations in which we cannot be certain of how our acts will turn out, rationality cannot tell us how to balance the goal of allowing for the possibility of something great against the goal of securing a guarantee that things will not turn out too badly. And so, with this recognition that decision-makers have more freedom than we previously thought, comes a realization that decision-makers have more responsibility than we previously thought. Since there is no unique answer to the question of how a decision-maker should treat risk, an individual not only may, but must, decide for himself how he will take risk into account when making decisions.

Appendices

Appendix A. Representation Theorem

For readability, I will repeat all of the technical information from Chapter 3 here, but will omit intuitive explanations of the axioms. MS abbreviates Machina and Schmeidler (1992), and KW abbreviates Köbberling and Wakker (2003).

Spaces, Relations, and Notation

State space $\mathscr{S} = \{ \ldots, s, \ldots \}$, a set of states.

Event space $\mathscr{E}$ = the set of all subsets of $\mathscr{S}$.

Outcome space $\mathscr{X} = \{ \ldots, x, \ldots \}$, a set of outcomes.

Act space $\mathscr{A} = \{ \ldots, f(.), g(.), \ldots \}$ = the set of all finite-valued functions from $\mathscr{S}$ to $\mathscr{X}$, where $f^{-1}(x) \in \mathscr{E}$. For any act $f \in \mathscr{A}$, there is some partition of $\mathscr{S}$ into $\{E_1, \ldots E_n\}$ and some finite set $Y \subseteq \mathscr{X}$ such that f can be thought of as a member of Y^n.

Strictly speaking, f takes states as inputs. However, we will write f(E), where $E \in \mathscr{E}$, if f is constant on $s \in E$. Thus, f(E) = f(s) for all $s \in E$.

For any fixed partition of events $M = \{E_1, \ldots, E_n\}$, define $A_M = \{f \in \mathscr{A} \mid (\forall E_i \in M)(\exists x \in \mathscr{X})(\forall s \in E_i)(f(s) = x)\}$, the set of acts on M.

$\geq$ is a two-place relation over the act space.[1]

$\sim$ and $>$ are defined in the usual way: $f \sim g$ iff $f \geq g$ and $g \geq f$; and $f > g$ iff ($f \geq g$ and $\neg(g \geq f)$).

For all $x \in \mathscr{X}$, $\underline{x}$ denotes the constant act $\{f(s) = x$ for all $s \in \mathscr{S}\}$. We will also define a preference relation over outcomes in terms of preferences over constant acts: $x \geq y$ iff $\underline{x} \geq \underline{y}$ (for x, $y \in \mathscr{X}$).

For all $x \in \mathscr{X}$, $E \in \mathscr{E}$, $f \in \mathscr{A}$, $x_E f$ denotes the act that agrees with f on all states not contained in E, and yields x on any state contained in E: $x_E f(s) = \{x$ if $s \in E$; f(s) if $s \notin E\}$. Likewise, for disjoint events $E_1, E_2 \in \mathscr{E}$, $x_{E1} y_{E2} f$ is the act that agrees with f on all states not contained in E_1 and E_2, and yields x on E_1 and y on E_2: $x_{E1} y_{E2} f(s) = \{x$ if $s \in E_1$, y if $s \in E_2$, f(s) if $s \notin E_1 \cup E_2\}$. Similarly, $g_E f$ is the act that agrees with g on all states contained in E and agrees with f on all states not contained in E: $g_E f(s) = \{g(s)$ if $s \in E$; f(s) if $s \notin E\}$.

---

[1] Note: I use the "$\geq$" symbol for the preference relation between acts, for the preference relation between outcomes, and for the greater-than-or-equal-to relation between real numbers; but it should be clear from context which I am using.

We say that an event E is *null* on F⊆𝒜 iff (∀f∈F)(∀g$_E$f∈F)(g$_E$f ~ f) (MS 749).

When we say that an event is (non-)null without stating a particular F, it should be read as (non-)null on the entire act space 𝒜.

We say that outcomes x^1, x^2, ... form a *standard sequence* on F⊆𝒜 if there exists an act f∈F, events E$_i$ ≠ E$_j$ that are non-null on F, and outcomes y, z with ¬(y ~ z) such that for all k:

$$(x^{k+1})_{Ei}(y)_{Ej}f \sim (x^k)_{Ei}(z)_{Ej}f$$

with all acts contained in F (KW, p. 398).

A standard sequence is bounded if there exist outcomes v,w∈𝒳 such that ∀i(v ≥ x^i ≥ w)

We say that f,g∈𝒜 are comonotonic if (¬∃s$_1$,s$_2$∈𝒮)(f(s$_1$) > f(s$_2$) & g(s$_1$) < g(s$_2$)). C⊆𝒜 is a comoncone if every pair f, g∈C is comonotonic.

Alternatively, take any fixed partition of events M = {E$_1$, ... , E$_n$}. A permutation ρ from {1, ... , n} to {1, ... , n} is a *rank-ordering* permutation of f if f(E$_{ρ(1)}$) ≥ ... ≥ f(E$_{ρ(n)}$). So a comoncone is a subset C$_ρ$ of A$_M$ that is rank-ordered by a given permutation: C$_ρ$ = {f∈A$_M$ | f(E$_{ρ(1)}$) ≥ ... ≥ f(E$_{ρ(n)}$)} for some ρ. For each fixed partition of events of size n, there are n! comoncones (KW 400).

For each partition M, we define the relation ~*(F) for F ⊆ A$_M$ and outcomes x, y, z, w ∈ 𝒳 as follows:

$$xy \sim^*(F) zw$$

iff ∃f,g∈F and ∃E∈ℰ such that E is non-null on F and x$_E$f ~ y$_E$g and z$_E$f ~ w$_E$g, where all four acts are contained in F (KW, pp. 396–7).

We write xy ~*(C) zw if there exists a comoncone F ⊆ A$_M$ such that xy ~*(F) zw. (KW 400)

p: ℰ → [0, 1] is a finitely additive probability function iff:

$$p(\varnothing) = 0$$
$$p(𝒮) = 1$$

$$p(E_1 \cup E_2 \cup \ldots \cup E_n) = \sum_{i=1}^{n} p(E_i) \text{ for any finite sequence of disjoint events } E_1, \ldots, E_n \in ℰ.$$

Let the set of finite-outcome probability distributions over 𝒳 be denoted by 𝒫(𝒳) = {(x$_1$, p$_1$; ... ; x$_m$, p$_m$) | m ≥ 1, $\sum_{i=1}^{m} p_i = 1$, x$_i$∈𝒳, p$_i$ ≥ 0}) (MS 753).

We say that a probability distribution P = (x$_1$, p$_1$; ... ; x$_m$, p$_m$) *stochastically dominates* Q = (y$_1$, q$_1$; ... ; y$_n$, q$_n$) with respect to the order ≥ if for all z∈𝒳,

$$\sum_{\{i|x_i \leq z\}} p_i \leq \sum_{\{j|y_j \leq z\}} q_j$$

P strictly stochastically dominates Q if the above holds with strict inequality for some $z^* \in \mathscr{X}$ (MS, p. 754).

$r: [0, 1] \to [0, 1]$ is a *risk function* iff:

$$r(0) = 0$$
$$r(1) = 1$$
$$a \leq b \Rightarrow r(a) \leq r(b)$$
$$a < b \Rightarrow r(a) < r(b)$$

Axioms

Citations correspond to Machina and Schmeidler (1992), pp. 749–50, 761, or Köbberling and Wakker (2003), pages noted in parentheses.

A1. Ordering (MS P1 and KW 396): $\geq$ is complete ($f \geq g$ or $g \geq f$), reflexive ($f \geq f$), and transitive ($f \geq g \ \& \ g \geq h \Rightarrow f \geq h$).

Note that KW 396 only holds that $\geq$ is complete and transitive; however, completeness implies reflexivity. I list both conditions here for clarity.

Note further that ordering implies that the preference relation over outcomes is also complete, reflexive, and transitive.

Note finally that completeness implies that the agent must satisfy what is sometimes called the Rectangular Field Assumption: he must have preferences over all possible finite-valued functions from states to outcomes.

A2. State-Wise Dominance: If $f(s) \geq g(s)$ for all $s \in \mathscr{S}$, then $f \geq g$. If $f(s) \geq g(s)$ for all $s \in \mathscr{S}$ and $f(s) > g(s)$ for all $s \in E \subseteq \mathscr{S}$, where E is some non-null event on $\mathscr{S}$, then $f > g$.

A2 + A1 implies Event-Wise Monotonicity (MS P3):

A2′. Event-Wise Monotonicity (MS P3): For all outcomes x and y, events E that are non-null on A, and acts f,

$$x_E f \geq y_E f \text{ iff } x \geq y$$

(It follows that $x_E f > y_E f$ iff $x > y$.)

Proof: ($\Leftarrow$) Assume $x \geq y$. Then since $x_E f(s) = f(s) = y_E f(s)$ for all $s \notin E$ and $x_E f(s) = x \geq y = y_E f(s)$ for all $s \in E$, we have, by A2, $x_E f \geq y_E f$.
   ($\Rightarrow$) Assume $\neg(x \geq y)$. Then, by A1, $y > x$. Since $y_E f(s) = x_E f(s)$ for all $s \notin E$ and $y_E f(s) = y > x = x_E f(s)$ for all $s \in E$, we have, by A2, $y_E f > x_E f$. So $\neg(x_E f \geq y_E f)$.

A2 implies Weak (finite) Monotonicity (KW 396):

A2″. Weak (finite) Monotonicity (KW 396). For any fixed partition of events $E_1, \ldots, E_n$ and acts $f(E_1, \ldots, E_n)$ on those events (acts that yield a single outcome for all states in those events: that is, acts f such that $\forall i (\exists x \in \mathscr{X})(\forall s \in E_i)(f(s) = x))$, if $f(E_j) \geq g(E_j)$ for all j, then $f \geq g$.

Proof: If $f(E_j) \geq g(E_j)$ for all j, then $f(s) \geq g(s)$ for all $s \in \mathscr{S}$, so $f \geq g$.

A3. Preference Richness ((i)MS P5 Non-degeneracy, (ii)KW 398, Solvability):

(i)   There exist outcomes x and y such that $x > y$.
(ii) For any fixed partition of events $\{E_1, \ldots, E_n\}$, and for all acts $f(E_1, \ldots, E_n)$, $g(E_1, \ldots, E_n)$ on those events, outcomes x, y, and events E_i with $x_{E_i}f > g > y_{E_i}f$, there exists an "intermediate" outcome z such that $z_{E_i}f \sim g$.

A4. Small Event Continuity (MS P6): For all acts $f > g$ and any outcome x, there exists a finite partition of events $\{E_1, \ldots, E_n\}$ such that for all i, $f > x_{E_i}g$ and $x_{E_i}f > g$

A5. Comonotonic Archimedean Axiom (KW 398, 400):[2]
For each comoncone $F \subseteq A_M \subseteq \mathscr{A}$, every bounded standard sequence on F is finite.

A6. Comonotonic Tradeoff Consistency (KW 397, 400): Improving an outcome in any $\sim^*(C)$ relationship breaks that relationship. In other words, $xy \sim^*(C) zw$ and $y' > y$ entails $\neg(xy' \sim^*(C) zw)$.

A7. Strong Comparative Probability (MS P4*): For all pairs of disjoint events E_1 and E_2, all outcomes $x' > x$ and $y' > y$, and all acts $g, h \in \mathscr{A}$,

$$x'_{E1}x_{E2}g \geq x_{E1}x'_{E2}g \Rightarrow y'_{E1}y_{E2}h \geq y_{E1}y'_{E2}h$$

Theorem (Representation): If the relation $\geq$ satisfies (A1) through (A7), then there exist:

(i)   a unique finitely additive, non-atomic probability function p: $\mathscr{E} \to [0, 1]$
(ii)   a unique risk function r: $[0, 1] \to [0, 1]$
(iii) a utility function unique up to positive affine transformation

such that for any $f \in \mathscr{A}$, each of which we can write as $\{F_1, O_1; \ldots; F_n, O_n\}$ where for all i, $f(s) = O_i$ for all $s \in F_i \subseteq \mathscr{S}$, and $O_1 \leq O_2 \leq \ldots \leq O_n$,

$$REU(f) = u(O_1) + r\left(\sum_{i=2}^{n} p(F_i)\right)(u(O_2) - u(O_1)) + r\left(\sum_{i=3}^{n} p(F_i)\right)(u(O_3) - u(O_2)) + \ldots$$
$$+ r(p(F_n))(u(O_n) - u(O_{n-1}))$$

represents the preference relation $\geq$ on $\mathscr{A}$.

That is, there exist a unique probability function p, a unique risk function r, and a utility function u unique up to positive affine transformation such that for all outcomes $x_1, \ldots, x_n, y_1, \ldots, y_m \in \mathscr{X}$ and events $E_1, \ldots, E_n, G_1, \ldots, G_m \in \mathscr{E}$,

---

[2] KW add another condition in their statement of the Comonotonic Archimedian Axiom: see discussion in Part one, case (ii) of the proof of the theorem here.

$\{E_1, x_1; \ldots; E_n, x_n\} \geq \{G_1, y_1; \ldots; G_m, y_m\}$ iff

$$u(O_1) + r\left(\sum_{i=2}^{n} p(F_i)\right)(u(O_2) - u(O_1)) + r\left(\sum_{i=3}^{n} p(F_i)\right)(u(O_3) - u(O_2)) + \ldots$$

$$+ r(p(F_n))(u(O_n) - u(O_{n-1}))$$

$$\geq$$

$$u(Q_1) + r\left(\sum_{i=2}^{m} p(H_i)\right)(u(Q_2) - u(Q_1)) + r\left(\sum_{i=3}^{m} p(H_i)\right)(u(Q_3) - u(Q_2)) + \ldots$$

$$+ r(p(H_m))(u(Q_m)) - u(Q_{m-1}))$$

for some rank-ordering permutations Δ and Ψ such that $x_{\Delta(1)} \leq \ldots \leq x_{\Delta(n)}$, $O_i = x_{\Delta(i)}$, and $F_i = E_{\Delta(i)}$, and $y_{\Psi(1)} \leq \ldots \leq y_{\Psi(m)}$, $Q_i = y_{\Psi(i)}$, and $H_i = G_{\Psi(i)}$.

If there are three such functions so that REU(f) represents the preference relation, we say that REU holds.

Furthermore, in the presence of (A3), if REU holds with a continuous r-function, then the remaining axioms are satisfied. Therefore, if we assume Preference Richness (A3), we have:

(A1), (A2), (A4), (A5), (A6), (A7) are sufficient conditions for REU.
(A1), (A2), (A4), (A5), (A6), (A7) are necessary conditions for REU with continuous r-function.

Proof

Assume we have a preference relation that satisfies (A1) through (A7).

Part one. Derive a Weighting Function of States (following Köbberling and Wakker (2003))

Köbberling and Wakker (Theorem 8, pp. 399–400) show that if the relation $\geq$ on $\mathscr{A}$ satisfies (A1), (A2″), (A3ii), (A5), and (A6), then for each fixed partition of events M $= \{E_1, \ldots, E_n\}$ and acts $f(E_1, \ldots, E_n)$ on those events which form a subset $A_M \subseteq \mathscr{A}$, there exists:

(i) A *weighting function* W: $2^M \to [0, 1]$ such that $W(\emptyset) = 0$, $W(M) = 1$, and $A \subseteq B \Rightarrow W(A) \leq W(B)$

(ii) A *utility function* U: $\mathscr{A} \to \mathfrak{R}$, such that preferences can be represented by:

$$\text{CEU}: f \mapsto \sum_{j=1}^{n} \pi_{\Phi(j)} u(f(E_{\Phi(j)}))$$

where the "decision weights" $\pi_{\Phi(j)}$ are non-negative and sum to one; and for some rank-ordering permutation Φ on $\{1, \ldots, n\}$ such that $f(E_{\Phi(1)}) \geq \ldots \geq f(E_{\Phi(n)})$, we have:

$\pi_{\Phi(j)} = W(E_{\Phi(1)} \cup \ldots \cup E_{\Phi(j)}) - W(E_{\Phi(1)}, \ldots, E_{\Phi(j-1)})$ for all j (and $\pi_{\Phi(1)} = W(E_{\Phi(1)})$).

Furthermore, three cases are possible:

Case (i): the trivial case where at least one comoncone has only null events. In this case, all comoncones only have null events, the preference relation is trivial, utility is constant, and the weighting function can be chosen arbitrarily.

However, (A3(i)) rules out the case in which the preference relation is trivial, so this case (which is possible on Köbberling and Wakker's axioms) is ruled out by our axioms.

Case (ii): the degenerate case in which there is exactly one non-null event in $\{E_1, \ldots, E_n\}$ for each comoncone. Köbberling and Wakker add an additional restriction to their Comonotonic Archimedian Axiom (that there is a countable order-dense subset of $\mathscr{X}$) to determine a unique utility function in this case. Here, the weighting function is uniquely determined, only taking the values zero and one. (This holds, for example, for the preferences of a maximinimizer or a maximaximizer: the only event that will matter in each comoncone will be the event with the worst outcome, or the event with the best outcome. It holds also when the partition on events is so coarse that the agent assigns probability 0 to all but one of the events.) I do not add their restriction, but I will return to this case shortly to show that it cannot hold on all finite partitions of $\mathscr{A}$, given the additional axioms of the theorem.

Case (iii): the non-degenerate case where at least one comoncone has two or more non-null events. In this case, utility is unique up to positive affine transformation, and the weighting function is uniquely determined.

In Section 5.1 (p. 402), Köbberling and Wakker extend the result to arbitrary state spaces (our $\mathscr{S}$), with finite valued functions from $\mathscr{S}$ to $\mathscr{X}$ (our act space $\mathscr{A}$). As noted above, every act can be denoted as a member of some A^M. They point out that for all partitions for which case (iii) holds, we can again derive a unique weighting function defined over all events in $\mathscr{E}$ and a utility function unique up to positive affine transformation. These representations are made to agree, yielding a utility function that is unique up to positive affine transformation, and a weighting function that is uniquely determined. Thus, the only case we must worry about is the case in which for all partitions, case (ii) holds. (In this case we would not get a unique utility function.) However, this case is ruled out by our other axioms:

> We now show that case (ii) cannot hold on every finite partition of $\mathscr{A}$. (Intuitively, this will rule out the case of the maximinimizer and the maximaximizer, and imply that there must be some partition on which the agent assigns probability to more than one event.)

> We start by showing that there is some finite partition of events M on $\mathscr{E}$ such that two of the events on this partition are non-null on A_M. By (A3i), there exist outcomes x and y such that $\underline{x} > \underline{y}$. By (A4), there exists a finite partition of events $\{F_1, \ldots, F_m\}$

such that for all i, $\underline{x} > x_{F_i}\underline{y}$. If m = 1, then $\underline{x} = x_{F_i}\underline{y}$, so m $\geq$ 2. Furthermore, for all i, $\neg F_i$ is non-null, because $\neg F_i$ is null implies $\underline{x} \sim x_{F_i}\underline{y}$. Therefore there are at least two non-null events on $\{F_1, \ldots, F_m\}$ (if there is only one, F_j, then $\neg F_j$ will be null).

We next show that for all finite partitions of events $N = \{E_1, \ldots, E_n\}$ on $\mathscr{E}$, if there is exactly one non-null event in $\{E_1, \ldots, E_n\}$ for each comoncone $\subseteq A_N$, then there is exactly one non-null event in $\{E_1, \ldots, E_n\}$ on A_N. For assume there are at least two non-null events on A_N: E_1 and E_2. By (A3(i)), $\exists x \exists y (x > y)$. Now consider the gamble $y_{E_1}y_{E_2}\underline{y}$ $(= \underline{y})$ and the gamble $x_{E_1}y_{E_2}\underline{y}$ $(= x_{E_1}\underline{y})$. Since E_1 is non-null, by (A2) we have $x_{E_1}y_{E_2}\underline{y} > y_{E_1}y_{E_2}\underline{y}$. Now consider the gamble $x_{E_1}x_{E_2}\underline{y}$. Since E_2 is non-null, by (A2) we have $x_{E_1}x_{E_2}\underline{y} > x_{E_1}y_{E_2}\underline{y}$. But $y_{E_1}y_{E_2}\underline{y}$, $x_{E_1}y_{E_2}\underline{y}$, and $x_{E_1}x_{E_2}\underline{y}$ are comonotonic: they are part of any comoncone whose rank-ordering permutation orders the events from worst to best starting with any ordering of the events in $(\neg E_1 \cap \neg E_2)$, followed by E_2, followed by E_1. So there are two non-null events on that comoncone; this is a contradiction, so there is only one non-null event in $\{E_1, \ldots, E_n\}$ on A_N.

Therefore, on the partition $M = \{F_1, \ldots, F_m\}$, at least one comoncone $\subseteq A_M$ has two or more non-null events.

We can reorganize the terms of Köbberling's and Wakker's equation:

$$\text{CEU}(f) = \sum_{j=i}^{n} \pi_{\Phi(j)} U(f(E_{\Phi(j)}))$$

$$= \sum_{j=1}^{n} (W(E_{\Phi(1)} \cup \ldots \cup E_{\Phi(j)}) - W(E_{\Phi(1)} \cup \ldots \cup E_{\Phi(j-1)})) U(f(E_{\Phi(j)}))$$

$$= \sum_{j=1}^{n-1} (W(E_{\Phi(1)} \cup \ldots \cup E_{\Phi(j)}))(U(f(E_{\Phi(j)})) - U(f(E_{\Phi(j+1)}))) + U(f(E_{\Phi(n)}))$$

where, again, Φ orders the states from best to worst.

This is equivalent to

$$\text{CEU}(f) = U(f(E_{\Delta(1)})) + \sum_{j=2}^{n} (W(E_{\Delta(j)} \cup \ldots \cup E_{\Delta(n)}))(U(f(E_{\Delta(j)})) - U(f(E_{\Delta(j-1)})))$$

where Δ is a rank-ordering permutation on $\{1, \ldots, n\}$ that orders states from *worst* to *best*.

Part Two. Derive a Probability Function of States (following Machina and Schmeidler (1993))

Machina and Schmeidler (Theorem 2, p. 766) show that if the $\geq$ relation over $\mathscr{A}$ satisfies (A1), (A2′), (A3(i)), (A4), and (A7) then:

There exists a unique, finitely additive, non-atomic probability measure p: $\mathscr{E} \to [0, 1]$ and a non-constant, mixture continuous preference functional $V(P) = V(x_1, p_1; \ldots; x_n, p_n)$ on the set of finite-outcome probability distributions such that V(.) exhibits monotonicity with respect to stochastic dominance (that is, $V(P) \geq V(Q)$ whenever P stochastically dominates Q and $V(P) > V(Q)$ whenever P strictly stochastically dominates Q), and such that the relation $\geq$ can be represented by the preference functional:

$Y(f(.)) = V(x_1, p(f^{-1}(x_1)); \ldots ; x_n, p(f^{-1}(x_n)))$, where $\{x_1, \ldots, x_n\}$ is the outcome set of the act $f(.)$.

This implies that an agent will be indifferent between two distributions of outcomes over states that give rise to the same probability distribution over outcomes (see also Theorem 1, MS, p. 765). That is, if $p(f^{-1}(z)) = p(g^{-1}(z))$ for all outcomes z, then $f \sim g$.

By the claim that p is non-atomic, we mean that for any event E with $p(E) > 0$ and any $c \in (0,1)$, there exists some event $E^* \subset E$ such that $p(E^*) = c \cdot p(E)$. (MS, p. 751, fn. 12).

Part Three. Derive a Risk Function

So far, since case (iii) is the only remaining case that is consistent with our axioms, we know that there is a utility function u: $\mathscr{X} \to \mathfrak{R}$ unique up to positive affine transformation, a unique weighting function W: $\mathscr{E} \to [0, 1]$, and a unique probability function p such that:

(I) $\geq$ is representable by:

$$CEU(f) = U(f(E_{\Delta(1)})) + \sum_{j=2}^{n} (W(E_{\Delta(j)} \cup \ldots \cup E_{\Delta(n)}))(U(f(E_{\Delta(j)})) - U(f(E_{\Delta(j-1)})))$$

where Δ is a rank-ordering permutation on $\{1, \ldots, n\}$ that orders states from worst to best.

(II) If two acts f and g give rise to the same probability distribution over outcomes—that is, if $p(f^{-1}(x)) = p(g^{-1}(x))$ for all $x \in \mathscr{X}$—then $f \sim g$, so, by (I), $CEU(f) = CEU(g)$.

(III) For all $c \in [0,1]$, $\exists N \in \mathscr{E}$ s.t. $p(N) = c$. This holds because $p(\mathscr{S}) = 1$, $p(\emptyset) = 0$, and since p is non-atomic, $\forall c \in (0,1)$ there exists $E^* \subset \mathscr{S}$ such that $p(E^*) = c \cdot p(\mathscr{S}) = c$.

Now for each $c \in [0,1]$, define $r(c) = W(E)$ for any E such that $p(E) = c$.

We can show that this is well-defined, since any two events that have the same probability p must have the same weight. Assume there exist E and F such that $p(E) = p(F)$ but $W(E) > W(F)$, and take outcomes $x > y$. $CEU(\underline{x}) > CEU(\underline{y})$, so $u(x) > u(y)$. $CEU(x_E\underline{y}) = u(y) + W(E)[u(x) - u(y)]$, and $CEU(x_F\underline{y}) = u(y) + W(F)[u(x) - u(y)]$, so $CEU(x_E\underline{y}) > CEU(x_F\underline{y})$, and thus $x_E\underline{y} > x_F\underline{y}$ because $CEU(f)$ represents $\geq$. But $Y(x_E\underline{y}) = Y(x_F\underline{y})$ because the two acts give rise to the same probability distribution over outcomes, so $x_E\underline{y} \sim x_F\underline{y}$ because Y represents $\geq$. Since this is a contradiction, $p(E) = p(F) \Rightarrow \neg(W(E) > W(F))$. An analogous argument shows that $p(E) = p(F) \Rightarrow \neg(W(F) > W(E))$. Therefore, $p(E) = p(F) \Rightarrow W(E) = W(F)$.

We also know that r is unique, since W and p are unique.

So for all $E \in \mathscr{E}$, $r(p(E)) = W(E)$.

Furthermore, r has all the properties of a risk function:

(1) $r(0) = 0$, because $p(\varnothing) = 0$ (by definition of a probability function), and $W(\varnothing) = 0$ (by the properties of the weighting function, given in part one).

(2) $r(1) = 1$, because $p(\mathcal{I}) = 1$ (by definition of a probability function), and $W(\mathcal{I}) = 1$ (by the properties of the weighting function).

(3) r is non-decreasing: Assume $a \leq b$. Pick F such that $p(F) = b$. Now pick $E \subseteq F$ such that $p(E) = a$ (we know such an E exists because p is non-atomic). Therefore, by the properties of the weighting function, $W(E) \leq W(F)$. So $r(p(E)) \leq r(p(F))$: that is, $r(a) \leq r(b)$.

(4) r is strictly increasing: Assume $a < b$, and pick $E \subset F$ such that $p(E) = a$ and $p(F) = b$. If $r(a) = r(b)$, then $W(E) = W(F)$, and so for outcomes $x > y$, we will have $CEU(x_E \underline{y}) = CEU(x_F \underline{y})$, and so $x_E \underline{y} \sim x_F \underline{y}$. But by stochastic dominance, $V(x_F \underline{y}) > V(x_E \underline{y})$, so $x_F \underline{y} > x_E \underline{y}$. Since this is a contradiction, $\neg(r(a) = r(b))$. And since $r(a) \leq r(b)$ by (3), we have $r(a) < r(b)$.

Therefore, for an act $f = \{E_1, x_1; \ldots; E_n, x_n\}$, we have:

$$U(f(E_{\Delta(1)})) + \sum_{j=2}^{n} (W(E_{\Delta(j)} \cup \ldots \cup E_{\Delta(n)}))(U(f(E_{\Delta(j)})) - U(f(E_{\Delta(j-1)})))$$

$$= U(x_{\Delta(1)}) + \sum_{j=2}^{n} r(p(E_{\Delta(j)} \cup \ldots \cup E_{\Delta(n)}))(U(x_{\Delta(j)}) - U(x_{\Delta(j-1)}))$$

Note that $p(E_{\Delta(j)} \cup \ldots \cup E_{\Delta(n)}) = \sum_{i=j}^{n} p(E_{\Delta(i)})$ by finite additivity.

Now for all members of the act space, finite valued functions $f = \{x_1, E_1; \ldots; x_n, E_n\} \in \mathcal{A}$, where $f(s) = x_i$ for all $s \in E_i$ let $REU(f) =$

$$u(x_{\Delta(1)}) + r\left(\sum_{i=2}^{n} p(E_{\Delta(i)})\right)(u(x_{\Delta(2)}) - u(x_{\Delta(1)})) + r\left(\sum_{i=3}^{n} p(E_{\Delta(i)})\right)(u(x_{\Delta(3)}) - u(x_{\Delta(2)}))$$

$$+ \ldots + r(p(E_{\Delta(n)}))(u(x_{\Delta(n)}) - u(x_{\Delta(n-1)}))$$

for some rank-ordering permutation Δ such that $x_{\Delta(1)} \leq \ldots \leq x_{\Delta(n)}$.

Therefore, for any $f \in \mathcal{A}$, each of which we can write as $\{E_1, x_1; \ldots; E_n, x_n\}$ where $f(s) = x_i$ for all $s \in E_i$ and again as $\{F_1, O_1; \ldots; F_n, O_n\}$ where for some rank-ordering permutation Δ such that $x_{\Delta(1)} \leq \ldots \leq x_{\Delta(n)}$ we have $O_i = x_{\Delta(i)}$ and $F_i = E_{\Delta(i)}$, there exists

(i) a unique finitely additive, non-atomic probability function $p: \mathcal{E} \to [0, 1]$

(ii) a unique risk function $r: [0, 1] \to [0, 1]$

(iii) a utility function u unique up to positive affine transformation such that

$$REU(f) = u(O_1) + r\left(\sum_{i=2}^{n} p(F_i)\right)(u(O_2) - u(O_1)) + r\left(\sum_{i=3}^{n} p(F_i)\right)(u(O_3) - u(O_2))$$

$$+ \ldots + r(p(F_n))(u(O_n) - u(O_{n-1}))$$

represents the preference relation $\geq$ on $\mathcal{A}$.

Part Four. In the presence of (A3), REU with a continuous *r*-function implies the remaining axioms.

Again, REU holds if there exist:

(i)   a unique finitely additive, non-atomic probability function p: $\mathscr{E} \to [0, 1]$
(ii) a unique risk function r: $[0, 1] \to [0, 1]$
(iii) a utility function unique up to positive affine transformation

such that for any $f \in \mathscr{A}$, each of which we can write as $\{F_1, O_1; \ldots; F_n, O_n\}$ where for all i,

$f(s) = O_i$ for all $s \in F_i \subseteq \mathscr{S}$ and $O_1 \leq O_2 \leq \ldots \leq O_n$, $\mathrm{REU}(f) = u(O_1) + r\left(\sum_{i=2}^{n} p(F_i)\right)(u(O_2) - u(O_1)) + r\left(\sum_{i=3}^{n} p(F_i)\right)(u(O_3) - u(O_2)) + \ldots + r(p(F_n))(u(O_n) - u(O_{n-1}))$ represents the preference relation $\leq$ on $\mathscr{A}$.

(i) KW's axioms: (A2''), (A5), and (A6).

If REU holds, then CEU holds; let $W(A) = r(p(A))$.
   KW's Theorem 8 (p. 400) shows that if (A3(ii)) holds, and if CEU holds, then (A2''), (A5), and (A6) hold.

(ii) MS's axioms: (A1), (A2'), (A3(i)), (A4), and (A7).

MS's Theorem 2 (p. 766) states that if there exists a unique, finitely additive, non-atomic probability measure p: $\mathscr{E} \to [0, 1]$ and a non-constant, mixture continuous preference functional $V(P) = V(x_1, p_1; \ldots; x_n, p_n)$ on the set of finite-outcome probability distributions such that V(.) exhibits monotonicity with respect to stochastic dominance (that is, $V(P) \geq V(Q)$ whenever P stochastically dominates Q and $V(P) > V(Q)$ whenever P strictly stochastically dominates Q), such that the relation $\geq$ can be represented by the preference functional $Y(f(.)) = V(x_1, p(f^{-1}(x_1)); \ldots; x_n, p(f^{-1}(x_n)))$, then (A1), (A2'), (A3(i)), (A4), and (A7) hold.

We know that p is unique, finitely additive, non-atomic, and by (A3(i)), we know that REU(f) is non-constant. We must show that (1) REU(f) is mixture continuous and (2) $\mathrm{REU}(f) \geq \mathrm{REU}(g)$ whenever f stochastically dominates g and $\mathrm{REU}(f) > \mathrm{REU}(g)$ whenever f strictly stochastically dominates g:

(1) Since we have a probability function of states, we can identify an act f with its probability distribution $f^* \in \mathscr{P}(\mathscr{X})$ such that all acts identified with that probability distribution have the same REU; we can write REU(f*). As defined on p. 755 of MS, REU(f) is mixture continuous if, for any probability distributions f*, g*, and h* in $\mathscr{P}(\mathscr{X})$, the sets $\{\lambda \in [0,1] \mid \mathrm{REU}(\lambda f^* + (1 - \lambda)g^*) \geq \mathrm{REU}(h^*)\}$ and $\{\lambda \in [0,1] \mid \mathrm{REU}(\lambda f^* + (1 - \lambda)g^*) \leq \mathrm{REU}(h^*)\}$ are both closed.

Consider the set of outcomes $\{x_1, \ldots, x_n\}$ such that x_i is an outcome of f* or an outcome of g*, and $x_1 \leq x_2 \leq \ldots \leq x_n$. Then we have:

$$f^* = \{x_1, p_1; \ldots; x_n, p_n\} \text{ for some } \{p_1, \ldots, p_n\}$$
$$g^* = \{x_1, q_1; \ldots; x_n, q_n\} \text{ for some } \{q_1, \ldots, q_n\}$$
$$\lambda f^* + (1 - \lambda)g^* = \{(\lambda p_1 + (1 - \lambda)q_1, x_1; \ldots; \lambda p_n + (1 - \lambda)q_n, x_n\}$$

For each i, $\lambda p_i + (1 - \lambda)q_i$ is continuous in λ. So for each k, $\sum_{i=k}^{n}(\lambda p_i + (1 - \lambda)q_i)$ is continuous in λ. Since r is continuous, $r\left(\sum_{i=k}^{n}(\lambda p_i + (1 - \lambda)q_i)\right)$ is continuous in λ. So,

$r\left(\sum_{i=k}^{n}(\lambda p_i + (1 - \lambda)q_i)\right)[u(x_k) - u(x_{k-1})]$ is continuous in λ. So the sum of these terms from k = 2 to n is continuous in λ. So REU(f) is continuous in λ. Therefore, $\{\lambda \in [0,1] \mid \text{REU}(\lambda f^* + (1 - \lambda)g^*) \geq m\}$ and $\{\lambda \in [0,1] \mid \text{REU}(\lambda f^* + (1 - \lambda)g^*) \leq m\}$ are closed for all m, in particular for m = REU(h*), so REU(f) is mixture continuous.

(2) Take two acts f and g, such that f stochastically dominates g. Consider the set of outcomes $\{x_1, \ldots, x_n\}$ such that x_i is an outcome of f or an outcome of g, and $x_1 \leq x_2 \leq \ldots \leq x_n$. Then we have:

$$f^* = \{x_1, p_1; \ldots; x_n, p_n\} \text{ for some } \{p_1, \ldots, p_n\}$$
$$g^* = \{x_1, q_1; \ldots; x_n, q_n\} \text{ for some } \{q_1, \ldots, q_n\}$$

Since f stochastically dominates g, for all k, $\sum_{\{i|x_i \leq x_k\}} p_i \leq \sum_{\{i|x_i \leq x_k\}} q_i$

Since $\sum_{i=1}^{n} p_i = \sum_{i=1}^{n} q_i = 1$, we have, for all k, $\sum_{\{i|x_i > x_k\}} p_i \geq \sum_{\{i|x_i > x_k\}} q_i$.

Thus, since r is non-decreasing, we have $r\left(\sum_{\{i|x_i > x_k\}} p_i\right) \geq r\left(\sum_{\{i|x_i > x_k\}} q_i\right)$ for all k.

Since $u(x_k)$ is non-decreasing,

$$r\left(\sum_{\{i|x_i > x_k\}} p_i\right)(u(x_{k+1}) - u(x_k)) \geq r\left(\sum_{\{i|x_i > x_k\}} q_i\right)(u(x_{k+1}) - u(x_k)) \text{ for all k.}$$

For each k, the above terms will either be equal to the (k+1)th term in the REU equation for REU(f) and REU(g), respectively (where the first term in both is $u(x_1)$); or else in the (k+1)th terms of REU(f) or REU(g), the "r" coefficient will be different than the above but the difference $u(x_{k+1}) - u(x_k)$ will be zero.

So REU(f) $\geq$ REU(g).

If f strictly stochastically dominates g, then $\sum_{\{i|x_i \leq x_m\}} p_i < \sum_{\{i|x_i \leq x_m\}} q_i$ for some m.

So, by the same chain of reasoning (using the fact that r is increasing rather than merely non-decreasing), $r\left(\sum_{\{i|x_i > x_m\}} p_i\right) > r\left(\sum_{\{i|x_i > x_m\}} q_i\right)$ for some m.

Take the least m for which the strict inequality holds. Then, for the least k such that x_k is preferred to x_m (we know there is some such k, otherwise both sums would be 1), the difference $u(x_k) - u(x_{k-1})$ will be non-zero, so we have:

$$r\left(\sum_{\{i|x_i>x_m\}} p_i\right)(u(x_k)-u(x_{k-1})) > r\left(\sum_{\{i|x_i>x_m\}} q_i\right)(u(x_k)-u(x_{k-1}))$$

This will be the kth term in the REU equation for REU(f) and REU(g), respectively; and for all other terms, the weak inequality will hold: that is, the jth term of REU(f) will be greater than or equal to the jth term of REU(g).

Therefore, by MS Theorem 2, (A1), (A2′), (A3(i)), (A4), and (A7) hold.

(iii) (A2). We want to show that if $f(s) \geq g(s)$ for all $s \in \mathscr{S}$, then $f \geq g$, and if $f(s) \geq g(s)$ for all $s \in \mathscr{S}$ and $f(s) > g(s)$ for all $s \in E \subseteq \mathscr{S}$, where E is some non-null event on $\mathscr{A}$, then $f > g$.

Assume $f(s) \geq g(s)$ for all $s \in \mathscr{S}$. Then, for all x, $\{s \in \mathscr{S} \mid g(s) > x\} \subseteq \{s \in \mathscr{S} \mid f(s) > x\}$, since if $g(s) > x$, then $f(s) > x$. Consequently, for all x, $p(\{s \in \mathscr{S} \mid g(s) > x\}) \leq p(\{s \in \mathscr{S} \mid f(s) > x\})$, by definition of a probability function. That is, f stochastically dominates g. To put it directly in terms of our definition of stochastic dominance: take a partition $M = \{E_1, \ldots, E_n\}$ of $\mathscr{S}$ such that $\forall i (\exists x_i, y_i \in \mathscr{X})(\forall s \in E_i)(f(s) = x_i$ & $g(s) = y_i)$. Then $\{s \in \mathscr{S} \mid g(s) \geq x\}$ and $\{s \in \mathscr{S} \mid f(s) \geq x\}$ are subsets of that partition, and $\sum_{\{i|y_i>x\}} p(E_i) \leq \sum_{\{i|x_i>x\}} p(E_j)$.

So $\sum_{\{i|y_i \leq x\}} p(E_i) \geq \sum_{\{i|x_i \leq x\}} p(E_j)$. That is, f stochastically dominates g. So, by (ii2) in Part Four, REU(f) $\geq$ REU(g). So f is weakly preferred to g.

Now assume $f(s) \geq g(s)$ for all $s \in \mathscr{S}$ and $f(s) > g(s)$ for all $s \in E \subseteq \mathscr{S}$, where E is some non-null event on $\mathscr{A}$. Take the set $\{x \in \mathscr{X} \mid (\exists s \in E)(g(s) = x)\}$. We know this set is non-empty. We also know this set is finite, because the outcome space of g is finite; so we can pick the most preferred member of the set, x^*. Now we want to show that $\{r \in \mathscr{S} \mid f(r) \leq x^*\} \subset \{r \in \mathscr{S} \mid g(r) \leq x^*\}$. Consider some element $t \in \{r \in \mathscr{S} \mid f(r) \leq x^*\}$. Since $f(t) \leq x^*$, we have $g(t) \leq x^*$, so $\{r \in \mathscr{S} \mid f(r) \leq x\} \subseteq \{r \in \mathscr{S} \mid g(r) \leq x\}$. Now consider some element $t^* \in E$ such that $g(t^*) = x^*$. We have $t^* \in \{r \in \mathscr{S} \mid g(r) \leq x^*\}$, but we have $f(t^*) > x^*$, so we have $\neg(t^* \in \{r \in \mathscr{S} \mid f(r) \leq x^*\})$. Therefore, $\{r \in \mathscr{S} \mid f(r) \leq x^*\} \subset \{r \in \mathscr{S} \mid g(r) \leq x^*\}$. Consequently, $p(\{r \in \mathscr{S} \mid f(r) \leq x^*\}) < p(\{r \in \mathscr{S} \mid g(r) \leq x^*\})$, and so f strictly stochastically dominates g. Again by (ii2) in Part Four, REU(f) > REU(g). So f is strictly preferred to g.

Therefore, (A2) holds.

So, assuming (A3), REU with continuous *r*-function implies (A1), (A2), (A4), (A5), (A6), and (A7).

Therefore, if we assume Preference Richness (A3), we have:

(A1), (A2), (A4), (A5), (A6), (A7) are sufficient conditions for REU.
(A1), (A2), (A4), (A5), (A6), (A7) are necessary conditions for REU with continuous *r*-function.

Appendix B. Axioms for EU theory

A1. Ordering: $\geq$ is complete, reflexive, and transitive.

A2. State-Wise Dominance: If $f(s) \geq g(s)$ for all $s \in \mathscr{S}$, then $f \geq g$. If $f(s) \geq g(s)$ for all $s \in \mathscr{S}$ and $f(s) > g(s)$ for all $s \in E \subseteq \mathscr{S}$, where E is some non-null event on $\mathscr{S}$, then $f > g$.

A3. Preference Richness ((i) MS P5 Non-degeneracy, (ii) KW 398, Solvability):

(i)   There exist outcomes x and y such that $x > y$.

(ii) For any fixed partition of events $\{E_1, \ldots, E_n\}$, and for all acts $f(E_1, \ldots, E_n)$, $g(E_1, \ldots, E_n)$ on those events, outcomes x, y, and events E_i with $x_{E_i}f > g > y_{E_i}f$, there exists an "intermediate" outcome z such that $z_{E_i}f \sim g$.

A4. Small Event Continuity (MS P6):

For all acts $f > g$ and any outcome x, there exists a finite partition of events $\{E_1, \ldots, E_n\}$ such that for all i, $f > x_{E_i}g$ and $x_{E_i}f > g$.

B5. Archimedean Axiom (KW 398): Every bounded standard sequence on $\mathscr{S}$ is finite.

B6. Unrestricted Tradeoff Consistency (KW 397): For all $A_M \subseteq \mathscr{S}$, improving an outcome in any $\sim^*(A_M)$ relationship breaks that relationship. In other words, $xy \sim^*(A_M) zw$ and $y' > y$ entails $\neg(xy' \sim^*(A_M) zw)$.

To show: In the presence of (A3):

(1) Any agent whose preferences obey (A1), (A2), (A4), (B5), and (B6) can be represented as an EU maximizer relative to a unique probability function and a utility function unique up to positive affine transformation.

(2) Any agent who can be represented as an EU maximizer has preferences that satisfy (A1), (A2), (A4), (B5), and (B6).

Part 1: Köbberling and Wakker (2003, Theorem 5) show that if (A3(ii)) holds and there are two or more non-null events on some finite partition $M = \{F_1, \ldots, F_m\}$, then any agent whose preferences obey (A1), (A2″), (B5), and (B6) can be represented as an EU maximizer relative to a unique probability function and a utility function unique up to positive affine transformation. Furthermore, we know from the proof in Appendix A that (A2) implies (A2″). Thus, it suffices to show that (A1), (A2), (A3), (A4), (B5), and (B6) imply that there are two or more non-null events on some finite partition:

By (A3i), there exist outcomes x and y such that $\underline{x} > \underline{y}$. By (A4), there exists a finite partition of events $\{F_1, \ldots, F_m\}$ such that for all i, $\underline{x} > x_{F_i}\underline{y}$. If m = 1, then $\underline{x} = x_{F_i}\underline{y}$, so m $\geq$ 2. Furthermore, for all i, $\neg F_i$ is non-null, because $\neg F_i$ is null implies $\underline{x} \sim x_{F_i}\underline{y}$. Therefore there are at least two non-null events on $\{F_1, \ldots, F_m\}$ (if there is only one, F_j, then $\neg F_j$ will be null).

Part 2: Köbberling and Wakker (2003, Theorem 5) show that if (A3(ii)) holds, then if EU holds, the preferences satisfy (A1), (A2″), (B5), and (B6). Furthermore, if EU holds, then REU holds with continuous r-function, and so it follows from the Representation Theorem in Appendix A that the preferences satisfy (A2) and (A4).

Appendix C. Tradeoff Equality and Utility Differences

Claim

For REU maximizers, xy ~*(C) zw holds just in case $u(x) - u(y) = u(z) - u(w)$.

Proof

Assume REU maximization, and assume xy ~*(C) zw. Then $x_E f \sim y_E g$ and $z_E f \sim w_E g$ for some $x_E f$, $y_E g$, $z_E f$, $w_E g$ that are comonotonic and E non-null on the comoncone. Therefore, there is some set of states $\{E_1, \ldots, E_n\}$ and some rank-ordering permutation Φ such that $x_E f(E_{\Phi(1)}) \geq \ldots \geq x_E f(E_{\Phi(n)})$, $y_E g(E_{\Phi(1)}) \geq \ldots \geq y_E g(E_{\Phi(n)})$, $z_E f(E_{\Phi(1)}) \geq \ldots \geq z_E f(E_{\Phi(n)})$, $w_E g(E_{\Phi(1)}) \geq \ldots \geq w_E g(E_{\Phi(n)})$ and:

(1) $E_{\Phi(i)} = E$ for some i.

(2) $\displaystyle\sum_{j=1}^{n} (r(p(E_{\Phi(1)} \cup \ldots \cup E_{\Phi(j)})) - r(p(E_{\Phi(1)} \cup \ldots \cup E_{\Phi(j-1)}))) u(x_E f(E_{\Phi(j)}))$

$\displaystyle = \sum_{j=1}^{n} (r(p(E_{\Phi(1)} \cup \ldots \cup E_{\Phi(j)})) - r(p(E_{\Phi(1)} \cup \ldots \cup E_{\Phi(j-1)}))) u(y_E g(E_{\Phi(j)}))$

(3) $\displaystyle\sum_{j=1}^{n} (r(p(E_{\Phi(1)} \cup \ldots \cup E_{\Phi(j)})) - r(p(E_{\Phi(1)} \cup \ldots \cup E_{\Phi(j-1)}))) u(z_E f(E_{\Phi(j)}))$

$\displaystyle = \sum_{j=1}^{n} (r(p(E_{\Phi(1)} \cup \ldots \cup E_{\Phi(j)})) - r(p(E_{\Phi(1)} \cup \ldots \cup E_{\Phi(j-1)}))) u(w_E g(E_{\Phi(j)}))$

See part one and three of the proof in Appendix A.

Since $x_E f$ and $z_E f$ only differ on $E_{\Phi(i)}$, and $y_E g$ and $w_E g$ only differ on $E_{\Phi(i)}$, subtracting eqn. (3) from eqn. (2) yields:

$$[r(p(E_{\Phi(1)} \cup \ldots \cup E_{\Phi(i)})) - r(p(E_{\Phi(1)} \cup \ldots \cup E_{\Phi(i-1)}))][u(x) - u(z)]$$

$$= [r(p(E_{\Phi(1)} \cup \ldots \cup E_{\Phi(i)})) - r(p(E_{\Phi(1)} \cup \ldots \cup E_{\Phi(i-1)}))][u(y) - u(w)]$$

This simplifies to $u(x) - u(z) = u(y) - u(w)$.

Claim

For EU maximizers, xy~*($\mathscr{A}$) zw holds just in case $u(x) - u(y) = u(z) - u(w)$.

Proof

Assume EU maximization, and assume xy ~*($\mathscr{A}$) zw. Then $x_E f \sim y_E g$ and $z_E f \sim w_E g$ for some $x_E f$, $y_E g$, $z_E f$, $w_E g$ in $\mathscr{A}$ and E non-null in $\mathscr{A}$. Therefore, there is some set of states $\{E_1, \ldots, E_n\}$ such that:

(1) $E_i = E$ for some i.

(2) $\sum_{j=1}^{n} p(E_j)u(x_E f(E_j)) = \sum_{j=1}^{n} p(E_j)u(y_E g(E_j))$

(3) $\sum_{j=1}^{n} p(E_j)u(z_E f(E_j)) = \sum_{j=1}^{n} p(E_j)u(w_E g(E_j))$

Since $x_E f$ and $z_E f$ only differ on E_i, and $y_E g$ and $w_E g$ only differ on E_i, subtracting eqn. (3) from eqn. (2) yields:

$$p(E_i)[u(x) - u(z)] = p(E_i)[u(y) - u(z)].$$

This simplifies to $u(x) - u(z) = u(y) - u(w)$.

Bibliography

Abdellaoui, Mohammaed, Carolina Barrios, and Peter P. Wakker (2007). "Reconciling introspective utility with revealed preferences: Experimental arguments based on prospect theory." *Journal of Economics* 138: 356–78.

Adams, Ernest W., and Roger D. Rosenkrantz (1980). "Applying the Jeffrey Decision Model to Rational Betting and Information Acquisition." *Theory and Decision* 12: 1–20.

Allais, Maurice (1953/1979). "The Foundations of a Positive Theory of Choice Involving Risk and a Criticism of the Postulates and Axioms of the American School." In *Expected Utility Hypothesis and the Allais Paradox*, ed. Maurice Allais and Ole Hagen (1979). Dordrecht: Reidel. English translation of "Fondements d'une théorie positive des choix comportant un risque et critique des postulats et axiomes de L'Ecole Americaine," in *Econometrie* (1953): 257–332.

Aloysius, John A. (2007). "Decision-Making in the Short and Long Run: Repeated Gambles and Rationality." *British Journal of Mathematical and Statistical Psychology* 60: 61–9.

Armendt, Brad (1993). "Dutch Books, Additivity, and Utility Theory." *Philosophical Topics* 21(1): 1–20.

—— (forthcoming). "On Risk and Rationality." *Erkenntnis*.

Arrow, Kenneth (1951). "Alternative Approaches to the Theory of Choice in Risk-Taking Situations." *Econometrica* 19: 404–37.

Axelrod, Robert (1984). *The Evolution of Cooperation*. New York: Basic Books.

Bell, David E. (1982). "Regret in Decision-making under Uncertainty." *Operations Research* 30(5): 961–81.

—— (1983). "Risk Premiums for Decision Regret." *Management Science* 29(10): 1156–66.

Bermúdez, José Luis (2009). *Decision Theory and Rationality*. Oxford: Oxford University Press.

Bernartzi, S. and R. H. Thaler (1999). "Risk Aversion or Myopia? Choices in Repeated Gambles and Retirement Investments." *Management Science* 45: 364–81.

Bernoulli, D. (1738). "Exposition of a New Theory on the Measurement of Risk." *Econometrica* 22(1) (1954): 23–36.

Broome, John (1990). "Rationality and the Sure-Thing Principle." In *Rationality, Self-Interest, and Benevolence*, ed. Gay Meeks. Cambridge: Cambridge University Press.

—— (1991). *Weighing Goods: Equality, Uncertainty, and Time*. Oxford: Blackwell.

—— (1993). "Can a Humean be Moderate?" In *Value, Welfare and Morality*, ed. G. Frey and Christopher Morris. Cambridge: Cambridge University Press, pp. 51–73.

—— (2007). "Does Rationality Consist in Responding Correctly to Reasons?" *Journal of Moral Philosophy* 4: 349–74.

Bruckner, A. M. (1964). "Some Relationships between Locally Superadditive Functions and Convex Functions." *Proceedings of the American Mathematical Society* 15(1): 61–5.

—— and E. Ostrow (1962). "Some Function Classes Related to the Class of Convex Functions." *Pacific Journal of Mathematics* 12(4): 1203–15.

Buchak, Lara (2009). "Risk and Rationality." PhD dissertation, Princeton University, NJ. Retrieved 31 July 2010, from Dissertations & Theses: A&I. (Publication No. AAT 3350817).

—— (2013). "Decision Theory." In *Oxford Handbook of Probability and Philosophy*, ed. Christopher Hitchcock and Alan Hajek. Oxford: Oxford University Press.

Chalmers, David (2002). "The St Petersburg Two-Envelope Paradox." *Analysis* 62: 155–7.

Chateauneuf, Alain (1985). "On the Existence of a Probability Measure Compatible with a Total Preorder on a Boolean Algebra." *Journal of Mathematical Economics* 14: 43–52.

—— and Michèle Cohen (1994). "Risk-seeking with Diminishing Marginal Utility in a Non-Expected Utility Model." *Journal of Risk and Uncertainty* 9: 77–91.

—— Peter Wakker (1999). "An Axiomatization of Cumulative Prospect Theory for Decision Under Risk." *Journal of Risk and Uncertainty* 18(2): 137–45.

Chew, Soo Hong, Edi Karni, and Zvi Safra (1987). "Risk-Aversion in the Theory of Expected Utility with Rank Dependent Probabilities." *Journal of Economic Theory* 42: 370–81.

Chew, Soo Hong, and Peter Wakker (1996). "The Comonotonic Sure-Thing Principle." *Journal of Risk and Uncertainty* 12: 5–27.

Christensen, David (1991). "Clever Bookies and Coherent Belief." *Philosophical Review* 100: 229–47.

—— (2007). "Epistemology of Disagreement: The Good News." *Philosophical Review*, 116: 187–218.

Davidson, D. (1973). "Radical Interpretation", *Dialectica* 27/3–4: 313–28.

Diecidue, Enrico, and Peter P. Wakker (2001). "On the Intuition of Rank-Dependent Utility." *Journal of Risk and Uncertainty* 23(3): 281–98.

Diamond, Peter A. (1967). "Cardinal Welfare, Individualistic Ethics, and Interpersonal Comparison of Utility: A Comment." *Journal of Political Economy* 75: 765–6.

—— and Joseph E. Stiglitz (1974). "Increases in Risk and in Risk-Aversion." *Journal of Economic Theory* 8: 337–60.

Dreier, James (1996). "Rational Preference: Decision Theory as a Theory of Practical Rationality." *Theory and Decision* 40: 249–76.

—— (2004). "Decision Theory and Morality." Chapter 9 of *Oxford Handbook of Rationality*, ed. Alfred R. Mele and Piers Rawling. Oxford: Oxford University Press.

Elga, Adam (2010). "Subjective Probabilities Should be Sharp." *Philosophers' Imprint* 10(5).

Ellsberg, Daniel (1961). Risk, Ambiguity, and the Savage Axioms." *Quarterly Journal of Economics* 75(4): 643–69.

—— (2001). *Risk, Ambiguity and Decision*. New York: Garland Publishing.

Eriksson, Lina, and Alan Hájek (2007). "What are Degrees of Belief?" *Studia Logica* 86: 183–213.

Feldman, Richard (2006). "Reasonable Religious Disagreements." In Louise Antony (ed.), *Philosophers without God*. Oxford: Oxford University Press.

Feller, William (1966). *An Introduction to Probability Theory and Its Applications*, vol. 2. New York: John Wiley and Sons.

Fermat, P., and B. Pascal (1654). Letters, collected as "Fermat and Pascal on Probability" and translated from the French by Professor Vera Sanford. In D. Smith (ed.), *A Source Book in Mathematics*. New York: McGraw-Hill (1929): 546–65.

Fishburn, Peter C. (1981). "Subjective Expected Utility: A Review of Normative Theories." *Theory and Decision* 13: 139–99.

Gärdenfors, P., and Sahlin, N. (1982). "Unreliable Probabilities, Risk Taking, and Decision-Making", *Synthese* 53: 361–86.

Gauthier, David (1997). "Resolute Choice and Rational Deliberation: A Critique and a Defense." *Noûs* 31(1): 1–25.

Gilboa, Itzhak (1985). "Subjective Distortions of Probabilities and Non-Additive Probabilities." Working paper 18-85, Foerder Institute for Economic Research, Tel Aviv University, Ramat Aviv, Israel.

—— (1987). "Expected Utility with Purely Subjective Non-Additive Probabilities." *Journal of Mathematical Economics* 16: 65–88.

Good, I. J. (1967). "On the Principle of Total Evidence." *The British Journal for the Philosophy of Science* 17(4): 319–21.

Hagen, Ole (1979). "Towards a Positive Theory of Preference Under Risk." In *Expected Utility Hypothesis and the Allais Paradox*, ed. Maurice Allais and Ole Hagen. Dordrecht: Reidel, pp. 271–302.

Hammond, Peter (1988a). "Consequentialist Foundations for Expected Utility." *Theory and Decision* 25: 25–78.

—— (1988b). "Orderly Decision Theory: A Comment on Professor Seidenfeld." *Economics and Philosophy* 4: 292–7.

Hampton, Jean (1995). "Does Hume Have an Instrumental Conception of Practical Reason?" *Hume Studies* 21(1): 57–74.

Handa, J. (1977). "Risk, Probabilities and a New Theory of Cardinal Utility." *Journal of Political Economy* 85: 97–122.

Hansson, Bengt (1988). "Risk-aversion as a Problem of Conjoint Measurement." In *Decision, Probability, and Utility*, ed. Peter Gärdenfors and Nils-Eric Sahlin. Cambridge: Cambridge University Press, pp. 136–58.

Harsanyi, John C. (1977). "On the Rationale of the Bayesian Approach: Comments on Professor Watkins's Paper." In *Foundational Problems in the Special Sciences*, ed. Butts and Hintikka. Dordrecht: Reidel.

Hume, David (1739/1978). *A Treatise of Human Nature*, ed. P. H. Nidditch. Oxford: Oxford University Press. First published in 1739–40.

Hurley, Susan (1989). *Natural Reasons, Personality and Polity*. New York: Oxford University Press.

James, William (1896). "The Will to Believe." Reprinted (excerpt) in *Reason and Responsibility*, ed. Joel Feinberg and Russ Shafer-Landau. Wadsworth/Thomson (2005). 101–9.

Jeffrey, Richard (1965). *The Logic of Decision*. University of Chicago Press. First published in 1965 (McGraw-Hill).

—— (2004). *Subjective Probability: The Real Thing*. Cambridge: Cambridge University Press.

Jensen, J. L. W. V. (1906). "Sur les fonctions convexes et les inégalités entre les valeurs moyennes." *Acta Mathematica* 30(1): 175–93.

Joyce, James M. (1999). *The Foundations of Causal Decision Theory*. Cambridge: Cambridge University Press.

—— (2010). "A Defense of Imprecise Credences in Inference and Decision-making." *Philosophical Perspectives* 24(1): 281–323.

Kahneman, Daniel, and Amos Tversky (1979). "Prospect Theory: An Analysis of Decision under Risk." *Econometrica* 47: 263–91.

Kahneman, Daniel, Jack L. Knetsch, and Richard H. Thaler (1991). "Anomalies: The Endowment Effect, Loss Aversion, and Status Quo Bias." *Journal of Economic Perspectives* 5(1): 193–206.

Kavka, Gregory (1983). "The Toxin Puzzle." *Analysis* 43(1): 33–6.

Kelly, Thomas (forthcoming). "How to be an Epistemic Permissivist." In *Contemporary Debates in Epistemology*, ed. Mathias Steup and John Turri. Oxford: Blackwell.

Keysar, Boaz, Sayuri L. Hayakawa, and Sun Gyu An (2012). "The Foreign Language Effect: Thinking in a Foreign Tongue Reduces Decision Biases." *Psychological Science* 23(6): 661–8.

Köbberling, Veronika and Peter P. Wakker (2003). "Preference Foundations for Nonexpected Utility: A Generalized and Simplified Technique." *Mathematics of Operations Research* 28(3): 395–423.

Kolodny, Niko (2007). "How Does Coherence Matter?" *Proceedings of the Aristotelian Society* 107(1).

Lehman, R. Sherman (1955). "On Confirmation and Rational Betting." *Journal of Symbolic Logic* 20(3): 251–62.

Levi, Isaac (1991). "Consequentialism and Sequential Choice." In *Foundations of Decision Theory*, ed. Michael Bacharach and Susan Hurley. Oxford: Blackwell, pp. 92–122.

—— (1974). "On Indeterminate Probabilities", *Journal of Philosophy* 71: 391–418.

Lewis, David (1969). *Convention.* Cambridge, MA: Harvard University Press.

—— (1974). "Radical Interpretation." *Synthese* 23: 331–44.

—— (1981). "Causal Decision Theory." *Australian Journal of Philosophy* 59: 5–30.

Loomes, G., and R. Sugden (1987). "Disappointment and Dynamic Consistency in Choice Under Uncertainty." *Review of Economic Studies* 53: 271–82.

Lopes, Lola L. (1984). "Risk and Distributional Inequality." *Journal of Experimental Psychology: Human Perception and Performance* 10(4): 465–84.

—— (1987). "Between Hope and Fear: The Psychology of Risk." *Advances in Experimental Social Psychology* 20: 255–95.

—— and Gregg C. Oden (1999). "The Role of Aspiration Level in Risky Choice: A Comparison of Cumulative Prospect Theory and SP/A Theory." *Journal of Mathematical Psychology* 43: 286–313.

Luce, R. Duncan. (1988). "Rank-Dependent, Subjective Expected-Utility Representation." *Journal of Risk and Uncertainty* 1: 305–32.

—— (1992). "Where Does Subjective Expected Utility Fail Descriptively?" *Journal of Risk and Uncertainty* 5: 5–27.

—— and Howard Raiffa (1957). *Games and Decisions.* New York: John Wiley and Sons.

Machina, Mark J. (1982). "'Expected Utility' Analysis without the Independence Axiom." *Econometrica* 50(2): 277–323.

—— (1983). "Generalized Expected Utility Analysis and the Nature of Observed Violations of the Independence Axiom." Originally in *Foundations of Utility and Risk Theory with Applications*, ed. B. P. Stigum and F. Wenstop. Dordrecht: Reidel, pp. 263–93. Reprinted in *Decision, Probability, and Utility*, ed. Peter Gärdenfors and Nils-Eric Sahlin. Cambridge: Cambridge University Press, 1988, pp. 215–39.

—— (1987). "Choice Under Uncertainty: Problems Solved and Unsolved." *Journal of Economic Perspectives* 1(1): 121–54.

—— (1989). "Dynamic Consistency and Non-expected Utility Models of Choice Under Uncertainty." *Journal of Economic Literature* 27(4): 1622–68.

—— (2004). "Nonexpected Utility Theory." *Encyclopedia of Actuarial Science*, ed. Jozef L. Teugels and Bjørn Sundt. Chichester: John Wiley and Sons.

Machina, Mark J. and William S. Neilson (1987). "The Ross Characterization of Risk-aversion: Strengthening and Extension." *Econometrica* 55(5): 1139–49.

—— and David Schmeidler (1992). "A More Robust Definition of Subjective Probability." *Econometrica* 60(4): 745–80.

Maher, Patrick (1990). "Symptomatic Acts and the Value of Evidence in Causal Decision Theory." *Philosophy of Science* 57(3): 479–98.

—— (1993). *Betting on Theories.* Cambridge: Cambridge University Press.

Malinvaud, E. (1952). "Note on von Neumann–Morgenstern's Strong Independence Axiom." *Econometrica* 20(4): 679.

Markowitz, Harry M. (1959). *Portfolio Selection: Efficient Diversification of Investments.* New Haven, CT: Yale University Press.

Marschak, Jacob (1950). "Rational Behavior, Uncertain Prospects, and Measurable Utility." *Econometrica* 18(2): 111–41.

McClennen, Edward F. (1983). "Sure-Thing Doubts." Originally in *Foundations of Utility and Risk Theory with Applications*, ed. B. P. Stigum and F. Wenstop. Dordrecht: Reidel, pp. 117–36. Reprinted in *Decision, Probability, and Utility*, ed. Peter Gärdenfors and Nils-Eric Sahlin. Cambridge: Cambridge University Press, 1988, pp. 166–82.

—— (1988). "Ordering and Independence: A Comment on Professor Seidenfeld." *Economics and Philosophy* 4: 298–308.

—— (1990). *Rationality and Dynamic Choice: Foundational Explorations.* Cambridge: Cambridge University Press.

—— (1997). "Pragmatic Rationality and Rules." *Philosophy and Public Affairs* 26(3): 210–58.

MacCrimmon, Kenneth R. (1968). "Descriptive and Normative Implications of Decision Theory." In *Risk and Uncertainty*, ed. Karl Borch and Jan Mossin. New York: St Martin's Press.

—— and Stig Larsson (1979). "Utility Theory: Axioms versus "Paradoxes." In *Expected Utility Hypotheses and the Allais Paradox*, ed. Maurice Allais and Ole Hagen. Dordrecht: Reidel.

Nakamura, Yutaka (1995). "Probabilistically Sophisticated Rank Dependent Utility." *Economic Letters* 48: 441–7.

Nozick, Robert (1993). "Decision-Value." Chapter 2 of *The Nature of Rationality*. Princeton, NJ: Princeton University Press.

Oliver, Adam (2003). "A Quantitative and Qualitative Test of the Allais Paradox using Health Outcomes." *Journal of Economic Psychology* 24(1): 35–48.

Pettit, Philip (1991). "Decision Theory and Folk Psychology." In *Foundations of Decision Theory*, ed. Michael Bacharach and Susan Hurley. Oxford: Blackwell, pp. 147–75.

Pratt, John W. (1964). "Risk-Aversion in the Small and in the Large." *Econometrica* 32(1–2): 122–36.

—— (1976). "Risk-Aversion in the Small and in the Large: Erratum." *Econometrica* 44(2): 420.

Prelec, Drazen (1998). "The Probability Weighting Function." *Econometrica* 66(3): 497–527.

Putnam, Hilary (1986). "Rationality in Decision Theory and Ethics." *Critica* 18: 54.

Quiggin, John (1982). "A Theory of Anticipated Utility." *Journal of Economic Behavior and Organization* 3: 323–43.

—— and Peter Wakker (1994). "The Axiomatic Basis of Anticipated Utility: A Clarification." *Journal of Economic Theory* 64: 486–99.

Rabin, Matthew (2000). "Risk-Aversion and Expected-Utility Theory: A Calibration Theorem." *Econometrica* 68(5): 1281–92.

—— and Richard H. Thaler (2001). "Anomalies: Risk-Aversion." *Journal of Economic Perspectives* 15(1): 219–32.

Rabinowicz, Wlodek (1995). "To Have One's Cake and Eat It, Too: Sequential Choice and Expected-Utility Violations." *Journal of Philosophy* 92(11): 586–620.

—— (1997). "On Seidenfeld's Criticism of Sophisticated Violations of the Independence Axiom." *Theory and Decision* 43: 279–92.

Raiffa, Howard (1968). *Decision Analysis: Introductory Lectures on Choices Under Uncertainty.* Reading, MA: Addison-Wesley.

Ramsey, Frank (1926). "Truth and Probability." In Ramsey (1931). *The Foundations of Mathematics and Other Logical Essays*, ch. VII, pp. 156–98, ed. R. B. Braithwaite. London: Kegan, Paul, Trench, Trubner & Co.; New York: Harcourt, Brace and Company.

Resnik, Michael D. (1987). *Choices: An Introduction to Decision Theory.* University of Minnesota Press.

Ross, Stephen A. "Some Stronger Measures of Risk-aversion in the Small and the Large with Applications." *Econometrica* 49(3): 621–38.

Rothschild, Michael, and Joseph E. Stiglitz (1970). "Increasing Risk: I. A Definition." *Journal of Economic Theory* 2: 225–43.

—— (1972). "Addendum to 'Increasing Risk: I. A Definition.'" *Journal of Economic Theory* 5: 306.

Rottenstreich, Yuval, and Christopher K. Hsee (2001). "Money, Kisses, and Electric Shocks: On the Affective Psychology of Risk." *Psychological Science* 12(3): 185–90.

Samuelson, Paul A. (1952). "Probability, Utility, and the Independence Axiom." *Econometrica* 20(4): 670–8.

—— (1963). "Risk and Uncertainty: A Fallacy of Large Numbers." *Scientia* 98: 108–13.

Savage, Leonard (1954/1972). *The Foundations of Statistics.* Dover: John Wiley and Sons.

Schervish, Mark J., Teddy Seidenfeld, and Joseph B. Kadane (1990). "State-Dependent Utilities." *Journal of the American Statistical Association* 85(411): 840–7.

Schick, Frederic (1986). "Dutch Bookies and Money Pumps." *Journal of Philosophy* 83(2): 112–19.

—— (1991). *Understanding Action.* Cambridge: Cambridge University Press.

Schmeidler, David (1989). "Subjective Probability and Expected Utility without Additivity." *Econometrica* 57(3): 571–87.

Schmidt, Ulrich (2004). "Alternatives to Expected Utility: Formal Theories." Chapter 15 of *Handbook of Utility Theory*, ed. Salvador Barberà, Peter J. Hammond, and Christian Seidl. Boston: Kluwer Academic Publishers, pp. 757–837.

Segal, Uzi (1985). "Some Remarks on Quiggin's Anticipated Utility." *Journal of Economic Behavior and Organization* 8: 145–54.

Seidenfeld, Teddy (1988a). "Decision Theory without 'Independence' or without 'Ordering.'" *Economics and Philosophy* 4: 267–90.

—— (1988b). "Rejoinder." *Economics and Philosophy* 4: 309–15.

Sen, Amartya (1993). "Internal Consistency of Choice." *Econometrica* 61(3): 495–521. Originally the Presidential Address of the Econometric Society, 1984.

Skyrms, Brian (1980). *Causal Necessity.* New Haven, CT: Yale University Press.

Slovic, Paul, and Amos Tversky (1974). "Who Accepts Savage's Axiom?" *Behavioral Science* 19: 368–73.

Smith, Michael (1987). "The Humean Theory of Motivation." *Mind* 96(381): 36–61.

Sobel, Jordan Howard (1986). "Notes on Decision Theory: Old Wine in New Bottles." *Australasian Journal of Philosophy* 64: 407–37.

Starmer, Chris (2000). "Developments in Non-Expected Utility Theory: The Hunt for a Descriptive Theory of Choice under Risk." *Journal of Economic Literature* 38: 332–82.

Sugden, Robert (2004). "Alternatives to Expected Utility: Foundations." Chapter 14 of *Handbook of Utility Theory*, ed. Salvador Barberà, Peter J. Hammond, and Christian Seidl. Boston: Kluwer Academic Publishers, pp. 685–755.

Tversky, Amos, and Eldar Shafir (1992). "The Disjunction Effect in Choice under Uncertainty." *Psychological Science* 3(5): 305–9.

Tversky, Amos and Daniel Kahneman (1981). "The Framing of Decisions and the Psychology of Choice." *Science* 211: 453–8.

—— (1992). "Advances in Prospect Theory: Cumulative Representation of Uncertainty." *Journal of Risk and Uncertainty* 5: 297–323.

van Fraassen, Bas (1984). "Belief and the Will." *Journal of Philosophy* 81(5): 235–56.

van Inwagen, Peter (2010). "We're Right. They're Wrong." In *Disagreement*, ed. R. Feldman and T. Warfield. Oxford: Oxford University Press, pp. 10–28.

Velleman, J. David (2000). "The Story of Rational Action." Chapter 7 of *The Possibility of Practical Reason*. Oxford: Oxford University Press.

von Neumann, John, and Oskar Morgenstern (1944). *Theory of Games and Economic Behavior*. Princeton, NJ: Princeton University Press.

Wakker, Peter (1988). "Nonexpected Utility as Aversion to Information." *Journal of Behavioral Decision-making* 1: 169–75.

—— (1990). "Under Stochastic Dominance Choquet-Expected Utility and Anticipated Utility are Identical." *Theory and Decision* 29(2): 119–132.

—— (1994). "Separating Marginal Utility and Probabilistic Risk-aversion." *Theory and Decision* 36: 1–44.

—— (1996). "The Sure-Thing Principle and the Comonotonic Sure-Thing Principle: An Axiomatic Analysis." *Journal of Mathematical Economics* 25: 213–27.

—— (2005). "Decision-Foundations for Properties of Nonadditive Measures: General State Spaces or General Outcome Spaces." *Games and Economic Behavior* 50: 107–25.

—— (2010). *Prospect Theory for Risk and Ambiguity*. Cambridge: Cambridge University Press.

—— and Amos Tversky (1993). "An Axiomatization of Cumulative Prospect Theory." *Journal of Risk and Uncertainty* 7(7): 147–76.

Watkins, J. W. N. (1977). "Towards a Unified Decision Theory: A Non-Bayesian Approach." In *Foundational Problems in the Special Sciences*, ed. Butts and Hintikka. Dordrecht: Reidel.

Weber, Michael (1998). "The Resilience of the Allais Paradox." *Ethics* 109: 94–118.

Weirich, Paul (1986). "Expected Utility and Risk." *British Journal for the Philosophy of Science* 37(4): 419–42.

—— (1987). "Mean-Risk Decision Analysis." *Theory and Decision* 23: 89–111.

—— (2008). "Utility Maximization Generalized." *Journal of Moral Philosophy* 5: 282–99.

White, Roger (2005). "Epistemic Permissiveness." *Philosophical Perspectives* 19(1): 445–59.

—— (2009). "Evidential Symmetry and Mushy Credence." In *Oxford Studies in Epistemology*, ed. Tamar Szabo Gendler and John Hawthorne. Oxford: Oxford University Press, pp. 161–88.

Yaari, Menahem E. (1987). "The Dual Theory of Choice under Risk." *Econometrica* 55(1): 95–115.

Zynda, Lyle (2000). "Representation Theorems and Realism about Degrees of Belief." *Philosophy of Science* 67(1): 45–69.

Index

Italic numbers denote reference to illustrations.

Printed and bound by CPI Group (UK) Ltd, Croydon, CR0 4YY